ROB JOHNSON

The Afghan Way of War

Culture and Pragmatism:
A Critical History

HURST & COMPANY, LONDON

First published in the United Kingdom in 2011 by
C. Hurst & Co. (Publishers) Ltd.,
41 Great Russell Street, London, WC1B 3PL
© Rob Johnson, 2011
All rights reserved.
Printed in India

The right of Rob Johnson to be identified as the author of
this publication is asserted by him in accordance with the
Copyright, Designs and Patents Act, 1988.

A Cataloguing-in-Publication data record for this book
is available from the British Library.

ISBN: 9781849041065 *hardback*

This book is printed using paper from registered sustainable
and managed sources.

www.hurstpub.co.uk

This book is dedicated to Ingrid

CONTENTS

PREFACE AND ACKNOWLEDGEMENTS

'*Tawan be halq firu burd ustakhan-i darusht, walay shikam bedarad chun bigirad undar naf*'.
(You can swallow a rough bone, but once it is embedded in your bowels, it cuts up your guts.)[1]

The purpose of this book is to offer a fresh perspective on the various conflicts that have beset Afghanistan from the nineteenth century to the present. The scholarship that exists on the Afghan wars and frontier actions of Pakistan, worthy though it may be, is written almost entirely from a Western viewpoint. It is disappointing to note that, in these Western military histories, Afghans are often deprived of 'agency' and are portrayed as capable only of reacting to external pressures. Even modern accounts have tended to reduce the Afghans to stereotypes and to deprive them of strategic, operational or even tactical initiative. Ironically historical commentators with direct experience of the country were rather more generous, and, it has to be said, that Western Coalition forces operating 'on the ground' in Afghanistan have been acutely aware that the Afghan insurgents exhibit great skill and adaptability in the tactical arena. However, there is also a tendency to gloss over the intrinsic problems faced by Afghan insurgents and to attribute to them capabilities which they do not possess.

This book, part of the Changing Character of War series, represents more than just another military history of the Afghan Wars. It seeks to open a new chapter in the debate about Afghanistan using methodology that not only makes use of several disciplines, but also attempts to reconstruct changing historical encounters with Afghan perspectives. It is not the intention to suggest that the Afghans have a fixed method of fighting, a way of war, that is unchanging through time. Scoured by the strategic shocks of the past, the Afghans are pragmatic and adaptive. It is change, not continuity, that characterizes warfare in Afghanistan. Thus, military officers and policy-makers looking for strong lines of continuity from the campaigns the British fought against the Afghans in the nineteenth and twentieth centuries in order to grasp lessons that can be applied instantly may be disappointed. This is a history of transformation. That said, there are characteristics of conflict in Afghanistan that endure, not least the difficulties presented by its human and physical geography, and Afghans have often interpreted events through a cultural lens that is distinct from the West, leavened, of course, with that strong sense of pragmatism.

This book has been formulated over many years and after frequent visits to Afghanistan, although I am deeply conscious that, since I am not an Afghan, attempts to reconstruct the Afghan perspective will be seen by some as inherently flawed and distorted. Anthropologists and other scholars will, no doubt, find fault with the methods and the shorthand nature of the terminology used. Space does not permit a full exposition of all the literature, while endless definitions, although useful to the academic scholar, would interrupt the line of argument too frequently. At best, this book is an interpretation which brings a new dimension to the debate about Afghanistan's security. Criticisms of its brevity and assumptions I can leave to others.

I am deeply grateful to a great range of people and institutions for support in producing this book. I have been able to reflect on the work that many scholars, service personnel and policy-makers have brought to the Oxford Changing Character of War programme. Thanks here are due to Professor Hew Strachan, the Chichele Professor in the History of War at All Souls College, Oxford, who directs the programme and never ceases to labour for a greater understanding of war and a more intellectual application of strategy. I am also deeply grateful to Professor Henry Shue, Professor Anne Deighton, Professor Richard Caplan and Dr David Rodin, who have brought their own disciplinary expertise to bear and exposed me to new thinking. This is also true of my other colleagues at Oxford and friends at Cambridge, King's College London, London School of Economics and Exeter, including Professor Judith Brown, Dr John Darwin, Dr Georg Deutsch, Dr Faisal Devji, Dr Adrian Gregory, Professor Chris Bayly, Professor Anatol Lieven, Professor Theo Farrell, Dr Antonio Giustozzi and Professor Jeremy Black. I am indebted to the British Army and RUSI for the contacts they have made available and the chance to gain a better insight into recent Western military operations. I am deeply grateful to Michael Dwyer for his support in the commissioning and production of this book. There are those in the United States who have contributed to my understanding of Afghanistan, including the War College at Fort Leavenworth, the

Tribal Analysis Center, RAND Corporation and friends in Washington DC and Kabul. Special mention must be made of the men and women who work 'on the ground', including the service personnel of the British and the United States armed forces, government agencies and civilian NGOs; especially those who have made courageous efforts to go and speak with and work amongst the Afghans in the cause of a 'better peace', like Michael Webb and Rory Brown. They have each given me unprecedented access to their work and to their Afghan interlocutors across the country. Most important are my Afghan friends and colleagues, including Nadir, Latif and Mohammed, the Afghan Army officers who have hosted me on several occasions, and all the Afghans who endure the current conflict with great stoicism but still make time for warm hospitality to foreign visitors.

GLOSSARY

Amir	commander (*Amir al mu'minim*—commander of the faithful)
Andaran-i Khas	royal guards
Badal	justice, retaliation
Badmash	criminal
Barat	assignment
Bashi	head of service
Beg (Baig)	chief of a village
Buluk Musher	lieutenant of artillery
Chalweshtai	group of forty men raised by clans of the Suleiman Khels for the defence of a community
Dafadar	cavalry sergeant
Dahbashi	militia section commander
Darra	valley
Dunbalapur	double-barrelled breech-loading rifle
Eljari	dismounted warrior levy
Feringhee	foreigners
Ghar	Pashtun title for a faction
Ghat Mushr	General
Ghaza	religious war
Ghulum-i Shah	royal guards (lit. slaves)
Hawaldar	Corporal
Hazarbashi	leader of a thousand men
Hazirbash	cavalry formed under Shah Shuja in 1840
Imam	prayer leader, member of the *ulema*
Izzat	honour
Jagir	government grant to collect revenue; payment on any land held by a landowner

GLOSSARY

Janbaz	light cavalry formed in 1840
Jezail	long-barrelled musket
Jihad	struggle in the way of Allah (lit.); conflict in the defence of Islam
Jirga	(lit. circle), a village council
Lashkar	war party
Kalla minar	tower of skulls, made up of enemy dead after battle
Khan khel	leading clan
Khassadars	tribal militia raised by British in North West Frontier Province
Khassadar Muhassil	militia for the collection of taxes
Khutba	Friday prayers noting the name of the sovereign to whom the people owe allegiance
Kiftan	Captain
Kohna Nokar	feudal cavalry in Balkh
Kotal	mountain pass
Kotdafadar	Sergeant Major in the cavalry
Kufr	unbeliever, infidel
Landakwar	sergeant in artillery and infantry
Maijir	Major
Malik	elder
Mingbashi	commander of a thousand militiamen
Mirata	murder committed to seize a victim's estate
Mushr	elder
Na'ib	lieutenant or viceroy
Nala	ravine (sometimes *nullah*)
Nam girak	(lit. name-calling), assassination at night of named persons
Nanawatai	hospitality offered to fugitives
Nang	honour (Pashtun)
Nap	Adjutant
Paira	division of an infantry company
Pashtunwali	customary code of Pashtuns; note that the Pakistan variant may be Pushtun or Pakhtun, and the English version Pathan, but this book adopts Pashtun consistently in the author's text
Panza Mushr	Brigadier General
Park Mushr	Sergeant Major of artillery

xiv

GLOSSARY

Pinjabashi	commander of fifty militia men
Pultan	regiment
Qala	high walled village compound or fort
Qarawel khana	border cavalry
Qawm	system of loyalty based on community, family or location
Risala	cavalry regiment
Risala'dar	Captain in the cavalry
Sadbashi	leader of a group of one hundred men
Safar mina	(lit. sappers and miners) pioneer regiment
Sartip	commander of one hundred militiamen
Sarwara	cavalry
Sarwara-i kushada	feudal horsemen
Sharia	Islamic Law
Sil Mushr	Captain in the artillery or cavalry
Sipahi	soldier
Sipahi ghair-i-munazzam	irregular army
Sipahi i-munazzam	regular army
Taliban	students of Islamic studies
Tarburwali	conflict between first cousins
Thahans	military posts
Tiyul	land granted for military service
Topkhana	artillery
Ushr	Islamic tax
Wahhabi	follower of Mohammed abd' al Wahhab (1707–87) who aims to abolish all innovation that has developed since c.300 AH (c.AD 1000).
Waqf	religious foundation
Watan	fatherland
Yuzbashi	leader of one hundred
Zabit	officer tasked with the collection of revenue
Zar	gold; money
Zar Mushr	Colonel
Zan	women
Zamin	land

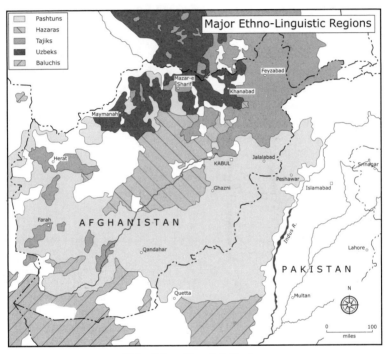

Major Ethno-Linguistic Regions

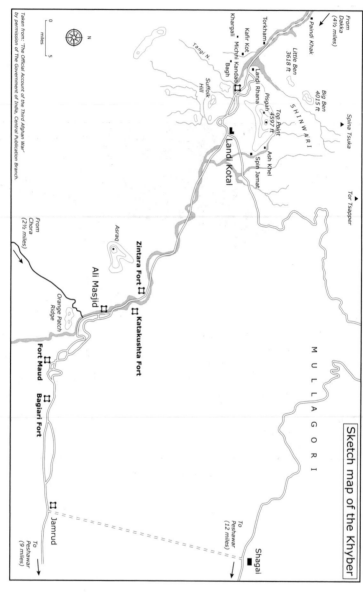

Sketch map of the Khyber

The Khyber Pass

From Dakka
(4½ miles)

Paindi Khak

Torkham

Little Ben
3618 ft

Big Ben
4015 ft

Spina Tsuka

Tangi N.

SHINWARI

Kafir Kot

Michni Kandao

Khargali

Bagh

Landi Khana

Suffolk Hill

Pisgah
4597 ft

Top Point

Ash Khel

Spin Jamat

Tor Tsapper

Landi Kotal

Asraq

From Chora
(2½ miles)

Zintara Fort

Ali Masjid

Orange Patch Ridge

Katakushta Fort

MULLAGORI

Fort Maud

Bagiari Fort

Jamrud

To Peshawar
(9 miles)

To Peshawar
(12 miles)

Shagai

N

0   miles   5

Taken from: 'The Official Account of the Third Afghan War' by permission of The Government of India, Central Publication Branch.

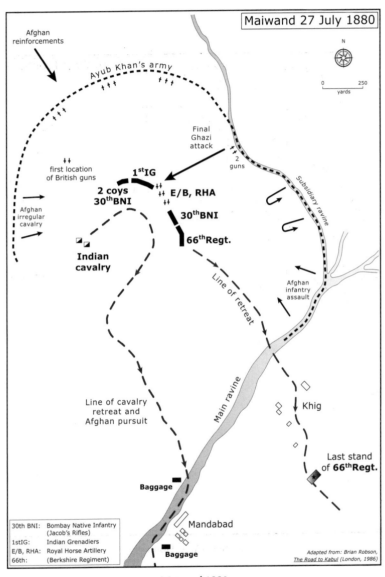

Maiwand 27 July 1880

N

0 ———— 250
yards

Afghan reinforcements

Ayub Khan's army

Final Ghazi attack

2 guns

Subsidiary ravine

first location of British guns

1stIG

2 coys 30thBNI

E/B, RHA

Afghan irregular cavalry

30thBNI

66thRegt.

Indian cavalry

Line of retreat

Afghan infantry assault

Line of cavalry retreat and Afghan pursuit

Main ravine

Khig

Last stand of 66thRegt.

Baggage

Mandabad

30th BNI:	Bombay Native Infantry (Jacob's Rifles)
1stIG:	Indian Grenadiers
E/B, RHA:	Royal Horse Artillery
66th:	(Berkshire Regiment)

Baggage

Adapted from: Brian Robson,
The Road to Kabul (London, 1986)

Maiwand 1880

The North West Frontier

Central Area 1919 (The Third Anglo-Afghan War)

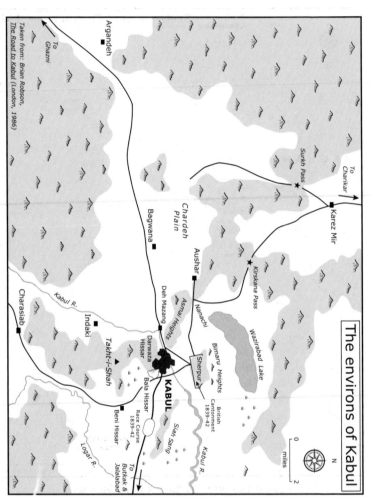

The Environs of Kabul

Taken from: Brian Robson, *The Road to Kabul* (London, 1986)

The environs of Kabul

To Charikar

Argandeh

To Ghazni

Surkh Pass

Karez Mir

Chardeh Plain

To Charikar

Bagwana

Aushar

Kirskana Pass

Charasiab

Kabul R.

Deh Mazang

Asmai Heights

Nanachi

Wazirabad Lake

Indaki

Darwaza Hissar

Bimaru Heights

Takht-i-Shah

Sherpur

British Cantonment 1839–42

Bala Hissar

KABUL

Siah Sang

Kabul R.

Beni Hissar

Race Course 1839–42

Logar R.

To Butkak & Jalalabad

N

0   miles   2

1

INTRODUCTION

A CONTESTED HISTORY

The difficulty in defeating the neo-Taliban insurgency has compelled the Western armed forces to investigate the socio-cultural aspects of their adversaries, and to look deeply into the British and Soviet historical experience of fighting the Afghans.[1] However, one of the immediate problems in this regard is that almost all the prominent historical sources on the various Afghan conflicts are written from a Western perspective. The paucity or absence of written records from the Afghan side, certainly until very recent times, has meant that analysts are deprived of one crucial element: what the Afghans thought, judged and decided when they conducted their operations. Much, of course, has been written on the tactical prowess of the Taliban and the Mujahideen, or on Islamic Jihadism and Afghan history, and there is now an increasing body of literature on the conflicts between various social groups in Afghanistan, but there is still precious little analytical history on military operations in the region which illustrate the difficulties, achievements and decision-making from the Afghan side.[2]

In Western military histories, Afghans and 'tribesmen' have invariably been presented as simply reactive to British or Soviet manoeuvres. As a consequence, various contemporaries and scholars constructed stereotypes about the Afghans, and these have accumulated to the extent that it appears there was a simplistic Afghan 'way of war', a phenomenon consisting almost entirely of religious mobilization and individuals' fanatical courage but deficient of any concepts of tactical evolution or of strategy. Patrick Porter has recently challenged this assumption and notes that the pursuit of victory is not a purely Western convention, but a sound and understandable first principle of war. Thus, when we return to the historical record, we are given the opportunity to reappraise Afghan conflicts. By re-examining the narratives of British military expeditions in Afghanistan and along the North West Frontier between 1838 and 1947, Afghan civil wars, the Soviet occupation and recent Western military intervention, this book seeks to show that a reinterpretation and, more importantly, a review of our understanding of the Afghan approach to conflict are long overdue. A process of historical reconstruction, through careful reading of the British and Soviet sources, assisted by the insights from history, anthropology and oral testimony, can create a new perspective on the Afghan character of war.

The literature on the existence and influence of a 'way of war', or 'military culture' as it is now known, has grown rapidly.[3] Culture is a difficult concept to pin down. It is not always clear whether the current search for 'culture' as a means to explain historical or contemporary phenomena is conveniently constructed and imagined to suit modern academic parameters. The British colonial personnel, much criticised for their distortions and obvious misconceptions, nevertheless offered some empirical references that were not completely devoid of objectivity. Indeed, we might use an evaluation of the Pashtuns and Afghans historically to re-examine and reassess tacitly the orthodox assumptions about their portrayal in British scholarship, and to challenge the idea that culture 'explains', or even determines, behaviours. It is not the intention to create some ambitious revisionism. The aim is merely to ask whether there was something distinctive about the Afghan approach to war, or whether there was a recognizable set of phenomena common to almost all Afghan wars. This question is of some importance, not least because Western nations are struggling to find a solution to the conflict in Afghanistan through reconciliation, enlistment in new security forces and participation in state-building using Western models. At the same time the state of Pakistan is facing serious challenges from radical elements of its own Pashtun population.

The Western world's view of the Afghans and the adjacent Pashtuns of the Khyber Pakhtunkwa (North West Frontier Province) of Pakistan draws on a legacy of half-understood and often misconceived ideas from a long period of colonial contact, and distant memories of the Mujahideen struggle against Soviet occupation in the 1980s. Since 2001, a variety of interpretations have been offered on Afghanistan's history: from academic studies that often combine anthropological fieldwork and observations on the Western military intervention in the country, through political commentaries and media reports, to the emotional reactions of the Afghan and Pashtun diaspora. Given the centrality of current political and military interest in the Afghans and Pakistan's Pashtuns, this particular field of history not only has contemporary resonance, but is also much contested. History is used to reinforce particular agendas and score moral points either in favour of continued intervention, or against it.

This introductory chapter seeks to offer a framework to examine an Afghan way of war, with explanations of the approaches taken to the subject and the problems that have evolved. It illustrates the varieties of history that have emerged, some of the reasons that lie behind different interpretations, and attempts to uncover why particular myths about the Afghan and Pashtun way of fighting have proved so enduring. In this, we owe a great debt to Patrick Porter whose *Military Orientalism* pointed to a predilection to stereotyping in the Western episteme which is so pervasive as to threaten to prevent accurate judgements being made in the policy sphere.[4] What is particularly fascinating is how the construction of knowledge about Afghanistan, from the West's contacts in the eighteenth century onwards, influenced subsequent scholarship so strongly. It is also noticeable that views of the Afghans were shaped and coloured by Europeans' views of themselves and of comparable realms across the Middle East. Initially, Afghans were defined and known in contrast or similarity to Persians, Ottoman Turks and South Asians. In the nineteenth century and first half of the twentieth century, British views were based on direct contact, particularly in the wars and confrontations of the period 1838–1919. Subsequently it was the Cold War that acted as the lens for the Western view: the Mujahideen were, on the whole, 'heroic' underdogs struggling to throw off the yoke of Soviet occupation. This view was even reinforced by popular literature and film.[5] The illusion was shattered by the protracted civil war of the 1990s and the Afghans faded from the West's field of vision until 1998, when it became apparent that the Taliban were in the process of building an austere emirate and acting as the host of Osama bin Laden's al Qaeda movement.

There are some distinctive trends in the way that the Western world wrote about the nature of Afghan and Pashtun society and about British and Soviet encounters with the Afghans and Pashtuns, which have an important bearing on the descriptions of the Afghan way of war. In many cases, British views of the Afghans and Pashtuns actually tell us more about the British than they do about the Afghans and Pashtuns themselves. Soviet interpretations, so often filtered through the lens of communist ideology and the anxieties of the Cold War, suffered from a similar form of partiality. By examining the Afghan approach to war more critically, we may understand more clearly why, for example, the West believed the Afghans were 'natural guerrilla fighters', why occupations in the modern era were short-lived, or why recruitment drives by foreigners so often ended in failure. In addition, narratives of Afghan civil wars can help fill the gaps in our understanding of the Afghan way of war.

The purpose of this book is to provide an historical assessment of the changing character of warfare in Afghanistan and to review some of the long-held assumptions about the Afghans as fighters. In recent operations, Western forces have tried to 'win hearts and minds', that is, to influence the way that Afghans think and behave. There has been a desire to isolate the insurgents of Afghanistan from the rest of the population. To access the 'Afghan mind', policy-makers have turned to academics and specialists to provide answers that can be translated directly into practice. While some anthropologists have rejected the 'unethical taint' of collaboration with military personnel, others have provided detailed support not only from Europe, but also in Afghanistan and Pakistan on the basis that ignorance amongst Western policy-makers is far more lethal to the Afghans than trying to assert the moral high ground.

Despite the current interest in the conflict in Afghanistan and some remarks pertaining to it, this book takes a longer, historical view and cannot be considered a policy guide. Afghanistan in the early twenty-first century is experiencing rapid change. It is subjected to a variety of new ideologies, the interests of neighbouring states, and the bewildering speed and accessibility of new information technologies. Each of these is being harnessed by different generations and communities in Afghanistan, and few can predict, long-term, where this is taking the country. Equally, after thirty years of civil war, with its infrastructure ruined and its economy still feeble, many Afghans have experienced a collective trauma that is likely to have profound repercussions. In essence, war has shaped Afghanistan in a very comprehensive way, Afghanistan's recent transformation is rendering many old certainties redundant and this book can only attempt to begin to understand that effect.

This chapter is structured in three parts. The first is an examination of the problem of a 'way of war', including a brief discussion of the historiography and conceptual framework, the place of Islam as a mobilizing force in Afghan warfare, the nature of civil war, the question of ethnic warfare and the relative importance of negotiations in war. The second part of the chapter offers a brief overview of the existing histories of war in Afghanistan, particularly those of the Afghans, British and Soviets. The third and final part deals with methods and approaches, indicating that each comes with its own problems and flaws. With these caveats and parameters outlined, navigation of the rest of the book will, hopefully, be much easier.

Ways of war: theories of war and military cultures

The phrase 'a way of war' was coined by the British historian and former soldier Basil Liddell Hart at a lecture at RUSI in 1931 to describe a deep-seated British preference for the 'indirect approach' through armoured doctrine or other technologies, or naval and expeditionary warfare, rather than continental alliances and commitments.[6] Liddell Hart was reacting to what he termed the 'Clausewitzian fallacy', the erroneous belief that waging absolute war against the main force of the enemy would produce victory, because he had witnessed costly attacks against German entrenchments on the Western Front in the First World War.[7] The notion of a way of war was subsequently taken up by G. S. Graham, Michael Howard, Graham Weigley, Paul Kennedy, Brian Linn and others.[8]

In the attempt to identify distinctive characteristics through time, one must remain aware of diversity in what appear to be common or collective features of war, noting that history is contingent and not obedient to general principles. In his many studies of warfare, historian Jeremy Black has often warned not only against ignoring cultural difference but also the risks of assuming consistency and continuities with the benefit of retrospection.[9] Various writers have attempted to characterize different national 'ways of war', and there are now works on America, China, the Soviet Union, India, South Africa and the Arab nations.[10] Most dramatically and conclusively Victor David Hanson developed Liddell Hart's original ideas and posited a 'Western way of war' that emerged in the ancient world, suggesting that certain forms of organization and fighting were distinctive to Europeans thereafter. These included: advanced technology, superior discipline, an ability to adapt through an intellectual tradition of innovation, civic militarism (where the population broadly supported the military effort), an inclination towards seeking decisive battles, a preference for infantry, particularly those using bladed weapons rather than missiles, highly organized logistics with an economy geared to war and, finally, a moral opposition to aggression and violence that resulted in limited war, or justification and reasoning for war.[11] John Lynn was deeply critical of this attempt to construct an over-arching theory of Western war, arguing that such consistency over two and a half millennia was surely impossible.[12] Indeed, Hanson's assumptions and the problems Lynn identified would affect any attempt to construct a similar 'Eastern way of war'. There should be scepticism about such a project if the context of changing relative military power between East and West in the nineteenth and twentieth centuries is not acknowledged.

Equally, any relativism through ethno-centric analyses seems fraught with difficulties, as Ken Booth noted in his work on strategic culture.[13] Booth argued that strategic culture, of which a way of warfare was a subset, was 'a nation's traditions, values, attitudes, patterns of behaviour, habits, customs, achievements and particular ways of adapting to the environment and solving problems with respect to the threat or use of force'.[14] Such studies, Booth asserted, could assist in a better understanding of what appeared to be irrational decision-making because strategy was a 'created world' where strategic realities were 'in part culturally constructed as well as culturally perpetuated'.[15]

Michael Doyle also argued that culture had a part to play in decision-making and that we should see domestic and foreign policy as harnessed together. He noted that 'a coalition or conglomerate of ... interests' shaped policy.[16] Paul Schroeder made a similar point, offering a critical evaluation of international relations theory to show that 'rational' choices and balancing of costs and benefits were conditioned by cultural factors and contingencies, sometimes producing a 'band-wagoning' effect.[17] However, there have been numerous attempts to show that states are capable of producing more than one culture. Alastair Johnston believed that within a country there could be 'contested strategic cultures [and] crossnational or transnational strategic cultures' because states were invented and essentialized 'ethno-territorial entities'.[18] This would certainly seem an appropriate assessment for Afghanistan.

War, a ritualized and encultured approach to violence, suggests that there are common characteristics that we should acknowledge when it comes to how strategy is conceived and the fighting is conducted. Colin Gray noted: 'human beings are encultured as people who live in communities, and because, alas, those communities are communities for security, humans have no choice other than to undergo a process of strategic enculturation'.[19] Rituals and beliefs in a section of society may also affect behaviours towards violence including the tactics employed.[20] Yet, as Patrick Porter warns, the rush to find the distinctive in others, especially 'the exotic and the bizarre', can produce a tendency to see 'foreigners as eternally separate and primordial, an alien species with their "ancient hatreds" or "primal urges"'.[21] War itself has an effect on beliefs and perceptions, and can affect the strategy, operations and tactics employed regardless of culture. As Porter notes, Afghans set out to win just as their Western adversaries do, but all too often, historically, interpretations of Afghan actions were quick to condemn pragmatism as a form of treachery and untrustworthiness. Referring to the First Anglo–Afghan War, the nineteenth-century historian J. P. Ferrier argued that 'the Afghans do not attach the same importance to some words as Europeans do; "country" and "honour" are to them as empty sounds, and they sell them to the highest bidder without scruple'.[22] Ferrier could not appreciate that for the Ghilzais, to whom he referred, national identity meant little if the more immediate threats arose from neighbouring clans, and that they made a living from taxing caravans which wend their way through the passes of the Khyber districts. John Kaye concluded: 'It was a moot point whether revenge or avarice is the stronger feeling in the Afghan breast. Both were now arrayed against us. The [policy of] bayonet and the money-bag were failing to do their work'.[23]

Lady Sale, a prisoner of the Afghans in 1842, believed: 'there is also a peculiarity in the Affghan [sic] mode of fighting' which involved the ruthless mass murder and mutilation of their enemies.[24] Archibald Forbes, the war correspondent of the late nineteenth century, wrote in his history of the First Anglo–Afghan War that, in the destruction of a retreating British column: 'all the bodies were stripped. There were children cut in two. Hindustanee women as well as men—some frozen to death, some literally chopped to pieces, many with their throats cut from ear to ear'.[25] As Keith Stanski recently noted, British contemporary accounts emphasized that: 'Afghan violence was not restrained by any logic, such as the pursuit of wealth. Rather, violence was seemingly an expression of Afghan backwardness and lack of restraint'.[26] There was no acknowledgement of the need to annihilate those who would otherwise return to seek revenge.

Defeats and strategic shocks have been capable of altering apparent 'ways of war', or perhaps reaffirming a preference from which there had been a deviation, as in the case of Liddell Hart's original analysis.[27] The degree of change is often contested by scholars, since 'culture' suggests some deep-seated practices and fundamental behaviours. Nevertheless, a culture that is in a constant state of re-evaluation, which would seem to be true of most cases historically, might mean that change and adaptation are, in fact, norms in any 'way of war'. Geoffrey Parker, in his work on the grand strategy of early modern Spain, suggested that there were strategic considerations which did not change over a period of 500 years, namely command and control, communications and intelligence (sometimes referred to as C3I), which had informed Spain's 'strategic vision and influence[d] the selection of its strategic priorities'.[28] Jeremy Black, who had contested Parker's exclusive focus on Western ways of war and assumptions about a 'military revolution', was consistent in his analysis that 'it is all too easy to reify national attitudes and policies, to make them appear clearer, coherent and more obviously based on readily-agreed national interests' than is the case.[29] He attacked the obsession with theories that created an 'overly-fixed use of the concept of strategic culture' and throughout his many works has emphasized change in warfare. The risk of searching for continuities and patterns is teleological: we tend to find what we are looking for and derive a theory from it. Parker, though, was prepared to acknowledge a challenge-response mechanism in warfare in Europe where 'each innovation broke the prevailing equilibrium and provoked a phase of rapid transformation and adjustment'.[30] Colin Gray also identified a 'punctuated equilibrium' where revolutions in warfare created antidotes which could take tactical, operational, strategic or political forms.[31]

The argument of this book is that there is no fixed and unchanging way of war for Afghanistan, and the selection of historical episodes in this book is an attempt to illustrate the changing nature of Afghan warfare. Approaches to war were conditioned and altered by the prevailing circumstances at specific points in time, being shaped by new technology, new invaders with their own methods of fighting, the degree of unity that could be mobilized, or the relative strength that could be mustered. The nature of war, like principles of strategy, may consist of timeless concepts and themes, but not all are applied equally throughout time, nor with the same significance. While Afghan perceptions and decisions were shaped through a cultural lens, the appropriateness of each principle depended on the circumstances prevailing.

One of the few constants in Afghanistan's situation is its geography. Terrain, climate and distance have imposed considerable limitations on the conduct of war in the region.[32] Before the twentieth century, the scarcity of resources limited the size of occupation armies, and even during the Soviet intervention huge volumes of food and materials had to be shipped in. High altitude affects heavily armoured troops and helicopter deployment, while mountain ranges limit manoeuvre and the deployment of mobile land forces such as cavalry or tanks. High temperatures and fine dust in the deserts of the south debilitate soldiers and increase the wear and tear on high-tech equipment; freezing conditions and deep snow in the winter in the mountains have similar effects. The mountains and intensely cultivated areas of Afghanistan have provided concealment for generations of fighters. In terms of a way of war, the need to find solutions to repeated failures by Afghan conventional forces against the sheer military power ranged against them compelled the Afghans to exploit the strategic and tactical advantages of the terrain and climate. Afghans had to avoid destructive direct encounters and concentrate on cutting logistics, using the element of surprise in ambush and manoeuvre, and adding time and cost to an occupation force. Only by these means could they hope to defy the asymmetry of power that confronted them.[33]

The Islamic framework of Afghan resistance and warfare

While geography provided a physical constant in Afghan warfare, it was religion that offered certainty in the spiritual realm. Islam has a charismatic appeal in war: it offers a radical break with the past, a form of enlightenment, the sense of unity or solidarity with the dispossessed against oppressors, and the certainty of the righteous and supporting power of the Almighty against whatever forces are arrayed against the Muslims.[34] Periodically, when faced with crisis, Islam has been the rallying point for many communities, and Afghanistan is no exception. Paradoxically, while the precepts of the Qur'an urge repeatedly the value of a peaceful and sober approach to living one's life, the West is more familiar with its defensiveness and, latterly, with a phenomenon called the 'offensive Jihad'.

There is no theological basis for an 'offensive Jihad' in modern Islamic scholarship, although there are vestiges in historical tracts. Much of what contemporary internationalist Jihadists claim to be the 'true faith' is in fact a false and manipulated version of Islam.[35] The relevant passages on war are selected to give an entirely different meaning to them, and it is not unknown to find text attributed to the Qur'an by Jihadists which does not actually appear in it at all. More typically, mullahs and Jihadists have often used the same style of rhetoric as that which appears in the Qur'an to give the impression these words are derived from it. In rural Afghanistan, understanding of the finer points of Islamic jurisprudence has been rare. We might even refer to a 'folk' version of Islam, or note that, since the 1970s, after years of war and in the presence of foreigners, Islam has just become a cipher or a metaphor for other agendas. Consistently one finds examples of how Islam has been used to galvanize resistance to 'foreign occupation' or to fight sectarian rivals. Three areas are particularly important: the concept of Jihad; a sense of individual honour; and collective obligation.

Jihad, strictly defined, has two aspects. It is a daily personal struggle to live out one's faith, *al-jihad fi sabil Allah* (striving in the way of Allah). It is also the defence and obligation to protect the people (Muslims), and Islam itself (its culture, integrity and 'purity'). Jihad is subject to qualification and limitation including concepts of proportionality, self-defence, last resort, necessity, collateral damage, manslaughter, discrimination and pure intention. The 'offensive Jihad' is a reinvention of a concept, based on a crudely selective reading of history, which suggests one has to defeat or convert the unenlightened or heretical in a war, or even simply to wage total war as the means to arrest the overbearing power of the West. Despite the absence of any single head or authority of Islam, a process of precedence and scholarly debate has determined the 'right path' in defining Jihad. Nevertheless, from the beginning of Islamic history there have been bitter divisions and even civil wars over what constitutes the right direction, including the great Shia–Sunni schism. Islamic scholars and teachers (*ulema*) exercise varying degrees of authority based on decades of study, and they constantly reinterpret Islam in light of new situations. While very few have the authority to issue fatwas to initiate Jihad, the desire to defend the faith is a widespread and pragmatic reaction to events.

Interpretations and justifications for Jihad are particularly revealing and indicate how Muslims can be mobilized.[36] Ethics and meta-ethics can be harnessed to persuade, morally coerce and ultimately recruit personnel for military operations. Historically, for example, a special value has been attributed to martyrdom (*shahada*) as the means to honour the fallen and to provide solace to families and communities that are bereaved. Martyrdom has also been used a means to inspire sacrifice from others. More recently, Jihadists argue that martyrdom is justified and even obligatory in the defence of Islam. They emphasize that widows of martyred fighters are particularly blessed, and the redemption of immediate extended members of the family is possible. It is interesting to note that there is no Qur'anic basis for suicidal martyrdom. The justification was really no different from the call for extraordinary efforts from combatants in the West in previous conflicts, including the total wars of the twentieth century. The common theme for both Western armies and Muslim ones was the elevation of the idea of sacrifice for the greater good.

There is a long-standing dispute in Islamic jurisprudence over *fard al-kifaya* (collective obligation) to wage Jihad and *fard al-ayn* (individual duty) to carry out Islamic responsibilities. For those distant from a conflict, Islamic scholars indicate that *fard al-ayn* only applies if the local Muslims require assistance and have not enough men, or power, to expel an invasion of Muslim territory.[37] Permission from the correct authority, such as parents, mullah and/or scholars, is required. Modern Jihadists dispute this, arguing that the situation merits action anyway. In rural Afghanistan, historically communications and infrastructure were so bad that it was very difficult to join the struggles of other communities, and divisions between social groups usually precluded any alliance. In the case of near communities, however, eyewitness records suggest that, regardless of divisions between communities, rural Afghans would rush to participate in any battle against a common rival or a foreign force because of the chance it offered for the improvement of one's status.

For modern Jihadists, training is an alternative obligation, hence the willingness of some Muslims resident in the West to make visits to training camps in Afghanistan and Pakistan, and their expressions of a readiness to serve when called. They cite the Qur'an: 'And prepare against them whatever you are able and with steeds of war...'[38] In an effort to mobilize the entire global *umma*, modern Jihadists also condemn Muslims who protect their personal savings while a Jihad is taking place and believe that *fard al-kifaya* takes precedence over *fard al-ayn*. It is worth noting that, in Afghanistan, customs of obligation are to be found alongside the theoretical aspects of Islam. Notions of justice and solidarity are central to the Qur'an: a sense of discipline is intrinsic, and a feeling that effort must be made towards the common good, for example by worshipping together and supporting the community (*umma*) with *zakat*. In Afghanistan, rural communities in the south and east also have a strong sense of egalitarianism and cohesion, although it is often fractured even between near-families. There is a customary justice system where issues are settled by *jirga* and then implemented by a 'village constabulary' (styled as *arbakai* in the south-east but as a concept it exists in other parts of the Pashtun belt), involving destruction of property or removal of land.

While Islam is predicated on the idea of achieving *salama* (peace) through the submission to the will of Allah, in the contested lands of Afghanistan it has often seemed that such noble injunctions are ignored. Cosmic Dualism is central to Islam and, given its position amongst believers as the 'final revelation', the defence of the faith is seen as particularly critical. There are several types of threat, and a permanent occupation, erosive interaction and constant contact with non-Islamic ideas and practices would increase the level of these significantly.[39] However, historically, perpetual feuding or protracted warfare could be abated by negotiation. In village communities, mullahs were the primary brokers for peace, but civil war since 1979 has eroded this capacity and now ideological arguments in favour of armed struggle tend to attract more attention, support and leverage. Nevertheless, in Islam there is no justification for any form of indiscriminate violence: 'Anyone who has killed another except in retaliation, it is as if he has killed the whole of humankind'.[40] Rural Afghans were similarly regulated by customary codes. The obligation to retaliate when members of the family or clan were killed by another was supported but also tempered by the injunctions of customary justice. It would be unjustified to kill any greater numbers of a family than one had lost oneself, thereby imposing a code of proportionality. Moreover, those taking their revenge were expected to do so with discrimination, targeting male members of the specific family that had carried out the act.

At the higher level, war, rather than communal infighting, was only justified if it was to defend Islam as a *harb al-Muqadis* or *ghaza* ('holy war'). Failure to adhere to the ethical code of Islam in this struggle would mean that an individual or a community could face judgement, for the Qur'an states: 'Those who believe fight in the way of Allah, and those who disbelieve fight in the way of Shaitan'.[41] Accordingly, a set of principles were established by Abu Bakr, the Prophet's companion and a cavalry commander, during the expansion of the seventh century. It specified that soldiers should not: 'commit treachery; deviate from the right path [deceive]; mutilate the dead; kill a child, woman or old man; cut down or burn a fruitful tree; harm a weak person; slay the enemy's flocks, except for food, or hurt those who worship God in remote places [monastic orders]'. The references to trees and flocks indicate the origins of these ideas, since food sources were vital to nomadic communities in Arabia. In Afghanistan, however, there was a more robust approach to the ethics of waging war. For example, regarding prisoners of war, the Qur'an states: 'Allah forbids you, with regard to those who fight you for (your) religion or who drive you out of your homes, from not dealing kindly and justly with them; for Allah loves those who are just'.[42] But in the struggle against what Afghans perceived were the enemies of Islam, and against those they believed had acted without justification, many fighters felt they were not obliged to follow this Qur'anic injunction. Sheer anger replaced any adherence to the code on many occasions.

Ghaza (holy war) was probably conceived in the earliest Muslim conquests, but certainly can be traced to written records as early as AD 983 (361 AH) and the catechism written by Abu al-Layth al-Samarkandi.[43] Whereas Jihad emphasized the defence of Islam and Islamic civilization, *ghaza* was a duty discharged by a section of the *umma*, if sanctioned by the Caliph, to invade infidel lands or defend distant territory. Once again there were rules and restrictions on making war and peace, the division of spoils, commission of atrocities, and the offer of either conversion or death to prisoners.

Yet, for all the neat academic interpretations, the reality on the frontiers of the Islamic world was different. Faced with numerous and committed enemies, Muslim polities had to fight for their survival and aggrandizement with the rules of *realpolitik* rather than jurisprudence. In the Ottoman context, the concept of *ghaza* was co-opted to provide legitimacy for heroic but arbitrary military leadership, or to justify the prosaic acquisition of land, property and loot.[44]

Ghazi came to refer to particular military leaders who conquered territory, but also to volunteers who converted to Islam and fought alongside the armies of the Ghaznavid Empire. In many cases the term referred to full-time soldiers who, when unemployed in periods of peace, became bandits.[45] Some leaders took the title of '*al-Ghazi*' to denote their status, and many volunteers were recruited by the Ghaznavids from Afghanistan and Central Asia to fight in India as *ghazis*. It was here that the emphasis on forced conversion and enthusiasm for the faith reappears strongly. According to the eleventh-century historian Utbi, the volunteers exhibited a 'zeal for Islam, ... striking their numerous swords, and uttering the shout of the holy war: "God is Great"'.[46] Utbi records that they were prominent in battle, although details of their motivations and tactics are omitted. Later Mughal records suggest that *ghazis* were indistinguishable from other warriors, and were especially given to collecting loot and hunting. During the Mongol invasions, *ghazis* were those who defended Muslim territory in South Asia.[47] In the Near East in the tenth and eleventh centuries, *ghaza* was a term used to justify all manner of military operations, even against other Muslim states. Tribal groups on the periphery of the Ottoman Empire who were commissioned to raid others were styled *ghazis*, but at the same time *ghazis* had entered the written and oral traditions of many Middle Eastern communities and were associated with courageous actions that glorified Islam.[48] Afghans therefore reached for this lexicon in their conflicts with non-Muslim foreigners. Significantly, Amir Amanullah (r.1919–29) was awarded the title *Ghazi* for his apparent 'victory' over the British in 1919, but he was later to betray that faith and was deposed in an insurrection led by religious conservatives.

Islam has been an important cultural lens for Afghans' perceptions of and approaches to warfare. The concept of Jihad, the struggle to protect the faith, has been deeply enmeshed with a desire, particularly in rural areas, to preserve a way of life from outsiders or alien contaminants. Islam also emphasizes a sense of obligation that lends itself to military service, and this too is reinforced amongst rural communities with obligations to protect and serve one's family, clan or *qawm*. The more ecstatic forms of Islam, heightened in times of crisis, have sometimes corresponded with and strengthened support for charismatic leaders, while clan cultures celebrate acts of heroism. Equally, Islam has provided the framework for negotiation and restoring peace, and the rural mullahs were often the individuals who acted as intermediaries in inter-clan disputes. Rural clans stressed the pragmatism of survival which could, at times of extreme scarcity, take a ruthless form. Islam could act to temper violence but also provide the legitimacy and regulatory element for it under particular circumstances.

13

'Ethnic Warfare' and civil war in Afghanistan

Curiously, the notion of a 'way of war' is not normally applied to civil war in the way that it is for conventional wars between states, although it is sometimes attributed to a category of warfare in wars of liberation. This inconsistency reflects a disciplinary preference for the study of state-on-state conflicts in international relations and to some extent in military history too. To explain repeated episodes of civil war, or the ethnic nature of conflicts in Afghanistan, sociologists, anthropologists and political scientists emphasize comparable behavioural traits and practices, whereas historians tend to look for empirical explanations through the specificities and contingencies of events and evidence. For social scientists that align themselves to 'primordialist' explanations, the focus is on traditions and beliefs that are antagonistic towards 'primordial objects', the biological features of a group or their territorial location.[49] This would certainly seem to explain the deep-seated conflict between Pashtuns and the Hazaras, for example. Afghans seem to have an instinctive ability to identify ethnic difference and confront rival groups.[50] Historians prefer to show how these are dependent on time and circumstance.

James Fearon and David Laitin argue that conflicts that appear to be 'ethnic' are in fact driven by other conditions: political instability, weak governance, economic inequality and structural conflicts that can be traced back into the past.[51] They posit that these conflicts often become civil wars or insurgencies because of the ideal conditions for such warfare, including 'rough terrain and large populations'. This would suggest that ethnicity was 'instrumentalist', a badge of identity that could be exploited by leaders to mobilize a part of the population against others. Those examining nationalism and ethnic identity have often referred to 'imagined communities' that are artificially constructed in order to differentiate from an 'Other', often because that Other is a threat or a competitor for scarce resources.[52] This 'constructivist' school of thought helps to explain the way that certain Afghan families have managed to change their identity and allegiances, often through marriages, to realign with a different clan and thereby join a stronger group and avoid destruction. The more temporary shift of allegiances might produce alliances. Stathis Kalyvas notes that there is a tendency in civil wars between fractured communities to side with whoever appears to be winning: this is the 'logic' of survival.[53] Post-constructivists, such as Monica Toft, are willing to embrace a hybrid of the other theories to show that, through the study of settlement patterns, it is possible to show that certain groups in a locality will opt for violence while others will not, because of a set of calculations based on 'constructed' identities, charismatic leaders, resource scarcity and precedent.[54]

However, recent research continues to dispute the idea of a purely ethnic conflict.[55] One of the chief criticisms has been that belligerents in ethnic conflicts seem to fight for zero-sum outcomes, such as battling over a landscape of no value or when there appears to be no 'rational' benefit to be gained at its conclusion. Yet, such critiques ignore the intrinsic importance of identity and what it represents in certain communities. An apparently 'worthless' landscape, besides its tactical or strategic value, may be important because it is something a clan believes it owns. In the case of the Ghilzais astride the Khyber Pass, the terrain was an important source of income as generations of merchants and traders had been taxed along its route. This would also be true of the Hazaras and the Panjshiri Tajiks, where mountain fastnesses offered income and security. In the case of the Pashtuns, identity and personal prestige were vital components that permeated every aspect of life.

Nineteenth-century ethnologists, British colonial officials and, subsequently, historians have attributed the ancestry of the Afghans, and particularly the Pashtuns, variously to Alexander's Greeks, the Scythians and White Huns, the 'lost tribes' of Israel, Turks, Aryans, and vaguely-defined 'aboriginal populations'.[56] The Pashtuns have been organized by segmentary, patrilineal descent groups from a common ancestor, Qais Abdul Rashid.[57] Lineages have been central to Pashtun identity, although they are subject to the vagaries of historical memory, and, as noted above, they are malleable when new alliances require legitimacy. The claims to descent were described by Fredrik Barth as an idiom to reflect social organization rather than an objective historical fact.[58] The fractured nature of the Pashtuns, and the competition between the clans for scarce resources, meant that the Pashtuns never acquired a single homeland, the Pashtunistan or *Pashtunkwa*. Only once did an Afghan Amir, Ahmad Shah Durrani, achieve a relatively united Pashtun-dominated state, but there was no sense of national identity. Internal divisions, dynastic rivalry and British strategic considerations resulted in the partition of the *Pashtunkwa* with the drawing of the Durand Line in 1893. The eastern *Pashtunkwa* was incorporated into the North West Frontier Province and was subsequently inherited by Pakistan with a separate enclave of the Federally Administered Tribal Areas (FATA), but even then there was little territorial, political or social unity. The traditional migratory patterns of the clans in the hills astride the Durand Line meant that the international border was largely ignored by local inhabitants, but, in contrast to their neighbours, the frontier Pashtuns failed to create a nation state.

Afghanistan came into being as the territory between the British, Russian and Persian Empires, continuing its historical role as a crossroads between Central and South Asia. Afghanistan had been a 'highway of conquest' from at least the fourth century BC, and, despite the frequent reference to Afghanistan's recent reputation as a 'graveyard of empires', historically it was Afghanistan that was repeatedly overrun and occupied because of the fragmented and weakened nature of its political organisation.[59] To maintain their meagre income and prevent permanent incorporation into neighbouring empires, the Afghans made use of the mountainous terrain to conceal themselves, harassed stronger adversaries and raided their rivals. The desire to maintain independence at the local level created an aversion to centralized authority, except in opposition to a more significant external threat.

Under the idealized version of the tribal code of *Pashtunwali*, a Pashtun will shelter, defend to the death, and offer generous hospitality to a stranger (*melmastia*), including an enemy who has become a fugitive (*nanawatai*). Charles Lindholm argued that this was due to a deep emotional need for an expression of love in a competitive, violent and barbarous society.[60] However, it was not 'love' that generated the code, but war. The struggle for limited resources in a marginal environment created intense competition and frequent outbreaks of violence. Hospitality evolved as a means of survival, and, like gift-giving, created obligations that had to be reciprocated. The emphasis on egalitarianism, '*har saray khan dey*' (every man a khan), ensured the fair distribution of limited resources or 'windfalls'. Heads of families sought to accrue honour and prestige as a form of deterrence: an accomplished warrior was less likely to be challenged. Anthropologists, like Barth, identified a 'structural violence' that characterized all relationships between different segments. This violence could be mediated by Sufi 'pirs' *ulema*, who used a neutral political position in order to broker peace deals, but warfare was as perpetual as the search for resources. Yet elders too had this responsibility: young men were expected to exhibit *tura* (hot-headedness) and older men were expected to exercise *aql* (restraint, and a lack of emotion unless representing the anguish of the clan or family).

Afghan Pashtuns were not entirely anarchic, forming alliances through marriage and relations in order to increase military power and deter rivals. However, once the *qawm*, or descent-locality group, reached a size likely to threaten the available resources, then suspicion and anxiety increased and served to undermine the very alliance to which a family or an individual might belong. Pashtuns valued the idealism of *gheryatmun* (courageous independence), rendering *qawm* alliances inherently temporary, unstable, and liable to disintegration. Solidarity to groups external to one's *qawm* were normally despised, but could be arranged for convenience or necessity. However, such a relationship would be even more temporary, lacking the solidarity that would be required to form a permanent bond of trust. The Pashtun needed to engage in alliances that were convenient but avoid military obligations that might incur his or his family's destruction. This helps to explain the fluidity of Afghans on the battlefield, rushing to assist another clan in the hope of spoils or an alliance, but equally quick to retreat and disperse if the engagement turned unfavourably against them. This dichotomy of engagement and independence can be expressed as *atrapi-y* (an Arabic term for 'freedom in all directions').[61] Life under a government, *hokumaat*, was thought to be the antithesis of that liberty.[62]

Afghan communal conflicts and civil wars, and the deep-seated rivalries that feature in them, should perhaps be understood as part of a long historical evolution. This may help to explain why inter-clan rivalries persisted so stubbornly through time and why negotiations so often failed to ensure a lasting settlement. The essence of the 'historical' argument is that the probability of ethno-nationalist conflict increases with the number of prior conflicts fought in the name of the same ethnic group. Moreover, history is used to reinforce Afghan concepts of conflict, notions of the enemy and the means for mobilization. Cederman, Wimmer and Min argue:

Ethno-nationalist mobilization and contestation are macrohistorical processes that operate over both short and long time spans. It may take decades until perceived humiliation and unfair ethnic status hierarchies give rise to political mobilization and conflict. Thus, rather than being an instant and ahistorical phenomenon, nationalist mobilization takes place in a historical context that might be characterized by previous episodes of ethno-nationalist violence. In extreme cases of path dependency, actors may find themselves trapped in self-sustaining cycles of violence.[63]

Cederman, Wimmer and Min suggest that the way in which Afghans remember selections of their military history, and living that history through conflicts in the present, fuels a violent form of ethno-nationalism:

... past conflicts influence the likelihood of present conflict through three mechanisms. First, ethnonationalists attempt to glorify their group's history through one-sided narratives that stress their own victories and attribute blame for military losses to traitors, weak-spirited leaders, or a ruthless enemy. This implies that leaders might not update their risk assessments and might take up arms again even when the chances of winning have not improved significantly.[64]

They emphasize that selective and militarist history has an important part to play: 'past experiences of traumatic violence may live as a part of oral tradition or they may sometimes be perpetuated in official history textbooks and public rituals, nourishing calls for revenge'. Above all, they emphasize that:

prior exposure to combat means that violence is no longer unthinkable but constitutes part of the accepted repertoire of action and may help create organizational structures and identities that can be reactivated at later points in history or even create a culture of violence. We express these three mechanisms of path dependency in our third main hypothesis.[65]

Negotiations in war

It has long been recognized that negotiation has been a constant feature of conflict, during the fighting as much as it is at the conclusion, and, according to British and Soviet accounts, this was certainly the case throughout Afghanistan's modern history. When there is an asymmetry of historical records from which to work, as is the case with the relative abundance of British and Soviet sources compared with the relative paucity of Afghan ones, an understanding of the processes can help to establish a baseline of types of negotiation, practices, assumptions, calculations and outcomes. Existing theoretical models give us frameworks that can be applied across a number of episodes in Afghan history, and they lend themselves particularly well to comparative work. Theoretical approaches also enable scholars to identify specific themes and test them against quite distinct historical eras, and make it possible to begin to analyze the decision-making of Afghans where we have relatively few written records. Five stages emerge as particularly useful: one, the decision to negotiate; two, the conditions prevailing (whether one side perceived imminent defeat or victory, for example); three, the terms proffered and the process of negotiation; four, the implementation of those terms and, finally, the perceived or desired outcomes.

One feature common to the Afghan conflicts is the fact that Afghans were forced to negotiate amongst themselves, across traditional lines of social and ethnic division as much, if not more than with the foreigners who had occupied their territorial space. Moreover, it is clear that negotiations with foreigners did not end the conflicts of interest between Afghans, and civil wars were the frequent result. Afghan groups were divided by collaboration and resistance, while some tried to utilize the presence of foreigners to manipulate their military power or to exploit the withdrawal of occupiers to reinforce their own prestige.

There are four main themes common to Afghan conflicts which are given treatment here, but several other observations can be made. First, both the Afghans and their Western adversaries knew that it was better to negotiate from a position of strength. This challenges the popular idea that belligerents are more likely to initiate negotiations when there is a stalemate or an impasse, perhaps of some duration. In the First Afghan War in the winter of 1841, when a British garrison at Kabul had been isolated and cut off from its supplies, and its main negotiators, Alexander Burnes and William Hay MacNaghten, had been killed, the Afghans were prepared to discuss terms with the British for a time, until the imminent collapse of the retreating British forces tempted local Ghilzai clans to kill and loot at will. Equally, Soviet authorities delayed negotiations for some time in the mid 1980s, believing that a more vigorous prosecution of the war would enable them to 'break clean'.[66] This view was abandoned when it was clear that no military victory was possible, but the Soviet Union still had the strength and capacity to withdraw 'with honour'.

Second, violence is often a form of negotiation. That is not to say that violence is used only as a selective device to 'up the ante' once negotiations have begun, and thereby to improve a bargaining position tactically, but rather that violence is a form of communication with another identifiable group. In a recent lecture, Mary Kaldor noted how violence was reciprocal and that in war both parties tended to develop a dynamic of dependency at least in rationalizing their actions.[67] Arno Mayer and Stathis Kalyvas have also examined the proportionality of violence and its reciprocal nature in revolutions and civil wars respectively.[68] Joanna Bourke examined the intimacy of violence and posited that it was a means to connect with, assert power over and subordinate an adversary.[69] Afghans have also used violence to 'send a signal' to rival factions and families, taking killing beyond the rational requirements of power and resources in order to establish prestige, hierarchy or reputation. Afghan women were as involved in this as much as men. In the Third Afghan War (1919), British officers noted how Afghan women flayed and dismembered the bodies of British or Indian dead or wounded to intimidate, avenge losses or express their anger.[70] In the Soviet War, Mujahideen factions could use violence against the Soviets to prove their worth to the Pakistani Inter-Services Intelligence agency that supplied them with arms, ammunition and money. Their attacks on the Soviets, even if strategically insignificant, were a useful means of communicating to a third party.

Third, negotiating a truce or ceasefire can be a pragmatic means of escape from defeat or the method by which a belligerent can achieve their aims by means other than fighting. There are clear examples of this occurring in the Afghan context. Abdur Rahman, as a pretender to the Afghan throne in 1880, had not the means to defeat the British Army which was in occupation at Kabul. Instead, while protected by the Hindu Kush mountain range, he negotiated with the British to become Amir in return for concessions over Afghan foreign policy. In a contrasting example, the warlord leader Ahmad Shah Masoud settled a truce with the Soviets in order to relieve pressure on his guerrilla forces in the Panjshir Valley in the mid 1980s and as a means to 'break out' to more secure base areas in the north-east. His manoeuvre, while not without controversy, was a success, enabling him to resume resistance later on more favourable terms.

The fourth major theme for negotiation appears to be the need to find a surrogate. Both the British and the Soviets were prepared to negotiate with their enemies and the local powerbrokers to form and leave behind a government favourable to their own interests. In the case of the British in 1842, they accepted the return of Amir Dost Mohammed as the figure most likely to guarantee stability on the western flank of their growing Indian Empire. In 1880, they accepted Abdur Rahman as a ruler likely to keep Russian interests out of Afghanistan. Both of these Afghan leaders saw advantage in negotiating directly with the British, but also making use of the presence of Russia, as the means to wring concessions from the government in Calcutta or London. For the Soviets, the appointment of Dr Najibullah as a candidate likely to serve their interests but also be acceptable to the Afghan people appeared to be the means to ensure a strategic victory.[71]

In addition to these themes there are a number of further observations that can be made about negotiations in the Afghan context from a theoretical point of view. The first is that the role of a third party was important to the Soviet–Afghan negotiations, although it was not possible in the British wars of the nineteenth century because of the absence of any international institutions for that purpose. Negotiations were used by Mohammed Akbar Khan in the spring of 1842 to ascertain the objectives of the British because there was no other way to be certain of their intentions. For the Soviets and the Afghans in the 1980s, by contrast, the intervention of regional and international protagonists was critical. The United States, Pakistan and Iran all had interests in Afghanistan which influenced Afghan positions towards the Soviets, brought competing agendas into play and distorted the chances of a settlement of the Afghan civil war which had begun even before the Soviet intervention in 1979. Furthermore, as many other case examples from around the globe have proven, it is an essential requirement to have institutions that can engage all parties, ensure grievances are met and offer security guarantees during the implementation of the peace terms. The failure to achieve this was a direct cause of the civil war in Afghanistan from 1992 onwards.

Many studies emphasize the importance of 'ground conditions' as the determining factor for negotiations to begin. This can be a rational decision of cost-benefit analysis, where the time, cost, chances of victory, likely pay-offs, resources remaining, degree of external support and the level of pressure from a domestic population wearied by war may have a part to play. The ground conditions can produce a 'balance of power', or a stalemate which, George Modelski argued, is probably the key factor in creating the environment for negotiation.[72] Domestic institutions have an impact on the decision to negotiate when ground conditions appear unfavourable or in stasis. The leaders of democratic states are more likely to be held accountable for the progress of a military campaign, and there may be considerable pressure from below to negotiate or end a conflict. Furthermore, democratic institutions lend themselves to negotiation because of their traditions of power-sharing, and they are perhaps more likely to reach for this solution. The British colonial authorities and the Soviets appear to have made their decisions to negotiate on the basis of the military situation and costs, although reputation in the wider world also had a significant influence on them.

The willingness to seek to resolve conflict through bargaining is seen by some scholars as more significant than ground conditions, and can explain why the decision to negotiate is taken when military victory is imminent. It is thought that the identity of the combatants (which includes their values and ideologies), the divisibility of the stakes (whether there are sufficient spoils to divide, for example), and the presence of external third parties can determine the initiation of negotiations. When ideological convictions preclude concessions, then negotiations will fail, just as they will when the demands imposed by one belligerent are impossible to fulfil, or when one side prefers to pursue a path to absolute military victory. The aims of revolutionaries, which are predicated on the overthrow of a regime, are unlikely to permit negotiation, which contrasts with separatists or those seeking moderate reform that may be prepared to accept a compromise. Popular clan revolts against British occupation in 1841 and 1879 would exemplify the former, while the cooperation and collaboration of certain Khans, such as the Khan of Kelat in 1880, eager to preserve their position and faced with overwhelming force, illustrates the latter.

The presence of a third party to push for negotiations and monitor the implementation of terms is regarded as a key factor in the lasting success of any settlement, although even then, as Barbara Walter observed, almost two-thirds of negotiations in civil wars fail.[73] Mediators and the 'Good Offices' of the United Nations were critical to the success of the Geneva Accords which led to the Soviet withdrawal from Afghanistan in 1989. Axelrod notes that these third parties can establish an agenda which keeps the belligerents on track, in spite of deteriorating ground conditions and a return to violence.[74] In some cases third parties can also provide the interventionist forces, from peacekeepers to more robust force structures with appropriate rules of engagement, which can impose a settlement and ensure security for the warring parties' populations.

However, military intervention to forestall civil war, as in the Soviet case in 1979, adds a new variable of violence and does not guarantee peace. The Soviets became the target of violence and actually united previously warring factions against them. Nevertheless, Walter argues that the ground conditions are not the determinant in the decision to negotiate. She believes that security guarantees, for which third parties are essential, are critical to the success or failure of any negotiations. Walter's 'Credible Commitment' thesis suggests that negotiations require more than the resolution of underlying grievances to succeed at all. Ceasefires may fail, for example, but negotiations can still work if the protagonists feel that their goals can be fulfilled and that their own personnel can be protected as they make the transition to peace. Confidence-building measures, such as verification, monitoring and security, are vital to success. Interventions to impose a negotiated settlement, and the deployment of peacekeepers after a settlement, may not guarantee success. It will invariably depend on the local situation whether full military interventions (such as Afghanistan in 2001 to the present) are effective.

Existing histories of the Afghans at war

There is a vast amount of material by British writers on the Afghans. This collection of travelogues, official literature and academic work is characterized by a desire to describe the history, geography, ethnography and politics of Afghanistan, and, above all, the behaviour, culture and habits of the people. Some, like Mountstuart Elphinstone, the first British envoy to Kabul in 1808, sought to understand the Afghans sympathetically, but amongst the others, the Political Agent Alexander Burnes was more instrumentalist in his assessments and manipulated or selected what he observed in order to concentrate minds at home or directly alter British policy.

British views of the Afghans were made in relation to their own experiences and in comparison to British rule in India. Elphinstone noted that the Afghans were 'decently attired' and not 'half-naked' like the Indians.[75] He admired their honesty and independence. Elphinstone captured the mixed feelings the British had of the Afghans from the beginning. He wrote:

The English traveller from India—would admire their strong and active forms, their fair complexions and European features, their industry and enterprise, the hospitality, sobriety and contempt for pleasure which appear in all their habits; and, above all, the independence and energy of their character–On the whole, his impression of his new acquaintance would be favourable—he would reckon them virtuous, compared with the people to whom he had been accustomed.[76]

Like many of the British that followed, Elphinstone was struck by their ability to offer hospitality to any stranger in their homes and yet rob and butcher those they found on the trails. He concluded: 'Their vices are revenge, envy, avarice, rapacity and obstinacy; on the other hand, they are fond of liberty, faithful to their friends, kind to their dependents, hospitable, brave, hardy, frugal, laborious and prudent'. He continued: 'Ruthless, cowardly robbery, [and] cold-blooded, treacherous murder, are to him the salt of life. Brought up from his earliest childhood amid scenes of appalling treachery and merciless revenge, nothing can ever change him. As he lived—a shameless cruel savage—so he dies'.[77]

The emphasis of nineteenth-century accounts was on observed 'character traits' and behaviours, but articulated in terms of difference, and as fighting qualities. The Pashtuns, with whom they had most contact, were accorded particular attributes by British observers, but almost all references repeat admiration for their fighting skills, condemnation of their bellicosity and the acknowledgement of their obligations under *Pashtunwali*. Colonel C. E. Callwell described them as 'Marauding cut-throats', 'exceptionally fine mountaineers', 'admirable marksmen', and 'ferocious adversaries'. He suggested, rather quaintly: 'Like most savages they can see far better in the dark than Europeans can'.[78] Colonel H. D. Hutchinson, who took part in the Tirah campaign against the Afridi Pashtuns, noted: '...these men are extremely bold, and they are as cunning and clever as they are audacious. They show much patience in watching and waiting for their prey, and great dash and impudence in their attacks when they make them'.[79]

By the 1890s, the theory of 'martial races' had become more firmly institutionalized in the Indian Army. The Pashtuns were regarded as natural hill fighters who, with the right discipline and training, could channel that prowess into military service for Britain. However, much has been written about the loaded nature of the term 'tribesman', with all its connotations of savagery and ignorance, and when subjected to the brutal attacks of Pashtuns, particularly where the dead and wounded were cut up, it was understandable perhaps that British observers made this pessimistic and pejorative assessment. In common with many analysts of non-European races in the nineteenth century, Henry Bellew, an administrator among the Yusufzai, wondered if they were governable at all: 'The most notable traits in their character are unbounded superstition, pride, cupidity and a most vengeful spirit–They despise all other races–They glory in being robbers, admit they are avaricious, and cannot deny the reputation they have acquired for faithlessness.'[80]

Bellew, who took part in the First Afghan War, was unimpressed by the Afghans and drew attention to their 'fanaticism' and their tenacity as formidable fighting qualities, as a way of influencing others at home. Later writers were similarly divided. Lord Frederick Roberts and R. I. Bruce, who were exponents of the Forward Policy against Afghanistan in the 1880s, felt the Afghans should be chastised and, if necessary, occupied, in order to bring Afghanistan into a colonial scheme of defence as well as being integrated economically and politically into South Asia. Sir Robert Warburton, the half-Afghan Political Officer who supervised the Khyber Afridis, and Sir Henry Mortimer Durand, the Foreign Minister of the Government of India in the 1890s, were more sympathetic and attempted to work with the Afghans and frontier Pashtuns. They felt more could be gained by getting the cooperation of the Afghans and border clans, but there were still limits: British policy interests always came first.

There was rather less appreciation by the British of the effect of the environment on their views of the Afghans, although they were often given to describing the 'wild landscape' and relate this to the 'wildness' of Afghans. Given the mountainous nature of much of Afghanistan, the population had been confined to marginal terrain and ribbons of cultivable settlement. The heavy winter snows cut off Afghanistan's passes and restricted access for caravan traffic, leaving the people isolated. The presence of neighbouring states and empires, including the Persians, Sikhs, Russians and British, hemmed in the population, and eventually political divisions carved away portions of the country, adding to the natural divisions created by mountain systems and distance. Although the British saw the Afghans and the Pashtuns as frontier peoples in relative poverty, the Afghans regarded themselves as survivors, dependent on subsistence agriculture, transit tolls, raiding and smuggling. These economic activities coloured British views of the Afghans and Pashtuns as a whole. Bellew concluded that the Afghans were: 'a race of robbers, ... quarrelsome, ... faithless and intractable without appreciating their situation'.

These critical perspectives became more prevalent after military setbacks in the nineteenth century and as more rigid views of South and Central Asians took hold. Racial interpretations and a frustration with the continued resistance of the Afghans and Pashtuns meant they were condemned as fanatics, given to irrational beliefs. British observers pointed to the endemic violence of Afghan society as evidence of their lawlessness. Yet while Pashtuns seemed so irreconcilable, the concept of martial races more suited to service in the Indian Army gained greater purchase; a number of Pashtuns were enlisted in frontier formations and line regiments because of their martial qualities as warriors. Pashtuns were especially admired for their 'strong, self-sufficient' attributes. The British tended to see the Afghans and the Pashtuns as a collection of tribes readily suited to military service, but the concept of the 'noble savage' espoused by Rousseau in the eighteenth century had been replaced, by the late nineteenth century, with more negative connotations. British officers noted that Pashtun soldiers were often divided by clan rivalries and family feuds that spilled over from their home life, or indeed, were a consequence of their military service. This gave the impression that Pashtun soldiers were unreliable when, in fact, their first loyalty was to their family and *qawm*, and not to the mercenary service with the British. The British Indian Army tried to circumvent local rivalries by grouping personnel into specific frontier corps, companies or regiments, and Political Officers were despatched to work with specific sections, but they never overcame the first loyalties of the Pashtuns they employed.[81]

The generally negative British assessments appear to have deprived the Afghans and Pashtuns of being anything more than 'wild tribesmen'. Yet, the British also had respect for their spirit, skill and endurance in the mountain environment. The frontier was described as both grim and romantic. Its landscapes seemed untamed and service there offered the opportunity for military leaders to be free to exercise their own judgement, not least because they were so often involved in small unit actions where junior officers were responsible for key decisions. There was also admiration for the 'frontier' lifestyle of the Pashtun fighters, which seemed to contrast with the unhealthy aspects of urban living in Britain. Robert MacDonald suggests that the British appreciated the masculinity of the Pashtuns who lived a strong, independent and self-sufficient life, and, alongside Britain's experience of fighting the South Africans in 1899–

1902, this drove the movement for national efficiency, scouting and greater physical fitness in the early twentieth century.[82] Alan Moorhouse believes the North West Frontier provided an opportunity to enhance individual reputations in the context of an imperial mission: amongst participants, skirmishes were referred to as 'scraps' and sporting metaphors were common. Casualties were born 'cheerfully' and there was often genuine praise for the *sang froid* of the troops.[83] British Political Officers who served amongst the Pashtuns were expected to be of good character, with tact, flexibility, stamina, gentlemanly bearing and the ability to command.[84]

It was through Elphinstone that the British inherited the idea that the Afghans were stereotypically tribal. Strongly influenced by his observations of the groups in the south and east of Afghanistan, Elphinstone listed 392 Pashtun groups, although he remained less familiar with the Uzbeks, Tajiks, Hazaras and Aimaqs, and several other minorities. Yet his interests were wider than pure ethnography. Elphinstone compiled no fewer than nine volumes of data on geography, commerce and government on Afghanistan, which finally found its way into just two volumes published in 1815. Although it has been suggested that Elphinstone was building a system of knowledge that ultimately sought to control Afghans, it seems pretty clear that he was far more interested in the scientific value of his research.[85]

Systems of government amongst Afghans and Pashtuns also created particular British viewpoints. During the diplomacy and military operations in 1839–42, the British were eager to establish a surrogate monarchy that could serve their interests, and they failed to grasp that Afghanistan depended on a variety of systems of governance, including village *jirgas* in Pashtun mountain areas, Khans wielding various degrees of power amongst the people, baronial Khans with their own fiefdoms, viziers and *wakils*, and 'Amir' Dost Mohammed of Kabul. There was no monopoly of power, no Caesar and no senate. Afghanistan was still in the throes of civil war when the British intervened, and even in times of peace rulers in Kabul, Ghazni and Kandahar were forced to be far more consultative than the British assumed. The clans of the eastern Ghilzais paid little attention and owed no loyalty to the Khans of Kabul or Kandahar. The realization that Afghan politics was so fractured prompted the British to seek to install a more stable and powerful Amir, a ruler better able to resist Russian encroachments from the north, which was the perennial concern of the Great Game. For this, the British were willing to pay a substantial allowance and donate weapons, rendering Afghanistan into a 'rentier state'. The British were also eager to elevate *maliks* and *arbabs*, leaders and middle men, within the egalitarian Pashtun society, to act as interlocutors, to distribute allowances and keep the peace. The military authorities in India were keen to maintain a pacified border lest it threaten their lines of communication which lay astride the mountain belt into Afghanistan. However, allowances paid by the British were a frequent source of friction between clans and families and they were an imperfect means to address the poverty of marginal mountain communities. Allowances could not guarantee an end to the tradition of raiding for material gain or as a means to demonstrate their culture of worthiness.

To some extent, the contradictory nature of British impressions of the Afghans and Pashtuns stemmed from the many shifts in frontier policy from 1849 to 1947 as they attempted to manage, manipulate and manoeuvre the Pashtuns.[86] Unable to sustain the costs of permanent occupation, the British instead set about turning Afghanistan into a client buffer state, whilst weakening the Pashtuns on their immediate frontier with punitive military expeditions, boundary demarcation and the deployment of Political Officers. Of these the latter proved to be the most successful, not because of the skills of the officers *per se*, but because Politicals could work through the social networks which characterized Pashtun society. The British learned to appreciate that negotiation, particularly after skirmishes, was an integral part of Pashtun culture. They also looked to recruit the 'martial races' of the hills into the Indian Army, turning 'poachers into gamekeepers', as a solution to the security threat the Pashtuns posed to the British settled border areas. By the 1940s, it was clear that employment and negotiation with tribal leaders were more lasting solutions than punitive military operations.[87]

Some caution is required in reading the historical record to make judgements about the present. Assumptions about Afghan preferences based on distinct historical circumstances have often created inaccurate generalizations. That said, in Afghanistan's military history it is clear that standard military principles have been applied by both regular and irregular forces, such as the search for alliances as part of a grand strategy, the pursuit of victory in conventional war, or the harassing of the lines of communication of occupation forces. Cultural preferences do seem to influence Afghan decision-makers, creating assumptions and misconceptions as readily as they do for any other group, but they do not determine those decisions. The historical records indicate that, quite often, the Afghans and their adversaries shared perceptions. A careful examination of British military records in the late nineteenth century, for example, suggests that Pashtuns in the frontier districts understood war as a tool for the accumulation of honour as much as an opportunity to achieve specific tactical outcomes, not unlike the British themselves. In other conflicts, when the British felt they had achieved victory through occupation or a particular decisive battle, the Afghans often felt they had fulfilled all their culturally-informed obligations and 'won'.

Soviet knowledge of the Afghans was, to some extent, better than the Western agencies of the twenty-first century because there had been a period of cooperation for almost two decades before the war of 1979. The resistance fighters came to be known as *dhukis* (ghosts) because they were so unknown and elusive, but, despite the general familiarity with the country, many Soviet soldiers regarded the Afghans with contempt. There were episodes where Soviet troops would fire on Afghan communist soldiers, and vice versa, and the history of the war is littered with accounts of atrocities.[88] Given that Soviet soldiers found themselves killed randomly by snipers, mines, and even by women and children, it is easier to understand, if not condone, why the troops took such severe reprisals. These incidents embittered both sides. However, there were also episodes of cooperation between the belligerents. While the Mujahideen executed some Soviet prisoners, others were exchanged through intermediaries. For example, a Soviet Tajik soldier in Shindand, Feliks Rakhmonov, frequently paid for prisoners, and in one transaction bartered three men for some flour and seven cans of diesel.[89]

Lingering historical perceptions or misperceptions, and strategic errors, led to a number of problems in Western military operations in Afghanistan in the period after 2001. Subsequently, to achieve a victory in counterinsurgency, the Coalition powers believed that they required a more thorough understanding of the Afghans in order to exploit weaknesses and divisions, to isolate 'irreconcilable' fighters, to recruit supporters and to 'win hearts and minds'. The experiment with Human Terrain analysis has had mixed reviews, not least amongst American anthropologists, and familiar problems of categorization from the past have reappeared.[90] Social surveys attempted to reveal what the Afghan people wanted, which policy-makers and journalists seized upon to reinforce or critique particular political agendas. The result is misconception and confusion, a situation which was in fact exploited by the Afghans themselves.

Misunderstandings have characterised Afghan perceptions too. Afghan histories, both oral and written, have tended to reflect a political purpose, either reinforcing genealogical achievements of particular clans or nationalist values. Louis Dupree embraced oral traditions to glimpse an Afghan world view and the values that supported it, and discovered how the memories of the three

Anglo–Afghan Wars were used to reinforce a sense of clan identity.[91] At Malik Khel in the Khyber Pass, Amanullah of the Babur Khel clan of Ghilzai Pashtuns related that his ancestors had fought the British in 1842, and, confusing his chronology, he stated:

The holy war began. A real hot war. Then the British appealed for another jirga and asked permission to leave and give up Afghanistan. They said ... We must decide who will be king of the Afghans. And that will be Abdur Rahman Khan, son of Amir Afzal, who was living in Moscow ... The British left Kabul and the Afghan patriots chased them. Wherever the British camped the ghazis were after them... when the British entered the Khord Kabul Valley, the Afghans shouted and began the battle. The British troops lost many of their people. Some were killed by the water, some by swords, some by guns, but all by the hand of Allah. The ghazis had flintlocks, some breechloaders. Hour by hour the British received losses... only three, four or five got back to their homeland.[92]

Archival material and official Afghan analysis on the Anglo–Afghan Wars is also subject to interpretations that stress national achievements. The work by Sayyid Mohammed Qasim Rishtiya emphasized the courage of Afghan fighters, the treachery of the British and victorious outcomes.[93] The Swiss ethnologist Pierre Centlives argued that the wars against the British were the defining elements in modern Afghan national identity: 'For many people in Afghanistan ... [the] embryo of national feeling is rooted in history and in the heroic imagery of the struggle against the English in the nineteenth century. It is also the source of popular political thought'.[94] However, it was a very selective form of nationalism that stressed the achievements of Pashtuns. Nazif Shahrani complained that the 'invisibility of non-Pashtun groups ... was particularly evident in official histories taught in the school system'.[95] Rishtiya was attacked by certain minorities for failing to play up each community's individual role, but also because he was a Shi'ite historian. Hasan Kakar nevertheless challenged the orthodoxy with his work on early-modern Afghanistan, and Mir Ghulam Mohammed Ghobar, a leading historian of the 1940s who wrote a critical history *Afghanistan in the Course of History*, had his book banned by the Afghan government. The state radio and later television services tried to construct the Afghan national consciousness, but they were never able to resolve the tension between Islamist and communist interpretations of the past. Both emphasized a particular ideological position and seemed intolerant of pluralism. Communist party ideologues borrowed from Marxist–Leninist theory, and practically the only sentiment they could share with the radical religious idealists of 'Political Islam' was hostility to foreign, imperial interventions.[96] War, especially the 'allure for Afghans of the concepts of jihad and martyrdom', has been promi-nent.[97] Ironically, these 'national' and militarist interpretations depended heav-ily on transnationalist critiques. In the 1990s, the Taliban also seized upon an isolationist, anti-foreign sentiment that defined nationalism in opposition to the Western world.

Methods and approaches

James Belich's study of the New Zealand Wars provides us with a possible frame-work to recover the Afghan and Pashtun perspectives in the British campaigns along the frontier and in Afghanistan, of various factions in the civil wars (as reported and recorded by Afghans and British personnel in Western records) and of Afghan operations against the Soviets without the loss of objectivity.[98] Belich argued that nineteenth-century British sources tended to stereotype the Maori in such a way as to deprive them of any tactical or strategic sense and instead emphasized certain attributes such as determination, savagery and elu-siveness.[99] He studied the British sources and written accounts by settlers to piece together the Maori approach to war. He located Maori formations in time and space, and extrapolated a set of operational and strategic plans. Whilst critics might challenge the conclusiveness of his analysis, there is no doubt that his work offered a chance to reclaim the Maori perspective and therefore cre-ate a far more thorough understanding of the decision-making on both sides.

The problem of interpreting the actions of those who fought the colonial powers, but who have few or no written records, has led in recent years to greater interest in oral tradition. This has its merits, of course, but historians remain sceptical of its value, especially when events experienced by people sev-eral generations ago are collected.[100] It can sometimes reveal a deep-seated sense of grievance, wrapped into the cultural metaphors of the society in question, but often events of great antiquity and recent memory flow together and are constantly re-interpreted by each generation.

Post-colonial scholars have also attempted to recover the 'silenced subal-terns' of empire by offering their own interpretations which strip away West-ern assumptions, conceptions and an emphasis on the rulers. Ranajit Guha's introduction to the first volume of *Subaltern Studies* criticized the emphasis of 'elitist histories' of the intelligentsia and denounced the idea that the masses had responded along 'vertical lines' of command rather than possessing any agency of their own.[101] Certainly it would seem sensible to assess the degree to which the highly democratized and fragmented Pashtun groups acted independently of their 'leaders', but equally, it would be just as crucial to keep in mind the part played by charismatic leadership, not least from influential religious figures, as well as the influence of khans, elders and chieftains of non-Pashtun Afghans.

Some more recent post-colonial scholars are so concerned to remove the 'taint of colonialism' in their analyses that they have suggested that a bricolage of myth and memory should take the place of 'empiricism' as *the* history of those peoples as they see it. Edward Said pointed to European constructions of the Asians which were so pervasive as to render them subordinate, and it was evident that he railed against the racist stereotypes of the colonial era that had, unwittingly or not, continued into modern analyses.[102] Critics of Said's work demonstrated that there were several flaws in his polemic, and the very existence of the Pashtun resistance, spread over many decades, suggests that, for all the ideological justifications the British or Soviets invented, there was no question of this being a substitute for exercising power or actual occupation.[103]

Indeed, despite the assertions that British Orientalist assumptions were largely myths, there could be no escaping the fact that other groups from the region also described the Afghans and Pashtuns in similarly stereotyped terms. The Orientalist debate thus turned from the polarities of constructive 'discourses' about the 'Other' to embrace the idea of dialogues, and the interpenetration of assumptions, knowledge and ideas. By studying a wider range of material, it was thought that scholars might gain a better understanding of the Europeans and the colonial 'other', and this might therefore include the narratives, stories and myths of the frontier generated by the Afghans and frontier Pashtuns.[104] Historians, with their preference for the empirical, have still been circumspect. Myths are not a substitute for what Leopold von Ranke called the past '*wie es eigentlich gewesen*' (essentially as it happened); they may augment our understanding of the cultural world view of those who confronted the Europeans, but they do not give us the rendering of strategy or tactical decision-making that would satisfy a rigorous military analysis.

There are some fragments of written testimony which, rather like the Western historian of the medieval period, one must piece together carefully. It is clear from the letters of leading Afghan and Pashtun participants which do survive that, as so often in history, it is not so much what happened as what people believed was happening which determined their decisions. A letter from Kazi Mira Khan (representing the Adam Khel Afridis' *Jirga*) to Mullah Said Akbar of the Aka Khel clan on 28th Jamadi-ul-Awal 1315AH (25 October 1897) on the British side of the Durand Line referred to reports that had come via Kabul to the effect that Aden, the British coaling station, and the Suez Canal had been seized by the Ottoman Sultan. This meant that it would take the British 'six months to send reinforcements to India'. The letter continued:

The Sultan, the Germans, the Russians and the French are all in arms against the British at all seaports and fighting is going on in Egypt too against them. In short the British are disheartened nowadays–British troops are required in Egypt and other seaports.–In the case of the Mohmands and the peoples of Ghandab, who had killed ten thousand British troops and had inflicted a heavy loss of rifles and property on them, the British, in their great dismay, concluded a settlement with them for 24 rifles only–when the British get rid of their other difficulties they will turn back and demand from the Mohmands their remaining rifles and compensation for their losses,–I have thus informed you of the deeds and perplexities of the English.[105]

This single letter hints at local interpretations of international events, and one detects the British concerns with the recent Franco–Russian Alliance in 1894 and the spat with Germany over the Kruger Telegram in 1896. This example hints at a functional alternative to the oral tradition that utilizes British and indigenous documents. A re-examination of British sources to reconstruct the movements, actions and comments of the Afghans and frontier Pashtuns may give some idea of their strategy, operational plans and tactics, although it must be said that this can in no way constitute a definitive and conclusive solution to the absence of Afghan accounts.

We should also consider the approaches of other disciplines that can help to illuminate the Afghan decision-making. Political anthropology, for example, examines both power and culture, and the role played by ideology, symbols and organizations, particularly during conflicts. Comaroff and Comaroff argue that it is not just the narrative of decisions which emerges from the participants that matters, but also the context of that narrative.[106] They have to be 'situated in the wider worlds of power and meaning'. For decades, Fredrick Barth's anthropological study of the fragmented and feuding Swat Pathans and his description of the tribal code of *Pashtunwali* stood as the definitive study of all Pashtuns.[107] However, there were several assumptions in Barth's work which have subsequently been challenged. The idea that, in Pashtun society, there was endemic and deadly feuding was, in fact, the result of specific land arrangements implemented by the British, which led to a particular peak in internal unrest. His analysis seemed to suggest that the tribal code, with its polarizing demands for *melmastia* (hospitality), the preservation of personal *nang* (honour) and *badal* (revenge against all enemies), was immutable. Akbar

Ahmed, whilst critical of Barth's assumption that the Swat Pashtuns were typical of the entire frontier region, nevertheless repeated his assertion that the martial tradition and predilection for embracing Jihad were unchanging Pashtun attributes.[108] He also perhaps rather overstated the case that, in their approach to war, Islamic unity and tribal cohesion could overcome the sort of Hobbesian anarchy that Barth had portrayed.

David Edwards' study of the Pashtuns during the Soviet occupation of Afghanistan in the 1980s suggested a far more selective use of the Afghan behavioural codes, warning us to be circumspect about the creation of some over-arching hypothesis.[109] Rather than compelling action, the code acted as a guide to assess and react to changing situations in particular ways. The code itself was therefore subject to constant re-interpretation, depending on the nature of each crisis.[110] This code was also balanced against the demands of Islam and the particular understanding of the faith by largely illiterate clans. Religious teachers frequently acted as the translators of religious injunctions, but also initiated them. The response of the Afghan and Pashtun population was, however, far from certain: mullahs sometimes found that their calls for action or neutrality were not heeded. Village *jirgas* might decide that it was simply not prudent to follow a particular mullah's advice, and they would deploy their own references to Islamic injunctions to serve their purpose. Moreover, whilst the *ulema* might be accorded respect in legal matters, in the settlement of disputes or moral questions village imams and mullahs had far less influence.[111] Generational differences could play their part just as strongly. Young men without employment and in need of the opportunity to prove their worth as fighters for the sake of personal honour would carry out raids and ambushes in defiance of the local elders. In other words, the Afghans and frontier Pashtuns did not adhere to a rigid system but lived and negotiated through the code and their personal or collective circumstances. Capable of unity in the face of an external threat, or the combination of enemies from rival clans, lineage or family, they were just as likely to abandon the alliance as soon as circumstances changed. Although responsive to the call for armed defence of Islam, they might abandon any struggle if it was more pragmatic to do so. Moreover, whilst old men counselled one course of action, the younger generations might equally pursue their own agendas.

The notion of a dynamic tribal culture certainly appears to offer a far more satisfactory historical explanation for the actions of the clans of Afghanistan and the North West Frontier. The idea of a dynamic within tribal society continues to be the case in Pashtun-dominated regions of Afghanistan, even where decades of civil war have sliced through and disrupted older hierarchies, social and political jurisdictions, and land claims.

However, there is another caveat. Decisions and actions were not only the result of dynamics within tribal societies, but also of reactions to external influences. Unity could be forged by an alien threat. Language, a segmentary structure and acephalous organization, endogamous marriage rules and egalitarianism could all help the coherence of the tribes in the sense that they all understood and endorsed a particular way of life and defined themselves with reference to the difference of outsiders. Moreover, groups and families made frequent reference to a patrilinear descent using the suffix of *zai* (family) or *khel* (clan) to identify themselves. The oldest groups might be able to trace their ancestry back generations, and these connections could form the basis of a temporary alliance, but equally clan identities could be changed for survival or convenience. The *parajamba* (taking sides) in disputes within Pashtun society might involve a calculation of one's proximity, from a lineage point of view, to the protagonists. The process was so common that it was termed *tarburwali* (conflict between first cousins). One British officer recalled how shooting could break out within a village, but after a few had been killed or wounded and the ammunition exhausted, 'a quarrel could be settled by an interchange of marriages'.[112] Groups conjoined by intermarriage between lineages were styled *quom/qawm*, and decisions about these, in common with all other clans, sections and families had also to be calculated against a system of prestige. Refusing a challenge or failure to respond to an insult would reduce the individual's prestige, *izzat*, or *nang*. Accepting challenges or proactively seeking to enhance one's prestige increased the individual's and the clan's social standing. Making war on the British and later the Soviets was, of course, far more clear-cut since they were regarded as alien in clan terms, infidel in their religion (or *kufr*, without religion) and without prestige as a consequence of their coercive policies.

Historically, particular aspects of the Pashtun code do appear to have been influential in fighting. The key issue for the Pashtuns of the frontier region in the late nineteenth century, for example, was that the occupation of any of their lands constituted a direct threat to their way of life, and they believed that the British had deliberately and consistently eroded their honour. For generations after the Pashtuns had occupied the mountain region of the Suleiman range, this marginal land was periodically redistributed to the *daftari* (shareholders) in a process known as *wesh*. Considerable tracts were sometimes exchanged, requiring some nomadism between sections. The exchange of land also served to reinforce the *pashtunwali* code, since it ensured that each tribesman had the means, along with women and weapons, to sustain his personal honour.[113] By contrast, *faqirs*, former prisoners, servants, the dispossessed, and non-Pashtun artisans could neither compete as *daftari* nor participate in *jirgas*. Yet the Pashtuns did not have habitual leaders; even men of influence rarely possessed any authority beyond the immediate issues presented at the *jirgas*. The only exception might be those who could demonstrate a consistent piety in their religious devotions and deeds. Nevertheless, the erosion of this system was not due solely to foreigners. Before British rule, the system of *wesh* and *nang* was already under threat. The centralization of the Mughals and then the Kabuli monarchs meant that tributes and revenues were extracted. Landowning and the possession of private property further challenged the tribal system. Several decades after the British had taken control of the Punjab, the more efficient extraction of land revenue, the jurisdiction of their courts and the rise of the landowners still affected only the margins of tribal territory. The changes imposed on the Settled Districts (areas within the British 'Administrative Border' from 1849) nevertheless caused considerable anxiety amongst the tribesmen of the frontier region.[114] Permanent private landowning, which the British favoured, directly challenged the notion of land exchanges. Money lenders, many of them Hindus, and unscrupulous land speculators or *Arbabs* (middle men) represented the unworthy to the Pashtuns, and yet it was these very people who seemed to profit from rising land values at the expense of Pashtuns. When the British built fortifications and roads along the edge of tribal lands, it seemed to be only a matter of time before they imposed their rule throughout the region, and, when they did, they would be depriving the tribesmen of the ability to assert their *nang* and perhaps of being a Pashtun at all.

For the British trying to control the frontier, it made sense to create a landowning class to provide a leadership to do business with and to lead the tribesmen into less 'criminal' activity. Settled and wealthy landowners had a stake in the Raj and shared its interests in terms of stability and order. Smaller landowners, who aspired to share the prestige of the larger landowners, also collaborated willingly. When faced by feuding and raids, the British put pressure on the *jirgas* of the Settled Districts to produce far more draconian and punitive sentences than the traditional, more ambiguous assemblies had done. An increase in population put more pressure on the land, whilst rising rents and prices towards the end of the century increased the tension between families and clans, and increased disaffection with British influence. There was still more anger at the British habit of paying 'political pensions' for the continued loyalty of certain landowners. Both the British and these 'sub-imperialists' assumed they could exercise some control over the clans of the settled areas. In the remote areas, Political Agents were despatched to create communication channels and to exercise some supervision, but, whilst these agents were generally treated with respect, they nevertheless represented another step towards direct colonial rule. The result was armed resistance. This desire to protect the land and way of life was perhaps typical of the Afghan situation.

This book attempts to examine the Afghan 'way of war', reflecting on the ways in which Afghans could define victory, conceive of strategy, carry out operational planning and execute those plans during campaigns. It evaluates force structures, troop types and tactical evolutions. It attempts to show strategic preferences that occurred under particular circumstances. However, the emphasis is on change over continuity. It attempts to explain how motivation changed, showing how the emergence of ideologies subverted traditional allegiances based on dynasts and *qawm*. It illustrates the problem of disunity, clan dynamics, the values and ethos that affected decision-making, and the role of the *ulema*. There is a brief overview of how negotiations, alliances and coalitions were undertaken during conflicts in Afghanistan.

The book is not limited to Afghan conflicts against foreign interventions; episodes of civil war are included. However, a limitation on the available space has meant that the book is necessarily selective. It has not been possible to include the fighting in the border areas of Pakistan since 2001 and many of the minor conflicts of the late nineteenth and early twentieth centuries. However, readers should understand that the aim is to illustrate through examples rather than offer a definitive history that lists every encounter. The key point is that there was no single Afghan way of war in the country's history. Every response has been dependent on the situation that confronted the Afghans, and it is hoped that the number and breadth of examples will be sufficient to demonstrate that process of change.

Having set out some of the problems and framework, the second section of this book tackles three particular and inter-related themes concerned with British attempts to manage, manipulate and manoeuvre the Afghans and frontier Pashtuns from 1849 to 1947. Willing to sustain the costs of permanent occupation, the British instead rendered Afghanistan into a client, buffer state, whilst weakening the Pashtuns on their immediate frontier with punitive military expeditions, boundary demarcation and the deployment of Political Officers. The British learned that it was more effective to work through the social networks which characterized Pashtun society. The British came to appreciate that negotiation, was an integral part of Pashtun culture. They also looked to recruit the 'martial races' of the frontier into the Indian Army and local corps, as a solution to the security threat the Pashtuns posed to the British settled border areas. It is clear that employment and negotiation with tribal leaders proved to be more lasting solutions than punitive military operations. This section also examines how the Afghans and Pashtuns reacted to these British efforts.

The third section of this book offers chapters on the period of civil war, including the unrest in 1978, Soviet intervention, the insurgency against the communist government, the post-Soviet civil war and the emergence of the Taliban. The final chapter brings the past into the present to show how historical perceptions and myths cloud Western analyses of the Afghans and Pashtuns and how this has led to misconceptions in Western military operations since 2001. To achieve a victory in counterinsurgency, the Coalition powers believe that they require a thorough understanding of the Afghans, to exploit weaknesses and divisions in order to drive a wedge between the population and the insurgents, to recruit a robust Afghan National Security Force, to encourage a democratic ethos in order to establish effective governance, and to 'win hearts and minds' through the protection of the population.[115] However, frequent changes of strategy has created confusion, while insufficient force rations a situation which is in fact exploited by the Afghans themselves, for, as the Pashtuns say in one of their proverbs: 'when two men go to fight, who holds their horses?'. The insurgents since 2003 have sustained their resistance and made significant effort to align themselves with the grievances of the population.

In the light of these initial reflections, some questions might now be posed: Are we any nearer understanding Afghans and the manner in which they waged war in the past? Can historical assessments be re-applied to the present? Are cultural analyses mere academic exercises that lack empirical foundation, but which serve the purpose of reassuring the hubris of the academy that it somehow 'understands' while practitioners do not? The current state of the literature resembles a minefield of stereotypes, fragments of empiricism, and shards of constructed knowledge, all liable to explode if mishandled or inadvertently trodden on. Different disciplines approach the subject with their particular methods and assumptions, and this work, a practical military history, is perhaps as guilty as any other of this charge. As Patrick Porter has pointed out in *Military Orientalism*, the West is prone to construct curious caricatures about its Asian adversaries. This book challenges stereotypes whilst trying to avoid creating new ones. It seeks to make a contribution to the scholarship and to provoke thought as to the methods by which we recapture the manner and purpose of those who fought. It will, I hope, cause us to rethink the British and Soviet accounts of the Afghans at war and appreciate the determination and courage of the Afghans as a whole. It may perhaps even provoke more research into the military histories on Afghanistan written by westerners over the last two hundred years. However, my hope is that this will drive us all to recover Afghan perspectives about the history of war in the region. I also believe that a better understanding of the record of Afghans at war actually shows that British and Soviet efforts were more remarkable than is usually acknowledged. This study may enable us to accord them the respect they deserve.

The conclusion thus draws together the various themes, showing, through more recent historiography, how enduring misconceptions obscured some fundamental elements of Afghanistan at war and relations between the Afghans and their adversaries. Western observations, working through Afghan interpretations, the distinctive circumstances and character of warfare, and changing Afghan approaches to making war all feature in the concluding argument, which is, specifically, that the British, Soviets and Americans often did not understand the Afghans and saw a people that threw their own reflections into sharper relief; that working with the 'grain' of Afghan society and negotiating have proved as effective in the past as waging war, although coercion and negotiation are themselves tools of power amongst Afghans; and finally, that the recent Western approaches in Afghanistan have required a significant shift to produce the strategic effects the West desired.

2

DYNASTIC STRUGGLES AND
POPULAR RESISTANCE IN AFGHANISTAN

THE ERA OF THE FIRST ANGLO–AFGHAN WAR

In the thirty years before British military intervention in Afghanistan, there had been a steady erosion of the strength of the first modern Afghan emirate. The territorial expansion of Ahmad Shah Durrani, the 'founder' of Afghanistan, proved to be an illusion of success. Indeed, even before his death in 1772, lands on the peripheries were restive and rejected Ahmad Shah's authority. When he died there was no obvious successor, which meant that fratricidal warfare between his heirs broke out around the country. The succession of pretenders and usurpers undermined the legitimacy and authority of the institution of monarchy, and contributed to the heightened sense of rivalry between *qawms* and regions. At one point, violent Shia–Sunni sectarianism erupted in Kabul, while Durrani factionalism, and conflict between Durranis and Ghilzais, weakened the nascent polity of Afghanistan still further. More remote communities were nevertheless largely unaffected by dynastic struggles, while regions on the northern periphery were governed independently by 'warlord' figures, or chieftains, who ruled without penalties or fear of retribution. It was against this background of political instability and regional division that the British formed their initial judgements about Afghanistan and its peoples, and, in turn, formulated their policies.

The Durrani empire was built on the successes of its army and not its administration. Ahmad Shah himself admitted to his treasurer in 1751 that this was, in effect, a military state that depended on the warriors: 'it is by their unanimity, and with the help of their swords, that I have been raised to this position–I should certainly look upon my soldiers as partners in this wealth'.[1] Although there were *jagirs* and offices to be sold, the imperial coffers had to be replenished with raids on the Mughal territories to the east. The Afghan rank and file were enthusiastic about these attacks since they offered large personal profits through looting, the chance to exhibit their courage and gain promotion, and the legitimacy of waging holy war against Hindus and Sikhs. Descending from the passes and mountains, the Afghans could fan out rapidly from the logistics hub of the Vale of Peshawar. In Ahmad Shah's reign, eight offensives were launched over a span of twenty years. However, the majority of the troops were irregulars who refused to sustain their operations for any longer than a few months. Frequent raiding, rather than occupation with a permanent garrison, was the norm. Any attempt to override these preferences meant that the army was reduced through desertion.

The anatomy of the Afghan army in this period also indicates the character of the regime and its methods of war. The original force under Ahmad Shah Durrani's control numbered 16,000 feudal cavalry, known as the *sawara-i kushada* or *sawara-i khudaspa*, but this was expanded when he took power to 40,000. The army was composed of Durrani and Ghilzai Pashtuns with a bodyguard of Kizilbashes ('redhead' Turkic mercenary cavalry), augmented on campaign with more irregulars to reach a maximum strength of 120,000. The Durrani cavalrymen were supplied by the clan elders in return for grants of rent-free land. If their land produced insufficient revenue, they could be granted *barats* (stipends) from other sources, such as transit duties. Additional cash allowances were received if they increased the number of horsemen in the Shah's service. Because of their association with the 'royal' clan, the Durrani elders assumed the mantle of a *noblesse oblige*, and, like the baronial order of Britain in the thirteenth century, they took the view that they had the right to govern in the name of their selected monarch. If that monarch failed to serve their interests, they took it as a *sine qua non* that they could intervene to remove that head of state.

Ahmad Shah's capital at Kandahar was guarded by 12,559 cavalry, of whom 5,710 were Durrani.[2] The rest were non-Durrani *qawm* from neighbouring districts, such as the Ghilzai Hotaks, and the separate Kakars, Darwais and Barechis. When Timur moved the capital to Kabul, additional cavalry were raised under the title *Kara Nokars*. Again, non-Durrani Pashtuns and ethnic groups like the Tajiks were strongly represented. In an effort to extend the monarch's reach, every landowner was supposed to provide soldiers, and pay them, in return for a remission of land taxes. In reality, only the region around Kabul ever submitted their full quota, and then only when an emergency arose. Remote areas either sent a token few men or none at all. Nevertheless, the *Kara Nokars* were formed into units under the command of their own maliks, and these were grouped under five Durrani sirdars.[3] These men, like all those paid in some way by the Shah, were expected to act as civil administrators in times of peace, fusing the military and civil structures still further. While ensuring a single line of authority, the risk was that, in periods of tribal unrest or rebellion, the Shah was often unable to enforce their authority without bringing in troops from elsewhere.

It was significant that Ahmad Shah Durrani and his son Timur attempted to incorporate their rivals, the Ghilzais, while subordinating the other ethnic groups of Afghanistan as subjects to be farmed and managed by the army. Nevertheless, sustaining this vast host was problematic, and supplies were stripped from the lands through which the force passed like a plague of locusts. Even the structure of the army was oriented towards the acquisition of plunder. A third of the 'regular' army was mounted, and a variety of light guns were drawn, but the irregular forces, the *sipah-i ghair-i munazzam*, were a mixture of cavalry and dismounted warriors. Some accounts suggest that a majority of these irregulars were mounted to suit their role as raiders, emphasizing mobility and mass over strength: corps consisting of thousands of horsemen could generally swarm around foreign garrisons and overwhelm them before they could be reinforced, or cascade through the countryside to acquire booty and then ride away before their enemies could concentrate against them. Each cavalryman was armed with a variety of weapons for the diverse military tasks he might have to perform on extended expeditions: shield, long spear, matchlock, sword, pistol and long knife.

Officially, the army could be paid in cash or granted *jagirs* or lucrative appointments in Afghanistan, or in conquered parts of India. Irregular forces were raised not just by asking for levies of men from chieftains in return for an annual tax remission, in the hope of loot (that would be shared by the victorious troops) since the same *jagirs* and cash rewards enjoyed by the standing army often proved a greater draw. On the borders, irregular light cavalry were maintained more or less permanently to patrol the frontier, impose taxation (from which they took a share for themselves) and to pursue enemies of the Shah. They were paid in the same way as other tribal levies. In an attempt to garrison the troublesome north, a permanent military colony was established at Balkh.[4] Here too the *Kohna Nokars*, as the northern cavalry were known, were paid by assigning them land which they could pass on to their sons and heirs.

Elsewhere, fortresses were supposed to control entry points into the Afghan realm. At Herat, the earthen walls were many feet thick and provided with a variety of cannons; and the citadel, the Maruchaq, occupied an area that was equivalent to two-thirds of the size of the city itself. The fort of Dehdadi in Mazar-i Sharif was also notable for its size and strength, and the Bala Hissar of Kabul was famous throughout Central Asia.[5]

The relatively lawless nature of the rural areas meant that almost every village community and family house resembled a small fortress, known as the *qala* (tower or compound). Compound walls not only concealed women and valuables, but kept at bay rival families or clans. Towers were built at the corners of compounds for observation and for shooting platforms. The thick vegetation of cultivated terraces or ditch-lined fields could also provide cover. However, it was the mountainous nature of much of Afghanistan that rendered the country a natural fortress. High summer temperatures, freezing winter conditions, long routes without abundant pasture or water, high altitudes and narrow passes and defiles closed by winter snows all meant that even relatively poorly armed Afghans could harass a regular army even if they could not halt its progress. Like the desert raider, safety lay in the environment and one's ability to raid and slip away, rather than in the strength of arms. Nevertheless, the precarious nature of Afghanistan's food supply and infrastructure meant that invaders practising a policy of scorched earth could defeat Afghan resistance, even if they could not sustain a large army of occupation in the country.

There were three significant problems, though, that affected the Afghan military forces specifically. First, they lacked any secure financial-logistical system, so that if chieftains failed to pay their men, or there were sustained periods without the rewards of loot, there were mutinies. Second, the frequency of raids fell hardest on the Sikhs of the Punjab, and they reorganized their forces in such a manner that resistance against the Afghans stiffened. Third, their loyalty was often in doubt. Afghan forces were raised by local chieftains and communities and their first loyalty was to them and not the Durrani rulers. The governors of regional cities were also aware that loyalty could be purchased. Durrani Shahs faced the dilemma of staffing governorships with weak men who might be unable to rule effectively, or stronger men who might be tempted to rebel. A traditional proverb maintained that: 'An Afghan Amir sleeps upon an ant heap'.

To offset this problem of disloyalty, Ahmad Shah had established another independent military force, the *ghulam-i shah*. This bodyguard, based on the Persian *shah-sevan*, excluded Durranis from its ranks and recruited kizilbashes. Troopers were enlisted for life and paid in cash, and their units were commanded by respected officers, or *qular aghasis*. Yet, for an army made of feudal levies without professionalized systems such as regular terms of service, the Afghan army's strength often ebbed and flowed. Although it was traditional to try to garrison regions with troops drawn from other parts of the country, to avoid sympathies and fraternization developing, in practice this was far harder to achieve. Soldiers would simply vote with their feet if conditions did not suit them. Officers might use greater coercion to prevent desertion, but irregular pay or simply a desire to return to one's home could not prevent the army from fading in strength. Far more serious was the problem of local insurrection, and Afghan troops drawn from the same communities were not reliable. Ghilzais, who had traditionally made up the majority of the Afghan forces, were often in the forefront of resistance to the Shah. Although Ahmad Shah, like those who followed, tried to adopt Persian practices, such as the reading of statements of fealty to the monarch at the *khutba* (Friday prayers), the Ghilzai elders were aware that the Shah did not control their districts. Financial rewards might induce cooperation, but they did not ensure loyalty. Ghilzai clans were also conscious that they could exact tolls at will on caravans that made their way from Kabul and Kandahar, or across the Suleiman range into the subcontinent, and this financial independence reinforced the sense that they were politically autonomous too.

The bulk of fighting forces in wartime were the *eljaris* (dismounted levies), men who were raised during foreign raiding expeditions, to resist invasion, or to crush rebellions of rival *qawm*. Given the proximity of the plains of India, many of the *eljaris* were drawn from Ghilzai clans, but the forces were a mix of groups organized in tens, fifties, hundreds and thousand-strong formations under leaders correspondingly styled as *dahbashi, pinjabashi, sadbashi (yuzbashi)* and *hazarbashi (mingbashi)*. Governors of the provinces were given overall jurisdiction, but real authority rested with the elders who selected them and paid them.[6] Real money, as noted before, came from looting, and *eljaris* were permitted to retain four-fifths of what they stole, the rest being handed over to the Shah, that is if they couldn't get away with keeping more.

Exhibitions of personal courage were deeply ingrained in the Pashtun code, and were common to other Afghan minorities. It was considered a means to acquire greater honour and prestige by performing acts of daring, either against rival clans, or in wartime against an enemy. There was much to be gained, there-fore, by being at the front, and no honour at all in serving as some logistician or victualler. Equally, accepting orders from others was seen as a limitation on their opportunity to demonstrate their courage. Every man thought himself a *khan*, '*har saray khan deh*', and every man thought himself the equal of anyone else. This had a number of unfortunate effects. In battle, many would try to get straight into the fight, regardless of the odds against them, and there would be little restraint or patience. Equally, once a line started to collapse, the whole army tended to fragment and melt away. In periods of stalemate, the absence of any logistical support meant that the army had to break up for foraging.[7]

The sudden influx of looted property and cash nevertheless had a profoundly destabilizing effect on the Ghilzais and Durrani Pashtuns. If one clan acquired more than its 'fair share' in the eyes of other clans, the tribal code ensured that these feelings of jealousy could be transferred quite legitimately into violent action. These disputes might last some years, as deaths in one family obligated another to seek *badal* (justice).

In the chaos following the death of Ahmad Shah Durrani in 1772, it was one of his sons, Timur Shah, who succeeded in crushing another favoured heir from his Durrani *qawm* to take power. However, to reduce the threat of being overthrown in a subsequent *coup d'état*, Timur had moved the capital from Kandahar, out of the Pashtun heartlands. For greater security, he looked to develop the Kizilbash to provide the core of an army that would be loyal to him, through cash rewards, and not to Afghan clan affiliations. This attempt to break with tribal linkage was significant, and Timur, like his father, was clearly trying to establish a hereditary monarchy that could bind all Afghans under a single ruler in emulation of the Persian or the Mughal empires. Yet the Pashtun clans of the south distrusted, collectively and universally, any attempt to assert one individual or family over all others. Pashtunwali emphasized egal-itarianism, and, despite the creation of a *majlis* or advisory council of elders, Durrani and Ghilzai elders were not convinced that Timur was content to be a mere *primus inter pares*. Nevertheless, although he was forced to deploy the kizilbash cavalry to break a series of Pashtun revolts, Timur hoped to continue the policy of avoiding taxation and to foster support through consensus and a network of patronage. He also ensured that garrisons were maintained to pre-vent any large faction, like the Ghilzais, taking possession of Kandahar, which they might use as a base for operations and a recruiting ground to overthrow him. Most importantly, he tried to keep the Durranis, the closest *qawm* to the seat of power, divided. A British observer wrote: 'the King's policy is to keep the Douranees in subjection to himself, while he exalts them over other Afghauns', continuing: 'For this purpose he protects the Taujiks, and all others whose power he can use to depress the nobles, without endangering the ascendancy of his tribe'.[8] In practice this meant intervening in the internal politics of the Durranis, and keeping up the demands for soldiers in return for grants of land, whereas, with non-Pashtun groups, Timur could afford to spend less time concerning himself with their affairs.[9]

Mullahs and those closest to the Shah regarded Timur's power as absolute, but tribal elders were not persuaded, and the more remote those tribal factions were from the main urban centres, the more independent they considered themselves. To offset this problem, Timur tried to keep certain Durrani elders close to him at court, where they could not foment rebellion. He appointed new men to positions of authority, hoping their privileges would mean that they would owe him their loyalty. Conscious that his sons and relatives might be the first to revolt, in an attempt to invoke their own royal legitimacy, he refused to appoint them to positions of power, such as the governorships of the major cities.

To reduce expenditure, he avoided military expeditions beyond the border zones, and concentrated his army against internal disorders. However, the net effect was that peripheral regions were less and less influenced by the court at Kabul. When Timur died in 1773, the factions of the country made further attempts to assert their autonomy. His sons waged civil war against each other, or used intrigue and assassination to capture, maim and murder each other. Zaman Shah (r. 1793–1800) succeeded for a time and tried to reunite Afghan factions by marching on India, but Mahmud Shah (r. 1800–03), the governor of Herat, rebelled and then captured Zaman.[10] Mahmud Shah was in turn captured and imprisoned by Shah Shuja (r. 1803–9; subsequently 1839–42). Mahmud nevertheless returned to power (r. 1809–18) and drove Shah Shuja into exile. The constant fighting broke up the Afghan armies and squandered any support for the Sadozai clan of the Popalzai Durranis. More importantly, it allowed the Barakzais, one of the largest Zirak Pashtun clans, to emerge from under the Durrani dynasty. Barakzai elders had served as allies and viziers to different Sadozai pretenders and were, in many respects, the 'kingmakers'. Payinda Khan, a prominent Barakzai, had worked as the chief advisor to Timur Shah, and had acted as the governor responsible for the suppression of a Ghilzai uprising. Payinda Khan had also been charged with gathering support for Zaman Shah in 1793. Zaman subsequently had Payinda executed to suppress his power, but Payinda's son, Fitih Khan, captured and blinded Zaman in revenge and then ensured that his rival, Mahmud Shah, succeeded to the throne. Moreover, it was the loyalty of the Barakzais that ensured Mahmud returned to the throne against Shah Shuja in 1809. However, Mahmud betrayed this loyalty by having Fitih Khan tortured, blinded and executed. The Barakzais then deposed Mahmud in favour of two Sadozai rulers, Sultan Ali Shah (1818–19) and Ayub Shah (1819–23), while they retained real power, and wealth, for themselves.

It was another of Payinda Khan's sons, Dost Mohammed, who emerged from the maelstrom of intra-Barakzai feuding to become the ruler of Ghazni and Kabul in 1826. However, Dost Mohammed's realm extended only as far as the region around the two cities, since rival factions held northern and eastern territories, Kandahar (half-brothers of the Mohammadzai clan) and Herat (ruled by the Sadozai Durranis). Remote areas that might once have considered some suzerainty to the Durranis, like Kashmir and the Pamirs, were lost. Ghilzai lands in the south and east also considered themselves entirely independent. Despite this evident weakness and fractiousness, it was the intervention of foreign and 'infidel' forces that would weld some sort of unity amongst the Afghans, particularly in defence of Islam.

In the late 1820s, Dost Mohammed and his clan were regarded as usurpers with the impertinence to emulate Ahmad Shah Durrani. The weakness of the new regime only seemed to be underlined by the Sikh victory in 1834, when Peshawar was wrested from Afghan control. Despite later historiography that portrayed Dost Mohammed as a national leader, he was weak. As Mountstuart Elphinstone observed:

the internal government of the tribes answers its end so well that the utmost disorders of the royal government never derange its operations, nor disturb the lives of the people. A number of organized and high-spirited republics are ready to defend their rugged country against a tyrant; and are able to defy the feeble efforts of a party in a civil war.[11]

Dost Mohammad lacked the means to extend his power. Land grants accounted for more than 50 per cent of the potential revenue, and the number of troops he could raise was limited to the area he controlled. The most valuable eastern provinces were lost, and any attempts to increase taxation in his own small realm would almost certainly have provoked a revolt. Dost Mohammad therefore tried to extend his authority piecemeal and then introduce taxation to areas that had just fallen under his control, using the coerciveness of the army to extract funds. The Tajik Kohistanis, the Ghilzais of Laghman and Ghazni and the Hazaras of Bamian were all forced to pay. Formations of

1,000 cavalry were divided into detachments in each district, and these billeted themselves in houses and villages, eating everything, until the villagers paid the revenue required. The largesse was then ferried back to Kabul, turned into cash for the troopers or exchanged for goods, while a portion of collected grain was either stored or given to the soldiers' families. Slaves too could be taken and sold for the Amir's profit. Villagers and clans therefore took the view that their army was a predatory organization to be resisted if possible, and peripheral areas often rebelled.

These internal fissures meant it was difficult to sustain operations beyond the fiefdom of Kabul. Although Dost Mohammad managed to mount an expedition against the Sikhs, winning a battle near Jamrud in 1836, he was simply unable to recover Peshawar. He looked to open up diplomatic relations with the British to outflank the Sikhs, and in 1837 the British seemed to be moving closer to the Afghan position when they compelled the Persians to abandon a siege of Herat. However, it soon became evident that the British, who had succeeded in annexing most of the Indian subcontinent, were a formidable adversary. The Afghans were aware that the British possessed a large and modern army with a great deal of mobile artillery, and they had augmented their forces with Hindu sepoys and sowars. Dost Mohammad had believed that a careful diplomatic approach to the British would avoid ever having to confront them in war, but his diplomacy with Russia and Persia merely fuelled British suspicions that Dost Mohammad was looking to join Britain's enemies. As a result, Afghanistan was to find itself defeated and occupied.

In the prelude to the Anglo–Afghan War, the British believed the Afghans were unable to withstand a modern, disciplined army. Herat had withstood the siege of 1837 by a narrow margin of success. Although the ruler was Kamran, the descendant of Ahmad Shah Durrani, the city and the Hari-Rud valley was governed by Yar Mohammed, and he had assembled the inexperienced city militia to withstand the onslaught of the Persian army. The Persians had long-standing claims to western Afghanistan, and had occupied the city in 1805. They compelled the Afghans to pay tribute to the Shah of Persia, until a revolt in the neighbouring Khorassan province enabled the Heratis to cease their payments, and in 1816 the rebels seized the Persian fortress at Ghurian.[12] It was not until 1832 that the Persians regained full control of Khorassan and destroyed the Turkoman border settlement of Sarakhs. The Persians renewed their demands for tribute, but the Heratis refused to comply.[13] Although the Persians started to march on Herat, Abbas Mirza, the Crown Prince and commander of the expedition, died en route at Mashad, and a truce was concluded.

However, Herat's defences were also reduced by a persistent outbreak of cholera and a steady migration of the population away from the city. By 1829, when Shah Mahmud died and his son Kamran took over, the city population had more than halved from an estimated 100,000 to 40,000. However, Yar Mohammed, as Vizier, tried to organize the city's recovery and even extended the area under his control southwards into Seistan. The Persians regarded this as part of their own dominion and there were preparations to reduce Herat's power.

Shah Shuja's return to Kandahar in 1834, Dost Mohammed's need to counter that threat, and the annexation of Peshawar by Ranjit Singh indicated to the Persians that the Heratis were unlikely to get reinforcements. The defeat of Dost Mohammed's forces by the Sikhs at the Khyber Pass in May 1835 also suggested that the Afghans were weakened. However, the Persians were locked into a struggle with the Ottoman Empire on the south-western border, and consequently they could take no action against the Afghans until 1837. Russia, which was eager to assert greater influence over the Persians, faced disturbances in the Caucasus (1834) and Kazakhstan (1836–7) and was unable to intervene.[14] In a further twist, in 1837 Dost Mohammed offered to accept Persian suzerainty of Herat in return for military assistance against both the Sikhs and the Heratis.[15] Dost Mohammed made a second attempt to defeat the Sikhs and his son Akbar Khan won an action in April 1837, but he was then driven back by Sikh reinforcements from the Punjab; once again the Persians interpreted this as the moment to strike against Herat. Conscious that an offensive was likely, Yar Mohammed recruited more men into his own army, repaired the city walls and did his best to hunt down and drive out Persians in his territories. On the eve of their offensive, the Persians were delighted by another offer of assistance, this time from the Kandaharis led by Kohendil Khan, a rival of both Dost Mohammed in Kabul and also of Herat. Kohendil was prepared to submit to Persian rule if military assistance was forthcoming to deal with Kabul. The Persians, who had been delayed yet again by an unexpected and protracted border conflict with the Turkomen in 1836, were finally able to concentrate their army against Herat in the spring of 1837.

The British tried to broker a last minute compromise, and Yar Mohammed offered to restore the Persian tribute while refusing to accept full Persian sovereignty. The British accepted the Heratis' position, as they were concerned about growing Russian support for Persia and wanted to see Herat remain independent. The Persians reacted by sending an army, 30,000 strong, across the border in October. The Heratis tried to slow this advance by a scorched-earth policy, destroying any forage, although they declined to defend the fortress at

Ghurian. On 23 November the Persians reached the ruined north-western suburbs of Herat, but after some skirmishing the Afghans took refuge behind the vast walls of the city. For the first few months, the Persians struggled to maintain their investment. Their logistical system was under severe strain, especially when bad weather hampered supply columns. There were no lines of circumvallation, and the Afghans were able to use three of the five city gates to move in and out of the city, even grazing cattle on lands to the east. Persian artillery fire was desultory and ineffective, although trenches were dug to within yards of the base of the walls and a half-hearted effort was made to mine underneath them. If the morale of the Persians wasn't affected by their meagre rations, Yar Mohammed did his best to terrorize them by displaying the heads of captured Persians along the battlements.

In April 1838 the Persians finally effected a breach in the walls and prepared to storm the city. The attack was planned for the night of the nineteenth, but the British arranged a truce and the assault was cancelled. It was not until June that the Persians were able to reinvigorate the offensive, assisted by Russian advisors. The city was finally sealed off, and it was not long before disease broke out in the unsanitary streets. Yar Mohammed ordered that all remaining stocks of food be seized, and suspected 'fifth columnists' were summarily executed.[16] Some 600 civilians were also driven out of the city on Yar Mohammed's orders, only to be turned back by the Persians, beaten and shot at by the Herati garrison, before finally escaping through Persian lines. Meanwhile in the Persian camp it became clear that the British intended to take military action, and the Shah thus ordered a final assault on 24 June. Five columns were launched at the gates and breaches. Two were driven back easily but, at the south-eastern corner of the city walls, the Persians managed to get 400 men into the breach. The British account, reported by Lieutenant Eldred Pottinger, emphasized the last-ditch nature of the defence and the temporary loss of will by Yar Mohammed. However, with defeat imminent, Yar Mohammed was suddenly restored to his usual determination, and drove his men by sheer fury back into the mêlée.[17] By contrast, a French officer in the Persian army explained the defeat of the Persian assault as the result of treachery, claiming that many Persian soldiers hung back from the fight and shot some of their officers. General Semineau suggested that this was because the Persian troops had been bribed by the British, but there was no British presence at the Persian camp at the time of the assault.[18] Having failed to break through, and faced with war against Britain, the Persians withdrew in September.

However, Herat had been reduced to a population of little more than 8,000 with no supplies. Yar Mohammed was driven to selling prisoners as slaves to the Turkomen across the border. He accepted British money, but was eager to avoid any control from the government of India and prepared to re-open negotiations with the Persians to obtain support against the British if that proved necessary.[19] The greatest threat, though, came from Kandahar, as Kohendil Khan considered mobilizing against the Heratis. When the British invasion force arrived to forestall this move in support of Shah Shuja, Kohendil fled to Persia. Yar Mohammed, realizing that the Persians were in no position to resist, quickly concluded a treaty with the British and received Major D'Arcy Todd as the British envoy. However, Yar Mohammed continued his intrigues against his rivals, avoided any British influence, and paid only lip service to the idea of submission to Shah Shuja.[20]

The first Anglo–Afghan war, 1839–42

The British invasion of Afghanistan with the 21,000-strong Army of the Indus in 1839 was designed to force the abdication of Dost Mohammed, the Amir ('leader', rather than Shah) of Kabul, in favour of the Sadozai claimant to the throne, Shah Shuja. This ruler, rightfully restored to the throne of the Durrani clan, would serve British interests, it was thought, by acting as an ally against Russian influence. Shah Shuja's pro-British Afghanistan would also serve as a counterweight to the powerful Sikh kingdom of Ranjit Singh, whose dominions lay adjacent to British possessions in India. The British had tried for several years to persuade the Amir of Kabul to yield to their interests through negotiations, but Dost Mohammed's insistence on the recovery of Peshawar, the city-state lost in 1834 to the Sikhs, and his negotiations with the Persians and Russia in 1836, persuaded the British that the Amir had to be removed.

Dost Mohammed anticipated that Russia and Persia would augment his bargaining positions against the Sikhs and, indeed, against his own internal rivals. The last hope of a compromise was the British proposal that Dost Mohammed's brother, Jubber Khan, should serve as an Afghan viceroy of Peshawar under the Sikh's suzerainty, but Dost Mohammed did not trust his brother and believed that he would simply foment intrigues against him and recruit local Turan Ghilzai Pashtuns to march on Kabul. Indeed, it was Jubber Khan who warned the British that Dost Mohammed had received a Russian envoy, Lieutenant Jan Vitkevich, carrying the offer of financial support and closer diplomatic relations. Eager to avoid Russian influence growing on their Indian borders, the British issued an ultimatum, the Simla Manifesto, on 1 October 1838. They made little secret of their desire to turn Afghanistan into a protectorate, and had no sympathy with Dost Mohammad's attempt to remain in power.

Dost Mohammad's strategy was to remain on the defensive against the British. He could muster about 38,000 feudal cavalry, of which 8,000 were Durrani, and most of the army, augmented with tribal levies, was placed under the command of his son, Akbar Khan.[21] Akbar Khan feared treachery by the Afridis in the Khyber Pass region, and lacked funds to secure a passage, so he drew up the army in reserve while sending envoys to encourage the Afridis to resist any foreign force attempting to come from the east. Dost Mohammad believed that the British would use the Khyber Pass as their main avenue of attack, and he did not seem to realize until the offensive had begun that the British were in fact sending the bulk of their forces through the Bolan Pass and on towards Kandahar. Major General Henry Marion Durand later wrote:

Dost Mohammad's attention had been occupied by the direct advance which was apprehended from ... Peshawar, where [Lt. Col. Sir Claude] Wade [the British Political Agent from Ludhiana], playing at royalty with Shahazada Timour in his camp, had since the end of March [1839] been assembling a motley levy, and endeavouring to attract partisans to the Shah's cause.[22]

As soon as Dost Mohammad realized that the axis of the British offensive was towards Kandahar, he hoped to delay General Keane's invasion force by enlisting the help of the chiefs at the Bolan and Khojak Passes, and perhaps even the Kandaharis themselves. His principal objective was to hold his two urban centres of power and wealth, namely Ghazni and Kabul, and he was less concerned about the fall of the rival fiefdoms in Kandahar or Herat. Short of funds and men on this southern front, Durand noted: 'he evidently selected the most judicious course in resolving thus to await the nearer approach of his foes', judging that, as the exhausted British became strung out along the Kandahar–Kabul route, 'intercommunications between [the British forces] would be at his mercy'.[23]

Sending another of his sons, Hyder Khan, to fortify Ghazni by building an additional curtain wall to the fortress, making repairs, and blocking up all but the northernmost gate, he reinforced the garrison there to 3,000 men and ordered that six months' provisions be laid up for a siege. Dost Mohammad calculated that a delaying action would give him time to muster both his army and the Ghilzai clans. With greater numbers and in the barren terrain about Ghazni, he aimed to overwhelm the invaders. Subsequently he could then turn to deal with the British forces at the end of the Khyber Pass. But Kandahar fell without resistance. Shah Shuja was greeted with great enthusiasm at first, although the subsequent cool reception on the following days may have been caused by the presence of so many foreign troops and the realization that a Sadozai restoration did not necessarily mean an end to arbitrary governance and civil war. The Kandahari Sirdars had fled across the Helmand to Persia fearing reprisals. Locals were more concerned by the economic effects of occupation. The British and Indian forces, and the Indian and Afghan exiles which furnished much of Shah Shuja's army, had suffered from acute shortages for much of the advance, not least because 38,000 camp followers who accompanied the army added to the gargantuan logistical needs of this force in an environment that was marginal and where the agriculture was based on subsistence. Yet, despite some skirmishing from local raiders, the Afghans had been unable to gather in sufficient strength to contest the passage of the southern passes. Nevertheless the fall of Kandahar to Shah Shuja was a significant blow to Dost Mohammad's prestige which affected his ability to raise levies.

As General Keane advanced towards Kabul, he was informed that Dost Mohammad was urgently trying to complete the fortification of Ghazni and 'exciting the Ghilzais'.[24] This intelligence was brought in by Afghans loyal to Shah Shuja, but Dost Mohammad also had his spies and the Amir was given a detailed and accurate picture of the strength of the British force approaching from the south. Dost Mohammad feared that the British might screen and bypass the fortress, so a force of cavalry, led by Afzul Khan, assembled to harass the British flanks. Keane, however, was relieved that the Afghans intended to make a stand at Ghazni, since his greatest concern was that 'the enemy, avoiding the risk of defeat in a general action, would confine himself to guerrilla warfare and the defence of fortified posts'.[25] The British duly arrived at Ghazni, where they discovered that the fortifications were too strong to be breached by the field artillery they had brought with them, but an Afghan deserter, a nephew of Dost Mohammad, informed them of the relatively less well-defended Kabul Gate which could be blown open with a charge of gunpowder.[26]

Before the assaulting forces had assembled, a detachment of Dost Mohammad's cavalry made a raid on Shah Shuja's camp. Most accounts suggest that the horsemen were *ghazis*, warriors of Islam immune to fear and eager to die in order to enter Paradise. Certainly they pressed home their attack with determination and engaged in close-quarter fighting with swords, but fifty were captured and the rest killed, wounded or driven off. Some British accounts described their attack as hasty and spontaneous. In fact, there is evidence of a more coordinated Afghan plan. As soon as the *ghazi* cavalry commenced their charge, artillery on the ramparts of the fortress gave supporting fire. One 48-pounder brass gun, known as the *Zubur Zun* (hard-hitter), hurled round-shot that ricocheted the 2,000 yards into the Shah's encampment. Nevertheless the raid, which may have been an attempt to decapitate the pretender to the throne, failed completely. Interestingly the prisoners, who were paraded in front of Shah Shuja, took the opportunity to insult the erstwhile monarch. One of them was so enraged that he stabbed a member of the royal bodyguard, and the Shah ordered their execution en masse. One British officer noted that the prisoners were 'young and old' but were butchered by brutal men who seemed to 'enjoy their work'.[27]

On 22 July the fortress was stormed. The Afghan garrison fought almost to the last man, with a counter-attack made against the blown gateway and a sharp close-quarter battle. It took several hours to secure the entire fortification, and 500–1,200 Afghans were killed, with a further 300 wounded and 1,500 taken prisoner. The firepower of the British was exemplified by their contrasting moderate losses: 17 killed and 65 wounded. Hyder Khan was spared by Shah Shuja when he was taken captive, while Afzul Khan, who was astonished to see Ghazni in British hands, rode his entire force back to Kabul without fighting. The news was received with similar shock elsewhere, indicating just how much faith had been placed in the strength of the fortress at Ghazni.

The initial military operations were thus a great success for the British. Dost Mohammed sent his brother Jubber Khan to negotiate a settlement, as was the Afghan custom after a decisive battle. The Amir had accepted that his surrender might prevent the 'further effusion of blood' and that he would hand over 'the state of Cabool into the hands of Shah Shooja'.[28] However, he refused to live 'under surveillance in the British provinces' and he demanded, as head of the Barakzais, to serve as the *wazir*, a return to the Barakzai tradition under the Sadozais, and therefore be, as one British officer put it, 'the maker and controller of kings'. The British took the view that this would simply lead to plots against Shah Shuja, but Sir Henry Havelock, who was present, noted that Jubber Khan 'felt, or affected, the utmost indignation at their rejection'.[29]

Dost Mohammad therefore tried to rally his troops for a final battle outside Kabul. News of the power of the British Army had now become widespread and there was little appetite to die needlessly for the Amir. The Kizilbash deserted, and one officer, Hajj Khan Kakar, joined the British. Dost Mohammad apparently appealed to his soldiers on the basis that they had 'eaten my salt these thirteen years... grant me but one favour in requital for that long period of maintenance and kindness—enable me to die with honour'. He continued: 'stand by the brother of Futteh Khan while he executes one last charge against the cavalry of these feringhee dogs; in that onset he will fall; then go and make your own terms with Shah Shuja'. The speech, if it ever really took place, apparently met with a stony silence. There were reports that Dost Mohammad's call for a Jihad had similarly failed. With just 3,000 followers, he was forced to retreat over the Hindu Kush mountains into Central Asia. He was joined *en route* by Akbar Khan, who had fallen sick during the vigil on the Khyber. His British pursuers had chosen Hajj Khan Kakar as their guide, but the turncoat had no wish to betray his former Amir so directly, and he did his best to delay and mislead the British cavalry. The Amir got away.

When Dost Mohammed escaped into Central Asia, the British conceived a plan to march a strong column to the Oxus to impress upon the Emirs of Bokhara and Kunduz that they should under no circumstances attempt to assist the Afghan exile. The military force was designed partly to protect their envoy, Dr Percival Lord, but also to persuade the local potentates that resistance to the British was hopeless. However, military officers advised against the scheme, arguing that sending a column over the mountains so late in the year when supplies further north were uncertain, and when potential enemy strengths were unknown, courted disaster. Even sending individual envoys was known to be hazardous. Two British officers were imprisoned and subsequently executed by the Emir of Bokhara in 1842, after allegations that they were spying for the Khanates of Khiva and Khokand.[30] Dost Mohammed was also imprisoned briefly, but escaped.

What was more troubling for the British was the evident lack of enthusiasm in Kabul for Shah Shuja, and the obvious resentment of the presence of a foreign army of occupation. Keane, on his departure for India, made the ominous prediction that: 'It will not be long before there is here some signal catastrophe' because of Shah Shuja's growing tendency to govern by coercion and use 'harsh measures'.[31] Kabulis were dismayed to find that those who had fled the advance of Shah Shuja had had their property confiscated and were barred from returning. There were also mutterings about 'licentious infidels' buying up property in the city. The dispossessed men of means were more likely to provide the leadership to any resistance, and, gradually, the incidents of abuse were transmitted further out from the capital.

Dost Mohammed remained weakened and unable to mount further resistance because of desertions from his cause, but he had no advantages or concessions to offer in any negotiations either. Indeed, when he attempted to re-cross the Hindu Kush in September 1840, his forces were intercepted, and, although he managed to defeat an Indian cavalry regiment sent against him, his call for a Jihad against the British still went unanswered. Dost Mohammed and his son Afzul Khan had managed to capture the former British post at Syghan, 30 miles from Bamian, because the levies there had called upon the Dost for support. Other levies began to mutiny the moment Dost Mohammed's cavalry arrived. Yet the Ghilzais, Kandahari Durranis and the population of Kabul remained silent. The 6,000 Uzbek Afghans on whom he depended for irregular cavalry were little more than mercenaries, and they were ready to capitulate once they had faced British forces.[32] Lord Auckland remarked that, despite the mutiny of the levies, even the Bamian population 'behaved well towards us'.[33]

To some extent a British military victory at Bamian on 18 September 1840 had obscured the sentiments of the population. The British artillery had achieved a decisive effect, and the British Indian troops had 'crowned the heights' to outflank a chain of forts that lay astride a defile occupied by Dost Mohammed's force. The collapse of the two flanks had caused the Afghans to waver, and, despite rallying four or five times, Dost Mohammed's troops had broken. As the Uzbek cavalry lost cohesion, the British unleashed their own horsemen and the pursuit was not broken off until the Afghans had been driven back 4 miles. It is noticeable that local *khans* escaped and, despite the punitive destruction of their forts and compounds, they remained at large. Dost Mohammed also got away with 200 followers. The Wali of Khulum immediately sued for peace with the British, but the rest of Kohistan remained angry and defiant. Small groups of fighters raided and sniped against British troops during the systematic destruction of Tajik–Afghan property in October 1841. Reflecting on the potential for insurrection, Macnaghten concluded that 'the Afghans are gunpowder, and the Dost is a lighted match'.[34]

The British were therefore delighted when Dost Mohammed surrendered and he was promptly sent into exile at Ludhiana in British territory. Nevertheless, what the British did not grasp was that Dost Mohammed's surrender was a political and military calculation. In conflicts in Afghanistan, rulers expected to be able to surrender and gamble on the chance of returning to power at some later date. Not all were this fortunate, of course, and the murder or mutilation of rival brothers, rebels and usurpers was just as common, but many chieftains had been granted the opportunity to serve under new authorities after tendering their submission, sometimes literally placing nooses around their necks or placing grass in their own mouths.[35] Dost Mohammed was also following a long tradition of seeking exile in a neutral neighbouring state as a base for future operations, just as Shah Shuja had done. Dost Mohammed saw his defeat as a temporary setback, not a permanent condition.

The British occupation and Afghan insurgency

In 1839 British objectives were achieved and the war appeared to be over. Within two years, however, the British would be confronted with a series of localized insurrections and a serious rebellion in Kabul that ended with the destruction of a British brigade.

There were two inter-related causes of unrest: the reform of the Afghan armed forces and the distribution of money. Although the revolts against the British were legitimized by invoking the name of the Shah and the defence of Islam, the elites who provided the leadership were concerned to acquire power, wealth and military forces to assert their position. In effect, despite the presence of the British forces, the conflicts that occurred between 1839 and 1842 were really a continuation of the dynastic struggle and civil war that had begun in 1803, or perhaps even earlier. Western writers have tended to emphasize the errors made by the leading British political and military figures, and the antagonism caused by cultural affronts, but a more detailed examination of the Afghan situation and the concomitant communal rivalries shows that the fissures in Afghan society, prised open by military reforms and money, were of great importance. The British errors were chiefly to attempt economies in security in the face of growing unrest. Because of the costs of occupation and the extended lines of communication, the military garrison was reduced with small pockets left in key urban areas, each of which proved vulnerable to insurrection or isolation. The British presence also polarized the Afghans. During the occupation, Shah Shuja's lack of traditional consultation and the high-handedness of his subordinates caused considerable resentment, but it was his association with foreign backing that eroded his legitimacy by 1842. The death of Shuja at the hands of an assassin created further instability and a civil war, weakening the resistance that Afghans could offer to a British counter-offensive in August 1842. These internal divisions were not resolved for years after the departure of the British garrisons, and they resurfaced when Dost Mohammed died in 1863.

A large proportion of the revenue gathered by Afghan rulers was to pay for the army, and it was common for officials to take a share of the whole and for individual clan leaders to claim financial allowances for larger numbers of men than they had actually raised, the corrupt practice of 'ghost-payrolling'. The siphoned income was used as patronage pay-offs. Dost Mohammed had seen the need for a regular corps at the heart of the Afghan army, but he also knew that it would be fatal to attempt to change the system of feudal cavalry and its financial-patronage networks while the clans remained so powerful. Even Captain Trevor, who later opposed the idea of payments to the feudal horsemen, recognized the political role the light cavalry of the army played:

We must not look on the Irregular Cavalry as merely a military body; in that light 3 Regiments might annihilate it tomorrow, but, as an instrument which enables H.M's principal subjects to appropriate a greater part of his revenues without making any return, and which has continued so long that its destruction would certainly be considered an invasion of private property.[36]

It was the reduction in the payments of allowances to *khans* and elders that caused an outbreak of violence during the British occupation. The payment of allowances was a long-established practice, and encouraged the local leaders and democratized clans to keep the peace. Men would be mustered, providing their own arms and horses, and then disband almost immediately afterwards. The *khans* received 6 *tomans* (120 Kham rupees) per horseman, or sometimes a grain equivalent, and the *khans* would keep a proportion of the allowance for themselves.[37] If the *khans* did not receive their stipend, they in turn could not pay off their own retainers or other sub-contracted followers. Ghilzai clans would increase the degree of brigandage and raiding to compensate or, *in extremis*, to combine to rebel against the rulers of the fiefdoms of Kandahar, Qalat, Ghazni and Kabul. Yet, after the accession of Shah Shuja, payments to the *khans* and clan elders fell by 25 per cent, from 1.3 million rupees in 1839 to 1 million in 1841. To make matters worse, there had been an expectation that, since Shah Shuja was backed by the wealthy British, allowances would have increased. To add insult to injury, the cuts did not fall equally across Afghanistan. The allowances of the Eastern Suleiman Khel Ghilzais fell by 50 per cent, from 80,000 to 40,000 rupees. The Ghilzais therefore reacted in the traditional fashion, by cutting communications, raiding and attacking symbols of the ruler's authority, not to overthrow him, but to obtain concessions. This might be interpreted as using violence as a form of 'communication', but the effects of material loss to a community living in such marginal conditions would have had serious consequences. It is worth noting that regions not affected by changes in the allowances system did not revolt in 1840 or 1841.

The other financial effect of the British occupation, particularly in Kabul and Kandahar but less so in Herat, was inflation. The influx of rupees, brought by the troops and the traders, victuallers and camp followers who came in their wake, had a dramatic effect on prices. The inflation polarized the commercial classes of Kabul, who made large profits, from the *khans* and elders, whose income fell in relative terms. This overturned the carefully calibrated hierarchy of prestige and created a sense of humiliation for the traditionalist *khans*.

Inflation also increased the price of food in and around Kabul, increasing the relative poverty of the urban inhabitants. The introduction of cash crops for exports added further upward pressure on food prices, and the approach of winter, when there was a traditional scarcity and higher prices anyway, increased anxiety.[38] The *ulema*, who relied on a fixed stipend, found their income suddenly inadequate, and the state's seizure of the *waqfs*, the religious endowments, to augment tax revenue incensed the religious leadership. When combined with proposals for the replacement of the feudal cavalry, which represented an income, greater efficiency in the collection of taxes, and rumours that the British intended to seize and exile certain mullahs and *khans*, the old Kabuli elites felt compelled to resist. The entire traditional order appeared to be in jeopardy, and, since the British showed no signs of leaving, armed resistance seemed obligatory.

In order to cut the costs of occupation and keep order, the British returned to the long-established practice of raising their own auxiliaries. Two cavalry formations were created, the Janbaz and Hazirbash. The Janbaz were designed to be a well-trained and disciplined force, initially just 1,600 strong.[39] It was assumed that some of the feudal cavalry could be absorbed into the new unit, but, given the tendency of the feudal horsemen to put loyalty to their clan above that of the Shah, the Janbaz were seen as a new, more reliable internal security force. Pay was either by assignments of land, determined by Shah Shuja, or in cash by the British. Rates of pay were higher, with troopers receiving a regular salary of 15 rupees a month. The difficulty for Shah Shuja was that the 1,200 Janbaz cavalry raised in Kabul knew that the British were the real paymasters, and the fact that they were officered by Europeans reinforced the sense that their first loyalty was not to the ruler of Kabul.

The Hazirbash were auxiliary cavalry raised at the same time for the purposes of local security and tax collection.[40] Numbering 800, they were paid only a third of the Janbaz rates but with assignments direct from the Shah. The British provided 'Inspectors' who 'supervised', which in practice meant that they led the new formation, and they also underwrote the Shah's payments. Dispatching parties of ten men to different districts in the Kabul region, tax collection became far more organized and increased the revenue of the Shah significantly.[41] While middle-ranking elders and *khans* embraced the Hazirbash as a means of earning income, tax collection was never popular, and the more senior leaders in and around Kabul viewed the innovation with suspicion.

The rebels in Kabul were not drawn exclusively from the feudal cavalry, although some of the urban population who had mustered in the past did subsequently join the revolt. The strongest support would come, in fact, from the Ghilzais and the Kohistani Tajiks, and the *ulema*, rather than the Durrani Pashtuns. Mohammed Akbar Khan, who eventually came to direct the revolt against the British garrison, had to rely on the Ghilzai *khans* and elders because the Durrani factions were so divided and opposed to him as a leader. Zaman, who assumed the position of Shah for a time, was a committed rival of Akbar Khan. Faction fighting came to the fore as soon as the British garrison had been driven from Kabul, reached a peak after the assassination of Shah Shuja and continued even when the British were poised to launch a counter-offensive against Kabul with the so-called Army of Retribution. Unity, even in the face of a common enemy, proved impossible to achieve.

The first signs of armed resistance to the British occupation can be traced to the attack on a large column on the road to Ghazni by 2,000 Ghilzai horsemen in May 1840. The Ghilzais had not been engaged by the main army during the invasion and were not prepared for the firepower that the British possessed. Although the Ghilzai cavalry made an attempt to envelop the 1,200-strong British force while pinning their centre with a frontal attack, disciplined musketry and artillery fire inflicted an estimated 200 casualties, and the Ghilzais were forced to retreat.[42] General Nott at Kandahar decided to improve the fortification at Qalat in order to provide a secure base for his communications and garrisoned it, much to the irritation of the local clans. Nevertheless, Nott was confronted with the problem that a revolt by the Baluchis further south had effectively cut off his logistical link with India through the Bolan Pass. Although a punitive column was sent towards Quetta, the Baluchis fell back in front of it, and then returned once the British column withdrew. Concurrently Yar Mohammed, the governor of Herat, was intriguing with the Persians and encouraging them to strengthen their claims to Kandahar. With Persian backing, Yar Mohammed sent an expedition in the hope of defeating the rivals in the south and earning the favour of the Persian Shah. Curiously Shah Shuja appeared to have acquiesced in the idea that he was an undisputed leader in Afghanistan, and he made no attempt to build the patronage networks that Dost Mohammed had exploited, even amongst his squabbling governors. Instead of asserting his influence over Herati or Kandahari *khans*, Shah Shuja relied on British military backing.

In the east of the country, the Ghilzai clan elders had been summoned to Kabul in September 1841 to be informed that, owing to economies, their allowances were to be reduced drastically. The news was received without complaint, but as soon as the elders and *khans* had returned to their homelands, violence began immediately.

The first revolt broke out in Zurmat in the form of resistance to revenue collection. An attempt to occupy a local fort failed, which fuelled the fighting, and so a larger force was dispatched to destroy compounds and forts and to seize stocks of grain.[43] The destruction and looting of a caravan on its way up from India to Kabul was the next indication of Ghilzai anger. The clans cut communications to Jalalabad completely soon after. The British used troops who were not only due to return to India under the command of Brigadier Robert Sale to clear the route, but also, through negotiations, threatened to replace the elders as recipients of the remaining allowances with new beneficiaries. On 9 October 1841 the Ghilzais made a night attack to avoid the firepower of Sale's two regular regiments encamped in bivouac. They inflicted twenty-five casualties before drawing away. Three days later the Ghilzais took up positions along the cliffs of the Khoord–Kabul Pass and had to be dislodged by an infantry assault. As soon as the defile was cleared, the Ghilzais made a second night attack on the British and Indian encampment. At Tezin, the British opened negotiations and offered a quarter of the old allowances. Although this was accepted by the clans in the immediate vicinity of the pass, the next day more Ghilzais shot at the column as it passed below them at Jugduluk. The main body was subjected to a steady fusillade of *jezail* fire, but the baggage column that came up behind offered a richer reward. As it reached the summit of the 3-mile-long pass, the volleys of Ghilzai fire were accompanied by a charge of swordsmen.[44] The rearguard fell back, was rallied, but only a portion of them counter-attacked. Exhibiting their anger at the British, the Afghan swordsmen were at that moment busy dispatching the wounded British and Indian soldiers, and were driven off. The British lost 120 men killed and wounded, but Ghilzai losses are unknown.

More importantly, the swordsmen had created a psychological effect on their adversaries. Hemmed in by the terrain, the British and Indian troops had been unable to do much damage with volley fire. The steady attrition of their ranks, where 300 had become casualties in the space of a week's march through the pass, and the resolute attack by men armed with Khyber knives had clearly unnerved the soldiers. Something of the strength of feeling of the Afghans is suggested by the fact that even some of Shah Shuja's personal bodyguards rode out to join the fighting against the British, although there were many reported cases of joining a fight regardless of who was involved for the thrill of action and the chance to be tested in battle. At Gandamack, Sale halted his brigade and was subjected to sniping from the nearby hills, but then news arrived that a revolt had broken out in Kabul.

In the far west, Yar Mohammed, the vizier of Herat, was continually search-ing for the opportunity to subvert the presence of the British and Shah Shu-ja's apparent suzerainty. Correspondence was maintained with the Persians, and both money and men were sent to support Akhtar Khan Alizai in a revolt against Shah Shuja in December 1840.[45] Todd, the British agent in Herat, was so exasperated with Yar Mohammed's intrigues that he cut off financial subsi-dies, demanded that British troops be stationed in the citadel and delivered an ultimatum in February 1841. When the frustrated British envoy left, Yar Mohammed rounded up those who had made profits through the British and had their assets seized. The sons of Kamran, the ruler of Herat, made an attempt to seize power in a palace coup, but although they held the citadel for fifty days, they were forced to capitulate. Yar Mohammed appropriated all Kamran's trea-sury and exiled his sons. However, the tide turned when Akhtar Khan's revolt was defeated by Shuja in August 1841 and Herat remained isolated.

There was also developing unrest of a small and localized character in the Pashtun south. General Nott at Kandahar had to deal with a minor insurrec-tion in January 1841, but his troops were able to contain the resistance. By August the rebels had been dispersed. Rawlinson noted that: 'The only "irrec-oncilable" was Akrum Khan, with whom promises and threats were alike pow-erless... A fellow countryman, therefore, having been induced to reveal his whereabouts, the unfortunate Doorani chief was surprised and seized. Nott carried him to Candahar, where, after consultation with the Envoy and the puppet monarch, he was executed, being blown from a gun'.[46] It is not clear whether this inducement was driven by hard cash or clan rivalry, but the Brit-ish were able to use Afghan interlocutors and agents throughout their occu-pation and were never deprived of vital intelligence in the south. In the north, however, the situation became critical.

The Kabul revolt and the question of Islamic or national resistance

It is often assumed that Afghan resistance was constant and united through-out the British occupation, with a desultory low level of insurgency as the norm. In fact, as the episodes of 1840–41 show, unrest was localized, sporadic, and closely related to the provision of allowances or clan politics. The Afghan view is that opposition to foreign occupation was inevitable, universally popular and that success was assured. The reality was that many collaborated with the British or used the presence of the foreign forces to pursue their own agendas. Afghan society remained as divided as before, but new alliances and coalitions were formed under the political dispensation of Shah Shuja. The myth that Afghanistan was the 'graveyard of empires' has proved persistent, despite the historical fact that Afghanistan has been overrun, incorporated and rendered into a 'rentier' territory many times. Moreover, the defeat of a British brigade at Kabul in 1841 at the hands of an irregular force was the exception rather than the rule. Afghan forces had found it impossible to hold ground against the disciplined battalions of British and Indian troops. The lack of coordination between Afghan factions, and occasions of outright hostility to each other, has often been overlooked.

The emphasis on the 'inevitable' defeat of occupiers in the historiography emerged because of several related factors. The first, and most recent, was the Soviet withdrawal in 1989, but ironically there was also an echo of the determinism of Soviet ideology in the narrative, namely that revolutionary forces would always overthrow an imperial power. Western Whig histories also emphasized the inevitability of outcomes. It suited the authors of British histories in the nineteenth century to use the destruction of the brigade at Kabul to prove that it was impossible to hold Afghanistan, which was also the contrasting case for India or other parts of the empire. Afghan exceptionalism was easier to assert, and consequently the characteristic of 'fanaticism' was emphasized. The strategic situation for the British after 1841, specifically to reduce costs and render Afghanistan a client buffer state rather than assume the burdens of occupation, has too often been ignored. The biggest oversight has been the failure to acknowledge that it was the under-resourced nature of the occupation, with small and isolated garrisons, both those of the Shah and the British, and the consequent under-financing of the project, that led to the crisis of 1841. Each generation rewrites its history to suit changing values, expectations and interpretations, and nationalist agendas in Afghanistan have been reinforced by the case of the First Anglo–Afghan War. The notion that the Afghans conducted a 'national revolution' against the British and their puppet leader ignored the fact that Shah Shuja enjoyed greater legitimacy than Dost Mohammed and the Barakzais.

The populist aspect of the resistance to the British had a strong Islamist character, and leaders found this factor a useful tool for mobilizing the people in large numbers. This had an obvious and critical military value. The employment of mass was in effect the only way to overwhelm the military power of small, professional British and Indian forces. However, there is another tendency, used by Afghans, to see this as the exclusive element of the resistance. In reality, the prospect of loot was just as important in motivating men to fight.

Shah Shuja noted: 'these men are not influenced by considerations of religion, they give their lives for the wealth of this world and do not fear death'.[47] The British also felt that religion was being used cynically as a rallying call by the *khans*.[48] In such an impoverished society the evident wealth of the foreign forces made identification of the enemy much easier, and men were prepared to take risks to acquire some share of it. At Qalat, the rebels soon drifted away when there was no material gain to be made. Religion became a useful way to justify action, and so were claims that clan sensibilities or interests had been adversely affected. The Reverend Gleig, who took part in the war, concluded:

...the Afghans proved themselves to be especially skilful. Though individually brave, they seldom stood to oppose our men, either in a stand up fight upon the plain, or in a smart skirmish; but wherever they found an opening whereby to approach our baggage and rear guards at a disadvantage, no troops in the world knew better how to turn it to account. They slew ... a good many men, and carried off no inconsiderable amount of booty.[49]

In many ways, resistance to the foreigners and even to Shah Shuja was conservative rather than revolutionary. The emphasis of the rebel leaders was on preserving the status quo and the 'old order'. Rebels in Kabul invoked the name of the Shah to gather support, claiming that the British were forcing their ruler to make decisions against his will, and evidence suggests that documents favouring the rebellion of 1841 bearing the Shah's name were forgeries.[50]

The resistance in Kabul and the Khyber Pass

In Kabul on 2 November 1841, the British faced a small but serious revolt which broke out in the bazaar and quickly spread to other parts of the city. Amongst the first to be killed was Sir Alexander Burnes who had been a key negotiator with the Afghans and was due to succeed Sir William Macnaghten as the senior political figure in the British administration. The crowd, estimated initially at 300, was reported to have gathered at Burnes' house in the old city in the early morning in the hope of acquiring the cash that was said to be stored at the property. The crowd appears to have started with verbal abuse and vocal protest, and Burnes is reported to have attempted to remonstrate with them from the balcony of his house. The protest turned violent and Burnes was hacked down. This murder of a British officer committed the crowd to further action. One of the first buildings to be stormed was the Treasury under the command of Captain Johnson, the Paymaster of the Shah's army.

According to Mohan Lal, Burnes' secretary and spymaster, the uprising was led by disaffected court nobles, Barakzai *khans* and the middle-ranking *ulema* not in the service of Shah Shuja's court.[51] Very few Kizilbash were involved, and certainly none of the Afghan minorities. The *ulema* had been eager to proclaim a Jihad, and Mohan Lal reported that they had rushed through the streets making an announcement to this effect soon after the outbreak of violence.[52] Nevertheless, against the background of rapidly rising prices, the news that the Treasury had been broken open was an important incentive to join the fighting. Lal noted that the crowd swelled rapidly after the initial violence.

The leaders who had planned the protest and revolt were keen to protect their privileges and their incomes, and, in the secret meeting the night before the outbreak, there were frequent complaints about British high-handedness towards them. They were angry that their prestige, so crucial to social relations in Afghanistan, was undermined and that Afghan women, especially wives and consorts, were being attracted by British money to the foreigners. There was concern that the influx of revenue was being redistributed to other factions, and not shared according to the former hierarchy of clans. Resistance to the Hazilbash and Janbaz cavalry was especially marked in this regard. Some of the *ulema* argued that the new uniforms and forms of discipline were un-Islamic, but the real motive was to register their protest at the growing influence of the British over political affairs and their own relative loss of power.[53] The rebels were eager to restore the Shah's power too. He had complained of the dictatorial manner in which the British were insisting on economies and the lack of control he had even over his own contingent of troops.[54] As early as July 1840, some Durrani *khans* had asked him to lead the resistance to the British, but he had refused.[55] Shah Shuja had tried to negotiate an end to the revolt shortly after the outbreak, but shooting had broken out against Shuja's men and the attempt was abandoned. Some 200 of the Shah's troops were killed or wounded in the street fighting and two cannon were lost. The Shah's son had allegedly made a last-ditch attempt to recover control by announcing that the rebels should strike against the British, but the Shah continued to negotiate with the British and hoped to see the rising suppressed by them.[56]

British histories of the rising tend to focus on the inactivity of the British forces after the initial outbreak of fighting in Kabul and the failure of decisive leadership. From the Afghan perspective, the lack of British initiative gave the rebellion a chance to gather momentum, and an estimated 15,000 fighters assembled at the city. Kohanistanis, deeply affected by the punitive campaign of the autumn, poured into the city from the north. Kabulis eager to avenge themselves or take part in plundering were joined by rural inhabitants directed by local *khans* and elders over a period of three weeks. Mir Aftab became prominent in Kabul, but there was no single leadership. It was some time before Nawab Zaman Khan Barakzai declared himself Shah, while Amanullah Khan Logari became his *wazir* and Abdullah Khan Achakzai became commander of the military forces. Despite the lack of British military response, negotiators were much more active. Mohan Lal was responsible for buying off some Ghilzai elders who took their men away from Kabul. The Kazilbashes also stayed out of the rebellion, but it is not clear whether they were paid off or not. There was a risk that, at this point, the rebellion might collapse, not least because of the rivalries between the Afghan factions and the precedence that acquiring some of the British revenue now took.

More effective military leadership was established by Mohammed Akbar Khan, the son of Dost Mohammed, who arrived in Kabul around 25 November. He arranged for the *ulema* to move into the villages to persuade the farmers to stop selling supplies to the British cantonment at Sherpur.[57] A commissary depot containing the British garrison's supplies was first cut off and then captured in a series of night assaults. He sent fighters to Beymaru and the cluster of villages that lay adjacent to the cantonment to prevent food reaching the garrison, and his men burned bridges that linked the cantonment to the city. Ringing the British base to cut off supplies and then gradually squeezing the weakened garrison avoided the problem of making costly frontal assaults, although the defences around Sherpur were hardly formidable.

The Afghans also made good use of a fortification that lay close to the British cantonment, known as Mohammed Shareef's fort. They loopholed the walls so as to be able to shoot down any British attempt to sortie from the gates. As before, the prospect of acquiring loot was a strong incentive to join the fighting. When the commissary was overrun, the scene of Afghans scrambling to get a share of the goods was said to resemble 'an anthill'.[58] The bonanza of looting even persuaded the Kazilbashes to join the rebellion. The abandonment of the Bala Hissar by the last remaining British detachment there on 9 November 1841 fuelled the enthusiasm of the Afghans for victory, and the news of these successes acted as a magnet for the Ghilzais too. Mohan Lal estimated that the numbers of fighters who assembled at Kabul was 50,000.

On 10 November, the Afghans tightened the ring. The heights above the two sides of the cantonment, if occupied, offered the chance to thin out the defenders manning the ramparts and to dominate the entire position. If artillery could be established on the heights as well, this would hasten the fall of the British defences, although finding trained gunners proved difficult. On the eastern side of the cantonment, Afghan cavalry managed to get on to the high ground and then ride forward to occupy a walled enclosure called the Rikaba-shee fort. Dismounting here, the Afghans opened fire on the ramparts. The British assembled a force to clear this position, but when their attempt to open a breach in the enclosure walls only created a small gap, the Afghans inside were able to pick off the attackers as they tried to get in. Seeing the British assault, the Afghan cavalry still on the heights above charged down and took the infantry in the flank. The British 44th Regiment was driven back, rallied, and rejoined the troops who had managed to get inside the Rikabashee enclo-sure. The Afghans therefore abandoned the position but their cavalry managed to mount a second charge, and dismounted Afghan troops made a counter-attack up to the main entrance. The British troops at Rikabashee were unable to close the gates, were driven back into a stable block and wiped out. Once again, the British fought their way back. This time, the 37th Native Infantry managed to push the Afghans out and straight into the fire of the 44th Regi-ment. Meanwhile the rest of the British force had skirmished up to the Siah Sung Hill on the eastern side of the cantonment from where they could use cannons to fire onto the remaining Afghan formations. In this sharp engage-ment, the Afghans had proved that they could contest positions they knew to be of tactical value and that they understood the importance of momentum and shock action in attack. They also demonstrated perseverance by launch-ing a second major attack three days later.

On 13 November, the Afghans manhandled two field guns up onto the Bey-maru Heights that stood to the immediate west of the cantonment. They began to fire through the British encampment as soon as they reached the summit, and it was clear that, once again, the British would need to clear the high ground. The Afghans had anticipated this move, and as soon as the British were in the open they launched a cavalry charge from the hillside. The Afghan horsemen rode into and through the British and Indian ranks, causing com-plete confusion. However, the British cavalry were able to mount an effective counter-attack and the Afghan horsemen fell back. The British artillery joined in, inflicting losses on the Afghans streaming back across the plain to the south. The British infantry then scaled the heights, spiked one gun and hauled away the other. The Afghans may have abandoned the guns because they lacked ammunition, although the hilltop location would have made it extremely difficult to extract them under fire. There is no record of the Afghans having fought to defend the guns. The shortage of ammunition may also explain why they did not use them to attempt to make breaches in the walls of the cantonment.

The British planned to remain in possession of the Beymaru Heights until darkness, but their withdrawal proved to be the opportunity the Afghans needed to close with their enemies. As soon as it got dark, distinguishing friend from foe became impossible and the Afghan cavalry rode deep into the British lines causing chaos. At this point a second wave of 400 Afghans advanced from the north-east, which suggests that there had been some coordination in this attack. In the confused fighting, the British managed to extract themselves and returned to the cantonment, firing for some time from the walls. The Afghans, realizing the impossibility of preventing the British from recovering their position, drew off.

The contemporary British accounts of the fighting in and around Rikaba-shee and Beymaru focus strongly on the errors of the commanders and the gradual demoralization of the British and Indian garrison. The shortage of supplies, caused by the failure to secure their commissary depot, also features prominently. Rather less attention was given at the time, or indeed by subsequent authors, to the Afghan perspective. In many ways the Afghan attacks on 10 and 31 November were premature. Having taken the British supplies, or at least a substantial portion of them, they were not prepared to sit out a siege and wait. The decision to secure the Rikabashee compound appears to have been a hasty decision, which contrasts with the careful siting of forces on the dominating heights. Getting drawn into a fight for a relatively unimportant position, albeit one close to the cantonment walls, caused unnecessary casualties. At Beymaru a great deal of effort was made to get two guns above the British cantonment, perhaps to cause a demoralization of the garrison rather than any substantial physical effect. The action of the Afghan cavalry when the British left the security of the cantonment walls gives the impression that an ambush had been planned, but it was too small a force to defeat the British and was driven off. The night attack as the British withdrew suggests an attempt at coordination, but too few Afghan forces were deployed to create a decisive effect. This suggests that the Afghans had difficulty combining their various factions to act in concert, even when they were presented with a common enemy. When the British eventually withdrew from the Sherpur cantonment, only the Ghilzai factions pursued them beyond the Khoord–Kabul Pass, because this was, in effect, their own territory.

Macnaghten reluctantly agreed to offer 200,000 rupees to draw off all the Ghilzais, but perhaps sensing that they now had the upper hand and a greater reward awaited them, the Ghilzai elders rejected the offer.[59] In the meantime General Nott was ordered to send a relief force from Kandahar, and Brigadier Sale was instructed to fight his way back to Kabul if he felt he could manage it. In fact, Sale believed he could not provide security for his wounded and sick, or fight all the Ghilzai clans with just two reduced battalions. He had lost thirty-five killed and wounded to sniping in just one night, and this sort of harassing fire was kept up during the daylight hours too.[60] He marched to Jalalabad to await reinforcements coming up from India. In the south, Nott faced difficulties of his own. A body of 100 men had been wiped out in a well-executed Ghilzai ambush as it approached Ghazni. Nevertheless he held on to a brigade that was due to depart to India, and sent a reduced brigade on from Kandahar as ordered.

Meanwhile at Charikar, in Kohistan, a Gurkha regiment and its families and camp followers, who had attempted to fall back on Kabul, had been destroyed. Muslim gunners attached to the formation had been persuaded to cooperate with their Afghan co-religionists against the British and Indian troops. It appears that the survivors who tried to escape through the snows were cut down by fast-moving Afghan horsemen. Finally the reinforcements due to reach Jalalabad from India, a composite force under Brigadier Wild, had been defeated in the Khyber Pass. On the eve of the advance of this relief column, the Sikh auxiliaries had deserted and the remaining sepoys broke under the Afridis' *jezail* fire. The collapse of the force affected the garrison of the fortress of Ali-Musjid. They fled, and the Afridis rushed in to seize cattle, supplies and abandoned munitions. When news arrived that British reinforcements would not be coming from the south or through the Khyber, and with dwindling rations, Macnaghten once again tried to open negotiations.

The Afghans, however, were eager to inflict a decisive military defeat on the British first, partly to assert that the negotiating position was absolutely clear but also to satisfy their honour by reasserting their supremacy in battle. After another three days of preparation at Kabul, which the British observed was to manufacture more ammunition and collect more powder, the village of Beymaru was sealed off. Since the British garrison had been on half rations since the loss of the Commissary depot and had relied on Afghans to supply food and fodder via the village, it was decided a sortie should be made to recover control of this key terrain. The Afghans began to dig in on the heights above the cantonment, perhaps aware that the British were about to undertake some offensive manoeuvre. At dawn on 23 November, British and Indian infantry, with sappers, cavalry and a single cannon, started to advance on the village, but they were met by a considerable weight of *jezail* fire. The sound of the firing drew Afghans from the city and they concentrated on the heights. Estimates suggest that 10,000 assembled there. The single British gun, although effective, overheated and ceased firing.

At this point several hundred Afghan horsemen had assembled nearby, prompting the British infantry to adopt the 'square' formation for all-round defence against cavalry. However, the Afghan horsemen had no wish to throw themselves into the path of British volley fire and hung back, allowing the *jezail*-carrying foot soldiers to open up on the densely-packed British ranks.

While the British and Indian troops were pinned in one place, Afghan swordsmen approached them via dead ground, using a gully that concealed them from both the infantry and the fire of British guns in the cantonment. Emerging at close quarters in large numbers, the nearest square collapsed and this was the signal for the Afghan cavalry to surge forward. The single British gun was overrun. However, the British held their ground and counter-attacked with bayonets accompanied by an Indian cavalry squadron. In the mêlée, Abdullah Khan, one of the original leaders of the Kabul revolt, was mortally wounded. This caused the Afghans to pull back, abandoning the hill and the British cannon. However, the British were still vulnerable when they halted. The Afghans took up positions on the slopes amongst the rocks and proceeded to cut down the standing ranks, taking care to keep out of range of the muskets and under cover when volleys were fired overhead. The skirmishing continued for some hours until a second force of swordsmen again worked their way up to the British position using the cover of a defile. They assembled for a final assault while concealed and then made a sudden attack. This compelled the British to fall back and the Afghan cavalry, still hovering nearby, seized its chance to pursue and destroy the collapsing line. The Afghans were soon mixed in amongst the retreating redcoats and victory was so certain for the Afghans that many of them chose to spare the British troops rather than slaughter them. Captain Trevor noted that 'several times' Afghans had stopped short of killing him, waving a sword above him instead. Curiously the Afghans also let the British return to the cantonment.

This fighting on 23 November at first sight suggests a far more coordinated operation, and the obvious suggestion has been that Akbar Khan had taken command of the various factions to achieve a victory. In fact, although there was a picquet line of Afghan *jezailchis* in Beymaru village, most of the Afghans who took part in the battle had to assemble from their billets in Kabul. This fact, and the decision by the cavalry not to attack, had little to do with a coordinated plan but were based on the experience of having faced a cohesive line of British musket fire in the past. For the second time, Afghan cavalry and infantry had been unable to hold the Beymaru Heights or stand their ground in the open, but they had been most effective when the British insisted on using close-order formations (a precaution against rushes by swordsmen or cavalry-men) and the Afghans could make use of cover and fire against them. This was simply a pragmatic decision on the part of the Afghans against the key British assets, namely cohesion and massed fire from the infantry, not forgetting the effectiveness of their artillery. It was not an enduring Afghan 'way of war' but a classic example of adapting to a new situation.

The reason why the British personnel were spared, especially after such bit-ter fighting in the previous weeks, might be explained by the desire not to cre-ate the conditions for revenge. Amongst Afghans, their culture dictated that to kill or die in the heat of battle was quite legitimate, but unnecessary killing might compel the victim's family members to seek *badal*. The Afghans who spared the British officers may have believed that they were simply worth more alive than dead, perhaps as hostages, but it may also have been connected with the idea that, since the British were clearly defeated, there was no need to anni-hilate them. It certainly casts doubt on the oft-repeated assumption that the Afghans were simply 'thousands of fanatics' whose 'fervour was directed at the destruction of the infidels', as one writer put it.[61] For the Afghans, a subsequent breach of honour by the British nevertheless negated any ideas of sparing these men, and this led to the disaster of January 1842.

The failure of a negotiated settlement at Kabul and Ghazni

The loss of key resources, a reduced garrison, paralysis in the military leader-ship, the defeat and massacre of a garrison at Kohistan, the loss of the Khyber Pass, and then the defeat of British and Indian troops at Beymaru Ridge on 13 and 23 November 1841 completely altered the conditions for negotiation. Macnaghten knew the critical nature of the military situation and he initiated overtures to Mohammad Akbar Khan, who had come into the city of Kabul soon after the revolt, and to the tribal leaders of the Ghilzais from the neigh-bouring districts.

The Afghans demanded that Shah Shuja and his household be handed over to them, and that the British garrison at Jalalabad should evacuate and return to Peshawar. They insisted that the Kabul garrison should give up all its arms and ammunition, make over all the European officers and families as hostages, and that the Indian troops should march back to India.[62] The Afghan demands amounted to the full capitulation of the British forces, but they also ensured that, by taking hostages, they were insured against any further military incursions, they could demand the release of Dost Mohammed (whom they regarded as being held hostage) and, perhaps, the means by which they could trade for the return of all the other Afghan settlements under occupation, including Kandahar and Ghazni. They may also have intended to obtain Peshawar by these means. Certainly the hostages who were later taken were treated with hospitality, particularly by Akbar Khan himself. Disarming the British and Indian forces would simply prevent any further British resistance against Kabul and was not unlike the terms the British would have themselves demanded.

The British rejected the Afghan demands, but 'back channels' were kept open. One of the key negotiators, Mohan Lal, was still active in this regard. It is alleged that Macnaghten, or perhaps Mohan Lal himself, had offered cash to any Afghan who would assassinate at least two of the tribal leaders, although there is no documentary evidence of such a plot.[63] Macnaghten was accused of being the architect of treachery, but, even if there was a conspiracy, Mohan Lal had refused to pay any bounties to those who claimed to have killed two tribal leaders.[64] The delay by the British and the suspicions that were harboured by the killings, feared to be part of a wider assassination effort, merely hardened the Afghan position. On 11 December, Macnaghten again met the Afghan leaders and announced that the British would not accept dishonourable terms and would rather die 'in the last ditch'. However, he was aware, as were the Afghans, that the Kabul garrison's supplies were almost exhausted and that wintry weather was causing a great deal of suffering. Macnaghten therefore also drew up a treaty that amounted to surrender, the terms stating that the British would now withdraw and would permit Dost Mohammed to return to the throne in Kabul. In return, the British asked for safe conduct out of the country via the Khyber Pass.

Macnaghten still hoped that divisions amongst the Afghans would give the British the edge in negotiations and perhaps permit a recovery of the situation. Indeed, Akbar Khan appeared to have great difficulty in persuading the tribal leaders, particularly the Ghilzais, to accept any deal at all. The British lacked sufficient transport animals, and disorganization prevailed in the cantonments at Sherpur such that the original deadline for departure, 15 December, passed without any movement at all. This served to increase the suspicions of the Ghilzais. On 22 December, on the second date set for departure, Akbar Khan offered a new treaty which stated that, in return for making him Wazir and donating supplies to get the Kabul garrison through the winter, he would support Shah Shuja. He even offered to arrest Amanullah Khan, the serving Wazir of the 'shadow government' and one of the leaders who had started the revolt in Kabul in November. Macnaghten famously signed this instrument, which was duly shown to the tribal leaders by Akbar Khan as final evidence of the infidelity of the British.

Macnaghten had hoped the new treaty would actually divide Akbar Khan and the clans, but it united them in a determination to abandon negotiations and destroy the British garrison altogether. On 23 December Macnaghten was summoned to a meeting on the banks of the Kabul River, where he was murdered and dismembered. The weakened state of the garrison was then exploited, and while some British officers still favoured fighting their way out or seizing the Bala Hissar fortress, the garrison in fact attempted to march out expecting the 'safe conduct' which they believed Macnaghten had secured. It took six days to wipe out the British force, which included hundreds of civilians and the families of many of the troops.

The Afghan forces at Kabul began to loot the cantonment even before the British had completed their evacuation on 6 January 1842. Several *jezailchis* opened fire as the rear of the column left the immediate vicinity, and a number of the garrison were killed before they could escape. The first 5 miles of the retreat was marked by abandoned baggage and some despairing camp followers. Many of the Afghans who pursued the column simply looked to acquire this baggage or valuables still held by the British. After all, the British had a reputation for wealth and so waves of raiders would move in, largely under cover of darkness, to seize anything of value. The British continued to resist and the looting parties were driven off on repeated occasions. Akbar Khan eventually caught up with the column to acquire more hostages which he could use for bargaining and insurance against any British counter-offensive. Conscious of the expectations of his peers, that all fugitives deserved to be offered hospitality under *nanawatai*, and perhaps reminded that his father might be humiliated if he did not ensure that British captives were well-treated, he ensured that his British prisoners survived.

As the British column struggled towards the Khyber Pass, each Ghilzai clan looked to acquire some sort of compensation to make up for the loss of their allowances. It seems unlikely that the Afghans, collectively, had set out to annihilate the entire British force, but rather this was the cumulative effect as the column passed through each clan territory. There must have been a steady stream of clansmen moving to and from the retreating column's route encumbered by valuables, or setting off to acquire a share. The acquisition of plunder had always been a divisive issue amongst Ghilzai families and villages, and the sudden input of these goods must have generated a good deal of rivalry which may have lasted for years. One of the reasons why the Ghilzais proved unable and unwilling to confront Dost Mohammed in the years after his return to power may, perhaps, have been because of the increased frequency of internal disputes and faction fighting caused by this sudden influx of goods. While we have no written records to support this assumption, similar episodes from other periods point in this direction.

In the defiles of the Khyber Pass, some Ghilzais attempted to halt the British column altogether with barriers. There were also British attempts to negotiate a path through the clans. At the Khoord–Kabul Pass, however, the Ghilzais tried to kill as many foreigners as possible, and once again, according to eyewitnesses, they concentrated their fire wherever the baggage was clustered most densely or where animals or loot might be acquired. On 8 January 1842, the third day of the retreat, some Ghilzais rushed in to try and wrest weapons from the Indian soldiers. They also used the herding masses of civilians as cover so as to get closer to the valuable goods without being shot down by the soldiers still offering resistance.

After the British had pushed their way through the Hoft Kotal defile, suffering more casualties, Akbar Khan offered to negotiate and demanded that the British surrender entirely. The British refused and tried to make a night march to reach Jugduluk while the Ghilzais slept, but the mass of panicking civilians destroyed any hope of secrecy. Conscious that the British and their valuables might soon be out of reach, the Ghilzais therefore launched a series of attacks on the rear of the column. The British nevertheless created a defensive position, using the walls of the village at Jugduluk as cover, and this forced the Ghilzais to sustain their fire from some distance away. But on entering the Jugduluk defile, the British were subjected to more intense fire as they tried to dismantle a holly oak barrier. Almost all the remaining officers were killed at this point and the camp followers were massacred. A handful of troops reached Gandamack and formed a defensive ring. The Ghilzais, according to Captain Souter who survived, initially approached without firing, possibly in the hope of disarming the British and acquiring their weapons. When the British resisted, they were all cut down. Another survivor, Dr Brydon, also noted that villagers had used a red flag to signal the approach of the British, whereupon Afghan cavalrymen concentrated to attack. This suggests that a system of warning signals may have been in use in and around the Khyber Pass, perhaps to summon *lashkars* for a defensive action.

The key Afghan accounts of the negotiations in November 1841-January 1842 were analyzed by the Afghan historian Sayyid Mohammed Qasim Rashtiya, and, as expected, they emphasized the treacherous nature of the British negotiators.[65] However, Afghan versions of events share a lack of critical reflection, generally only praising the Afghan forces' courage, character and military success. There is no mention of the frequent division of Afghan factions which the British had exploited, and there is even the suggestion, disputed by Malcolm Yapp, that a nascent nationalism had emerged.[66] Subsequent Afghan work in the 1960s copied British condemnations of the adventurism of the East India Company and its negotiators, but failed to acknowledge the subsequent British invasion of 1842 by the so-called 'Avenging Army' or negotiations and operations elsewhere. Studies influenced by communism made great play with the defeat of British capitalist-imperialism by Afghan revolutionary forces. Popular Afghan accounts, including those recorded by Louis Dupree in 1967, make no mention of the negotiations at all, except attempts by individual British female fugitives to barter for their lives or become Muslims, the emphasis on women reflecting their importance as symbols of success in war in local folk culture.[67]

After the destruction of the retreating column, the British garrison at Jalalabad had initially hoped to negotiate with Akbar Khan and the Ghilzais, but it was clear that the Afghans believed they had all the advantages and they attempted to storm and then besiege the fortress there.[68] The British troops nevertheless withstood the Afghan assaults, despite an earthquake destroying their walls, and they were relieved by British forces coming up from India. The breakdown of trust, essential for negotiations, was evident on both sides, with one officer commenting that 'I am surprised that anyone should suggest—an Afghan's word as worth anything'.[69] This sentiment was reinforced when the garrison at Ghazni, which was also offered a safe passage back to India, was ambushed and massacred after leaving the protection of the fortress walls. The prospect of seizing goods and cash had spurred on the clans in each of these attacks. Afghan divisions were also partly to blame for the offers of 'safe passage' that were subsequently ignored. Agreements made with one faction had no binding effect on another, particularly when they saw the opportunity for loot or revenge. Clearly many Afghans felt they had a religious obligation to defeat the foreign, non-Muslim occupation. However, not all the British garrison were driven from Afghanistan. Qalat was besieged and, despite determined attacks, held out, as did Kandahar, and these garrisons were only withdrawn in 1842, long after the sacking of Kabul.[70]

The collapse of unity

The view in London, which was shared by the Governor General in India, was to abandon Afghanistan, but there was a general feeling that some restoration of military prestige was required. Major General George Pollock, who commanded the forces below the Khyber Pass, argued that without a new expedition against Kabul 'our character as a powerful nation would be entirely lost in this part of the world'.[71] On 31 March 1842, the Duke of Wellington had written to the Governor General: 'It is impossible to impress upon you too strongly the Notion of the importance of the Restoration of Reputation in the East'.[72] He was particularly eager that action should be taken against 'the Moslem chief who had with his own hand murdered Sir William Macnaghten, the Representative of the British Government at the Court of the Sovereign of Afghanistan'. At the local level, negotiations were attempted with the Afridis to open a route through the Khyber, but generally the British chose to re-assert their military prowess because of their new objective: the restoration of prestige. Consequently, the British marched back into Kabul, and they won military victories at Qalat, Ghazni and in the Khyber Pass at Tezin, often perfecting the skills of mountain warfare and maintaining a relentless pursuit.[73] British hostages were released. At Kabul, Akbar Khan tried to discuss a new treaty, but the British commanders were ordered not to enter into any negotiations.

What British histories tend to overlook is the bitter divisions that had opened up amongst the Afghans. When the British garrison first left Kabul, the sick and wounded that became hostages were bargaining tools to be traded between the various factions. Legitimacy to govern and loyalty were also part of a currency for exchange. Zaman Shah could look to the Barakzai for his support, but not all followed willingly and some felt that Shah Shuja was still the true authority of Kabul. Others looked to Akbar Khan, who had organized the resistance and who represented the link with Dost Mohammed, although Akbar was engaged in trying to control Ghilzai *khans* and elders as they pursued the British towards the Khyber. The court nobles of Kabul, led by Amanullah Khan, drew upon the support of the Logaris. They derived their finances from pressure on the Hindu bankers left behind by the British garrison, and this gave Amanullah the chance to enlist soldiers in a private army. In the Bala Hissar fortress of Kabul, Shah Shuja himself could count on the backing of 2,000 troops and a sizeable treasury, and, he hoped, he could call upon the British to return and restore his undisputed position. At first a compromise was agreed where Shuja would remain as Shah, with Zaman as Wazir and Amanullah as *na'ib*. But the agreement soon ran into problems.

The first dispute was over the raising and control of the Afghan military forces. Most of the khans had exhausted the cash they had acquired, and many turned to looting Kabul and the surrounding area in order to raise money to pay for troops. Amanullah threatened the commercial classes to obtain more money. Shah Shuja was also called upon to raise forces with some of his state revenue and then send one of his sons to lead an army against the British.[74] As the Barakzais became more insistent, so Amanullah moved closer towards the Shah, and persuaded the Kizilbash to back his faction. Zaman reacted by disputing Amanullah's right to collect revenue, raised 3,000 of his own militia and deployed captured British cannons.[75] Shuja still delayed and offered cash. Eventually he relented and started out on the march, only to be killed by Zaman's son, Shuja 'al-Dawla. Amanullah used the killing as an opportunity to install Shah Shuja's son, Fath Jang, and to increase the size of his own militia to 3,000, with 400 Saddozai Popalzai allies.[76]

The situation changed again when Akbar Khan was defeated outside Jalalabad. The siege of the British garrison there had begun on 12 November 1841, but the British had made a successful sortie and accumulated the stores they needed to withstand a long investment. A second attempt to storm the town had failed in late November, and the besiegers had settled down to appropriate the cash from Kabul without further fighting. In January 1842, Akbar had been unable to raise more men to overwhelm the British garrison and so he tried to repeat the strategy he had used against the Kabul forces, namely cutting off supplies from outside by occupying all the neighbouring villages. However, local Afghans were eager to make money and there were attempts to negotiate a new deal with the British. Then, on 5 April 1842, General Pollock pushed through the Khyber Pass, and just two days later he attacked Akbar Khan's camp. Kabul was thrown into panic by the prospect of the British marching on the city.

Zaman declared himself Shah and raised more troops for the defence of the capital.[77] Kohistani Tajiks refused to support either of the Pashtun factions, arguing that they had not been awarded a fair share of the loot taken from the British. Fath Jang, eager to avenge his father, refused to march against the foreigners at Jalalabad. Thus, on the eve of a British counter-offensive, the Afghan armed forces were preparing to fight each other, and only the intervention by Akbar Khan averted a civil war. Having been driven back at Jalalabad, Akbar managed to negotiate a settlement between the factions, insisting that Fath Jang provide the funds and Amanullah direct 6,000 Afghan troops to the east, while a garrison of 1,000 was left at the Bala Hissar.[78] However, on 30 April

1842, a dispute between Zaman's faction and Amanullah's men turned violent. Kabulis, angry with Amanullah's extortion and abuse of the *ulema*, flocked to Zaman's cause. Amanullah's militia simply deserted en masse.[79] Fath Jang, who had briefly bombarded the city with artillery, was besieged in the Bala Hissar.[80] In time, many of his supporters also deserted. Akbar Khan added his own effort to the demise of Shah Shuja's son. He laid siege to the Bala Hissar in the first week of May having opened negotiations with the British, partly to buy time and partly to ascertain British objectives. Fighting was sporadic but the demoralized soldiers in the Bala Hissar eventually capitulated on 7 June.[81] The key aspect of the contest was that, between fighting, Akbar insisted that Fath Jang was only holding the fortress for the British. The Sadozai faction, he argued, were discredited because they were, in effect, infidels themselves.[82] Forged documents were created to show that the British intended to sack Kabul, destroy the mosques and seize Afghan women.[83]

Akbar immediately garrisoned the Bala Hissar with Ghilzais and threw out the Kizilbash and the supporters of Zaman. Zaman, for his part, began intrigues against Akbar Khan, but Akbar Khan gained the support of some factions by arguing that keeping Fath Jang as Shah was, given his legitimacy, the most effective way of raising revenue which could be used to pay for troops to resist the British. Zaman once again responded by gathering what revenue he could and positioning troops.[84] He appealed to the *ulema* and the elders to back him. Akbar Khan retaliated by declaring that Dost Mohammed was the ruler of Kabul, and he sent troops to take control of the Customs House. There, after a brief skirmish, Zaman's troops were defeated.[85] Akbar Khan then called upon the Ghilzais for support, invoking the name of his respected father-in-law, Mohammad Shah, and asserted that the Kizilbashes should submit to his authority. Mirza Imam Wardi kept up the rhetoric of Islamic resistance against the British to cement Akbar Khan's legitimacy. However, it was not a smooth transition. From the outset, Ghilzai *khans* and elders resented the elevation of Mohammed Shah and Akbar Khan.[86]

Akbar Khan nevertheless believed he now had sufficient unity and control of the revenue of Kabul to build an effective resistance to the British. He appointed Salih Mohammed as the commander of a new composite Afghan force. Many had been trained by the British, but he also tried to establish regular patterns of pay with 10 rupees a month to cavalrymen and 7 to foot soldiers. By mid July he had raised 4,000 men.[87]

Even this modest force began to put the Kabul economy under strain. The revenue held in the Bala Hissar and Customs House had gone, farmers around

Kabul refused to relinquish any goods or cash, and Kabuli citizens had to be forced to pay. The arbitrary nature of the new regime began to stimulate opposition, and any popularity, based on stability after the disputes of the previous winter, had ebbed away.[88] Zaman and other leaders looked to re-open negotiations with the British against Akbar Khan. However, the former emphasis on Jihadism deterred any fruitful discussions with General Pollock.[89] Akbar himself also tried to negotiate with the British general, offering to release all the hostages in return for a British withdrawal. However, Pollock's orders had changed. He was now tasked to march on Kabul and obtain the release of the prisoners from a position of strength, and his army marched from Jalalabad on 20 August 1842. On 13 September, Pollock defeated the Afghans at the Khoord–Kabul Pass, entered Kabul and watched as the Kabulis established a new government. The elders selected Shapar, brother of Fath Jang, as Shah and pleaded with Pollock to provide arms, ammunition and money to hold the city, and to keep Dost Mohammed in India.

The Afghans were unable to confront the conventional forces of the British with any hope of success, but they still exercised a form of passive resistance. Major General Nott, who had marched from Kandahar to Kabul, reported that although his men were behaving well towards the Afghan population:

I believe the enemy (I mean Futteh Jung's party and the rest of the people) are organising a system to bring our men to the same state of starvation to which General Elphinstone's army was reduced in hopes of the same results—while I think it is my duty to state this, I must declare that I will not, to please a few Afghans, who have already washed their hands from the blood of our countrymen, allow my army to be destroyed and my country to be dishonoured. There is grain in the country and I think it ought to be brought in immediately the same being paid for'.[90]

However, Nott noted that 'the people are not inclined to sell even at the highest price'. A Soviet writer of the 1920s also commented on the means by which the Afghan people could remain defiant: 'The country is extremely well adapted to a *passive* resistance. Its mountainous nature and the proud and freedom-loving character of its people, combined with the lack of adequate roads, makes it very difficult to conquer and even harder to hold.[91]

The dilemma of trying to hold down a resistant population in such difficult terrain meant that garrisons had to be maintained across the country, but this entailed great cost and increased the security risks to isolated formations. Nott refused to allow small detachments to be sent out, stating: 'after much experience in this country my opinion is that, if the system of sending detachments should be adopted, disaster and ruin will follow'.[92] Nor was there any guarantee that local forces, raised by the British, would not abandon their paymasters. Nott was concerned about the lack of cash he possessed, which he claimed he needed for the irregular cavalry, presumably because he believed they would desert his force.[93] Once again, money determined Afghans' loyalties.

We should not, however, underestimate the importance of religion. Henry Rawlinson, the Political Officer stationed in Kandahar, noted that many Afghans were angry with the British on religious grounds and that 'it is indeed the rock upon which we split'.[94] Ata Mohammed, one of the rebels in the south, had tried to obtain the cloak of the Prophet to legitimize his cause.[95] The followers of Salu Khan Achakzai implored him to join the revolt because, according to a British report, 'all the Mussalmans are prepared to fight with [against] the kafirs in defence of their religion'.[96] These sentiments had a profound effect on Afghan negotiators working for the British. Sultan Muhammed Khan Alikozai, who acted as the go-between in Kandahar for the Heratis and the British, and who had been valuable in preventing an Alikozai revolt, found it hard to continue his work under the pressure of religious condemnation. Mirza Ahmad, another negotiator, succumbed to the arguments put before by Ata Mohammed, a rebel leader, and, according to Rawlinson, was 'lost to us by his religious feelings'.[97]

Each revolt, concluded the historian Malcolm Yapp in his coverage of the unrest in the Pashtun south, 'was conceived in religious terms'.[98] He believed 'the arguments, the propaganda, and the whole concept of the revolt were religious'. He also noted, however, that religion was not the cause but the means to legitimize violence. The revolts were localized and often organized by men whose interests were being affected adversely. But the defence of Islam provided a rallying cry that could overcome bitter *qawm* rivalries long enough to sustain resistance to the British and to subvert their Afghan allies. Rawlinson's own verdict was:

I believe all our troubles to be attributable to the countenance which we have shown to the chiefs, rather than to the pre-existence of any strong national or religious feeling against us; and I am sure that no Gov[ernme]nt either British or Native, can ever become efficient in this country until the privileged constitution of the Tribes is annihilated and the old Dooranee families who came in with Ahmad Shah are fairly crushed.[99]

Rawlinson was careful to ensure that, in Kandahar at least, the population believed that the British were still only the backers for the Saddozais led, in the south, by Shahzada Mohammed Timur. The chiefs to whom Rawlinson referred were nevertheless related to the Durrani rebels in Kabul, and it would be curious had they not communicated their feelings about the British position. Rawlinson reported that some Durani *khans* had travelled from Kabul after the outbreak of unrest there and had arrived near Kandahar in December.[100]

There was little immediate effect, partly because, perhaps, the British had suppressed comprehensively a series of risings through 1840. Nevertheless some sections of the Achakzais took up arms, and a detachment of Janbaz cavalry, led by the Achakzai *khan*, Salu Khan, mutinied. The catalyst for this defection had been the withdrawal of a post at Qala Abdullah at the northern end of the Khojak Pass. News that the post had gone encouraged some of the Barakzai, who lived to the south-east of Kandahar under the leadership of Ata Mohammad Khan Popalzai, to attempt to seize goods as they came up the pass from India. In fact, these hopes of loot were dashed when no caravans appeared. Salu Khan was induced back to the British side in May 1842 because of his rivalry with another Achakzai leader, a certain Abdullah Khan, and he hoped to benefit from his association with the strongest military power in the region. Nevertheless, Salu Khan was attacked for his decision by other Achakzais.[101] Similar clan divisions affected the Ghilzais around Kelat-i Ghilzai (Qalat) and arguments amongst the *khans* resulted in many of the assembled forces going home again. Around 500 remained, declaring that their religious convictions obliged them to sustain the resistance.[102]

In the Helmand Valley there were a few disturbances at Tirin and Dihrawat, but at Garmsir the Durrani clans were unwilling to advance on Kandahar for fear that the Baluchis and Brahuis further south might seize their lands. Other Durani *khans*, who were located closer to Kandahar, accepted subsidies from Rawlinson to remain quiescent. They expressed concerns about the empowerment of the Barakzais, and Rawlinson was able to persuade the *ulema* of the city to issue a fatwa that instructed Afghans to support Shah Shuja and his British allies.[103]

However, the mutiny of the 1st Kandahar Cavalry on 27 December reignited unrest. There was a hasty meeting amongst leading Durrani and other Zirak *khans*, which the Nurzais of the Panjpai Pashtuns joined, but many of the tribes hesitated to commit themselves. Fearing that unrest was about to break out in Kandahar, many of the Durrani families left the city, and Rawlinson estimated that 75 per cent of the inhabitants fled. Ata Mohammed believed the moment had come to move against the British and he marched steadily down the Arghandab River, collecting fighters from the Alikozai clans along the way. Nott estimated that, when he arrived at Kali Shak to fight on 12 January 1842, there were some 20,000 Afghans assembled, but Rawlinson believed the numbers were closer to 5,000.[104] Although Nott could drive the Alikozai off, his artillery breaking up the Afghan cavalry while his light infantry drove off the *jezailchis* trying to hold a river line, the most significant outcome was that news of Ata Mohammed's progress prompted the Durrani *khans* to join the rising. Thus, in and around Kandahar, the rural areas were in revolt against the British. As in Kabul, many of the clansmen thought the Saddozai monarchy was actually leading the rising. Two observations can be offered here. The first is that the Afghan forces gathered their own momentum as news, or rather rumours, poured in; and second, the growth of the revolt and the apparent sanction of the monarchy added to its legitimacy.

Nevertheless, the Afghans' chief problem was their internal divisions. The British were able to defeat the Afghans at Kandahar because the various factions would not agree on leadership and direction. Mirza Ahmad was recognized as the key leader amongst the Durrani Pashtuns, but Ata Mohammed claimed that he was better suited to take command. Arguments broke out between the Janbaz mutineers, the Ishaqzai and the Popalzai. No system of supply could be agreed and no one could be sure exactly how to pay for the support of the clansmen. Mirza Ahmad nevertheless attempted to organize the resistance and encouraged the mullahs of Kandahar to spread propaganda against the British, and to try to subvert the Muslim troops in British service.

However, in many cases, the appeal to join the Jihad against the British fell on deaf ears. Only a handful, barely 400, of the Barakzais from Helmand joined the rebellion. Dihrawat, under the jurisdiction of Yar Mohammed in Herat, also stayed quiet. It was not until late February that any more Helmandis felt compelled to fight, and then a *lashkar* of only 1,000 could be raised. This made one attempt to storm Gereshk but was driven off by a detachment of Indian troops. Supply problems in the harsh winter weather forced the force of 6,000 that had mustered outside Kandahar to break up again to search for food.[105] It was not until the very end of February that the rebels could concentrate their forces again, and when they did so they focused on attacking British foraging parties or arson against the villages of those *khans* they knew to be sympathetic to the British. They were hoping to intimidate these clans in order to isolate the British from the population. An ultimatum was also delivered to the British, demanding that they quit the city of Kandahar.

General Nott believed it was necessary to draw the rebels into a decisive battle, so he was content to see the Afghan *lashkars* concentrating around the city.[106] However, when he marched out to fight them, he was frustrated by their tendency to fall back. He fought a series of three engagements between 7 and

10 March, which he believed had dispersed the rebels. There is some evidence to suggest that the Afghans were following a plan conceived by Mirza Ahmad to draw Nott further and further away from Kandahar. After an assembly of other forces lasting the entire day, a night attack on 10 March was made on the Herat gate of Kandahar. It was only driven off with some difficulty. The wooden gates had been set alight, and when they collapsed the Afghans stormed through. British and Indian troops, stiffened with artillery firing case shot, held the portal of the city for three hours. The Afghans rallied several times but their losses were considerable: it is estimated that 600 bodies were found around the gateway. By dawn they abandoned the attempt to storm the city. Mirza Ahmad was blamed for the débâcle, and only the news that Ghazni had been retaken offered an encouragement to the rebels. However, the numbers remaining at Mirza Ahmad's side fell to 1,500.[107] Nott intercepted the rebels in the Arghandab on 25 March and pushed them further from the city. The Ghilzais near the Khojak Pass nevertheless enjoyed greater success. They intercepted Brigadier England's column of reinforcements for Kandahar and drove off his forces.[108]

This was, however, an isolated attack by local forces eager to capitalize on British weakness and to acquire their baggage. Elsewhere the local population was beginning to tire of the endless extortions by rebel fighters.[109] Villagers refused to sell produce to the rebel detachments that scoured the countryside. Some village elders of the Achakzai, Alikozai and Popalzai would not allow the rebels to enter their lands.[110] That is not to say that the British were any more welcome. Villagers complained that Nott's forces and camp followers had seized a great deal of their produce in order to withstand a siege for five months. However, Rawlinson noted that the local *ulema* were afraid of the punishments inflicted by the rebel *khans* and encouraged by the evident military success of Nott's army. The only difficulty for them was deciding how long the British might stay, and therefore they refused to commit themselves entirely to their side.

The rebellion in the south was saved, briefly, by the defection of Akhtar Khan. He brought with him a large number of Alizais, and the size of the force he deployed rewarded him with the offer of overall command. Consequently, on 29 May, 10,000 fighters began another advance on Kandahar.[111] They were stopped by Nott and defeated, and then forced to fall back to Ghorak. A second counter-attack by the British on 16 June compelled the rebels to split up, with Ata Mohammed and Mirza Ahmad journeying to Kabul, while others remained with Aktar in Zamindawar. The Durranis, noting that the British seemed to be contemplating evacuation of Kandahar, now sensed that the foreigners might be a useful means to break the power of the Barakzais, and they began to cooperate. Nevertheless, once the British had left in early August 1842, the Barakzai Khans returned and, with threats of force, demanded to be able to join the administration. The Durrani government led by Safdar Jang collapsed under this pressure, but resentment increased to the point where, in September that year, the Durranis once again drove the Barakzais out of the city. Alikozai and Popalzai clans also clashed in and around Kandahar, reflecting the same termination of unity that the clans had achieved temporarily against the British at Kabul.

At Qalat, Ghilzais of the Tokhi and Hotak clans had assembled very suddenly, having been uninvolved in the fighting before. They made one attack on the British outpost there on 21 May, were repulsed and then dispersed. Without reports on the clans' politics and movements, it is difficult to determine why this brief aggression occurred. The best guess that can be offered is that the clans, when informed of the reinvigoration of the revolt around Kandahar, the news of the fall of Ghazni and the existing evidence of the defeat of the British at Kabul, believed that they might be able to sack Qalat and seize the wealth that was housed there.

What had influenced the decision of the various clans and factions of the south to side with the British or to rebel was the legacy of the civil war before the time of Dost Mohammed. Durranis wanted to keep Shuja on the throne, or a Saddozai candidate, as long as they could keep out their rivals the Barakzai. If the Barakzai took Kabul, then they were even more determined to ensure that the Saddozai kept Kandahar. Rawlinson observed: 'their detestation of the Baruckzyes appears to be only inferior to their jealousy of our monopoly of power'.[112] To add further confusion, there were elements within the Durrani who wanted to reduce rival families. The *wakil* at Kandahar, a Saddozai, was actively working to portray many Durranis as rebels in the hope that these clans would be destroyed, thus ensuring greater power for his own family.[113]

Ellenborough, the Governor General, brought the British troops out and announced he would 'leave it to the Afghans themselves to create a government amidst the anarchy which is the consequence of their crimes'. His only concession was to express his desire that any future Afghan ruler who could establish himself in power would be recognized by the Government of India. As soon as British forces were withdrawn from Kabul and Kandahar, the Kabul government fell apart. Akbar returned with the Barakzais and resumed control, but it was almost a year before Dost Mohammed was released from India.

The British had deposed Dost Mohammed but found the alternatives unsuitable for their purposes of keeping Afghanistan neutral and free of the interference of Russia or Persia. In the 1830s, the British had sent warships to pressure the Persians to relinquish any influence over Herat. In 1856, they went to war with Persia on Afghanistan's behalf to free that city. Their diplomatic pressure on the Persian Shah after that date was constant. They also used diplomacy to establish a détente with Russia, roughly demarcating their exclusive areas of interest in 1873 and threatened war with Russia when the northern borderline came into dispute in 1885 at Penjdeh.

The post-war dispensation

For the Afghans, Dost Mohammed was restored when Akbar Khan had defeated the rival factions of Sadozais and their allies. There were concerns that the British might return, but it was domestic security that was the perennial problem of the regime. With the Saddozai heirs driven off or discredited, Dost Mohammed was in fact in a stronger position, at least in terms of credibility and perhaps legitimacy. He and his supporters emphasized their role in having defeated foreign forces to ensure the independence of all Afghan Muslims.

However, he was aware that Afghanistan lacked an army that could ensure both internal security and hold off the British, a point driven home by the second invasion from India in 1842 which had stormed through the Khyber Pass, despite attempts to hold it. The difficulty was that, without changes in the means to acquire more revenue, including the taxation structure, it was difficult to raise a larger or more professional force. Nevertheless, the legacy of the British occupation was that the amount of tax being collected from the realm in the vicinity of Kabul had risen from 2.5 million to 7 million rupees. This was sufficient to raise a large enough force to wage war against his rivals in the north. Acquisition of the revenues of the north then offered the chance to sustain operations against the southern provinces, and subsequently against Herat.

The traditional army had preferred a core of light cavalry, some foot soldiers, and a collection of relatively poorly armed and untrained *eljari* militia, and success depended on being able to swarm en masse against isolated British or Indian detachments, or hold seemingly impregnable mountain terrain. The fact that large numbers of *eljaris* and clan warriors had been involved in the war, and had even enjoyed brief successes in the Khyber Pass, held out the possibility that a more universal military service might result.

The weapon that had proved surprisingly effective, as far as the British were concerned, was the *jezail* musket. The long barrel gave the Afghan *jezailchi* a greater range against the British and Indian musketeer, although the heavier ball and difficulty of reloading a fouled and hexagonal bore reduced the rate of fire to about one round every two or three minutes. To offset this problem, Afghans tended to carry two or three loaded weapons into action and, if advancing, all weapons were discharged before closing with sword and shield. The short sword, or 'Khyber knife', was much feared because of its ease of concealment and the damage it could do. The cutting up of wounded personnel with this weapon had a psychological effect on British and Indian witnesses, and was mentioned frequently by survivors of the 1841 retreat from Kabul. But the *jezail* was better suited to the Afghan defence of mountainous terrain. Firers could take cover to reload, whereas sword or mounted attacks, for all their spirit, were often destroyed by volley fire from the British. There is much disagreement about the range of these weapons, with some claims being made that they could hit targets out to 500 yards, but this seems an exaggeration and may be explained by the Afghans occupying positions in cliffs practically above their targets, or, in the retreat from Kabul, being virtually unable to miss the densely-packed camp followers in narrow defiles. According to Vincent Eyre, 'the Afghans shot down our men with ease, and laughed at the musket balls [fired back at them]'.[114] Some *jezails* could also be supported by stands or bipods which allowed them to be aimed, and therefore enhanced their accuracy.

Eyre observed that the Afghans were 'invariably taking steady deliberate aim, and seldom throwing away a single shot; whereas our men seemed to fire entirely at random, without any aim at all'.[115] The British and Indian infantry had been trained to shoot at massed targets at close quarters in the European style, but for Afghans, where arms and ammunition were expensive, they used their weapons more discriminately. Nevertheless, there is a risk of exaggeration in these assessments, not least because the British needed to explain the defeat of the Kabul garrison. According to John Kaye, 'The British muskets were no match for the Afghan jezails' but Major Yate, referring to other battlefields, observed, 'Yet with those same muskets did our soldiers and Hindustani sepoys defeat the Afghans at odds of 5 or 10 to 1'.[116] Another officer commented that the clouds of smoke discharged from a *jezail* gave away the positions of the Afghans, and enabled British commanders to determine where the flanks of their formation lay, an advantage the British lost when smokeless propellent and breech-loaders became the norm in the twentieth century.[117] The focus on the *jezail* as a weapon reflects a more general Western focus on technology in war, but British histories that emphasize the 'superiority' of the *jezail* do not offer explanations for the failure of the same weapon to halt the British counter-offensive through the Khyber in 1842.

Afghan foot soldiers lacked the mobility of the cavalry, and could be used to hold ground for cavalry to advance from, but horsemen could also deliver the infantryman to the front line, and the cavalry occasionally dismounted as dragoons to engage the British with their *jezails*. At Kabul, this ability allowed them to increase their manoeuvrability. Lady Sale remarked that, although the Afghans had a reputation for assassinations which provoked condemnation from the British, they 'show no cowardice in standing as they do against guns without using any themselves, and in escalading and taking forts which we cannot retake'.[118] She concluded that the Afghans were tough adversaries: 'The Affghans of the capital are a little more civilized, but the country gentlemen and their retainers are, I fancy, much the same kind of people as those Alexander encountered'.

The Afghans fought in the style of many South and Central Asian armies of this period, making use of gunpowder weapons and coordinating their use with the *arme blanche*. They understood the value of shock action, delivering charges with both infantry and cavalry, but they also knew not to attempt a stubborn defence when the odds were against them. Feudal cavalry were not prepared to risk losing their horses if the outcome was doubtful, and foot soldiers might make similar judgments if the chances of escape were in the balance. Withdrawing to fight another day when there were greater advantages and chances of success reflected the Afghans' pragmatic approach to warfare.

In terms of internal security, the feudal cavalry and militia forces were problematic. Local forces were likely to side with the rural population in times of rebellion, and the fact that so many had experienced the war against the British, and were so well-armed, was a concern for the rulers of Kabul. What was needed was a professional army led by an officer corps loyal to the Amir. Although the dynastic threat of rival leaders remained a perennial problem for the Amir, the threat of internal disorder and the loss of state revenue continued to bind the Afghan army into the administration in a fundamental way.

Dost Mohammed's initial operations had been modest, concentrating against Jalalabad and Bamian. The northern territories were absorbed between 1849 and 1850, although Badakshan was not incorporated until 1859 and Maimena remained under Herat's jurisdiction until 1863. Peshawar was retaken briefly in 1849 after the defeat of the Sikhs by the British in 1848, but fears that the British might use the seizure of the city as an excuse to attack Afghanistan persuaded the Afghans to withdraw. A negotiated settlement with the British in 1855 awarded Peshawar to the British. In return Afghanistan obtained British support against Persia. Kandahar was taken in 1855 when Dost Mohammed's brothers there died, but Herat remained defiant. The Persian army captured the westernmost city in 1856, prompting the British to launch an amphibious operation against the Persians in the Gulf. In the Treaty of Paris which followed, the Persians managed to retain sympathizers in the city and prevent Kabul regaining full control. The British nevertheless supplied Dost Mohammed with 8,000 muskets and ammunition, and 500,000 rupees, with a further 100,000 rupees a month while the Anglo–Persian War was underway in 1856–7 to support him. This had the effect of ensuring that Dost Mohammed remained neutral during the Indian Mutiny, despite the urgings of some of his followers, and it also enabled Dost Mohammed to equip his army and march on Herat in 1863. The westernmost city of Afghanistan had to be besieged, but it fell just a few months before Dost Mohammed's death that year.

Dost Mohammed believed that, sooner or later, the British would try to attack Afghanistan again and he was determined not to provoke any invasion. Diplomacy was the first line of defence. He had written to the Emir of Bokhara: '...I well know that my own kingdom, and that of Bokhara, will one day be annexed to the British territories. I have therefore entered into an alliance ... with the view to keeping my country as long as possible'.[119] Yet Dost Mohammed's political organization was rudimentary, with no state records or recognized ministries. Avoiding official appointments allowed him to ensure fluidity in his dealings with the *qawms* and ethnic groups of the country. Akbar Khan, who was associated with the successful resistance against the British in the Anglo–Afghan War, was a troublesome Wazir, but he died in 1847 and therefore did not participate in the long process of Kabul's aggrandizement. The Barakzai clan continued to exclude the other Durrani groups from power, although most rural areas were left under their own clan elders and *khans* as long as revenue could be extracted from them. Nevertheless, there was still intense rivalry between Barakzai leaders and amongst the twenty-seven sons of the Amir. This multitude of brothers and half-brothers was the cause of the struggle for power after the death of Dost Mohammed. The sheer number of factions ensured that many parts of the country were affected, and this threw the country into civil war for five years. Unrest in peripheral areas continued far longer.

Conclusions: the Afghan way of war

When the British invaded, Afghanistan had just come through a civil war and Dost Mohammad controlled only one fiefdom in the whole country. Afghanistan was divided, and Shah Shuja was eager to use the British military machine to obtain the restoration of the Sadozai line and exclusive power of the entire country. He needed an external backer to break the power of the Barakzai.

The British intervention exposed the divisions between Afghans, and although in the face of a foreign occupation these differences were settled temporarily, the fissures resurfaced soon after. Factions were prepared to use the presence of British forces to secure advantages for themselves, and the civil war resumed the moment the British had withdrawn. However, the Mohammadzai Barakzai could present themselves as the focus of the anti-foreign resistance. By contrast the Ghilzai were unable to assert themselves over the Zirak Durrani Pashtuns, despite being perhaps the most homogeneous fighting force. Loyalty to *qawm* was strong amongst Ghilzais when their autonomy was threatened, but they fragmented into parochial disputes which prevented the sort of unity the Mohammadzai could muster.

The Anglo–Afghan War had illustrated the weakness of conventional forms of resistance against a disciplined, professional army, but also the enduring advantages of guerrilla warfare, use of the environment and the power of 'mass'. Major Broadfoot, who took part in the fighting, concluded that the Afghans were:

masters in mountain warfare...; skilful in choosing ground, and of a coolness never to be disconcerted; swift to advance, timely in retreat, and expert in both; their masses were seldom shown, hardly ever uncovered to our fire, yet never far away when a blow could be struck... Better arms, organization, and leaders would make them troops of the highest order; the want of them rendered the largest assemblages unworthy of the name of armies.[120]

The defeat of the British brigade that withdrew towards the Khyber gradually became the only narrative of the war, and this 'victory' seemed to preclude the need to adopt foreign European practices, as the Sikhs had chosen to do. Indeed, the defeat and occupation of the Punjab in the 1840s reinforced the idea that Afghan irregular forces, surrounding a corps of professional cavalry and retainers, were sufficient to hold the country. That said, Dost Mohammed recognized the need for a modern regular army to defend the country and manage internal security. The Anglo–Afghan War had discredited Dost Mohammed's main rivals, the Sadozai, and also weakened the other Durani Pashtun clans, particularly the other Barakzais, and this gave him the opportunity to assert himself more decisively, and move towards a 'monopoly of violence'.

Both the Civil War of the 1830s and the Anglo–Afghan War had been characterized by intrigues and treachery as much as conventional fighting. The presence of foreigners made it possible to legitimize the quest for power and wealth as a religious struggle. Despite frequent negotiations between the leaders of the factions and the British, the ability to mobilize peasant farmers and mountain clansmen with a rhetoric of xenophobia and Jihadism was a lesson that the ruling Mohammedzai dynasty understood very well. To avoid civil war, Dost Mohammed hoped to exploit the weaknesses in his rivals and assert a more centralized government in which a loyal army would play a key role. The fact that Afghanistan had received an injection of Indian rupees, bullion and regular payments from the British in the 1850s greatly assisted Dost Mohammed's consolidation of power, but it could not prevent a new civil war.[121]

3

ASYMMETRICAL WARFARE

THE AFGHAN CIVIL WAR, 1863–8, AND THE SECOND ANGLO–AFGHAN WAR, 1878–81

On the death of Dost Mohammed, it was Sher Ali, the third son of his favourite wife, who took his place as Amir, and amongst his first acts as ruler he reinforced the diplomatic defence of the country by reassuring the British: according to the Afghan Wakil, the new Amir expressed his desire to stay on good terms with Britain.[1] He also stated his intention to establish better relations with Persia, despite recent events against Herat. With internal opposition brewing, Sher Ali had no wish to be confronted by a foreign threat at the same time. His accession had been opposed from the outset by other brothers, half-brothers and their sons. Mohammed Afzal Khan, the eldest son of the late Dost Mohammed, believed that he should have been accepted as the ruler of Kabul, not only on the basis of his rank but also because he was an effective and experienced leader. He had been serving as governor of the northern provinces of Turkestan for a decade, and, to back his claim to the throne, Mohammed Afzal commanded an army of 25,000 troops.[2]

Sher Ali was forced to meet this threat by marching north with his own troops, and there was an indecisive battle in June 1864. This was followed by negotiations in which Sher Ali asserted his right to rule. It appears that Mohammed Afzal accepted the terms offered to him. However, it was then alleged that Afzal's son, Abdur Rahman, opposed his father's decision to relinquish his claims to the throne and set out to seize and imprison Sher Ali, and then shoot dead the heir apparent, Muhammed Ali Khan. The British intelligence report of the time showed that: 'the ameer had ordered fetters to put on Sirdar Afzul Khan–[and] it is not improbable that disturbances in the Cabul territories will result from this extreme measure'.[3] However, the 'Ameer had confined Sirdar Mohammed Afzul Khan in the citadel of Tash Koorghan after his return from Mazar Shureef on 24 August–[because] intrigues by the Sirdar's son–had necessitated the measure'.[4] Abdur Rahman Khan and his family were ordered to surrender, but they fled to Bokhara. The orders to place fetters on his father were issued to Sirdar Mohammed Ossman Khan, but he begged not to have to do it since 'this was quite contrary to the customs of the Barukzai family' whereupon 'the Ameer turned from him in great wrath' and ordered General Sheikh Meer to do it. Mohammed Afzul Khan greeted the news by saying 'if it is God's will', and spat on his beard three times before being cast in irons. His property was confiscated, including his jewels, horses, camels and war material as well as a crore of rupees. Mohamed Afzul Khan's ally, Sirdar Soolham Ali Khan, fearing the same fate, had given himself up and expressed his regret at having resisted Sher Ali. He then requested to be able to proceed to Mecca. However, the humiliation of the family of Mohammed Afzul Khan was severe enough to provoke further resistance and Abdur Rahman remained a committed enemy of Sher Ali until the Amir's death in 1879.

On 22 September 1864 it was reported to the Assistant Secretary to the Government of the Punjab that unrest in Afghanistan was spreading. The chief complaint was the arbitrary conduct of Sher Ali. It was alleged that, although 'the Ameer had sworn on the Koran at Mazar Shareef to be true to his brother', the treatment of Afzul Khan turned the Sirdars and the chiefs away from Sher Ali.[5] The Amir's mood was 'so violent, no body would counsel the Ameer as a result except those seeking to gain personal advantage'.[6] The loyalty of the troops raised by Mohammed Afzul Khan was also reinforced. Rather than join the Amir, they dispersed, and 'those who have been induced to join are not trusted'. The report continued: 'In fact, thoughtful people assert that half the army and half the Cabul government have been lost, and the other half is destitute of the discipline and order which existed in the time of the late Ameer'.

While Barakzais and their supporters in Kabul grew restive, relatives of Afzal Khan made an attempt to rouse the Barakzais families living in the Pashtun south. Sikunder Khan took 800 regular cavalry, via the Hazarajat to Kandahar. Even those the Amir considered loyal began to desert him. Sirdar Wali Mohammed Khan, whom Sher Ali had only just appointed Governor of Turkestan, fled to Bokhara to join Abdur Rahman. Opportunists across the border sensed a weakening of the power of the Afghans too. 'Hearing of Afzul Khan, the Oozbecks attacked the Afghans settled in the Taktapool districts, and according to their custom, carried off about a thousand families with their wives, children and property across the border'. This slavers' raid created terror on the northern frontier and one report noted 'the Toorkistan chiefs are in much excitement'. Sher Ali was perhaps fortunate that the Bokharans were in no position to exploit this crisis or assist Abdur Rahman and thus extend their own power over Turkestan since they were at that time engaged in a war with Khokand. Interestingly, both these states sent envoys to the British hoping for assistance.[7] It was not long before the Kandaharis also looked for support from the British.[8]

Mohammed Amin Khan, the brother of the Amir who was also the Governor of Kandahar, cited the treatment of Afzul Khan as the reason for his decision to rebel against Sher Ali, but, in fact, he was also concerned that he was about to be replaced by one of Sher Ali's sons. The British saw no reason to risk a war with the Afghans over this domestic dispute and calculated that, 'The Ameer has a considerable army at his disposal and a well-supplied treasury; whilst the force at the command of Mohammed Ameen Khan does not exceed 8,000 men of all arms, and which has limited finances'. The only difficulty for Sher Ali seemed to be the fact that the bulk of his forces were at Balkh and therefore he was unable to mount operations against the Kandaharis until March 1865 at the earliest. The British were keen to support Sher Ali if he could maintain the integrity of the country, especially at a time when the Central Asian Khanates were aligning themselves to Russia, or in danger of falling to Tsarist control. To defeat the Kokandis, Bokhara concluded a treaty with Russia in March 1865, and news filtered through that the Russians wanted to establish cantonments at Charjui on the Oxus.[9] This, it seemed, would put the Russian army within striking distance of Afghanistan and it reignited fears about an advance towards India.[10]

In June 1865 Sher Ali's army marched to the south and was confronted by the Kandaharis. Sirdar Mohammed Rufeek Khan gave an account of the battle that took place.[11] 'On 5th June, the army arrived at Ussiab Hazara. The Candahar force endeavoured to bring on an action. The Ameer however would not allow his force to advance as the ground was covered with trees. Shots were fired by the enemy until the evening'. The Kabul newswriter Mirza Mausum Khan added: 'During the night Sirdar Mohammed Shareef Khan took up a position on a hill to the left of our camp and from there fired on us with some mountain brass guns. When day broke it was found that during the night the enemy had advanced and had prepared entrenchments on the right of our camp.

Each entrenchment was occupied by two guns and two companies of infan-try'. There was then a council of war. 'The Ameer ascended a hill and assem-bling all his officers round him declared the Heir Apparent and the sirdars of rank should advance with infantry and artillery and drive back the enemy'. Sir-dar Mohammed Rufeek Khan and Sirdar Mhd Ibrahim Khan were allocated four regiments of infantry and eight guns and sent to the left flank while the heir apparent commanded the right flank. Mohammed Rufeek Khan wrote:

Next morning the Ameer ordered an advance from both flanks; he directed the Heir Apparent to advance against Sirdar Mohammed Ameen Khan and ordered [me] to attack Sirdar Mohammed Shureef Khan. Both wings of our force advanced and arrived opposite to the entrenchments/sungars of the sirdar. Their force consisted of 12 regi-ments [c.9,600 men], 6,000 cavalry and 26 guns.

It seems the Amir's army struggled to get the upper hand, and Mohammed Rufeek Khan found it necessary to explain events through the framework of traditional Afghan battle narratives of individual heroic combat:

We were severely engaged for four hours; at last the Ameer came to the assistance of the Heir Apparent. The fight raged on all sides and the Heir Apparent and the Sirdar Mohammed Ameen Khan found themselves face to face. Sirdar Mohammed Ameen Khan wounded the Heir Apparent with his sword. He then fired at him with a pistol. The ball entered above the eye and the Heir Apparent fell dead. Sirdar Mohammed Ameen Khan received 3 sword wounds from the Heir Apparent before he fell. Seeing their leader fall, five foot soldiers fired at Sirdar Mohammed Ameen Khan who was killed. The two chiefs fell within a few paces of each other. The Candahar force was defeated, their camp plundered and Sirdar Mohammed Shureef Khan fled.

The newswriter in Kabul gave a different account, noting that, at first, the Amir was losing the battle: 'His force ... was being defeated and was dispir-ited'.[12] The Amir therefore:

ordered an advance to be made by his whole force in the plain and when he found that the Candahar force was pressing on, and gaining the advantage, he ordered the Heir Apparent in a taunting manner to charge the enemy—all this time the Cabul army was on the eve of being routed. But the Heir Apparent, although he lost his life in the effort, succeeded in driving back the enemy. The Heir Apparent and Sirdar Mohammed Ameen Khan fell on the field of battle. After the death of Sirdar Mohammed Ameen Khan, its leader, the Candahar army fell back. The disreputable men of the Cabul army stripped the body of Sirdar Mohammed Ameen Khan of all the clothes saving a vest and trou-sers. The body was placed in an old tent.[13]

The newswriter's account hints only at some sympathy with the rebel leader, but also admires the courage of the unfortunate Sirdar Mohammed Ali, the

Heir Apparent, in contrast to the description of the Amir whose conduct throughout the period is portrayed as dishonourable.

The newswriter noted that the battle had not been decisive: 'Sirdar Mohammed Shureef Khan with the Candahar army and several guns, is encamped at Gurinaha in the Julduk district. Sirdar Mohammed Shareef Khan's force has lost nothing; a few articles of small value belonging Mohammed Ameen Khan's army have been plundered. The Candahar army has lost 18 guns' but 'up the 7th of June, none of the Candahar force had tendered much enthusiasm to the Ameer'. Sher Ali attempted to resolve the conflict in the same way he had tackled the northern rebellion the year before, by offering to negotiate, but the rebels remained defiant. 'The Ameer held out an offer to Sirdar Mohammed Shareef Khan who replied on behalf of himself and the chiefs that they would only give up with their lives, [in] the hope of revenging the death of Sirdar Mohammed Ameen Khan, and that he did not consider the death of the Heir Apparent an equivalent to the death of the Sirdar'. Sher Ali was unable to make many decisions immediately after the battle because he was stricken with grief, retreating to the Shrine of the Cloak of the Prophet in Kandahar. When Mohammed Afzul Khan heard of the loss of the Heir Apparent, he reminded the Amir: 'You have done irreparable injury and have brought upon yourself a sorrow that you will carry with you to the grave'. The Amir's loyalists nevertheless took the view that the rebel leaders should be punished: Sirdar Mohammed 'Suvrier' Khan, son of Sirdar Mohammed Amin Khan, and Taj Mohammed Khan Popalzai were bound hand and foot, and it is reported that Taj Mohammed had his ears cut off and his nose slit. It is estimated that 2,500 were killed and wounded on both sides in the battle, but it is not recorded how many were subsequently executed. The Kabul newswriter noted that 'Many of the slain belonged to the royal family'.

The paralysis of the Amir and the news that some of the Kandahar rebels were still in the field encouraged Abdur Rahman and his brother Azam to exploit a new rebellion that had broken out in the north. The fighting began on 5 August with a mutiny amongst unpaid Kabuli and Turkistani troops at Takhtapul that local people joined.[14] The Governor of Turkestan, Sirdar Futteh Mohammed Khan, had to flee with just twenty loyal bodyguards as his army collapsed around him. Every garrison refused to give him sanctuary, including the fortresses of Mazar-i Sharif and Tashkurgan, and his property was plundered by the people.[15] When Abdur Rahman Khan and Sirdar Faiz Mohammed Khan arrived at Takhtapul they were hailed as liberators, and the Mullahs of the Uzbek Afghans read the Khutba in the name of the Emir of Bokhara.

In the midst of revolt, Sher Ali tried to exercise *divide et impera*. The Amir offered to appoint Mohammed Sharif Khan to be Governor of Kabul, ordering him to lead four regiments of infantry, each 400 strong, a battery of artillery and 1,000 horsemen against the northern rebels. Mohammed Sharif Khan refused.[16] The Amir then directed the Governor of Herat to march against the Turkistanis. However, Abdur Rahman gathered support over the entire north and gave his troops a year's pay in advance. Altogether he had six regiments of infantry, each battalion numbering 800 men, with four regiments of cavalry at a strength of 400, twenty companies of Jezailchis, 4,000 irregular cavalry and 30 heavy and light guns. Yet, his greatest strength lay in his popularity with the army and the people, which, if he could convert this into support further south, would give him a decisive advantage over Sher Ali.

Although Kabul was still secure, the Amir felt it necessary to remain in Kandahar, which 'he considered his capital'. While he was busy writing to Pashtun leaders to gain support, he did not at first announce news of the Turkistan revolt to the Kandaharis, fearing the consequences. However, he was aware that he could cultivate support amongst the Pashtuns and rouse them against a rebel army which was largely northern in composition. He also tried economic warfare by stopping caravans going north so as to prevent goods reaching the territories under Abdur Rahman's control.[17]

Sher Ali's greatest problem was a lack of money to raise or sustain troops to crush the rebellion. The Kabul garrison seemed unreliable. Soldiers there had demanded more money before they agreed to serve in Turkistan and were offered monthly pay.[18] However, there were no funds to pay for the troops at Ghazni, and they had received only one month's worth, a sum of 40,000 rupees, in the previous six months.[19] When the late Heir Apparent had fought in Kandahar, he had formed two regiments of cavalry, the 'khooduspas and the kujbaz', but now even these were not considered reliable.[20] The Amir knew he could not act decisively against the rebellion without money. He calculated that he needed 6 lakhs of rupees for his troops and a further 4 lakhs for the expedition, but his total finances amounted to 11 lakhs, with five more held in the treasury in Kabul and six in Kandahar. He was also aware that campaigning across the Hindu Kush with winter approaching would mean risking getting his supply lines cut off by snow-filled passes, but further delay would only consolidate resistance to his rule.

By the autumn of 1865, the Amir's authority appeared to be breaking down altogether. The Governor of Jelalabad, Shahmurd Khan, warned that Sirdar Mohammed Afzul Khan's supporters were preparing for revolt in his area and he wanted troops and guns to make a show of force against them. Neighbouring clans detected the opportunity to strike too. Turcoman raiders about 600 strong crossed the border to raid north-west Afghanistan, but were driven off by the forces of the Amir's son, Yakub Khan, in Herat. Many of the Amir's loyal followers pleaded with him to go to Kabul to take charge of the expedition to the north and snuff out the revolt before the situation got worse.[21] However, Ghilzai chiefs refused to supply troops as ordered and opened communications with Abdur Rahman.[22] A Herati regiment, which had been raised in Kabul, mutinied. The soldiers of 'Wuzeer ke Pultun' were ordered to be detained in Herat but they refused to be disarmed and, in the skirmish that followed, 70 were killed. News soon arrived of more Kabuli troops deserting due to lack of pay.[23] Some 2,000 men from Badakhshan and Kunduz had also joined Abdur Rahman, adding to the momentum of the revolt.[24]

As the passes cleared, Abdur Rahman decided to strike first, and in May 1866 he seized Kabul and freed his father Mohammed Afzul Khan, making him *de facto* Amir. Sher Ali tried to advance on Kabul but was defeated several times with heavy losses and fell back to Herat.[25] When Afzal died in 1867, his son Azam took his place as Amir, and Abdur Rahman became Governor of the northern territories. But the war was not over. Yakub Khan, Sher Ali's son, drew upon Herati supporters to continue the fighting, and it was he who managed to take back Kandahar from one of Azam's sons. Azam marched against Yakub Khan but was defeated outside Ghazni in 1868. Azam fled to Persia but died en route, and Yakub Khan continued his advance on Kabul and then into the north. Abdur Rahman was driven into exile in Samarkand in 1869, and Sher Ali returned to the throne to rule for the next decade.[26]

The civil war of the 1860s had demonstrated that support for any faction in Afghanistan was fleeting and largely dependent on money. In episodes of dynastic civil war, no party could depend on familial support or look to the *qawm* as a homogeneous body. Without control of the finances drawn from the whole country, it was difficult to sustain enough military force to achieve a decisive result. Financial weakness, as well as custom, had compelled Sher Ali to negotiate even when he not achieved a clear victory.

The solution to this breakdown was to develop further Dost Mohammed's idea of a professional standing army that owed its loyalty to the ruling dynasty and not the *qawm* and ethnic factions of the country. When Sher Ali made his first visit to India in 1869, a request for military assistance was at the top of the agenda. Britain refused to offer substantial aid, but did agree to the provision of some arms and the opportunity to recruit retired British Non Commissioned Officers as military advisors. The training teams would also bring with them engineering skills that could be used to develop a rudimentary arms manufacturing base.

The Afghan army of the 1860s and 1870s

In Dost Mohammed's second reign, regiments had been formed neither by conscription nor voluntarism, but by seizing quotas of men with threats to the family that they would either be imprisoned or ruined. Pay for foot soldiers, when it was paid at all, amounted to 5 rupees a month. Discipline was harsh with capital punishment or torture for minor infractions. Command was devolved to provinces and districts with no single chief of staff who might threaten the political order. For all its faults, this had produced a regular army that was, to quote Sir Bartle Frere: 'quite equal in armament, skill, and drill to any corps in our service'.[27] In 1879, Sher Ali had built up the army again to a strength of 56,173 troops, divided into 73 regiments of infantry, 42 regiments of cavalry and 48 batteries of artillery.[28] All of these units were based on the British Indian Army model. The bulk of the soldiers and the officer corps were drawn from Ghilzais and from Pashtuns of Wardak. Overall command of the army was given to Sipah Salar Hussayn Ali Khan Qizilbash, and advice was given by two former Muslim Indian Army instructors, General Karim Bakhsh and Sirdar Ghulum Bahadur Naqshband.[29] Infantry soldiers' pay was increased to 7 rupees a month while troopers of the regular cavalry were given 14 rupees a month. All the soldiers were expected to serve for life. There were very few Durrani and Zirak Pashtuns or minorities, reflecting the perceived disloyalty of the factions that had taken part in the rebellion of 1863–9. Dynastic marriages were also a convenient tool for a ruler to incorporate factions, but Sher Ali did not quite manage the extensive range that his father Dost Mohammed had done.[30] Instead the focus was on physical security. Each of the large cities was garrisoned and troops were held at strategically important locations ready to respond to any internal unrest or foreign incursion.[31] Nevertheless, there were still large numbers of irregulars whose loyalty was uncertain.

The Afghan *qawm* militia, especially in Ghilzai districts, believed they were 'born soldiers, excellent skirmishers and experienced foragers'.[32] However, they were 'impatient to restraint' and possessed no answer to artillery, believing that 'if other nations were, like themselves, armed only with swords instead of guns and other sophisticated weapons, Afghanistan could conquer the world'. There was still a strong faith in the idea that *ghazis*, the religious warriors of a determined frame of mind, could overwhelm greater numbers of infidels.[33] The

Amir knew he could not control these forces, but he also regarded them as a useful force that could provide a buffer against the British. He warned the Government of India, when it complained about potential foreign influences in Afghanistan: 'Before looking elsewhere, the English had better attend to their own house. Should they dare to move in this direction, they will first have the frontier tribes like hornets about their ears before they can ever attempt to cross the border'.[34]

The regular army consumed between 25 and 40 per cent of Afghanistan's revenue in the 1870s, and the extra expenditure had required a more efficient system of taxation.[35] Where possible, Sher Ali insisted on cash, not goods, as payment. Nevertheless, peripheral regions still lay outside the taxation system and were largely independent of Kabul, with Ghilzais practising *pashtunwali*, administering justice through a hybrid of Sharia and customary law and convening their *jirgas* as they had done for decades. Feuding and inter-clan violence continued unabated.[36] Moreover, family struggles for power affected the security of Afghanistan. Yakub Khan and Ayub Khan, Sher Ali's eldest sons, controlled Herat as a fiefdom of their own. When Sher Ali announced that a younger half-brother would replace them as governors, there was a threat of rebellion. Sher Ali used negotiations to settle the dispute, managing to outmanoeuvre Yakub Khan, who was imprisoned in Kabul, and forcing Ayub Khan to flee to Persia. Yet the army remained the cornerstone of Afghanistan's security, and therefore the foundation of its existence as a state.

Even with the growth and development of the army in the 1870s, Sher Ali feared it was no match for the modern forces of the British or the Russians. This was a decade of rapid technological change. The British had armed themselves with single-shot breech-loading rifles, rifled artillery, and there were experiments with machine guns. The British possessed telegraph communications, as well as tinned rations to sustain themselves on campaign all year long, and the railway network in India would soon terminate on the Afghan frontier.[37] The dilemma was that, in common with other Asian states, the Europeans were opening up a technology gap in warfare.[38] The *jezail* was rendered obsolete by rifles with much greater range and accuracy, and the *jezail*'s comparatively slow rate of fire was an additional disadvantage. Furthermore, a company of disciplined European troops was able to lay down a volume of fire that could cut down charges by *ghazis* before they could close with the British in hand-to-hand fighting. Howard Hensman, a journalist in Kabul in 1879, noted that, despite a mass attack, only a single *ghazi* reached the British defences at Sherpur, but he was shot down too.[39] Success for the Afghans

99

was dependent on the use of surprise or mass. In open battle, they were simply overmatched.

The Second Anglo–Afghan War: Amir Sher Ali's strategy

Relations with Britain had been strained for some years before the outbreak of the Second Anglo–Afghan War. Sher Ali had not been recognized as Amir by Britain in 1863 and the Government of India under Lord Lawrence, following the policy that had been announced in 1842 (specifically, that the British would recognize any government that could establish itself in Kabul), had actually recognized his rival Afzal Khan as Amir. Belatedly, Sher Ali had also been granted diplomatic recognition when he finally secured power in 1869, but he did not forget the slight. Sher Ali believed that the British policy had actually encouraged the coups and revolts of the 1860s. In fact, fratricidal and patricidal warfare, and faction fighting amongst the leading Pashtun *qawm*, had been an established element of Afghan politics for generations and the British view would have made little difference to the ambitions of Sher Ali or his rivals. Moreover, Sher Ali's reception at the ceremonial *durbar* at Ambala in 1869 had been lavish, with generous British support: the Government of India had told Sher Ali it would 'view with severe displeasure any attempt on the part of your rivals to disturb your position as ruler of Cabul and rekindle civil war'.[40]

However, the British priority was not to preserve Sher Ali *per se*, but to forestall a Russian annexation of Afghanistan.[41] The Tsar's armies had captured Tashkent in 1865 and rendered Bokhara a protectorate in 1868. It seemed likely they would try and annex the entire region, and negotiations commenced between London and St Petersburg to clarify where the boundaries of the British and Russian empires lay. In 1873, although no agreement could be reached on a neutral zone, a rough borderline for northern Afghanistan was treated as the limit of Russian influence. Sher Ali was satisfied since the line agreed by the British and Russians was the same as the historic line recognized by Bokhara and Kabul, namely the line of the River Oxus.[42] However, the Tsarist Asiatic Section of the Foreign Ministry, in collusion with the Russian Army, was eager to complete the process of annexation of all of Turkestan, the name they gave to Central Asia. Within months of the agreement, the Khanate of Khiva was annexed. Sher Ali was concerned that Afghanistan was next, and the British offered him more arms and money. Sher Ali accepted the arms but refused to take up the largesse he was offered, and he made a point of refusing entry to British travellers or a military mission which he feared might be the forerunners of another attempt to reduce his independence. The 1873 border agreement had given Afghanistan a guarantee of territorial integrity, and, fully armed, there was no need to offer further concessions to the British.

However, the fall of Kokend in 1876, the last independent realm in the region, seemed to herald another phase of Russian expansion. Operations were also being conducted by the Russians against the Turcomans, a nomadic people who lived astride the line determined in the European capitals. The British were themselves eager to acquire a secure frontier from which they could launch operations deep inside Afghanistan should the Russians attempt to advance on India. In 1876, the British took up a post at Quetta in Baluchistan and the following year began to assert their influence across this province. Afghanistan regarded Baluchistan as a feudatory principality, and so Sher Ali had cause to fear that his country was about to be crushed from two directions. The unwelcome arrival of a Russian delegation in Kabul in 1878, at the height of a confrontation between Britain and Russia near Constantinople, caused anger and alarm in India and seemed to confirm to Sher Ali that there was little to choose between the two European empires. His strategy was to continue to keep both empires at arm's length and, if attacked, to ally himself with one against the other.

The Viceroy, Lord Lytton, demanded that a British delegation be permitted to establish itself permanently in Kabul, but Sher Ali refused.[43] The Amir sent a belated attempt at concessions, but the message did not arrive in time. Even though a separate crisis between Britain and Russia off the Turkish coast had been settled, the Amir's appeal to the Russians for military assistance seemed to indicate a hostile intent towards the British. When Kabul was later overrun, Sher Ali's correspondence was published as the means to justify the invasion, not least because the British government had been thoroughly divided on the issue of military intervention.[44] The irony was that Lytton had arrived in India initially hoping to strengthen Sher Ali in order to bolster Afghanistan against the Russians.[45] But Sher Ali had been consistent in expressing his fear that a British mission would impose impossible demands on him, and that the Russians would almost certainly insist on making their presence permanent too. He also reiterated a warning that he could not guarantee the safety of a British residency in Kabul. Nur Mohammed, the Afghan negotiator with the British, had begged: 'you must not impose upon us a burden we cannot bear, and if you overload us its responsibility rests with you'.[46]

When war was imminent, Sher Ali took steps to resist the British. It appeared the British were planning to advance on three axes: the Khyber Pass, the Kurram Valley and the Bolan Pass. Half of the Afghan regular army was posted in Herat and Turkestan, so the defence of Afghanistan was dependent on the ability to hold the passes and on the willingness of the Ghilzai clans to harass the British lines of communication. The Amir's strategy has often been ignored because the Afghan conventional forces were swept aside by the British in a matter of weeks, but this overlooks the fact that the chief difficulties for the armies coming up from India were the lack of transport and the need to protect extended lines of communication.[47] Constant raiding on these vulnerable lines had the potential to paralyze the British forces.

The second element of Sher Ali's strategy was to obtain Russian support. He abandoned Kabul in order to concentrate the bulk of his army in the northern provinces where they could marry up with the Russians. General Kaufman had assembled 30,000 troops in Central Asia in the early summer of 1878 and Sher Ali expected to get, as he put it, 'financial and military assistance so that I may return to avenge myself'.[48] Kaufman refused to support him and suggested he make peace with the British. Sher Ali was forced to remain in Mazar-i Sharif, and after a severe illness he died in February 1879.

The Afghan army of 1879, while numerous, was unable to offer effective resistance to the British. There was considerable rivalry between regiments that were recruited from different localities, and the infrequent and irregular nature of soldiers' pay fostered desertion. Lists subsequently seized by the British in Kabul suggested that Sher Ali had wanted to introduce universal military service, but there was a lack of officers and trainers who could convert large numbers of conscripts into a modern army. There were, in common with other Asian countries in this period, attempts to emulate the Western model, even to the extent that British uniforms were copied, but this outward change concealed the lack of real transformation. One British journalist wrote: 'Shere Ali might be able to distribute Enfield and Snider rifles amongst his sepoys, fit out batteries with every kind of shot and shell, and teach his men such rudimentary discipline as would enable them to march in fairly good order; but he could not get beyond this'.[49] There was no military education, no attachés, no visits to foreign armies and no military academies or staff courses.

The British believed that the Afghan fighter was just unsuited to service in a regular army. One observer concluded: 'The Afghan does not lack native courage, and in hill warfare he is unrivalled so long as it takes the shape of guerrilla fighting; but once he is asked to sink his identity and to become merely a unit in a battalion he loses all self-confidence, and is apt to think more of getting away than of stubbornly holding his ground as he would have done with his friends, led by his own malik or chief'.[50] There was a practical reason for this attitude. If the battle swung against him, it was far easier to retreat to one's local community and blend in to 'play the part of a peaceful peasant', whereas regular troops could be pursued to destruction.

The artillery was regarded as the elite arm of the Afghan forces, having been developed by the introduction of British guns in 1869. Traditional brass smooth-bore guns of small calibre had been held in the various fortresses of Afghanistan, but the Amir was eager to replicate as many of the British rifled guns as he could. He ordered his chief military engineer and gunsmith, Surf-eraz, to copy the guns he had been given, but the experiments failed and Surf-eraz was imprisoned. He then dispatched another engineer to Peshawar, where the British obligingly showed him around the arsenal and allowed him to study the manufacturing of artillery and the means by which rifled bores were made. He returned to Kabul with model guns and scale drawings and was given an unlimited supply of metalworkers and cash by the Amir to turn out the new artillery. Iron was imported from India. The gun barrels were first fashioned by hand, and the bore was cut by machinery driven by a watermill at Deh-i Afghan, which was designed, according to the genealogies favoured by the Afghans: 'by a Hindustani named Muah Khan [who] learned his trade from a negro, named Belal, who was taught by one Ibrahim, a native of Isphahan, who came years ago from Persia in the service of Sultan Jan, late governor of Herat'.[51] The process was efficient and produced five guns a month. The chief engineers received generous pay of 70 rupees a month, reflecting the esteem attached to their work. Hensman, the journalist of *The Pioneer*, wrote: 'one cannot fail to be struck with astonishment at the rapidity with which guns were made, rifles imitated, and cartridges turned out by the 100,000 in a country which boasts of but few resources'.[52]

However, despite the enthusiasm for armaments, the quality of the imitation was low. The senior gunsmith for small arms manufacturing, Kutub-Udin, produced copies of 2,000 Snider and 8,000 Enfield (percussion) rifles. These weapons were breech-loading and enabled a trained rifleman to aim and fire ten rounds a minute, compared with the three rounds a minute achieved by muzzle-loading rifles and muskets. British Sniders also came with a complete manufactured cartridge, ending the need to insert a separate charge to the barrel and the lock, as had been the case until the 1850s. Afghans sought these new weapons eagerly, but they were disappointed in the copies made in the Bala Hissar. Extractor mechanisms frequently jammed and the rough boring caused 'leading' of the barrel, that is, where the rifling stripped lead from the bullet head and rendered the weapon useless after a few rounds had been fired. Percussion caps had been copied by 'two clever Cabulis, Safi Abdul Latif and Safi Abdul Hak', and, having built their own machinery, they could produce 5,000 a day. However, storage was a problem as the powder grains deteriorated after just two days, which caused misfires.

Similar problems of low quality affected Afghan gunpowder manufacturing. There were six major mills in Kabul and a number of smaller facilities around the country, which the British estimated could produce a ton of black powder every day in wartime. Sulphur was extracted at Bamian, saltpetre was made at Kabul and charcoal derived from the willow trees in Chardeh. However, the processes of mixing were rough and therefore the charges were lower than British ones, which tended to diminish the range of Afghan weapons. Fuses for exploding shells were also of poor design, causing accidents and duds. However, these defects did not detract from the Afghans' ability to develop their own armaments industry. The British underestimated the number of modern rifles the Afghans possessed, and were surprised by the weight of fire that the Afghans could lay down.

The greatest problem was the lack of training. Gunners were issued one artillery round with which to test the barrel, but there was no 'live-firing' practice. Consequently artillerymen were trying to learn how to operate their guns in combat for the first time. On 8 October 1879, Afghan gunners fought an artillery duel with the British in Sherpur from their position on the Asmai Heights. They did not inflict any casualties at all. By contrast, at Sang-i Nawishta, British gunners were able to score direct hits on the Afghan guns, which severely demoralized the Amir's men.[53] In the same vein, Afghan infantrymen were issued with only three live rounds per year for training, possibly because it was feared they might constitute a threat to the Amir if they were supplied with more, so fire control and marksmanship suffered accordingly. The British noted that fire tended to be too high 'and our men passed safely upwards with the storm of bullets rushing far above their heads'.[54] Lack of familiarity with the capabilities of the modern rifles meant that Afghan troops tended to fight at close quarters as they had always done. But the criticism of Afghan musketry also needs to be placed in context. British observers lamented the 'deplorably bad' shooting on their own side, with 'thousands of rounds expended with very poor results'.[55]

Sher Ali had a militia of 24,000 irregulars that he could call upon in wartime. These were paid through nominated *khans*, but in peacetime only 6,000 would be maintained for border duties or internal security. The figures were nevertheless nominal. As a British Intelligence report observed: 'In the hour of trouble every headman and chief of every clan or tribe is called upon and made to furnish levies... and 100,000 armed men could be assembled at Kabul without much difficulty'.[56] It was generally felt that, having dispersed and abandoned the formal discipline of the regular army when defeated in conventional operations, Afghan soldiers reorganized themselves as irregular fighters. Hensman observed: 'Occasionally we saw some sort of marshalling going on in the leading lines, in which the best-armed men were placed, but this was due more to the desire on the part of the leaders to make the most of their strength than to any idea of forming the mob into battalions'.[57] Despite the belief that the Afghans 'trusted to numbers and fanaticism', Hensman concluded that 'Afghanistan is a nation of soldiers, every adult being (apart from any military training he may receive) a ready swordsman and a fair shot'.[58]

Yet the Afghans were not just inherently hardy warriors schooled in warfare by blood feuds or the harsh environment, as they showed they were capable of rapid tactical innovation against the firepower they had recently encountered. They adopted dispersed formations to avoid risking heavy casualties from British artillery fire. They formed up in 'small scattered groups or on a line extending many miles across the country'. By doing so they maximized the number of firearms that could be brought to bear and took advantage of the cover afforded by the terrain. When battles went against them, they 'spread themselves broadcast across the country', hid their weapons in caches and sought to 'play the part of an innocent peasantry'. While the British intended this to indicate the treacherous nature of the Afghan fighter, it was in fact a purely pragmatic response to the asymmetrical situation they found themselves in.

In November 1878, at the outbreak of war, the British Khyber Line Force set out to seize the fortress of Ali Musjid at the mouth of the Khyber Pass.[59] The fortification stood on top of a detached hill 450 feet above the valley floor, protected by the Kabul River and three adjacent peaks. The ridges connecting these features had been lined with entrenchments, and ranges for the guns mounted in the fort or in the embrasures amid the trenches had been marked out on the landscape below. A deep gorge with precipitous sides protected another flank of the fortress, and, with its garrison of 4,120 men, the British assessments all agreed it was a 'strong position'. There were, however, too few Afghan troops to hold all of the high ground, particularly to the north and east, but the highest peak, known as the Rhotas, was defended by infantry in *sangars*.

The British decided on an encirclement of the position, using mountain paths to the north to get behind the defences. The advance took longer than expected because of the terrain; they were forced to bivouac overnight and then compelled to move in single file whereupon they arrived 'in a state of considerable exhaustion from exposure, heat and want of water'.[60] Had the Afghans had sufficient men to cover their flanks, this advance would almost certainly have been checked. Nevertheless, this flanking manoeuvre caused many Afghan troops to abandon their positions on the mountain, and a mounted force was ambushed by the British as it tried to escape.[61] The garrison of the fort, although isolated, kept up a steady fire with its artillery throughout the day on 21 November as the British deployed their brigades; and, as the British and Indian troops advanced up the slopes, they evoked 'a sharp reply in the shape of a cross fire not only from several entrenchments, but also from a series of *sangars* in front of them as well as from the conical hill redoubt on which the guns ... were now playing'.[62] The Afghan infantry not only held their mutually supporting trenches; they also managed to send forward small detachments which opened fire on the closest British artillery 'notwithstanding the fire of the escort and a few rounds of shrapnel'.[63] The British decided that, with a second flanking manoeuvre delayed, an attempt to storm the position from the front at this stage would prove too costly, although the withdrawal under fire was none too easy: the 27th Punjab Infantry lost thirteen killed and seventeen wounded, most of whom became casualties as they tried to pick their way down the slopes.

At dawn the next day, the British discovered that the Afghan garrison had slipped away under cover of darkness. Some 300 Afghans in the most forward positions had been left behind and were captured.[64] It was clear to the Afghan garrison commander, Ghulam Haider, that the position had become untenable, despite the defences being 'of great extent and... skilfully and formidably designed'.[65] The British assessments tended to focus on the strength of the position and the abandonment of the Afghan artillery as evidence of their success.

However, from the Afghan perspective, they had fought long enough to delay the British and took the pragmatic decision to abandon the fort when its fall seemed certain. Nevertheless, the action was clearly an Afghan defeat. The *Official History* noted that the Afghan camp had been left 'precipitously' because nothing had been taken with them. There was also reference to the fact that the Afghan troops were 'harried and looted' by Afridi Pashtuns as they withdrew. Certainly there were problems of command and communications. One relieving column of Afghan infantry, seemingly unaware of the battle at Masjid the day before, was scattered by a British ambush and its commander was persuaded to surrender with 300 of his men. The rest were eager to get away via the mountains.

Pashtun resistance in the Khyber Pass

In 1877, Major General Frederick Roberts had written that a military intervention in Afghanistan and the reorganization of the defence of India along the Hindu Kush should be accompanied by the recruitment of Afghan troops. This would ensure local security and be 'very different to the present, where, although we do hold the issues from the mountains, we are liable to be continually harassed from the existence of inimical neighbours on our immediate border'.[66] The North West Frontier of India remained a perpetual battlespace between the Army in India and the various clans of Pashtuns and Baluchis, and the British conducted several campaigns in the second half of the nineteenth century. During the Second Anglo–Afghan War, and drawing lessons from the first conflict of 1839–42, British political officers paid 'liberal' subsidies to nominated clan *maliks* amounting to 87,000 rupees per annum.[67]

Despite the payment of allowances to local Pashtun clans to keep the Khyber Pass open, there were punitive operations against them following raids on British lines of communications. Part of the British strategy was to distract the Afghan forces in the Khyber Pass area with demonstrations while the main force advanced towards Kandahar in the south.[68] Nevertheless the British were eager to avoid antagonizing the clans of the Khyber Pass, and there was a conscious decision to use as few Muslim troops as possible in the campaign because of fears of fraternization with the hill clans. Despite these efforts, baggage columns and picquets were attacked by raiders from the Zakka Khel and Shinwaris.[69] The British enlisted clan rivals, the Kuki Khel, and reinforced them with mountain guns and troops from the elite frontier force, the Corps of Guides. The Shinwaris disappeared as soon as this force appeared, and the destruction of a fort was deemed appropriate punishment for 'some outrages by the Mirzan Khels, a section of the Shinwaris'.[70] There was a brief attempt by irregulars to contest the Sissobi Pass in the Bazar Valley, but the lack of resistance may have reflected both the strength of the British forces in the area and the abandonment of Jalalabad by the Amir's army. The 'only danger', concluded the British report, 'was from discontented tribesmen and fanatics, such as are ever to be found in Afghan towns'. The British accounts stress the success of their advance and its organization, but there was very little acknowledgement that the Afghans were bitterly divided, despite the invasion.

News of the Amir's flight from Kabul was reported to be the prelude to the collapse of resistance in the capital: 'Before his departure the Amir appeared to have lost all authority at Kabul, while his army had been weakened by numerous desertions'.[71] It seemed that 'The country between Jalalabad and Kabul was

... in a state of anarchy'. Yakub Khan took command at Kabul and issued orders to the Ghilzai khans to assemble *lashkars* at Jagdalak, but they refused and sent 'submissive letters' to the British in January 1879, as did the inhabitants of Kabul. The Saiad (Sayyid) of Kunar, a much respected figure, had been urged by the Amir to preach a Jihad, but he 'seemed anxious to place himself on good terms with the Government [of India]'.[72] The lack of support for the Amir and an unwillingness to fight the main British force in the Khyber only partially explains this attitude.

Low-intensity raiding on the British lines of communication by Mohmands continued, although certain rival families saw advantage in siding with the British. The Zakka Khel Afridis continued to offer resistance, and there was sniping at night into British hilltop picquets.[73] When the British sent forces against them, they burned down their own houses and destroyed their own crops in a scorched-earth policy. 'None of the tribesmen showed themselves in daytime to the troops, but they hung about the hills and ravines, and fired on small parties when they had a chance'.[74] When a British reconnaissance team withdrew from the Bukar Pass, where a *lashkar* had gathered, it seemed to encourage the fighters. They 'showed in greater numbers' and harassed a British column, despite losing twenty men during daylight skirmishing. Once the British had withdrawn from their valleys they sued for peace, perhaps because they felt they had achieved their objectives and satisfied their honour.

Nevertheless, on 28 January 1879, the British received intelligence that their expedition into the Bazar Valley had created a fear amongst the neighbouring Afridis that they could also expect a visitation and punitive action. It seemed that news had passed quickly between the various clans and some attempt was being made to assemble all the Afridis, Mohmands and Utman Khels and to coordinate an attack from Kabul. Rumours suggested the attack would commence on 7 February. The objective appeared to be Jalalabad. The news that the British had taken prisoners and sent them into exile in India was particularly prominent as a cause of the unrest, and it was alleged that 20,000 men had been seen gathering on 2 February in Kunar 'on instructions from Kabul'.[75] In the event, only 5,000 Mohmands assembled and they refused to confront the British head-on, withdrawing into the hills and dispersing into villages *en route*. Throughout the disturbances, the British were at pains to protect one of their tribal allies, Akbar Khan, but it appears the Mohmands' *lashkar* had achieved its aim, having attacked his village in a night raid and killed his son. The incident revealed that, although the British felt that their security, particularly their vulnerable lines of communication, was the most important issue, the local people had not suspended their inter-clan rivalry, and they saw the British only as elements that could be utilized or opposed as necessary in these local struggles.

The various clans also had considerable problems in coordinating any anti-British resistance even when they agreed to cooperate. The Mohmands and Bajaurs had not heard that the Shinwaris, Khugianis and Ghilzais around Jalal-abad had called off their offensive. The reason for this is unclear, although con-temporary British accounts maintained that the death of Mir Akhor, a charismatic mullah who embodied the Afghan resistance, had been the cause. Conflicting rumours about the resistance were mirrored in various reports emanating from Kabul.[76] Some claimed that the Kabulis were anxious for the British to arrive and liberate them from the repressive actions of Yakub Khan, but others suggested that the Afghan regular forces were eager for revenge and hoped to defeat the British in the passes to the east of the city.

Lieutenant General Maude, who commanded British forces against the Zhaka Khels and Afridis, was eager to limit his operations, despite punitive measures in the first two months of 1879. He was conscious that fighting every village that resisted would invite 'a general Afridi war', and he was aware that the Government of India was eager to avoid unnecessary clashes with the bor-der clans.[77] Renewed efforts were made to reach settlements with the Pashtuns, and punitive columns withdrew to the main line of communications.

The deployments of the Afghan forces on the frontier confirmed a defen-sive strategy. Yakub Khan, Sher Ali's son nominated to be the garrison com-mander, held a reserve at Kabul on the Siah Sang heights numbering 7,800 with 25 guns. Another force was deployed at Butkhak, possibly with the bulk of the irregulars holding the passes. Another 9,000 men were held at Ghazni to prevent the southern flank being turned. Rather than being unpopular, Yakub Khan was 'most active in organizing his troops' and was 'greatly aided in this by the preaching of the mulla[h]s'. Although the Afghan leaders were attempting to generate a sense of the nation and the faith in peril, to the Brit-ish this anti-foreign sentiment was further evidence of the 'passions and fanat-icism of the Afghans'.[78] Despite these concerns, the Pashtun clans along the Khyber route had been paid, and, with their men posted at intervals along the Khyber Pass, they 'represented a very orderly and thoroughly effective system of police'.[79] Agreements with the various clans along the Khyber Pass estab-lished that the Pashtuns would 'abstain from outrages' in return for an annual subsidy of 85,860 rupees.[80] Moreover, the death of Sher Ali seemed to open the way to a negotiated settlement. Yakub Khan had sent a request to talk as early as 20 February, and so in early March the British opened a correspondence and offered their terms. After a month Yakub Khan seemed ready to accept all these, with the exception of territorial concessions in the Khyber Pass, no doubt on the basis that this would strip Afghanistan of its most important means of defence against future British incursions. Accepting a diplomatic settlement offered the best hope of preventing a long-term occupation.

While negotiations were underway, the British were forced to contend with aggressive Ghilzais who cared little for the diplomatic concerns of Kabul. Shinwari villagers attacked a British road survey party on 14 March 1879. The resistance appears to have been spontaneous, but was almost certainly sparked by anxiety that a road would assist foreign forces to enter and dominate the local area, perhaps leading to a complete loss of their independence. About fifty men, perhaps a hastily formed *arbakai*, attacked the survey group with long knives while villagers showered the British with stones, but they were no match for British firearms. By the time the survey party had reached open ground, they were being pursued by upwards of 300 fighters.[81] A punitive force was sent back to chastise the villagers. At Deh-Sarak the pattern was repeated against a British foraging party, as a *lashkar* of 300 took on an isolated group. When the British sent forward a reconnaissance team, the villagers beat tomtoms and fighters assembled on compound walls, in a *nala*, and in an open piece of ground between. The clans 'stubbornly disputed every tower and wall as long as possible' as they fought for their homes, but they had no answer to the rapid rate of fire of British carbines and breech-loading rifles. They were driven off by this gunfire and by cavalry, but they reassembled just 1,800 yards back on a line of hills, watching while their compounds and towers were blown up and their houses set ablaze. The moment the British started to withdraw, the fighters reoccupied the ruins and followed closely on the heels of the troops. The necessity of getting to close quarters to use their knives, and the short range of their firearms, meant that they used the available cover to keep within 50–100 yards of the British skirmish line. The running fight continued for 4 miles, and larger numbers of fighters assembled with each step until the column halted at Pesh Boldak. There the clans were held for a time, were shelled, and then gradually dispersed.

Meanwhile Asmatullah Khan, a Ghilzai leader, had gathered 1,500 men and travelled towards Fatehabad in order to encourage more Ghilzais and the Khugianis to join him, and to make an attack on those who were collaborating with the British. The despatch of a British column to intercept Asmatullah seemed to have succeeded in dispersing the *lashkar* by the beginning of April without a shot being fired, and the Ghilzai territories simmered, awaiting better opportunities. Once again, the difficulties for the Afghans and Pashtuns to achieve any coordinated resistance were evident. The British tried to minimize their presence and avoided occupations, choosing instead to make devastating raids on property, livestock and crops. At the same time British finances had neutralized the resistance of several clans, and, despite occasional raids to secure vulnerable goods, mules or horses, the Khyber Pass resistance was contained.

The Battle of Peiwar Kotal and the advance on Kabul

The neutralizing of the Khyber Pass left the Afghan army somewhat isolated against the British. What Major General Roberts, the commander of the Kurram Valley Field Force, hoped to do was to screen the pro-British Shia population in the Kurram valley and to inflict a decisive defeat on the Afghan regulars on the border. His instructions were to secure the cooperation of the Ahmedzai Ghilzais, who tended to migrate across the Suleiman range and winter along the Kurram, and to seize Khost inside Afghanistan.[82] As Roberts approached the border, he was informed by locals that the Afghans were retiring over the Peiwar Kotal pass in disorder, so, eager to catch them, Roberts pushed up through heavily wooded and broken country. However, when he arrived it was clear that the Afghans intended to contest the pass. They had dug trenches and *sangars* along ridges that formed a natural amphitheatre on three sides of the trail that led to the pass, while on the crest of the Kotal itself the Afghans had entrenched several field guns.[83] Roberts' advance guard was beaten back by intense rifle and cannon fire, which encouraged the garrison, numbering an estimated 4,000 with eleven guns, to continue to hold their position.[84] Indeed, Roberts conducted a thorough reconnaissance for two days, which must have been interpreted by the Afghans as an indication that their decision to remain had been correct. The volume of stores and equipment and the 'enormous natural strength' of the defences suggested that 'it was the intention of the Afghan government that their troops should remain in this position for the winter'.[85] Afghan reinforcements may have arrived as defences were extended further along the ridges on either side of the pass.[86]

Roberts elected to make a night attack, using a feint on the Afghan right and with his artillery harassing the centre of the Afghan line, while his main assault force weaved its way in a wide arc around the Afghan left. The element of surprise was lost when two Pashtun soldiers in the 29th Bengal Native Infantry not only tried to slow down the column but also fired warning shots when they approached the Afghan picquets.[87] Although the British captured the extreme left of the Afghan-held ridge at 0900 hrs, a deep ravine with a steep wall on the Afghan side enabled the Amir's troops to pin down the British assault force.[88] The Afghans were described as having 'defended [their positions] most obstinately' and many died at their posts.[89] One party of Afghan troops tried to mount a counter-attack to recover their *sangars* but without success. However, the advance on their right and centre by fresh British forces made it unclear exactly which of these thrusts was the main effort.

Resistance was maintained until 12.30 hrs, when Afghan units began to abandon the ridges and the *kotal*. British artillery fire, particularly from mountain guns brought up onto the ridge, was ranging down on the flanks and rear, having already destroyed a number of Afghan cannons. Roberts, still unable to get past the ravine astride the ridge, decided to break off his attack and push into depth behind the Afghan position.[90] This manoeuvre unhinged the Afghan defences: as soon as the Afghan troops were aware that their flank had been turned, they retreated. The irregular levies dispersed, but the regular forces were harried by the lancers of the 12th Bengal Cavalry as they struggled westwards, trying to avoid becoming encircled. The Afghan guns were abandoned along with stores and equipment. No attempt was made to hold the Shutagarden Pass that lay to the west, not perhaps because, as the British suggested, Afghan morale had been shattered, but because it afforded few natural defences and most of the Afghan artillery had been lost at Peiwar Kotal. Local Ghilzais, the Mangals in particular, had lost none of their fight. As a British baggage column passed through the Sapri Kotal, south of the Peiwar Kotal pass, it was assaulted by raiders.[91] During the course of the evening, as the British rearguard withdrew, the numbers of local fighters swelled and this persuaded Roberts that using subsidiary routes would prove too costly.

The British operations in Khost were less successful than hoped. Akram Khan, the governor, had agreed that, in return for a guarantee of order in the region, the British would ensure his personal safety.[92] Roberts hoped that this cooperation would ensure a peaceful occupation. Akram Khan seems to have been prepared to negotiate because of instructions he had received from Sirdar Wali Mohammed Khan, a half-brother of Sher Ali. Although it is not clear what the Afghan intentions were, it seems likely that an attempt to cooperate might limit the British incursion. If the British could be delayed, then there was still hope that the local clans astride the Suleiman range would offer more resistance. Indeed, on the day the British column was preparing to advance into Khost, the Massuzais of the Orakzai *qawm* had barricaded the entrance to the Karmana glen near Sadda on the British lines of communications, necessitating the deployment of more troops in the area.[93]

At Khost, some tribal elders were keen to negotiate with the British but others were not, probably reflecting the different results of various local *jirgas*. While Akram Khan was congratulated on his management of the province and its quiescence when the British arrived, it was soon evident that the local clans cared little for the injunctions of a member of the Kabuli elite. When elders were summoned by British Political Officers, only a handful obeyed. By mid-afternoon the following day, 7 January 1879, large numbers of Mangals, Makbhils, Zadrans, Khostwals and Gurbaz Waziris began assembling on three sides of the British encampment.[94] The British were compelled to make a demonstration of force, but the *lashkars* drew back onto higher ground. When the British attempted to attack them, hundreds poured out of nearby settlements, suggesting some sort of coordinated plan. Breech-loading rifles and carbines proved devastating against the local fighters and they were driven off, but as soon as the British began their withdrawal, they began edging closer again. Some local prisoners were taken and fighters attempted to mount a rescue at night, which resulted in the destruction of the raiders and the killing of a number of prisoners.[95] However, aware that to hold the area would require a brigade of troops, which he could not spare, Roberts decided to leave behind an Afghan administration, pay the clans to remain at peace, and withdraw. Within hours of leaving this surrogate leader, Sultan Jan, who was a Sadozai Durrani, on 28 January 1879 Roberts received a plea for rescue.[96] Roberts had to retrieve Sultan Jan and march off, leaving Khost once more in the hands of the Ghilzai Jirgas. From the Afghan perspective, their resistance had been successful.

Nevertheless, the main British thrust into Afghanistan was virtually unopposed. Kandahar fell on 8 January 1879 after token resistance by a force of Afghan cavalry at Ghlo Kotal outside the city.[97] The march from Quetta had nevertheless been arduous and the transport animals, procured hastily by the British in the Punjab or Baluchistan, died in large numbers.[98] Although General Sir Donald Stewart could push brigades out to Qalat and the Helmand river, resupplying them and transporting them was a constant difficulty. The British force that arrived on the Helmand found that supplies were inadequate and they were forced to divide into small foraging parties. It is likely that locals withheld food and fodder, and a local force of approximately 1,500 fighters assembled as a *lashkar* when the British commenced their withdrawal. A combination of British carbine fire and a cavalry charge inflicted losses of 200 on the Afghans, and the remainder dispersed to await a better opportunity.

The new Amir, Yakub Khan, who was son of Sher Ali, could see there was little hope of successful resistance. Kandahar had fallen. The British were at Qalat. The regular army had been defeated at Ali Masjid and Peiwar Kotal. The clans of the Khyber Pass, in contrast to their actions in 1842, were cooperating with the British. Khost had been occupied without opposition and, although the British had been driven out, the Khostwals were hardly favourably disposed towards his regime. In despair, Yakub Khan signed the Treaty of Gandamack in May 1879. By its terms, imposed deliberately at the very site of the last stand of the Kabul garrison in 1842 in order to expunge the memory of the British defeat, Afghanistan lost control over its foreign policy, was compelled to accept a British residency, was incorporated into the economic system of India and was forced to relinquish authority over the borderlands astride the Suleiman range. Afghanistan was rendered a British protectorate and Sher Ali's strategy had failed.

Major Cavagnari dictated the terms with some impatience. He wrote to the Viceroy: 'I found the whole lot to be pretty much of the ordinary Afghan stamp, and their avarice and suspicion were their leading qualities. Their arguments were so feeble and far from the point that I at once made up my mind to deal with the case as if it concerned an ordinary affair connected with border Pathan tribes'.[99] Many Afghans did not care about the issues of foreign policy and economic integration, but they were alive to the concession of land and the establishment of a permanent presence of foreigners in Kabul. The loss of land, so crucial to the hierarchy of Pashtun *qawm* along the frontier, was seen as a direct challenge to their way of life. Throughout the winter of 1878–9, there was desultory raiding against British logistical chains and an entire British division was devoted to protecting them between Jalalabad and Peshawar.[100] Yet, having achieved their strategic objectives, the British set out to withdraw all their forces, evacuating Kandahar and the positions along the border.

The operations resumed, 1879

Renewed violence against the British occurred soon after the Residency had been set up in the capital. In September 1879, soldiers from Herat who were stationed in Kabul mutinied and marched on the Residency because they had not been paid their arrears. Unrest similarly affected Herat and Kandahar where regiments had also not been paid. They understood that the British were the paymasters of the Afghan army, and the Amir Yakub Khan did indeed enjoy a subsidy of 600,000 rupees per annum from the Government of India. The mood of the mutineers in Kabul was evidently anti-British. They jeered the Kabuli regiments that had been defeated by the foreigners, and even when paid a portion of their salaries from the Bala Hissar they demanded to know why no one was throwing the British out of the city. Mullahs exhorted the Kabuli residents to action. To remove the threat, leave was granted for 40 days, which many took advantage of since cholera had broken out in the city and 150 soldiers had died from the disease in the 24 hours prior to the unrest.[101] Leading members of the court indicated to the British Resident that they had not been paid their salaries by the Amir either and the whole country was 'unsettled'.[102] On 3 September 1879, when the full back-pay to the mutineers was not issued, there was a riot and the Residency was overrun.[103] All the occupants were murdered and dismembered.

General Roberts immediately set out to reoccupy Kabul and the Amir was placed under house arrest. Intelligence had been procured that suggested the Amir had counselled his leading courtiers, the representatives of the Ghilzais, Kohistanis, Kabulis and Kizilbashes. It is alleged he asked them whether they all 'intended to join in a *ghaza* to fight the British'.[104] He had encouraged them all to send their families to the north of Afghanistan, perhaps anticipating that the British would return to sack Kabul. Yakub Khan tried to delay the British, claiming that he had it within his power to punish the mutineers and that, if the British moved into Kabul, the Amir would be seen as a puppet who could be overthrown and killed. The British simply did not trust Yakub Khan and it was evident they would soon be on their way.[105] Roberts noted that 'Ghilzais report that the Amir has called upon [them] to stop all roads leading from this [place] to Kabul'. Yakub Khan could perhaps have attempted to lead a popular resistance movement, but his brother in Herat, Ayub Khan, was conspiring against him. Moreover, Abdur Rahman was poised to overrun northern Afghanistan. Together, these figures were likely to erode any claim to be the leader of a national resistance. Members of his own family, including Wali Mohammed, had thrown in their lot with the British, and there was little sign that the Ghilzais or Kohistanis were inclined to back him. Finally, the British had already demonstrated their ability to crush the Afghan resistance, and unless he was seen to be submissive he might have been apprehended and held responsible for the death of the British Resident.

When Roberts made a rapid advance, Yakub Khan initially gave himself up, ostensibly for protection against his own people, and then abdicated soon after. The British believed that, if he could not protect a British envoy within a stone's throw of the Bala Hissar or even ensure his own safety, he was 'of no real use as an ally'.[106]

Before Roberts could enter Kabul, the Afghans prepared to defend the capital by occupying the heights at Charasiab.[107] Thirteen infantry regiments of regular Afghan troops and several thousand irregulars gathered and held a crescent of hills that extended for three and a half miles, with the largest concentration of troops near the Sang-i Nawishta valley. Roberts decided to attack this army on its weakest, western flank while pinning it in place with a feint. After just three hours, Roberts had managed to seize the western hills and began to push his men eastwards. The inability to hold the hills against disciplined rifle fire and mountain guns forced the Afghans to fall back. A small conical hill on the Afghan left was also taken and the main Afghan force, made up mainly of regular troops, was caught between two pincers. About 500 Afghans were killed, while the British lost only 18 with a further 70 wounded. The disparity of losses suggests the effectiveness of British artillery and firearms compared with Afghan weapons, although training and fire discipline also need to be taken into account.

The Afghans had abandoned the hills at Charasiab, but Roberts was aware that the population was hostile and that he dare not engage in street battles which would result in heavier casualties. Indeed, the day after the battle, large numbers of irregular fighters gathered to attack the British rearguard and transport, and were only driven off with some sustained volleys by two battalions. At Asmai, the hills overlooking the Chardeh plain to the east of Kabul, three regular Afghan regiments under Mohammed Jan Khan of Wardak had entrenched themselves with several guns. The British cavalry enveloped the position hoping to prevent their escape, and a force of British infantry with mountain guns made its way along the same ridge, but was unable to close with the Afghan force during the day.[108] That night, clearly cut off, the Afghans exfiltrated through the British cordon and dispersed.[109]

In the absence of any political alternative, Roberts, who marched into the city without opposition, was forced to impose military rule. While the British politicians debated the relative merits of partitioning the country, the Ghilzais and Kohistani Tajiks mobilized to take action against the occupation forces. Moreover, while Roberts had been advancing on Kabul, Afghan regulars consisting of six regiments of Heratis were marching towards Dakka and the Khyber Pass, right along the route that the British intended to use as their main line of communication through the winter.[110] There were reports that these troops and local mullahs were encouraging the clans to rise against the British, and it seems likely they were hoping to replicate the destruction of the Kabul garrison in 1842: ringing the city, cutting supplies and then attacking the inevitable withdrawal. Ghilzais near the Shutagarden Pass had deposed Padshah Khan in favour of his younger brother, Alaudin, who was anti-British, but a show of force by a brigade of Indian troops dissuaded the Ghilzais from taking action.[111] Nevertheless, the difficulty of holding open the line of communications along this route, and the penny-packets of British and Indian troops, which invited some sort of attack, meant this avenue was shut down. As they did so, Pashtuns from Mangal and Ghilzai clans attacked posts at Ali Khel, Shutagarden and Surkh Kot in storming parties of 2,000–3,000 men. These were only driven off with difficulty. At Shutagarden itself, the British garrison was surrounded.[112] The Ghilzais had initially tried to ambush a negotiating party, and then tried to form up for an assault under cover of darkness, making their attack at dawn with an estimated 1,500–2,000 men. Despite their knowledge of the local terrain, and use of dead ground to make their approaches, they were nevertheless surprised by British ambushes and counter-attacks. The arrival of reinforcements from other villages had, at times, restored the confidence of demoralized fighters, but British artillery and long-range rifle fire could reach across valleys and hills with considerable effect. Nevertheless, at Shutagarden the numbers of Ghilzai fighters eventually swelled to an estimated 17,000.[113] The Afghans cut off the garrison's water supply and severed its telegraphic communications. After a series of assaults, the Ghilzais offered to let the British withdraw in return for 2 *lakhs* of rupees. The British refused, and when relieving forces appeared they counter-attacked their assailants. The pattern was repeated at Ali Khel against a force of 5,000 Balesh Khel. A British column then set out to punish the Zaimukhts who had attacked their line of logistics further south, advancing to Bagh and Zawo, the latter being a settlement accessible up a ravine 8 miles long and in places only 10 feet wide. Fines were imposed and property destroyed. Two men accused of the murder of Indian camp followers were shot by firing squad, and the British withdrew without further resistance, as the locals, who for so long had put their faith in the impregnable terrain, were shocked into submission.[114]

To reopen the Khyber route, Brigadier General Charles Gough was ordered to overawe the Ghilzais with a rapid advance, but he found it impossible to intercept the Afghan regulars said to be near Dakka, or to push through the pass because of a lack of transport and crippling sickness amongst his troops.[115] Historian Brian Robson believes that, although swift retaliation for the destruction of the Residency threw the Afghans off-balance, the British forces had run considerable risks and were in danger of having their logistics completely severed. MacGregor confided in his diary that 'we've nearly eaten all our provisions and if we were to get worsted, not only would the whole country be up [in arms], but we should get no supplies'.[116] Nevertheless, Roberts managed to establish his garrison in the enlarged Sherpur Cantonment, the barrack complex started by Sher Ali but never finished. He also established a post at Buthak and sent a brigade to open communications with the Khyber Line Force and clear the entire route of fighters in November.

To the south, General Stewart had reoccupied Kandahar, again without opposition, and pushed up to Qalat in order to draw Afghan troops away from Kabul. Although he had insufficient transport to reach Ghazni, he managed to send forward a small screening force of 350 men to Shahjui (Shahjoy). These troops encountered a Ghilzai *lashkar* numbering no more than 900 that may have been assembling to contest Stewart's advance. The Afghans withdrew to a hill fort some 6 miles from the settlement and were immediately attacked there. Although the Ghilzai leader, Sahib Jan, managed to charge the British and Indian troops and get to close quarters, he and another sixty of his men were killed and the rest were scattered.

The Afghans were aware that Roberts' force at Kabul was relatively small, in fact 8,000 in total. They were also bitterly opposed to his presence near the city and incensed by the military tribunals that were carried out against the ringleaders of the attack on the British Residency. The difficulty in identifying the individuals responsible, and Lytton's private advice to Roberts that many Kabulis, indeed 'every civilian, be he priest, or layman, mullah or peasant', were guilty by association, made the atmosphere highly charged.[117] The Wazir to Yakub Khan, Shah Mohammed Khan, the Governor of Kabul, Yahiha Khan and his brother, Zakariah Khan, were all suspects. Secret meetings were held in order to acquire evidence and cross-examine witness reports. The Kotwal of the Kabul constabulary was tried and executed because it was believed he had disposed of the bodies of the Resident and his escort by dumping them on a rubbish tip. The number of executions is contested but the manner of their death, by hanging, and the accusation that they had rebelled against the will of the Amir, were lost on the population of Afghanistan. Their view was that the British had executed those who had resisted the British invasion. Indeed, not all the executions were carried out under the jurisdiction of the tribunal.[118] Five men were condemned to death for attacking the post at Shutagarden and six others were shot by firing squad by the 14th Bengal Lancers for being armed in the city contrary to the martial law imposed by the occupation forces.[119]

MacGregor felt that the measures were half-hearted and would generate more resistance: 'We are thoroughly hated and not enough feared... We have been cruel yet we have not made them quite acknowledge our supremacy; and they have not yet had time to appreciate our justice'.[120]

While the British government and the Viceroy considered breaking up Afghanistan into more manageable fiefdoms, Roberts was aware that popular resistance was stirring. The tribunals and executions, although not acknowledged as a cause, were nevertheless a significant spur to action. Roberts preferred to explain Afghan opposition as 'vivid fanaticism' which 'has ever formed a prominent trait in Afghan character'.[121] Roberts had issued an amnesty and opened a medical clinic, which enjoyed some success amongst Kabulis, but he was not prepared to admit that it was the fact of his occupation and his coercion that was generating resistance.

In order to obtain supplies for the winter, especially as the passes might be closed by bad weather or by harassing raids, Roberts dispatched foraging parties. On 22 November one of these was attacked by irregulars at Dara Nirikh valley in Wardak.[122] The fighters were driven off, the villages stripped of grain, livestock, forage and other supplies and the houses razed. *Maliks* from settlements nearby were ordered to witness the destruction as an example, but the British found that, with winter approaching, few villagers were eager to part with their provisions, regardless of cash or coercion. Four days later, a cavalry patrol was attacked at Bini Badam and, although there were no casualties, another village was burned. The village *malik* was made a prisoner. Rumours began to circulate that Mullah Mushki-i Alam of Ghazni was rousing people to fight, but in Nirikh, the centre of the resistance, was a local leader, Bahadur Khan. The Governor appointed by the British, Mohammed Hussein Khan, was subsequently murdered by Bahadur Khan's followers in revenge.

Further north, Mir Bacha, a Kohistani leader, drove out the British-appointed governor with popular backing. Links were soon established between communities in Maiden and Wardak under the leadership of Mohammed Jan, an Afghan regular army officer who had commanded the artillery at Ali Masjid. The conduit for negotiations between the various communities around Kabul was the *ulema*. Many had served as acolytes of Mushki-i Alam and so his calls for resistance had a particular resonance and made him an obvious choice as leader. The governor of Ghazni, Mohammed Syed, abandoned the city and arrived in Kabul on 18 November claiming the mullahs had taken control there, gathering 'several thousand tribesmen from the villages in the district'.[123]

Roberts decided to crush the gathering insurrection by contemplating a move against Ghazni, but the limited manpower and transport available ruled out this option. Instead, a concentric manoeuvre against the gathering clans in Wardak would, it was thought, secure Kabul and deter any further resistance from either Kohistan or Ghazni. Two columns, led respectively by Brigadier Generals Macpherson and Baker, would converge on the rebellious districts of Wardak from the north-east and the south. While Baker marched into position, Macpherson was expected to allow the Afghan irregulars to come on into the Chardeh Plain where they could be more easily destroyed.

However, the Afghans of Wardak were not simply heading for Kabul. They were attempting to link up with the Kohistanis and then advance together with overwhelming numbers against the British. Macpherson asked to be able to move instead against the Kohistanis who were assembling in large numbers at Mir Karez, just 10 miles north-west of Kabul. While pretending to fall back on Sherpur, he struck north-westwards and drove off the Afghans who held the Kriskana gorge and then scattered the Kohistanis assembling near Mir Karez. The Afghans did not withdraw northwards into their own territory, but evaded pursuing British cavalry as best they could and moved in groups of various sizes in a south-westerly direction. Roberts hoped to catch this movement on the horns of Baker's brigade that was now swinging through Wardak back towards Kabul. To ensure the destruction of the Afghans, a force of British cavalry under Brigadier General Massy was deployed to complete the encirclement. In fact, what the British had not realized was that the Afghans were not in retreat but moving to join 10,000 of Mohammed Jan's Wardak and Maiden fighters who had reached the Chardeh Plain. This area, full of cultivation and settlements, could conceal large numbers within striking distance of Kabul, and provide the supplies that such a vast force needed.

When the small cavalry force under Massy engaged Mohammed Jan's army, the Afghans had the advantages of numbers and cover. Moreover, they adopted more dispersed formations than Afghan regular troops. An officer of the 9th Lancers wrote: 'the RHA [Royal Horse Artillery] opened fire, but as they [the Afghans] were in such straggling order, only a few were killed'.[124] The Afghans kept rushing forward and so pressed Massy's small force that the British were forced to abandon or spike some of the guns. A British cavalry charge was also absorbed and defeated. However, Mohammed Jan's success was short-lived. Macpherson's brigade emerged onto the Chardeh Plain via the Surkh Pass and immediately attacked the Afghan rear.[125] Initially, Mohammed Jan thought this was the Kohistanis, but the British attack forced him to change direction.

He decided to move towards the Deh Mazang gorge, the gap in the Asmai heights that led directly into the city of Kabul. However, a small force of British riflemen from the 72nd Highlanders held this vital ground and Mohammed Jan's formation was forced to take up a new position on the Takht-i Shah mountain where it could overlook the city and the Bala Hissar. There was no further movement on either side for the rest of the day on 10 December 1879, but at night a number of attacks were launched against the Highlanders at Deh Mazang. *Sangars* were constructed amid the boulder-strewn slopes.

Meanwhile, Baker's brigade found itself under attack as it passed through Maiden from Wardak and Lohar clansmen, although initially it was only the baggage train that was targeted. At Argandeh, close to the Chardeh Plain, the Afghans tried to block a pass, but they were driven off. Baker was ordered to return to Sherpur where Roberts was concentrating his forces, but the rearguard was subjected to constant sniping. Meanwhile the British tried to dislodge Mohammed Jan from the Takht-i Shah with infantry assaults. The weight of Afghan fire proved to be so heavy and sustained, the slopes so steep and broken, that only the Sher Darwaza heights could be captured before ammunition started to run low. As darkness gathered, the British troops bivouacked in their positions and there was a renewed assault in the morning via the Beni Hissar spur.

Mohammed Jan seemed to be holding his position on the mountain awaiting the arrival of more fighters from Kohistan and elsewhere. He held the high ground, had checked two British attacks in two days and felt secure on the heights. Moreover, as the British started their new attack on 13 December, Kabulis emerged from the suburbs to join him. George White, who led the vanguard of the British assault with the 92nd Highlanders and the Guides, tried to prevent the Afghan reinforcements from linking up with those on the summit, and there was a close-quarter battle which the British won. These Afghans withdrew back down the mountain and reoccupied the villages and compounds as well as the lower slopes of the Beni Haissar. White then brought up mountain guns and, using a combination of fire and manoeuvre, fought his way to the summit, while the other British force pushed their way along the ridgeline to join them. The Afghans contested every yard of ground.

More importantly, while the British forces fought their way up the western slopes, Mohammed Jan directed some of his men to seize two villages which lay in their rear. Baker, the commander there, was forced to use his reserves to retake these villages with more close-quarter fighting. As soon as this was done, he was informed that another Afghan force was circling around his troops and heading for Sherpur, the British base. The British cavalry sent to intercept them was then pinned down with fighting around the Siah Sang heights. More fighters were gathering in Kabul and the local area. It was a situation where, as one historian put it, 'as fast as one gathering was dispersed another appeared in a different direction'.[126] But the Afghans were not working in a random and uncoordinated way. Mohammed Jan was in communication with other Afghan leaders, and while some of the fighters appearing on 13 December might be attributed to a spontaneous and opportunist reaction to events, the sheer size and coherence of the Afghans' movements suggests a more coordinated process.

Roberts was forced to give up the Deh Mazang defile because he lacked enough troops to hold the ground and thus concentrated his force at Sherpur, holding only the Takht-i Shah heights with a small detachment. He and many of his officers were encouraged by the fact that the Afghans often dispersed when attacked, but those with experience of fighting on the North West Frontier knew that this dispersal was temporary. By the morning of 14 December, Mohammed Jan had moved his men back around the Takht-i Shah and occupied a new position on the Asmai heights to the west of the British base at Sherpur. Roberts once again used a pincer movement to clear these hills, and the Afghan forces withdrew. However, the long-awaited Kohistanis arrived at the northern end of the heights and overwhelmed the British infantry and mountain battery there, despite a determined defence. Meanwhile, more of Mohammed Jan's forces had occupied the Siah Sang and others were moving north-eastwards around the British cantonment at Sherpur, attempting to join hands with the Kohistanis and complete the encirclement of the British forces. From the Asmai heights, still more Afghans could be seen streaming north and eastwards across the Chardeh Plain.[127] At 14.00 hrs that day, Roberts ordered his units to withdraw into the cantonment, abandoning the city and all the high ground that surrounded it. Extraction from the Takht-i Shah involved a fight more or less the entire way, and as they passed through the suburbs of Kabul they came under fire from walls and houses, but they reached the relative security of Sherpur by the end of the day. The Butkhak garrison was also brought in unscathed. However, the British forces had suffered losses of 81 killed and 213 wounded in a week, and found themselves 'locked up, closely besieged, after a jolly good licking and all communications with the outer world cut off'.[128]

As the British prepared to concentrate their various detachments on the Khyber Line, Asmatullah Khan, encouraged by news from Kabul, started to contact Ghilzai elders and prepared for an attack on the post at Jagdalak. The telegraph line was cut, and, as the clans assembled, the first few snipers began a long-range harassing fire into the British positions. The British commander, Gough, had just 1,260 men with which to march towards Kabul, later reinforced to 2,100, but he was compelled to maintain some detachments for later operations, replenish their supplies, and march with inadequate numbers of transport animals. The Ghilzais blocked the crossing points on the Kabul River, and while Gough marched to Sherpur to join Roberts, Asmatullah's men put in an attack on Jagdalak. The fighters got to within 150 yards of the walls but, even after eight hours of fighting, could not prevail against the sustained fire of the garrison.[129]

At Sherpur, Roberts tasked his men to complete a perimeter of entrenchments and obstacles, but he was aware that several compounds close to the walls could provide covered approaches and firing points for the Afghans. The heights and village of Beymaru actually lay within the defences, and every effort was made to turn the houses and other buildings into strongpoints. In contrast to the garrison of 1841, Roberts had four months of food supplies and his own water source. Yet Mohammed Jan had a vast host to feed over the winter and could not afford to remain inactive. He had to exploit the sense of momentum built up over the previous few days of fighting. He was also aware that a direct assault on the front of the Sherpur position would result in heavy casualties. He had no siege guns with which to demolish the defences, and a complex plan of assault would require sustained consultation with rival Afghan factions. Indeed, although there was unity about fighting the British, there was no agreement on who should govern Afghanistan once they were gone. The Kohistanis favoured Wali Mohammed Khan, while the Ghilzais argued for the restoration of Yakub Khan. Mohammed Jan declared that Musa Jan, son of Yakub Khan, was the new Amir, but, according to Howard Hensman, the journalist with Roberts, he sent his terms to the British which specified that Yakub Khan should be restored. He also allegedly called upon Roberts to surrender and march to India while leaving two senior officers as hostages. These terms were not relayed directly or formally and seem to have come in via couriers. Roberts ignored them.

For two days, the Afghans did not make any move against the British defences, and on 17 December, when a British cavalry formation left the perimeter, the Afghans who tried to attack it were subjected to accurate artillery fire. Nevertheless, at night, enterprising fighters would try to shoot sentries on the walls and a number of groups tried to get close to the ramparts and had to be driven off. In the city, Mohammed Jan's men loopholed walls, perhaps expecting the British to make a counter-attack.[130] Ammunition was also distributed from the Bala Hissar. The British officers were privately concerned that Muslim sepoys in Indian regiments might be tempted to change sides and join the Afghans, but they remained loyal throughout.

What determined Mohammed Jan's next actions was not Roberts' silence over the terms he had offered but the news from the Ghilzais that a British relief force was on its way. The Afghans believed they had to overwhelm the garrison at Sherpur or risk facing a larger force. The plan was for a diversionary attack to be made at night on 22/23 December on the southern walls, while the signal for the main attack on the eastern side would be the lighting of a large beacon on the Asmai heights. Once inside, the southern attack would be renewed. The aim was to split the British forces and make entry via the houses and narrow corridors and streets of Beymaru. News of the proposed attack spread to the Ghilzais on the Khyber Line who moved westwards to join in.[131] The prospect of final victory and plunder also appealed to Afghans from the whole region around Kabul, and they now poured in. However, the assembly of such a large force compromised the security of the plan. Roberts received intelligence the night before and the garrison was therefore ready and waiting for the attack.

The *ghazis* led the attack, but almost immediately the British threw up star shells which illuminated the entire battlefield. For three hours, the garrison used sustained rifle, artillery and machine-gun fire to cut down the assaulting Afghans, and at first light it was apparent that the Afghans had not broken through. Nevertheless three sides of the cantonment were under attack when, just before 10.00 hrs, the Afghans gained a lodgement on the eastern end of the Beymaru heights. However, some had begun to drift away believing that the British could not be overwhelmed, and this allowed the garrison to venture out and bring defilade fire on the lodgement made in the hills. As these men fell back, the British commenced a counter-attack, and pushed the attackers out of the Beymaru village area on the eastern side. Individuals and small groups tried to hold on to some houses and compounds, but it was clear the assault had failed. The retreat became general and the British, taking no chances, pursued the Afghans relentlessly. Roberts estimated that, for around 33 British and Indian casualties, the Afghans may have suffered more than 3,000 killed and wounded. The defeat was psychological as well as physical. It was evident that the British could not be defeated in a conventional battle, particularly if they held defensive positions. The lesson of the Battle of Sherpur was to return to attrition, severing British logistics and attacking more isolated detachments.

When the British sent a punitive force to destroy the villages controlled by Mir Bacha, Afghans in the surrounding districts were eager to make their submission. Supplies of food and fodder were handed over, despite the risk of hardship for themselves throughout the winter. Some livestock were killed because there was no longer fodder to feed them. Martial law was re-imposed in Kabul and more defences were constructed at Sherpur and in the surrounding hills. Compounds and houses close to the cantonment were destroyed and the inhabitants driven out. Along the Khyber Line, the Ghilzais found some villages temporarily occupied, but their attacks ceased when the assault at Sherpur failed.

Yet Afghan resistance was not entirely extinguished. With the defeat of the attack at Sherpur, the fighting clans drew off and sacked the wards of Kabul that belonged to the Hazaras and Kizilbashis, since they regarded them as pro-British.[132] Hindu businesses were also looted. A shadow government was established at Ghazni with the single objective of driving out the British. The spiritual leader of the revolt, Mushk-i Alam, asserted himself as a regent to Musa Jan and continued to preach Jihad. In early 1880, the Ghazni factions restated their objective to be the restoration of Yakub Khan. In the north, there were still Afghan regular forces as yet untouched by the occupation. Hensman wrote: 'In Turkistan [hostility] could scarcely be called a revival, as it never died out. In that province were still organized regiments ... whose sepoys had never suffered the disgrace of a defeat at our hands'.[133] Attempts to negotiate a settlement with Ghulam Haider, their commander, failed. However, Hensman also noted that the troops on which Haider relied had revolted and their generals had deserted.[134] Uzbek territories, including Maimena and Saripul, appeared to separate from Afghanistan under the leadership of Mohammed Shah. Badakshan appeared to be in revolt against the remnants of Yakub Khan's regime. Nevertheless there was still every chance that resistance would be sustained and that anti-foreign sentiments or the 'defence of Islam' would provide legitimacy, unity and motivation.[135] Hensman believed that 'with all the cunning astuteness of Afghans, the tribal leaders will come in and try to outwit us, as they have always tried before'.[136]

Operations in Southern Afghanistan

In January 1880, Abdur Rahman returned to northern Afghanistan to raise an army amongst the old regulars, the clans of the north and his relations amongst the men of Badakshan.[137] He also made an appeal to the Kohistanis, offering to lead them in a holy war against the occupation.[138] The British response to Abdur Rahman was to offer him control of northern Afghanistan, including Kabul, as long as he agreed to stand by the terms of the Gandamack Treaty. The Government of India added that it was 'not disposed to hinder' measures which he might take to obtain possession of the rest of the country.[139] In July 1880, Abdur Rahman accepted the terms and was recognized as Amir of Kabul. Yet, initially, the British believed that the dismemberment of Afghanistan was still a more satisfactory way of keeping control of the region. Kandahar had been quiet throughout the disturbances in Kabul. The governor, Sher Ali, a cousin of the late Amir Sher Ali, was widely regarded as a British puppet, but there seemed no reason to doubt his administrative abilities. He was to be given control of the entire south of the country, from Pishin in the east to Farah in the west, and he would have his own army, with a British garrison on hand to support him.[140]

When General Stewart marched a force up towards Ghazni in order to neutralize the seat of resistance, he encountered a scorched-earth policy. The British had always struggled with lack of transport and scarcity of resources with which to feed large numbers of soldiers, so the tactic by the Afghans was a shrewd one. Villages were deserted. Crops and animals had been removed or hidden in the hills nearby. Some food was found by foraging parties in pits, concealed under dung heaps or in karetz tunnels.[141] Moreover, intelligence reports indicated that the British column was being shadowed by a growing number of Ghilzai fighters, and there were indications that *lashkars* were forming on both flanks.

When the British bivouacked at Jan Murad, 70 miles south of Ghazni, a war party of Hazaras swept into the Pashtun settlement and looted the properties, killing anyone who offered resistance. The British believed that they would get the blame for this sectarian and ethnic pogrom, but the Hazaras understood that the Pashtuns would not bring in a retaliatory *lashkar* under the very noses of the British. They were exploiting the temporary shift in power for their own advantage.

On 18 April, there was more certain intelligence on the assembly of 9,000 Ghilzais who were moving on a parallel track just 10 miles from the British. This force encamped at a point only 4 miles from Stewart's division, but a reconnaissance patrol the next morning found that the camp was deserted and the fighters had moved off during the early hours. Later that day, this same Afghan force appeared astride the road to Ghazni, but its numbers had swollen to 15,000. They had moved from behind, passed the British and now blocked the route, while others had perhaps come down from Ghazni itself. While Stewart deployed to make an attack that would pin the Afghans astride the road and roll up their right flank, the bulk of the Ghilzai force swept off the hills straight for him. Despite this massed attack, some Afghan irregulars did not join the charge and held back.[142] By contrast, the extreme end of the Afghan right wing, a force of 2,000 horsemen was making a dash for the British artillery, perhaps hoping to overwhelm them before they could do much damage to the irregulars on foot. The effect of the Afghan attack, along an arc 5,000 yards in length, was to prevent the British being able to concentrate their fire at any single point. General Chapman, Stewart's Chief of Staff, wrote: 'The scene was one which defies description. Such an enormous body of Ghazi swordsmen had not been seen since the battle of Meeanee. Their bravery was magnificent, and ... nothing stopped them short of death'.[143] One British officer with the 59th Foot nevertheless remarked: 'Anyone with the semblance of a heart under his khaki jacket could not help feeling something like pity to see them advancing with their miserable weapons in the face of our guns and rifles'.[144] It was only their numbers, speed and courage that made them formidable, for the British knew that their firearms were designed for just this sort of encounter.

Despite the weight of fire, the Afghan swordsmen were able to crash into the British firing line and engage in hand-to-hand fighting. The British artillery on the right had started to run out of ammunition and was withdrawn when the Afghans reached within 30 yards of their muzzles. On the Afghan right, the horsemen punched through the 19th Bengal Lancers and rode into depth, through the medical posts. However, the Afghan attack lost momentum, and, without reserves, it had no means to exploit the success of the initial shock wave. The reserve Indian cavalry made flank attacks, while in the centre the disciplined British and Gurkha regiments did not break and run, but maintained their cohesion. They shot down large numbers of the Afghans immediately in front of them with volley fire. Reserve artillery plunged fire onto the Afghan horsemen that had ridden into depth and who were heading towards the column's baggage. The Afghans were hurled back, and then started to stream away. Some 2,000 Hazaras, waiting a mile or two from the battle, pursued the defeated Ghilzais, killing as many as they could.[145] The Afghans lost an estimated 3,000 killed and wounded, while the British suffered losses of 142. The whole battle, subsequently known as Ahmed Khel, had been concluded in just one hour.

When Stewart arrived at Ghazni, the 'shadow government' had deserted the city, but there were cavalry patrols that reported a force of 6,000 at Arzu and

Shalez, villages that lay just 5 miles from the British encampment. Moreover, it was said that 30,000 irregulars had assembled under Mushk-i Alam in the region. The British despatched a force of 2,800 men to disperse the Afghans at Arzu and Shalez, but the compound walls of these villages proved impregnable to British artillery fire and despite feigning a withdrawal to tempt the Afghans out, there was no movement. Yet the arrival of the British force appeared to have the effect of encouraging more local clans to join the original defiant band in the villages. The British brought up reinforcements, and when it seemed the escape route would be cut off, the Afghans evacuated the settlements. If there was any plan to repeat the charge at Ahmed Khel there was no evidence of it here.

Nor were the Afghans able to lure the British from their line of march into the hills. The British continued their advance to Kabul, while the resistance remained at large in rural areas. To underline the point, a force of 1,200 men of the Guides and the 92nd Highlanders who were patrolling Logar were confronted with a *lashkar* at Chikildukhtaran near Charasiab. The fighting began in the early morning and more irregulars arrived from nearby villages as the day wore on until about 5,000 were assembled. The Afghans used rifle fire to suppress the British movements and then used cover to inch forward until they were within 200 yards of the British firing line. An attempt was made to edge around the right flank but a detachment of British cavalry was deployed into a village to the right rear, and fire from here stopped the Afghan manoeuvre. It seems that efforts were made to encourage a final charge. One officer recorded: 'At one moment, they rose up all round with a shout and threatened to break over us like a great wave... men felt for their pistols and instinctively tightened their grip on their swords' but the attack never materialized.[146] The weight of British fire was sufficient to deter a final assault. The *lashkar* was subsequently driven off with losses of over 200. A British cavalry regiment surprised another Afghan *lashkar* in early July 1880 and inflicted heavy casualties on it.[147] Subsequent reports revealed that they had been waiting for reinforcements to join them from Mohammed Jan's *lashkars*.

Further north it was reported that Mir Bacha, the Kohistani leader, was eager to take revenge for the destruction of his property and the defeat of his forces at Sherpur. Along the Khyber Line there were repeated attacks, but almost all of these appeared to be for the chance of loot from the baggage trains constantly moving up to Kabul. At Jalalabad, an audacious raid resulted in 1,000 cattle being herded off into the hills. However, reports were also received of a mullah, Khalil, preaching Jihad against the British at Ghoshta and Besud.

A *lashkar* of 2,000 men affiliated to Khalil was surprised by a British ambush: 70 were killed and the rest dispersed. Khalil nevertheless escaped and continued to rouse the clans in Kama amongst the Mohmands. Another force of 1,000 Pashtuns under the charismatic leadership of Mullah Faqir was similarly destroyed near Abi Boghan, but Mullah Faqir reappeared later in Laghman in league with Asmatullah Khan, the latter keeping up resistance near Jagdalak. Yet, in August 1880, when the British garrison withdrew and took with it the entire Khyber Line detachments, a total of 24,000 personnel, the Ghilzais did not attack. They contented themselves with picking up abandoned stores, some of which became the scene of bitter inter-clan skirmishes.[148]

The Battle of Maiwand, 26 July 1880

The Battle of Maiwand has been elevated to legendary status in Afghanistan. The only war memorial in the country, other than those marking national independence in 1919 at the end of the Third Afghan War and a pillar to the fallen of the unrest in Khost in 1924, is dedicated to this battle and it stands at a busy road intersection in Kabul. The concrete structure, the *Minar-i Maiwand*, is covered in gaudy billboards and the details of the battle are largely forgotten or misinterpreted.[149] Every Pashtun in the modern province of Maiwand is convinced that his ancestors fought at the action, and when the British arrived with a task force in neighbouring Helmand in 2006, some expressed the sentiment that 'Fighting the British feels like unfinished business for many of us'.[150] In Afghan history this action has achieved its standing because, according to the national myth, it combines elements that Afghans recall with pride: a victory over a modern Western army achieved by enthusiastic irregulars imbued with sincere Islamic ideals and patriotism, which preceded the ejection of foreign occupiers. In public discourse, the accuracy of this interpretation does not matter; this is the keystone in the journey to national independence, part of the national story, and evidence of the agency and self-determination of the Afghan people.

Ayub Khan, the Governor of Herat, was aged twenty-nine in 1880, and had been a consistent critic of the Treaty of Gandamack. He had been in exile in Persia for intrigues against Sher Ali until his brother, Yakub Khan, became Amir in Kabul. But Yakub's decision to conclude a treaty with the British appears to have alienated him, and the arrest and deporting of the Amir offered the opportunity for Ayub Khan to claim the throne for himself. He possessed an independent military force, and his control of Herat gave him the power to rival occupied Kandahar and rebellious Turkistan. Intelligence reports suggested that he possessed seventeen infantry regiments and forty-four guns, some of the latter being modern breech-loading pieces. The appointment of the ageing and unpopular Sher Ali as Wali of Kandahar, the wealth of the Pashtun south, which was relatively unscathed by the war, and the chance of a British withdrawal, marked by the departure of Stewart's division for Kabul, all seemed to herald an opportunity to begin his march on the capital via the southern provinces.

However, Ayub Khan aborted his first attempt to advance on Kandahar in December 1879 because of significant unrest in Herat. His regiments were on the verge of mutiny and, with little revenue to pay them, he had to seek alternative methods to gain their loyalty. He tried to declare a Jihad and advocated an advance against Kandahar because of the Infidel presence there, both to claim legitimacy and offer its loot to his unruly troops.[151] To augment his invasion force, Ayub Khan tried to summon three Herati regiments from Maimena, but there was a revolt by his commander Fiazullah Khan in Herat, so Ayub Khan summoned four of his most loyal regiments (two Kandahari and two Kabuli) and defeated the Heratis, inflicting losses of 300 men as they sallied out. The Kabuli troops then plundered the city.[152] By January 1880, the Kabuli and Herati factions in the city had reconciled with each other for fear that Persia might try to exploit the situation. Nevertheless, there were rumours of fresh quarrels by the spring and even some references to Ayub Khan deliberately trying to divide the factions in order to break the grip of the army which held real power. It was alleged that Ayub Khan was practically their prisoner, held under house arrest for two months, and the relative status of Sirdar Khusdil Khan (known as the Luinab), his chief advisor, was uncertain.[153] Ayub Khan even sent an envoy to the British in Kandahar, hoping for their assistance while also looking to the Persians for support. In fact, he may have been trying to ascertain British intentions towards him as a potential monarch. The British gave little encouragement.[154]

The trigger for Ayub Khan to take action was the prospect of the coronation of his rival Abdur Rahman in Kabul. Rumours that Ayub was planning to advance southwards were being reported in Teheran and the bazaars of Kandahar in May 1880.[155] The Wali of Kandahar asked the British to send a brigade to the Helmand river where his own authority was weak and where he feared his troops might desert to Ayub Khan.[156] The problem was that the British had only 4,800 men at Kandahar, and although a brigade could be sent, the British believed its role would be purely to bolster local Kandahari troops.

Ayub Khan made a remarkable march from his base in Herat on 15 June, at the height of the hot weather, over a distance of 253 miles (407 km) with his artillery, completing the journey in just twenty-five days. This achievement rivals that of General Roberts, whose march from Kabul to Kandahar to relieve a beleaguered British garrison was celebrated in the contemporary press and, anxious for success, lauded by the British public. Like the British, Ayub Khan ensured that depots for supplies were set up in advance in Farah and possibly as far as Helmand.[157] On 2 July, the British got confirmation that Ayub Khan was en route with ten regiments of infantry, 2,500 horsemen and six batteries of guns, a total of between 6,000 and 8,000 men.[158] According to the Official History, news that Ayub Khan had left Herat had 'spread like wildfire all over the country, producing the most exciting and disturbing effect on the population, both in the city of Kandahar and in the surrounding country'.[159] Even then it was felt that only 2,500 British and Indian troops could be spared with a single battery of six guns. Of this force many were inexperienced, and the 30th Bombay Native Infantry (Jacob's Rifles) consisted of a large number of young Pashtuns.

When the British concentrated at Gereshk and news arrived that Ayub Khan's army was close at hand, the Wali's troops gradually became less reliable and then mutinied.[160] Although the British retrieved the six pieces of artillery they had tried to take away and killed over fifty of them as they escaped over the Helmand, they could not prevent the Wali's infantry from running to join Ayub Khan. To make matters worse, it was noticed that many Pashtuns in the 30th Bombay Native Infantry had either deliberately fired into the air, or exhibited a total lack of training about how to use their firearms.[161] General Burrows, the commander of the British brigade, decided to fall back on a more reliable supply base at Khusk-i Nakhud where he might be able to intercept any crossing further north. In fact, soon after the British left Gereshk, Ayub's cavalry arrived there in the hope of gaining information on the British intentions. The arrival of these horsemen also had the effect of encouraging Helmandis to join the resistance. Indeed, the perception that the British were withdrawing as Ayub Khan advanced created a great deal of enthusiasm. None of the local clans had any experience of British firepower in the way that had affected the Ghilzais and Kohistanis at Ahmed Khel or Kabul. Reports were received that 'hordes of tribesmen ...were coming in from all sides to swell the numbers of the Afghan camp'.[162]

There is some speculation that Ayub Khan may have been trying to avoid an encounter with the British and was perhaps hoping to move towards Ghazni, where he might have assumed command of the various factions of the resistance and challenged Abdur Rahman. However, General Burrows was ordered to intercept Ayub Khan as it was 'of the greatest political importance that his force should be dispersed and prevented by all possible means from passing on to Ghazni'.[163] Burrows therefore moved to intercept Ayub Khan at Maiwand, his cavalry keeping him informed as to the Afghans' movements. Spies informed him that Ayub Khan was still intending to move to Ghazni via the Khakrez Valley. On the morning of 27 July, Burrows was told that the Afghans had placed an advanced guard in Maiwand, and he hurried forward to prevent this forward detachment from being reinforced.[164]

At 10.00 hrs, the British observed a large number of Afghans moving across their right front towards Maiwand, which lay to the north, but the heat haze and dust obscured their view.[165] There was no sign of any guns, although a detachment of Afghan cavalry screened Ayub's army. General Burrows decided to advance across a deep ravine and past the villages of Mandabad (sometimes referred to as Mahmudabad) and Khig, drawing up his brigade facing north. The battle began at 10.50 hrs with British artillery firing on the Afghans, who were by now responding to the British presence.[166] Ayub's force moved to within 600 yards of the British firing line and many occupied a shallow ravine which ran parallel to the British front. More importantly, this ravine also ran around the British right flank and provided excellent cover against British artillery and rifle fire. Burrows appears to have been unaware of the presence of this feature until after the battle had begun. Ayub's men opened fire against the British right flank, forcing some companies of the 66th Regiment to manoeuvre and face east to meet this threat.

Meanwhile, some of Ayub's army continued to make their way southwards along the ravine until they were behind the brigade, and from here they made an attack on the baggage and its guards, although this was beaten off. On the opposite flank, Afghan cavalry edged its way further and further around the British left, until Burrows' brigade was completely enveloped. Lieutenant Fowle, a subaltern in the Royal Artillery, wrote that the Afghans 'kept pouring men round both flanks in some sort of loose skirmishing order'.[167] The British committed their reserve companies of infantry to form a left wing and suppressive fire, but this left only the British and Indian cavalry squadrons as a reserve.

For the first half hour of the battle, Ayub had no answer to the British artillery fire, hence the need for his men to find cover in the ravine. However, as more reinforcements arrived from the line of march he was able to bring his artillery into action. His batteries took up a position on the British left as soon as they arrived. Ayub had an estimated 10,000–15,000 troops under his command, dwarfing the British force by five to one, but it was in artillery that he possessed a particular advantage.[168] Ayub Khan's six Armstrong breech-loaders could hurl a heavier calibre shell at the British, although not always with great accuracy. However, Ayub Khan's dispositions, in an arc around the British, meant that all his guns could be brought to bear. Burrows later wrote that 'The former [Ayub Khan's artillery] were admirably served and with the exception of their Armstrong shells, which were generally too high, every shot was amongst us'. Lieutenant Fowle noted: 'Their artillery was exceptionally well served; their guns took ours in flank as well as directly, and their fire was concentrated. We were completely outmatched ... our guns seemed quite unable to subdue theirs... their smoothbore guns had great range and accuracy and caused great damage'.[169] The British and Indian troops were able to lie down in folds in the ground, but they were still rather exposed in contrast to much of the Afghan force, which was virtually entrenched along the ravine. Yet, any attempt by the Afghans to get forward and close with the British was met with withering fire from breech-loading Martini Henry rifles. Equally, the constant pounding by the Afghan guns was having a demoralizing effect on the Indian troops, and by 13.00 hrs eyewitnesses reported that some of the sepoys of the 30th Bombay Native Infantry were beginning to drift rearwards.[170]

The withdrawal of a section of smoothbore cannons to get ammunition added to the perception amongst these young men that the line was collapsing. The Afghan cavalry sensed that the British fire on the left was beginning to slacken and they tried to get closer. These were almost certainly the Kabuli horsemen and those formerly under the Wali, for it was reported that the 1,500 mounted Heratis 'would not fight'.[171] When the 30th were ordered to fire volleys, their fire proved inaccurate and ineffective. On the British right, Afghan irregulars had succeeded in passing right around the rear of the 66th Regiment and they opened fire. Several Afghan field guns were brought up to the ravine opposite the British centre and they were able to bring fire right into the middle of the British position.[172] The Afghans had clearly understood the importance of using the ground to protect and conceal their men, and to gain a tactical advantage. Moreover, they knew the importance of British firepower and did everything they could to compensate for it. However, there were at least two attempts to make a charge from the cover of the ravine that were stopped by devastating fire. Colonel Mainwaring wrote: 'I was twice enabled to give the order to cease firing, consequent on the enemy having been driven back'.[173] After firing, the British and Indian Grenadier companies lay down, but each

133

time they rose to fire at another assault their firing 'told heavily on the dense masses' of the Afghans.[174]

The fact that the British could wield such firepower and the decision to remain stationary, where the Indian cavalry were subjected to a long bombardment, was much criticized by British contemporaries after the battle.[175] One officer concluded: 'Maiwand was a defeat because the troops were not led promptly to the attack'. Comparing encounters in the First Anglo–Afghan War, the verdict was that 'the cavalry were kept inactive under the enemy's fire for hours'.[176]

At 14.30 hours, Ayub gave instructions to the guns to cease fire so that the irregulars could dash forward, and the main thrust of this attack came from the Afghan right.[177] The spectacle of this charge was too much for the 30th, which broke and fled. The Indian Grenadier battalion tried to form a square, but the irregulars were on them before the formation was complete and a hand-to-hand struggle ensued.[178] The demoralized Indian cavalry troopers made a charge, but then fell back contrary to their orders. The British infantry were also then engulfed, and the whole line tried to fall back in smaller groups. Several parties made a stand at Khig, particularly the remnants of the 66th.[179] One group, reduced from 100 to 11 men, even made a bayonet charge from a compound when its ammunition was exhausted. Many of the irregular Afghan forces actually made for the baggage at Mahmudabad, which allowed some of the fugitives to escape, but the Afghan cavalry, once it had crossed the battlefield, cut down the survivors of the 30th and pressed at the heels of the remainder.

The Afghans rode forward to ensure that they held the Maiwand Pass, the most direct route to Kandahar, which forced the retreating troops to curve away to the south-east. A rearguard provided a modicum of cover, but the rest of the British and Indian force was chased for miles across the plains, although it proved more difficult to come to grips with them once night came and Ayub called off the pursuit until daybreak. Survivors spoke of *jezails* and matchlocks being fired from villages along their line of retreat, and some were killed as they searched for water.[180] At dawn, attacks from the villages increased. The arrival of some of the British garrison from Kandahar on the banks of the Arghandab deterred any further action by large bodies of Afghan irregulars who had gathered to kill off the stragglers. The British gradually gathered in their forces, expecting a siege, but the defenders of Kandahar were shaken by their losses. Almost half of Burrows' brigade were killed and wounded at Maiwand.

Ayub Khan's losses were estimated by Mirza Mohammed Akbar to be 1,950 regulars and 800 irregulars. One of the Afghan participants, later interviewed by a British officer in 1881, felt the losses had been over 3,000 and it was reported that Ayub Khan admitted a similar figure. The general view given by Afghans at the time was that '*beshumar*' (countless) numbers had fallen and that it took seven days before the burials were complete. The losses were as shocking to the Afghans as the British and Indian ones were in London and Simla, and they explain why Ayub Khan did not make an immediate march on Kandahar.[181] If Ayub's force had numbered 15,000, as suggested, then his losses amounted to 20 per cent. If they had been 10,000, then the casualty toll was closer to a third of his strength. Mirza Mohammed Akbar believed that Ayub Khan's army had been at a disadvantage at the start of the battle, as most of the men were strung out on the line of march. It had taken almost an hour to assemble a fighting front, and the whole force was not in position until the middle of the day. Moreover, it seems that at several times the Afghans were in danger of retreating.[182] The presence of the ravine for cover and the gradual arrival of fresh fighters eager to join the fight probably helped sustain them. Once they had worked their way around each flank, the chance of victory became apparent.

The Afghans were willing to testify to the courage of the British soldiers of the 66th, especially those that held the compounds at Khig. However, they had their own icons represented especially by Malalai, a girl who lived, apparently, in the same village. Soon after the battle had begun, Malalai is said to have watched as the irregulars wavered under the rifle fire of the British troops and appeared to be on the verge of retreat. Malalai ran into the main ravine and, waving her veil over her head, encouraged the Afghans to hold on. Other accounts have Malalai replace an irregular fighter who had fallen while carrying a banner. She is said to have picked up the flag, or perhaps used her veil instead, and rallied the men by berating them about their honour. Other legends stress her care for the wounded. Shortly afterwards she was killed, but she was later buried in the village and for many years her grave was a site of special reverence. It was even said that Ayub Khan made a speech in her honour. The name Malalai has been a favourite for girls, schools and hospitals in Afghanistan ever since.

At Kandahar, the British placed the city into a state of defence and expelled much of the population.[183] Ayub Khan's leading elements arrived outside the city on 30 July, but the main body did not arrive until the next day. There was some desultory firing from guns on the ridges north and west of Kandahar, but there was also some speculation from spies that a night assault was imminent. However, Ayub Khan instead sent parties of his men to seize and fortify villages and compounds around the city walls.[184] An attempt by the garrison to drive off an Afghan force at Deh Khwaja was initially successful, but the Afghans pursued the British closely and inflicted some serious losses in the narrow lanes of the village, although their own losses were severe.[185]

Ayub Khan spent four weeks besieging Kandahar and therefore squandered the initiative. It was only a matter of time before the British sent a relief force up the Bolan Pass or down from Kabul, but Ayub Khan could not proceed to Ghazni while the remainder of Burrows' force lay at his back. Moreover, the inhabitants of Kandahar were eager to recover their city, and the clansmen in his army were almost certainly hoping that the fall of the city would offer the opportunity for looting. In contrast, a march on Ghazni would mean leaving their own homelands and would invite clashes with rival clans.

On 24 August, Ayub Khan was informed that a British relief column was approaching and his army decamped.[186] It appeared that Ayub Khan had demanded the irregulars assist in making a final assault, but they had refused. The intelligence about the size of the British force was sufficient to make Ayub Khan believe that he had to fall back to a stronger position. Accordingly, he moved his army onto the ridgeline of the Babi Wali hills, holding the pass there and filling the villages beyond the southern spur of the heights with both regular troops and his irregulars. His strength was estimated at 4,800 regular infantry, 32 guns and 8,000 irregular fighters, certainly a smaller total than he had commanded at Maiwand. Moreover Colonel St John, the British Political Officer at Kandahar, made contact with some of Ayub Khan's factions, and was informed that the Kizilbash and Kohistani elements were eager to desert.[187]

General Roberts, despite having just completed an exhausting march from Kabul, could launch 12,500 men into battle. The Afghans held on to the villages for as long as they could but were ultimately driven out. Some apparently tried 'shutting themselves up in underground chambers and firing upon our men as they passed'.[188] Once the flank was turned, and the British started fighting their way up the slopes of the ridge, even the regular Afghan troops could see that defeat was imminent. The whole line broke up and retreated, and the Afghan guns were abandoned or captured after hand-to-hand fighting. The Afghans were pursued for 15 miles until nightfall, having lost perhaps 1,200 killed and a similar number wounded. British losses were 35 killed. No attempt was made to push on to Herat, and Ayub reached the city with some of his mounted troops some time later. The Afghan irregulars dispersed to their villages, fearing punitive action, while others ran up into the Khakrez Valley.[189] 'All Afghan "armies"', it was said, 'have a power of dispersion which is unrivalled. Organized pursuit against them is almost impossible: unless every mountain path and torrent bed within 50 miles could be searched at once'.[190] In fact, there was no pursuit because the British were preparing for their evacuation and only the Achakzais were subjected to any fines because of their resistance near Kandahar. The Wali of Kandahar was persuaded to resign in the hope that Abdur Rahman Khan would simply take over, but the Amir had not yet consolidated his hold on Kabul and could not spare the resources to move south.[191]

The British victory of 2 September 1880 and relief of the city of Kandahar produced only a temporary setback for Ayub Khan. Although the irregular forces dispersed and Ayub Khan withdrew to Herat without his artillery, he nevertheless reconstituted an army and planned to make a raid on the British supplies being accumulated at Khusk-i Nakhund.[192] Moreover, he still hoped to negotiate his way to power, and he sent two envoys to the British laying claim to Kandahar. The British dismissed the idea and formally made over the city to Abdur Rahman in February 1881.[193] In April, Abdur Rahman's appointed governor, Mohammed Hashin Khan, arrived and received the British handover, but Ayub Khan advanced on Kandahar as soon as the British had left the city, arriving in June 1881. The Durrani Pashtuns welcomed his arrival, recognizing his legitimacy as a son of Sher Ali and the victor of Maiwand. Abdur Rahman, by contrast, was seen as being dependent on the British. Since he possessed a much smaller army he was also perceived as less powerful. However, Abdur Rahman marched on to Kandahar, following Roberts' steps, and engaged Ayub Khan outside the city on 22 September.[194] Abdur Rahman's men were generally better armed and, unlike Ayub Khan's approach to command, the fact that they were led by their Amir personally increased their motivation. At the critical moment, many of Ayub Khan's factions deserted him, and Abdur Rahman won the engagement.[195] Ayub Khan retreated again to Herat, but, despite surviving a revolt by repressive measures, he was eventually driven into exile.[196]

Until the last moment, Roberts had hoped Britain would retain Kandahar, because although Afghanistan was a 'wreck of her former self' he believed 'the warlike preparations carried on by Shere Ali in secret' revealed the Afghans' military potential. Roberts also wanted to keep Kurram and the Khyber Pass and therefore be within striking distance of Kabul. By 1880, after his victory at Kandahar, he felt that only the Khyber Line was viable and that, to hold the pass, local levies would be sufficient.[197] Roberts concluded that 'The less the Afghans see of us the less they will dislike us', and argued that since 'we have nothing to fear from Afghanistan, the best thing to do is to leave it as much as possible to itself'.[198] Abdur Rahman was also eager to keep the British at arm's length, but just as keen to obtain the generous subsidies on offer from the Government of India and the arms and munitions he needed to suppress his internal enemies.

The Afghan Army, 1881–1901

To the Afghan people, Abdur Rahman always argued that his army was organized purely for the defence of Afghanistan against foreign invasion, but in reality the Amir's troops were designed for internal security. Over forty separate disturbances were crushed by the army between 1881 and 1901. It was noticeable that senior officers were selected because they were mediocrities and they were given no training so as to prevent any chance of a *coup d'état*. The British consul at Meshed in 1886 noted: 'The company officers ... seem far superior to the General Officers, for the former do appear to have the instincts of soldiers, but General Officers [are appointed] merely as an act of favour bestowed on any but soldiers; a slave, a surveyor, or a contractor suddenly finds himself raised to the rank of General, and given to the command of an army'.[199] The sons of clan elders, *khanzadas*, were recruited and their promotion accelerated over that of career officers, *peshkhidmat*, in the hope that 'in times of emergency the leading men, having regard for the lives of their relatives, would not venture to rise against him'.[200] To protect the sensibilities of the clans, Abdur Rahman avoided foreign experts or military advisors. His aim was to ensure that the clan hierarchies became synonymous with the Afghan military.

The core of the army consisted of eight regiments, largely volunteers, that had accompanied Abdur Rahman from the north, and he made no attempt to retain the troops that had served Sher Ali.[201] Hazaras and Kizilbashes were also dismissed. Durrani Pashtuns were similarly generally excluded because they had fought for Ayub Khan in 1880–81. Ghilzais made up the bulk of the junior officers and the rank and file. Nevertheless, the outbreak of the Ghilzai revolt in 1886 had necessitated the mobilization of a larger force, particularly when many Ghilzai soldiers deserted, and it was easier to use Durrani Pashtuns, the old rivals of the Ghilzais, than to organize regiments from around the country. Despite the initial surge of recruits, service in the army was not popular amongst the Durrani Pashtuns.[202] The exception was a small corps of royal cavalry, the *Risala-i Shahi Kandahari*, which was drawn from the families of the Mohammedzais, and was retained in order to ensure loyalty.

By the 1890s, the composition of the Afghan army was far more balanced. Areas conquered after unrest were called upon to supply recruits, again to ensure future loyalty and to absorb some of the young men of particularly troublesome communities. The exception was the Hazaras, where only a handful of Besud and Jaghuris were enlisted for reasons of sectarian prejudice which might affect cohesion within the army. Some volunteers from beyond the Durand Line were incorporated, including Khattacks, Waziris and Afridis, and there was an increase in their numbers after the 1897 Pashtun Revolt. The army continued to be deployed with regiments stationed outside their place of origin in order to prevent fraternization with the locals, although intermarriages did occur. All regiments were organized on the *qawm* but it is striking that there was only one purely Pashtun regiment.[203]

In order to increase the size of the army, and make it the 'strongest in Central Asia', Abdur Rahman could neither rely on a purely voluntary system, nor on levying quotas of men from pacified districts. During the Penjdeh Crisis of 1885, when a Russian invasion seemed imminent, he attempted to impose a system of conscription on Herat, the *hasht nafari*, that demanded 15 per cent of all eligible males between fourteen and fifty years old, but the local economy could not function under such manpower demands and the regime could not afford the cost.[204] In 1887, the system was changed to one man in twenty, selected by the local mullahs and elders, while in Kandahar a system of *shasht nefari*, one man in six, was imposed.[205]

By the mid 1890s this system was being used amongst irregular levies as well as for the regular army. In 1894, in Logar, Nangahar and Ghazni, families had each been ordered to supply one man, but the unpopularity of the measure led to a steady emigration from border districts into British India. However, the Amir retained the notion of irregular levies that could be deployed in an emergency and he encouraged Afghan elders to 'keep their young men acquainted with the tactics of war'. The following year, Abdur Rahman introduced a more universal system of *char nafari*, the service of one in four, modified in 1896 to a selective system of *hasht nafari*. The British Government of India supported and funded the military expansion of Afghanistan as the best means by which to deny the country to Russian encroachments and therefore protect British India's landward frontier. In 1883, the regular army stood at 43,000, with a further 3,000 irregulars on a standing basis.[206] By 1890, the regular army totalled 60,000 and may have reached 90,000 by the time of his death.[207] There were around 100 infantry regiments and 24 cavalry regiments stationed around the country. Abdur Rahman, while conscious of the need to counter the threat of foreign invasion, nevertheless used the army to maintain internal security, consolidate his own authority and that of his dynasty. The army was, according to one biographer, 'the high point of his accomplishments'.[208]

The Afghan army was also changed in its role and structure as it expanded. When Abdur Rahman had made his bid to seize the throne with his army from the north, he had under his command a force of infantry and cavalry that fought as guerrillas even though they had a nominal regular army structure. Once in power, however, the army adopted the standard pattern of the period, with *piyada* (infantry) and *sawara* (cavalry) organized in companies, battalions or regiments, brigades and divisions, and the *topkhana* (artillery) in batteries.

The infantry was the largest and cheapest branch of the army. The smallest subdivision was the *paira*, a section of eight men under a *hawaldar*. Although theoretically infantry companies consisted of 100 *sipahis* (soldiers), few reached that strength and consequently the battalion, which should have been made up of six companies, was often less than the established strength of 600 men. That said, in some areas battalions were made up of 1,000 men, depending on local recruiting patterns and the state of the economy. Afghan regiments were identified by clan, city or region, but sometimes adopted a religious title, such as the *Mohammadiyya*, or simply the colour of their uniform, such as the *Zard-posh*. The fact that the troops were responsible for providing their own uniforms and clothes led to great variety in appearance. The only item that differentiated a regular soldier from an irregular was a leather belt issued by the Amir. All regulars were supposed to be armed with the modern Martini-Henry rifle, and irregulars with the Snider, but in reality there was again a great diversity in weaponry.

Afghan cavalry regiments had an established strength of 400 *sowars* divided into four troops and commanded by the *Zir Mishar* (leader of the thousand) or *Karnail* (Colonel).[209] Most units, though, appeared to have 316 in a regiment and 80 in each troop until the expansion of the 1890s when cavalry regiments were established at 600 men each. The horsemen were each armed with a carbine and sword, and, until the 1890s, some of these were still muzzle-loading Enfields. A few carried lances or pistols but, like the infantry, there were a variety of weapons in each troop. *Sowars* seem to have provided their own horses like the *sillidar* system in British India, but there also appear to have been some 30,000 horses of good quality provided by the government while 'Kataghani horses were most prized'.[210] Certainly if a horse was killed in action, the Afghan government would pay for its replacement; but in peacetime the *sowar* was expected to pay half the cost if a horse died, and each horse cost about 100 *kabulis*, although they were half that in Herat.

The efficiency of the cavalry was criticized by British observers. It was noted that Afghan cavalry never did drill and were scattered into small troops across the country to collect taxes rather than prepare for war. Nevertheless, Colonel Yate, the British Consul in Meshed, described Afghan cavalrymen as uncomplaining types and he praised the Kabuli *sowars* as 'the less bigoted and more energetic', noting that they 'learn quickly' and are 'strong, sturdy men as a rule'.[211] Afghan *sowars* could receive additional pay for bravery, or *bahadari*, equivalent to one *kabuli* rupee per month, but the chance of loot far outweighed the meagre pay he could receive every two months from the government. Yate was impressed that most Afghan *sowars* were different from the 'Pathans' enlisted in the British Indian Army: 'An Afghan will eat with anybody and do anything, whereas I have seen frontier Pathans call a native officer to account for sitting down to drink tea with his European officers [since] they are as bigoted in their habits as any Hindu'.[212] However the most serious drawback was that 'they are continually fighting amongst themselves'.

As in the reign of Sher Ali, under Abdur Rahman the artillery was the most prized branch of the Afghan army. To serve them the Amir possessed 860 guns of various types by 1891.[213] It was estimated that there were 5,500 trained gunners, but the quality of that training varied considerably. Some guns were confined to the defence of fortified positions, but of the mobile ordinance there were some machine guns, field guns and light mountain guns. Each of these was drawn by mules, horses or elephants, and there was some attempt at organization into field artillery batteries of six guns, as in the Indian Army.

In addition to the main branches of the army, the royal bodyguard consisted of three infantry battalions and four cavalry regiments, all of whom were better armed, well-fed and paid higher salaries. The *Anduran-i Khas* (the household guard) and the *Hazirbash* (bodyguard of the Amir) were hand-picked *khanzada* men from across the country, including Tajiks and Uzbeks, but with a disproportionate number of Kandahari Mohammedzais, Gardezis and Safis who were considered the most loyal. By contrast the Hazaras, who were regarded as an inferior minority of the country, were formed into pioneer battalions to carry out road building, mining and construction tasks. Despite their status they were constantly at work and therefore considered an efficient element of the army.[214]

The greatest strength of Afghanistan's defences lay in the ability of the irregular forces to maximize their use of difficult terrain to wage a guerrilla war. But to exercise a degree of control over them, Abdur Rahman gave special privileges to loyal *khans* and elders, including refined clothing, allowances or remissions on taxes, and tried to reinforce the sense of obligation to him with a notion of hierarchy within the clans.[215] *Khans* were given military ranks including adjutant, colonel and brigadier, and the numbers holding rank increased throughout Abdur Rahman's reign.[216] In return they were expected to raise a force of mounted levies, to parade these men annually for inspection and to hold arms and ammunition sold to them by the government. Some received payment for retaining a standing force of between three and fifteen light horsemen, the *sawar-i kushada*, which were loyal and could provide the sort of mobility needed to crush an insurrection in its early stages. Titles were sometimes inflated for reasons of prestige for the *khans*, rather than reflecting the actual number of levies under their command. Thus Mohammed Nazar Toqsaba Turkman of Akcha in northern Afghanistan was styled a *mingbashi*, but commanded only 400 men, not 1,000.

In Herat, where there was perceived to be a dual threat of foreign intervention or rebellion, there were some 2,400 permanent border cavalry, the *qarawal khana*, backed by 996 Durrani cavalry, 1,101 Aimaqs, 70 Ghilzais and 657 drawn from the Tajik, Kizilbash and other minorities.[217] There are no records of other areas, although there is reference to Hazara Khans of Dai Kundi and Dai Zangi being permitted to raise between 20 and 40 men each, while in Nangahar, Akbar Khan of Lalpura commanded 500 horsemen to crush the rebellious clans of the region.[218] Most of these forces could be grouped for the purposes of a military expedition or internal security operation, but they were not always supervised by a regular army officer. Personal connections of loyalty were preferred to impersonal chains of command.

Abdur Rahman was eager to embrace the idea of a 'nation in arms' to strengthen the defences of his country.[219] Following the destruction and forced conversion of Kafiristan in 1895, the expansion of the regular army, and the establishment of a system of espionage and surveillance, the Amir felt that there was no threat from internal opponents that could not be contained. However, he was still concerned about threats to the northern territories and the passes of the east.[220] In the north, every third man was supposed to serve as an irregular fighter, and elsewhere it was expected there would be a man in service for every thirty *jeribs* of land.[221] The estimated number of *eljaris* across the country in 1894 was 90,000, but the comprehensive system was dropped in favour of a more selective *hasht nafari*. The sheer expense may have played a part in the decision.[222] To meet the costs of the more modest *hasht nafari*, it was suggested that if one man in eight was picked by the *khans* or elders, then the other seven men should support the selected man while he served in the ranks.[223] The overall effect of the system, which appeared to vary across the country, was to create a cadre of trained men who could act as reservists in the event of a war.

In 1897, when there seemed to be a chance of war with Britain, military cantonments were established and all Afghan men were expected to attend training sessions.[224] Regular officers were also sent all to train villagers in the arts of musketry and some drill. Uniforms and rifles were issued, although as soon as the crisis had passed the practice was stopped. It was claimed that 100,000 reserves could be called upon in an emergency that year, but, as before, the quality of the forces varied and it was unlikely they could hold ground for long. Moreover, suspicions about the government's intent were aroused and there was opposition to the *haft nafari* proposals in Khost and Kunar, which resulted in some elders being imprisoned.[225]

The critical weakness of the Afghan army, both regular and irregular, was the social division between *qawm*, clan and ethnic groups. Skirmishes between regiments made up of rival entities were not uncommon.[226] In episodes of rebellion, soldiers were sometimes enthusiastic in their suppression. However, the Amir tried to create national unity through religion and fear of foreign invasion. He repeatedly emphasized the need for bonds between his rule, the *khans* and the people to withstand the pressures of confrontation and war. Yet there was resentment at the privileges of the Barakzais that were closest to the Amir, even though it was Abdur Rahman who broke up the largest clans of the Barakzai and deported them to the remote north-west and to unproductive lands in the north in a process of 'internal colonization' designed to provide better security against the threat of Russian annexation.[227] The first two attempts at colonization failed, but a third, after 1886, met with greater success. Abdur Rahman was eager to assert a national sentiment amongst the Afghans to override the fracture lines of society in the interests of national strength.[228] A national army held out the hope that this might be possible, but ultimately his regime was held together by coercion and terror. He attempted to establish himself as the sole authority on Islam in the state, punished rebels as enemies of his divinely ordained rule, and crushed armed resistance with a severity that was shocking even by the standards of customary and Islamic law in rural Afghanistan. He revived historic punishments, including the construction of *kalla minar* (towers of skulls) and claimed to have killed no fewer than 120,000 rebels in his reign.[229]

Abdur Rahman tried to emulate the British Indian Army and the Tsarist Russian forces by instilling greater discipline and focusing on loyalty. Officers were professionalized at the lower and middle ranks, and were no longer granted lands as rewards. Attempts were made to keep the troops separate from the civilian population to avoid cordiality or ructions with locals over the misbehaviour of individual soldiers. Soldiers of the 1880s and 1890s were certainly better armed and were just as willing to fight, despite the odds, as they had always been, but in the clashes between the Russians and the Afghan regular army, the Afghans were defeated. Despite the improvements in the army made under Abdur Rahman, and the success the regime enjoyed against large numbers of irregular, internal rebels, Afghanistan could not defend itself against external European adversaries in a conventional mode. This was certainly evident at Penjdeh in 1885.

The Battle of Penjdeh, 1885

In March 1885, a brigade of an estimated 1,200 Afghan troops positioned at Penjdeh, an oasis settlement at the junction of the Murghab and Kushk rivers, was confronted by a Russian force advancing southwards from Merv (Mari) under the command of Colonel Alikhanov, a Daghestani in Russian service.[230] The Russians claimed that the Afghan detachment was stationed beyond the agreed limit of the disputed northern border of Afghanistan, but the Afghans, who took tribute from the local Saryk Turcomans, believed this to be their sovereign territory. They dug trenches along the banks of the Murghab and on a hill feature known as Ak Tepe, threw forward their picquets and refused to let the Russians pass. Chahar Aimak *khassadars* took up their position on Ak Tepe, while 300 irregular horsemen and four light guns were stationed behind the trenches. The Russians reinforced their reconnaissance troops to a strength of 2,000 and General Komarov took command. For several days the Russians probed the Afghans' position and made a show of force with a flanking march.[231] The Russians also made efforts to provoke the Afghans into action, including an insult to the main Afghan negotiator, but the Afghan troops remained resolute.

At 06.40 hrs on 30 March 1885, the Russians sent forward a screen in an 'advance to contact'. There were disputes as to who actually fired the first shot, but in the engagement that followed, the Russians drove off the Afghan cavalry screen and then overran the Afghan trenches. It was reported that the defenders in the entrenchments 'died to a man', but there were eyewitnesses who stated that many of the Afghan troops tried to escape and drowned or froze to death trying to flee across the Murghab river. The Afghans lost 800; the Russians lost only fifty killed and wounded.

The incident caused a major international crisis.[232] Both the Governments of India and London announced that Afghanistan had to be defended against a Russian invasion, and preparations were made for the mobilization of the reserves and the deployment of the Royal Navy against Vladivostok. The Indian Army, already on manoeuvres, also prepared to advance into Afghanistan to hold the passes of the Hindu Kush and to secure Kandahar and Herat.[233] Fortunately, Abdur Rahman decided to concede Penjdeh in order to prevent an Anglo–Russian clash that might devastate his country. He described the loss of Penjdeh as 'less than nothing' in importance, and described the local population as a 'lot of thieving ruffians'.[234] In fact, he may even have been encouraged to make this decision by the Viceroy, Lord Dufferin, who deplored the idea of war over 'some sandhills' in Afghanistan. The British Prime Minister, William Gladstone, and Foreign Secretary, Earl Granville, also privately hoped to avoid an unnecessary and costly war with Russia. The British Boundary Commissioners, which had been present during the dispute, were aware of the unresolved nature of the border line, but they had been more interested in gathering intelligence and ensuring that, wherever the boundary lay, it could provide security against a further Russian advance. Abdur Rahman was simply reassured that the British were prepared to support his territorial claims, and he was awarded 10 *lakhs* of rupees, 20,000 breech-loading rifles, a heavy battery of four guns, two howitzers, a mountain gun battery and plenty of ammunition.

Captain Peacocke and a team of engineers helped the Afghans improve the defences of Herat to prevent a Russian *coup de main*. New bastions were constructed to take field guns, and the entire reconstruction bill was met by the Government of India. A total of thirty-one field guns and fifteen heavy guns were positioned there with provisions, munitions and accommodation for a garrison of 6,000 men. When it became apparent that a cemetery mound, the Talibankiyyan, outside the city walls could provide a platform for enemy artillery, a city meeting was convened to debate whether it could be removed or not. The elders agreed that their security considerations, for the defence of Islam, outweighed the survival of the burial grounds and the mound was levelled, although the *ulema* had to issue a fatwa to prevent rioting against the plan.[235]

Revolts in Afghanistan, 1886–94

Given the numbers of Ghilzais serving in the Afghan army, the revolt of the eastern Pashtuns in 1886 represented a serious threat to Abdur Rahman's rule and further limitations on Afghanistan's military power. The Ghilzai revolt was the culmination of a number of grievances about the imposition of taxation and more direct interference in local governance. Beyond the immediate environs of Kabul, Ghazni and the main roads, Ghilzais had enjoyed almost complete autonomy and had even been exempted from a poll tax in 1881 by Abdur Rahman during his struggle with Ayub Khan. When new measures of centralization were introduced and some of the key leaders who had resisted the British were imprisoned, including Muhammed Jan (Wardak) and Asmatullah (Jabar Khel), the clan elders encouraged their village *jirgas* to revolt. Two leaders emerged in October 1886 to direct operations, Mullah Abdal Karim Andar and Mohammed Shah Hotaki, and they scored victories over the garrisons at Muqur and Ghazni. In the spring of 1887, after a successful winter against the Amir's detachments, great numbers of Ghilzais assembled at Muqur, but there was no money and there were few modern firearms amongst the rebels, and, perhaps more importantly, they could enlist no support outside the Ghilzai districts. The Amir deployed his regular regiments and artillery with some effect, and it is estimated that approximately 30,000 *eljaris* accompanied the troops.[236] Fighting continued throughout the year until the autumn of 1887, and it is striking that irregulars generally preceded the regular army's offensives because of their familiarity with the terrain and because of the prospect of gaining loot. Crucially, the Amir could forge a closer alliance with the Durrani *khans* who had hitherto supported Ayub Khan.

In the repression that followed, the British were shocked at Abdur Rahman's ruthlessness. Sir Mortimer Durand, the Foreign Secretary of the Government of India, wrote: 'The Amir is a troublesome and unsatisfactory ally, and there is no doubt he is thoroughly detested throughout the country. His cruelties are horrible, and one feels reluctant to support him in power, especially as he shows the utmost jealousy of ourselves. If it were not for the fact that his fall would throw everything into disorder and give Russia an opening, I should not be sorry to see him driven out of the country.'[237]

Repressive measures were also used against the Hazaras in 1891–3. Attempts to centralize the administration of the Hazarajat led to corrupt and abusive officials seizing Hazara women, expropriating *qalas*, disarming the menfolk, and imposing new regimes of taxation. Soldiers, who made up part of an occupation force of 10,000, were particularly notorious for raping women and girls. When the population showed signs of armed resistance, the Amir invoked the idea of a sectarian war to garner support from the rest of the country. It is estimated that 100,000 troops and irregulars joined in the repression and individual soldiers were authorized to acquire their own slaves from amongst the defeated Hazaras.[238] Even so, it took three years to extinguish the resistance amongst the mountains and valleys of the region.

The rebellion of Ishaq Khan in August 1888 was the most serious of Abdur Rahman's reign. The rebels of Badakshan were a combination of mutinous troops and disaffected *khans* incited by Ishaq Khan, Abdur Rahman's cousin, but also driven by genuine anger and anxiety about Abdur Rahman's reforms. There were allegations that, having been given 20,000 rupees with which to recruit spies to watch the Russians in Tsarist Central Asia, Ishaq Khan had instead purchased 1,500 rifles to arm his loyal followers. The spark for the rebellion came amidst rumours that Abdur Rahman had died after a prolonged illness. The Hazaras threw in their lot with the rebels, although the population of Bamian remained quiet. Nevertheless, the British newswriter at Kabul warned: 'I do not believe that anyone will side with the Amir'.[239]

Undaunted, Abdur Rahman marched across the Hindu Kush and confronted Ishaq Khan at Tashkurgan. The battle that followed at Gaznigak (27 September 1888) was said to have ebbed and flowed for some time with no decisive result either way, but it is alleged that some of Abdur Rahman's cavalry, who galloped to Ishaq Khan's side in order to desert, terrified the rebel leader and precipitated his retreat. With their leader leaving the field, the rebel army collapsed and fled.[240] However, there is no reference to Ishaq Khan's cowardice in the intelligence reports of the Peshawar Diaries.

Interestingly, at the height of the rebellion, the Amir was so concerned that he requested support from the British, including the temporary military occupation of Kandahar and Jalalabad, and the appointment of a permanent Residency at Kabul. However, once the revolt was over, he dismissed any idea of cooperation. This incident nevertheless reveals Abdur Rahman's strategy and his priorities. He was eager to retain British support and even countenance military intervention in order to secure his power. For all the anti-foreign rhetoric, Afghanistan was still dependent on a foreign empire for its security. This was largely the reason for the Amir's acquiescence in the British terms for the Durand Line, the proposed border between British India and Afghanistan in 1893. Against a background of Russian advances across the Pamirs from 1887, and the defeat of a small detachment at Somatash (1892), the Amir needed the British as his best guarantee against Tsarist forces.[241] However, that did not preclude his own negotiations with General Kaufman, the Russian Governor of Turkestan in the 1880s, in order to ascertain Russian intentions.

Once the Durand Line was established, Abdur Rahman felt he had a free hand to deliver a decisive blow against the pagans of Kafiristan in 1895 that would also enhance his Islamic and dynastic credentials. The campaign, which was popular with the troops, resulted either in the forced conversion of the population of the province or slavery.[242] The Kafirs were divided by language and geography, but the terrain they occupied provided some protection, and for a while their 60,000 fighters, armed mainly with bladed weapons, bows and arrows and a handful of antiquated firearms, were able to offer some resistance to the regular Afghan troops. The campaign nevertheless was concluded with a victory for the Amir.

Indeed, the popularity of the campaign encouraged Abdur Rahman to invoke the defence of Islam as a concept whenever his popularity was jeopardized by coercive policies. This had proved successful during the Penjdeh crisis and was especially important when he exaggerated the idea of a foreign threat in 1887 and 1897.[243] The Amir urged all Afghans to support the concept of *rabat*, the defence of the frontiers of Islam, and this took a literal form when he demanded that men serve as guards in small forts built along the northern border.[244] To retain authority over the Afghan Jihad, Abdur Rahman insisted that only he could authorize mobilization and the defence of the faith. He denounced all other attempts to raise a Jihad, even beyond his own borders, and singled out for condemnation the 'Wahhabis' of British India (known as the Hindustani Fanatics to the British) and Mullah Hadda during the unrest on the frontier in 1897. Every aspect of the Amir's reign, from the expansion of the army, the creation of military ranks in the civil hierarchy, to the invoking of Jihad and the suppression of internal revolts, was driven by a desire to consolidate power. The legacy which this created in terms of an Afghan way of war was to establish a landmark in the transition between a bitterly divided 'feudal' and irregular resistance to a more homogeneous national security system.

4

THE PASHTUN RISING, 1897–8

We know that the general object of the expedition [in 1897] launched by us against the Afridis and the Orakzais was to exact reparation for their unprovoked aggression on the Peshawar–Kohat border, [and] for their attacks on our frontier posts–But that is only *our* view of the matter. We want to get behind this, and ascertain the *Afridi* view. Why did *they*, who had faithfully kept their agreements with us for sixteen long years, why did they rise against us, and commit these outrages? Were they altogether 'unprovoked' as we so confidently assert?[1]

The largest and most serious outbreak of fighting on the North West Frontier during the British colonial era was the 'Pathan Uprising' of 1897–8. The revolt was actually a series of local insurrections involving over 200,000 fighters, including Afghan volunteers, and it required over 59,000 regular troops and 4,000 Imperial Service Troops to deal with it. It was the largest British operational deployment in India since the Mutiny of 1857–8.[2] Its outbreak proved such an unexpected and significant shock to the British that they conducted detailed enquiries after the event. Various explanations were offered, but it was generally accepted that recent encroachments into tribal territory, with fears that the British meant to occupy the region permanently as a prelude to the destruction of Afghan independence and their way of life, led to the initial fighting. There were other contributory factors: a perception that the Amir of Afghanistan, Abdur Rahman Khan, would support an anti-British Jihad; rumours that the Christian Greeks had been defeated by the Muslim Turks and that the Christian world was finally in retreat; and local anxieties about women, money-lenders and road-building.[3] In fact, religious enthusiasm, such as it existed, had arisen from the failure of other forms of resistance and served to relieve the feeling of degradation while revitalizing indigenous culture. Colonel Sir Robert Warburton, the senior Political Officer in the Khyber Pass, recorded his interrogations which seemed at face value to indicate a religious revolt, but on the other hand, the prisoners were understandably keen to blame others:

What made you come down [from the hills to fight]? *The mullahs brought us down.*

Why did you obey the mullahs and not turn them out of your country? *They were too powerful for us.*

Have you any real grievance against the Government to induce you to fight against it? *No, we had not.*

Then why did you attack the posts? *The mullahs forced us.*[4]

This analysis of the causes, whilst important, has not been extended to the actual conduct of operations. Contemporary British accounts of the period tend to narrate and scrutinize British manoeuvres, leaving the Pashtuns as forces either incapable of strategic thinking or reactive to British decisions. Almost universally, however, British accounts remarked on the tactical skill of the Pashtun fighters and their great courage despite severe losses. A few accounts were even prepared to acknowledge that the Pashtuns had adapted their fighting techniques to take advantage of British operational procedures and that a few recent ex-Indian Army Pashtuns had returned to the hills to implement British tactics. Captain Nevill, an analyst of the North West Frontier Campaigns, concluded:

The Afridis are essentially a fighting race; we have little to teach them in the tactics best suited to their conditions of organisation and terrain. It is only in the higher branches of the art of war—the domain of strategy rather than tactics—that they have much to learn. Lack of organisation has always been the keynote of those guerrilla tactics which have baffled again and again the armies of civilised nations.[5]

Causes of the revolt: British Frontier Policy 1890–97

The British were concerned through much of the nineteenth century by the Russian threat towards India.[6] Despite the considerable distances, mountain ranges and deserts between Tsarist Central Asia and the subcontinent, the gradual annexation of the ancient khanates of Turkestan and Trans-Caspia brought the Russians to the borders of Afghanistan. The British were anxious that if the Afghans were also annexed or won over then this would give the

Russians an opportunity to bring to bear their vast land forces at any point on a long continental frontier. Twice in the nineteenth century the British had occupied Afghanistan, but the expeditions proved too costly and were too strongly resisted to be made permanent. Instead, Britain agreed to act as the guarantor of Afghanistan's sovereignty and territorial integrity, and controlled its foreign policy, thus achieving its strategic objectives by other means.

Nevertheless, in 1885 and in 1893, the Russian army clashed with the Afghans and compelled the British to clarify the delineation of Afghanistan's borders. Despite the Amir's reluctance to 'risk losing an arm' by taking responsibility for Wakhan, he was persuaded to accept this outlying district so as to give the British a narrow strip of territory between their own and the Russian possessions.[7] Nevertheless, the Government of India also felt it necessary to establish more influence and control over the strategic parts of the border. Gilgit and Chitral were furnished with listening posts, auxiliary Imperial Service Troops and supervisory British Political Officers.[8] The Khyber Pass and the Kurram Valley also had garrisons made up of local troops, whilst road-building projects were initiated in Waziristan and Dir to make it easier to move troops into any threatened district. These arrangements were part of the Forward Policy, designed to make the tribal areas, which stood astride potential lines of communication into Afghanistan, more secure. Military planners expected to have to race for the Hindu Kush passes inside Afghanistan if war with Russia seemed imminent, and that meant that the vulnerable supply routes had to be secured in advance.[9] The wide tribal belt on the Afghan–British Indian frontier owed little allegiance to either Kabul or Delhi, although historically Afghan monarchs had claimed the area as their own. In 1893 the British therefore negotiated the Durand Line as the definitive border. The Afghan Amir clearly felt that parts of the line, if not the entire boundary, were not in Afghanistan's interests, particularly as it cut away a proportion of Pashtuns at a time when the Pashtun ascendancy was under threat.[10] A number of internal revolts from the 1880s onwards had been suppressed with some difficulty, not least in the north, north-west and central Shia-dominated Hazarajat.[11]

For the British, the construction of the Durand Line was designed to bring to an end the troubles of jurisdiction of the Pashtuns, but there was a multitude of passes and routes across the mountains. The ethnic homogeneity of the Pashtuns astride the 'border' meant that it was a line with no significance to the indigenous peoples. Far from recognizing a boundary, Pashtuns ignored the Durand Line altogether. Consequently when fighting broke out in the 1890s, Pashtuns from the 'Afghan' side took part in the resistance and offered safe havens for those driven off by British troops. Moreover, the consolidation of the British side of the Durand Line provoked a degree of resistance even before the main revolt in 1897. British encroachments had gradually stirred resistance. The construction of fortifications along the Samana ridge created such unrest that General Sir William Lockhart had to form a column to fight its way through Orakzai country in January and February 1891.[12] He was forced to return and drive off an Orakzai *lashkar* that had attacked the Samana ridge posts that spring. British operations to secure the northern provinces of Hunza-Nagar and Chilas in the summer of 1892 (and thus secure routes to the Wakhan Corridor) led to fighting there too. In Waziristan, the construction of a road towards the Afghan border, prior to the formal demarcation, provoked a significant attack by *lashkars* at Wana in November 1894. A punitive column advanced through Mahsud country to suppress them. At Chitral in 1895, a small British force and the Political Agent were besieged after a local succession crisis and had to be relieved by two flying columns, both of which had to fight their way up the valleys through hostile Pashtuns and Chitralis.[13]

The British interpretation of the 'Pathan Revolt' and operations in Tirah, 1897

For the British, the causes of the Pashtun revolt appeared of 1897 at first to be little more than treachery and fanaticism.[14] There was universal acceptance that prominent and fiery mullahs had incited the tribesmen to attack the British, breaking previous agreements with impunity. The rising was initiated by an ambush on a small detachment at Maizar on 10 June 1897. In the engagement the British artillery soon ran out of ammunition and was forced to use blank rounds in the hope that this would deter a pursuit. Ironically, this fulfilled a prediction by the more enthusiastic mullahs: Sartor Faqir of Swat had assured the clansmen that the British shells would turn to stone and their bullets would turn to water the moment they hit the breast of a true believer.[15]

The leading mullahs demanded a Jihad to save the religion and condemned those that appeared to be profiting by association with infidels.[16] The rising appeared to have been premeditated, and the fact that the Bengal Lancers had been playing polo with clansmen until the very afternoon of a major attack at Malakand in Swat seemed to be evidence of a conspiracy. There had, in fact, been rumours of trouble for some time before the outbreak, but anxious messages were so common on the frontier that few paid much attention. The small Tochi Field Force which had set out to punish the initial ambush party met little opposition, which confirmed the idea that no further precautions were necessary. However, at 21.45 hrs on 26 July 1897, a large force of Pashtuns was seen approaching the Malakand Fort at the head of the Swat Valley. It took four days and nights to drive off a succession of attacks by several thousand fighters.

Crucially, attacks were being delivered at night because the Pashtuns dare not risk daylight assaults against the British who were armed with modern breech-loading weapons and entrenched behind prepared positions. 'It is possible', wrote one British officer shortly after, 'the frontier tribes have realized, as well as more civilized races, that rapid firing guns and rifles can best be faced when darkness nullifies aim'.[17] Reviewing the previous sixty years of Pashtun resistance, the same officer noted how rare night assaults had been, even if harassing fire had been typical.

As the British restored control in Malakand and Swat, more Pashtun groups joined the rising. On 26 August the forts of the Khyber Pass were attacked and captured, despite the resistance of some Afridi levies.[18] Ammunition and rifles were seized in large quantities, adding to the considerable arsenal of modern weapons they already possessed.[19] There was an attack on the Samana forts by the Orakzais soon after, and raids towards the Settled Districts by smaller parties.[20] At Sarigarh, a detachment of 36th Sikhs defended their isolated post to the last man, earning a great deal of admiration from British commentators. Against each rising, the British deployed fighting columns, and when they had won their pitched battles, they tried to tempt any guerrilla fighters into open warfare by destroying houses and crops. These methods also served to punish the tribes collectively and had the effect of forcing the Pashtuns into a negotiated peace. However, the Tirah campaign of 1897–8 proved to be one of the most difficult and its results were mixed.[21]

After the campaign, the British were keen to apply the lessons learned and to take steps to ensure more effective frontier security. Lord Curzon, who became Viceroy soon after the unrest, felt that the 'forward policy' of garrisons required modification because it acted as a catalyst for violence and defiance of the imperial authorities, and it simply cost too much. British garrisons were replaced by local militias and the deployment of more Political Officers.

Yet almost all studies of this campaign have focused on the British perspective.[22] To get a more comprehensive picture of the conflict, there is an imperative to recover the 'voice' of the Pashtuns. As already intimated, sources are scarce and fragmentary, but their narrative can to some extent be reconstructed through the records of their actions. The British accounts recorded the

Pashtuns' attacks, their strengths and their movements. They also recorded the comments made by fighters at the conclusion of the campaign. Through an analysis of these records, it is possible to reconstruct, tentatively, something of their tactics and, perhaps, of their intentions. A detailed study of the Tirah campaign, fought by the Afridis and Orakzais, was just one part of the 'Pathan Revolt' but illustrates the wider issues of the conflict and thus offers an opportunity to analyze the nature of the frontier in this crucial period in far greater depth.

The Pashtun Perspective: relative strength and fighting techniques

The Afridis and Orakzais knew from previous encounters with the British that it was impossible to survive an engagement from fixed positions or dense formations against their firepower. Instead they adopted dispersed 'light infantry' tactics, concentrating into larger groups for specific tasks such as an assault on a fortified post. The basic grouping was the *lashkar*, formed of an irregular number (which might range from 30 to 1,000) and based loosely on a particular leader, clan or a group of villages.[23] The clansmen moved great distances carrying the absolute minimum of rations, often at night, so as to appear without warning close to the British columns, or to avoid their pursuits. The British found it difficult to bring the fighters into a decisive battle, and as columns advanced through the mountains, the clansmen would give way in the front so as to bring harassing fire down on the flanks or to shoot at picquets that 'crowed the heights'. Winston Churchill, whilst serving as a lieutenant during the 'Pathan Revolt', noted: 'Great and expensive forces, equipped with all the developments of scientific war, are harried and worried without rest or mercy by an impalpable cloud of active and well armed skirmishers. To enter the mountains and attack an Afridi is to jump into the water to catch a fish'.[24]

Two British officers who analyzed the campaign noted that the tribesmen's tactics were superior to their own emphasis on rigid formations: 'The unusually heavy losses experienced by our troops ... were mostly due to the able manner which the Afridis ... took advantage of the ground and worked in unison ... to assist and support one another, and thus develop their fire so as to obtain the maximum value from it with the minimum exposure and loss to themselves'.[25]

The clansmen also knew that the British forces would be at a disadvantage when trying to withdraw down mountain slopes or from valleys which they had briefly occupied. Having offered merely token resistance to an advancing column, the moment a withdrawal got underway the *lashkars* would intensify their fire and pressure the troops with a close pursuit. Moreover, the Pashtuns liked to be certain of their kills and they would engage in hand-to-hand fighting quite readily. Traditional long knives were favoured in night attacks, and isolated detachments in *sangars* (temporary stone fortifications) were particularly vulnerable. Defiles, forests and other 'close country' made possible the use of surprise rushes of knife-wielding fighters, and this had the added advantage of preventing the British using their fire support or efficient command and control structures. Such was the threat that subsequent British analyses of the campaign in Tirah recommended pushing picquets further out to reduce the casualties from night-time sniping or the sudden charge of swordsmen.[26]

However, of greater concern was the ability of the Pashtun marksmen to pick off the British officers. This fact alone suggests that the Pashtun fighters knew how British assaults and the coordination of their fire were to a large extent dependent on the officers. Killing them was likely to seriously disrupt their ability to bring down effective fire and to manoeuvre. One officer noted that 'Hundreds of these [Pashtuns]–have been in our service, and they not only easily recognise our officers by their conspicuous head-dress and gallant leading, but they well know their value, and undoubtedly they select them for their attentions and pick them off'.[27]

By the 1890s a proportion of fighters had served in the Indian Army, but with their service at an end they had returned to the hills, where they set about training fellow tribesmen in the techniques of fire control and small unit tactics.[28] In addition, as Tim Moreman has indicated, a larger number of modern breech-loading firearms had reached the tribesmen either through theft of Indian Army weapons, from Afghan sources or through gun-runners based in the Persian Gulf.[29] Indeed, this campaign was the first in which British and Indian troops faced tribesmen armed in significant numbers with 'weapons of precision'. The British estimated that about half the fighters were armed with breech-loaders. Yet, even when armed with inferior weapons, the tribesmen were also crack shots. The fact that the Afridis secured 50,000 rounds of ammunition from the Khyber forts also enhanced their capability.

The British felt they had learned valuable lessons from the campaign of 1897–8, but there was some anxiety about the deficiencies exposed in their training and tactical doctrine. What is fascinating from the point of view of this study is the willingness to admit that the Pashtuns often had the upper hand. Major A. C. Yate noted that in the Tirah 'Our best frontier officers and soldiers found themselves foiled and at times worsted by these unorganised guerrillas'.[30] It was evident to British units that frontal attacks, volley-firing and quarter-column advances without the utilization of cover simply invited unnecessary casualties. One officer wrote that the elaborate preparations for volley-firing were easily evaded by the Pashtuns who 'never remained in position long enough for us to go through all the elaborate preliminaries'.[31] A new emphasis on marksmanship and musketry training was also the direct result of the experience of coming under the effective fire of the Pashtuns. The British aimed to bring down a sufficient weight of accurate fire to enable infantry to advance in extended order up mountain sides but still be in a sufficiently coherent body to be able to resist the weight of a sudden charge at close quarters.[32] Again, these precautions indicate something of the Pashtun Afridi tactics. Rather than abandoning every position, the tribesmen may well have calculated that a British or Indian force which was either too spread out or weakened by casualties could be overwhelmed by a counter-attack from dead-ground as they neared the crest of a hill feature. General Sir William Lockhart, the commander of the Tirah Field Force, was praiseworthy of the scouts of the 3rd and 5th Gurkhas because they were able to climb steep slopes, carry out ambushes at night and 'surpass the tribesmen in their own tactics'.[33] The British tended to avoid night operations, in part because of the difficulties in coordination, particularly the cooperation of their fire support assets with large mobile units, but also because it simply invited a surprise attack. The only exception to this was handfuls of picked Gurkhas who operated outside camp perimeters at night to 'hunt' snipers. The Pashtuns learned to keep their distance from these Gurkhas or to operate in larger groups.

Pashtun operations and strategy, 1897–8

The strategy of the Afridis was to clear the British from their lands astride the Khyber Pass and maintain the inviolability of the Tirah Maidan valleys, whilst the Orakzais, further south, aimed to drive the British from the Samana Ridge by destroying the forts there. The initial attack by the Afridis against the forts of the Khyber Pass was far more successful than anticipated and encouraged the Orakzais to commence their own attacks at Samana. A few isolated militia posts were easily engulfed and destroyed. A force of 3,000 tribesmen then sought to eject the Kurram militia from Sadda, but when a larger British force assembled, the tribesmen fell back. The focus therefore shifted to the Samana Ridge. As they advanced eastwards along the Khanki Valley a small British force withdrew, and this bought time for a considerable force of 10,000 clansmen to concentrate below the forts. Undermining the walls while protected by small arms fire, the Sarigarh fortification was overrun. However, the Orakzais, with an Afridi *lashkar* in support, failed to capture or destroy the two most important positions on the ridge, and when British reinforcements arrived with their artillery, the clansmen retreated. In these attacks, the Pashtuns seemed to focus on the symbols of British occupation, but while they had set out to uproot the British, they also intended to delay reinforcements and to concentrate wherever the threat appeared greatest. Despite their fragmented structures, the presence of an Afridi *lashkar* alongside the Orakzais was a significant commitment to inter-clan unity.

Through letters between prominent personalities, intercepted by the British in October, it is clear that the two tribes hoped to be able to count on the support of the Afghans. A delegation was sent to Kabul and, in accordance with protocol, it was treated with great courtesy by the Amir. There is little doubt that Abdur Rahman was concerned about the British insistence on the demarcation of the Durand Line.[34] The border meant that he lost the buffer zone of Pashtuns, some of whom, at least, owed a loose suzerainty to him. In the territories of the Mohmands and Bajauris this was acutely felt. The Amir reasoned that the British, who had twice invaded Afghanistan, might be more prepared to do so again if they had roads and frontier bases close by the border. Internal unrest within Afghanistan might just provide the British with a perfect pretext for intervention. He once expressed his desire to have a 'wall' around his country, suggesting he was keen to keep out the Europeans.[35] Yet the existence of ill-defined borders was actually the most pragmatic solution, because it made possible raids by the Afghan forces against peripheral communities on which the impoverished government sometimes depended. There was also the question of prestige. When challenged as to why he wanted to retain part of Waziristan during the border negotiations, he stated it was a question of *nang*: 'In cutting away from me these frontier tribes who are people of my nationality and religion, you will injure my prestige in the eyes of my subjects and will make me weak, and my weakness is injurious to your government'.[36] When the Amir was pressed by the British government to resist all entreaties by the Russians, he replied that it was little use being reminded of what his enemies might take when his 'friends' had already taken so much more.

To strengthen his domestic position, Abdur Rahman claimed to be *Zia-ul-Millat wa-ud-Din* (Light of Union and Faith) and the King of Islam, that is, of all the Muslims in his realm.[37] Although the British interpreted this as a sign that he was secretly fomenting unrest on the frontier, it was in fact a means to delegitimise any potential rebel. He was in effect saying that a rebellion against him would constitute a rebellion against the faith itself. In the same vein, Abdur Rahman produced a book, the *Taqwin-ud-Din*, which dealt with the central role of Jihad in Islam. At a series of meetings attended by frontier *fakirs* and *imams* alongside Afghan *ulema*, there were a number of anti-British tirades. These did not go unnoticed in India, but, as Sir Mortimer Durand noted, the Amir was known to invent a 'foreign threat' periodically to bolster his popularity. In 1887 Abdur Rahman had issued a *firman* exhorting Afghans to prepare to resist an invasion by infidels. Since the British harboured no such plans, Durand concluded it was a device to distract the people from a revolt by Ghilzais.[38]

Soon after the tribesmen had declared their war on the British in 1897, Abdur Rahman gave a deliberately ambiguous response: he had to be sure that he did not lose face in the eyes of his own people and he dare not publicly disown the call for support from Muslims in distress. Initially he told the tribal representatives, 'You should wait a few days, so that I may hold a consultation—and decide what steps should be taken. I will then either come myself or send you my son for Jihad with our victorious troops', but later he admonished the tribesmen and ordered them to settle their differences with the British, claiming he had made agreements he could not break.[39] His chief criticism was that the tribes had not informed him of their intentions before the outbreak of violence.[40] He also tried to prevent, where he could, Afghans joining the revolt, but, with such a porous 'border', this was really impossible.[41]

For the frontier tribes, however, great significance was placed on this apparent Afghan backing. A meeting of a *jirga* took place at the Musjid at Bagh, just 3 miles west of the Tirah Maiden, a spot which, according to one British officer, 'has always been known as a centre of intrigue and fanaticism'.[42] It appears that in June 1897, 130 mullahs from Tirah had attended a *jirga* convened by Hadda Mullah in Afghanistan where he had preached a vehemently anti-British sermon.[43] Once the revolt had begun in Swat and Mohmand territory, Hadda Mullah's *murids* (acolytes) moved through the mountains urging the Pashtuns to join the Jihad. The *murids* offered to end all clan feuds in order to facilitate this greater calling.[44]

Amongst the items the British later recovered were letters between the Pashtun leaders, including those as far afield as Malakand. The correspondence revealed that the Pashtuns had lobbied the Amir of Afghanistan for support because the British were 'day by day violating the former agreements,–forcibly encroaching upon our limits, [and] realising fines–from us for the arms stolen in the Khyber by their own servants [namely militia personnel in the Indian Army]'.[45] The letters stated that the Amir had promised to try to 'make peace between us and the British government'. The letters also indicated that Sayyid Akbar of the Aka Khels was a leading advocate of resistance and invoked the obligation of Jihad to mobilize his peers. Subsequent interviews with tribesmen revealed that they were also concerned about an increase in the salt tax and the refuge accorded to Pashtun women who fled the tribal areas to the British authorities in the Settled Districts. The Adam Khels and Jowakis were the most enthusiastic, but some Orakzais joined in more reluctantly. The 8,000 Zaimusht chose to remain outside the 1897 revolt altogether.[46] The fragmented nature of Pashtun society was a weakness the British would try and exploit, but it also created the more immediate problem of reducing the number of fighters available for the revolt. Out of the potential 50,000 men, there may have been fewer than 35,000 available. To make matters worse, after the initial attacks in August and early September many of the tribesmen unilaterally demobilized to bring in their crops.[47] Indeed there seems to have been a rapid waning in enthusiasm for any Jihad.[48] However, small-scale raiding was constant throughout September, particularly in the direction of Kohat.[49]

The failure to obtain Afghan support did not preclude Pashtuns taking refuge across the 'border', and offered a degree of 'strategic depth' in the guerrilla campaign. The strategic problem was that, although the tribesmen could operate on 'interior lines' in Tirah, they could not be sure which way a British force might come. A large number of Afridi tribesmen had to be retained in and around the Khyber Pass, which seemed the most obvious target for any British counter-offensive. It was also possible the British might advance due west from Kohat along the Khanki Valley or up the Mastura River from Peshawar. The final route was in fact the one that the British opted for, from the south across the Samana Range and then across the grain of the mountains towards the Tirah Maidan. There was nevertheless great faith amongst the tribesmen in the natural defences of the landscape. The Sampagha Pass above the Khanki Valley was a formidable obstacle in itself, but much of the region consisted of narrow defiles and mountainous terrain, where hard cover and concealment for dispersed defenders made it ideal for ambushes or fighting from prepared and entrenched positions.

In fact, the tribesmen appear to have believed, with fighting going on elsewhere across the frontier, that they may have in fact already won their campaign and no further precautions were necessary. They had achieved their objectives of taking the Khyber and had prevented any offensive action by the

British in the south. For eight weeks there was little sign of any British counter-attack, and the harvest had been gathered in without any hindrance. The British delay had in fact been caused by the difficulty in acquiring sufficient transport and troops for the campaign (some 20,000 ponies and mules, and 13,000 camels were required). When Indian pioneers appeared near Shinwari fort (south of the Samana Ridge), the tribesmen convened another *jirga* at Bagh. It seems that several leading spokesmen urged resistance, claiming that any attempt to conclude a separate peace would constitute a betrayal of Islam. Oaths were apparently sworn over the Qur'an. Nevertheless, an Orakzai delegation from the Kanki Valley tried to offer their submission to General Yeatman Biggs soon after. His refusal to accept their offer because of the raiding going on at the time compelled them to join the revolt.[50] British track-building parties were therefore soon under long-range fire, and there was evidence that *sangars* were being built along the Sempagha Pass from October 1897. Observation parties were despatched to all the valleys by which the British might come. The objective was clear: to keep the British at bay.

The British road-building activity south of the Samana Ridge had indicated to the Pashtuns the axis and the likely date of an offensive so that despite 'great secrecy in issuing orders', a number of tribesmen had gathered at Dargai to contest the advance. According to one British officer, the natural defile at Dargai not only made a defensive stance far easier, it also afforded 'excellent cover, naturally provided by the rocks and improved by walls, etc, built up by [the tribesmen]'. Light artillery could make no impression on the *sangars*, and there was a steep climb to the tribesmen's positions. It took the leading British and Indian troops six hours to reach the point where an assault could be made. The Pashtun riflemen put down some fire but gave way as soon as the British began to close on them, and they were prompted to retreat as soon as they came under fire from a flanking force under General Kempster. On the approach march and in the frontal assault across an exposed area barely 200 yards wide, the British lost nineteen killed and wounded; Pashtun losses were unknown.

The British decided that they could not retain this high mountain-top position because of a lack of water and manpower, and consequently the troops began to withdraw soon after 14.00. There was a great deal of controversy about this decision, not least because it became necessary to retake the Dargai heights just a few days later at a much greater cost in lives. However, in this debate, there was little thought given to the Pashtun perspective. The sound of the artillery fire at Dargai from 09.20 drew Orakzais and Afridis from the Khanki Valley, and they began to concentrate on the northern slopes, with a strength estimated at 12,000. Colonel Charles Callwell noted: 'As the afternoon proceeded, the enemy began to gather in great strength to the north of Dargai. Swarms of tribesmen were observed streaming up out of the Khanki Valley to participate in the fray'.[51] The original defenders also returned to their positions and began a cautious pursuit for 2 miles. Using firepower rather than trying to come to grips with the British, they focused on shooting down the men exposed on the hillsides below them, inflicting a further eighteen casualties. By nightfall the Pashtuns had regained all their defences and, from their point of view, had successfully driven off the British column.

It must have been evident to them that, if the British attempted a second attack on Dargai, it made sense to try to concentrate as much fire as possible on the narrow frontage they would have to take. They must also have reasoned, as their deployments subsequently suggest, that they had to avoid being outflanked. Tribesmen were pushed westwards along the ridge and also covered the spurs leading from the British forts on the Samana. General Lockhart, the commander of the British forces, originally considered bypassing Dargai, but these new dispositions indicated that any attempt to pass beneath Dargai to the west (below either the Chagru Kotal or Saran Suk) would simply invite a fusillade against his flank and possibly expose his column to a large attack.[52] General Kempster was thus compelled to make a second assault on the Dargai Heights.

The British account of the battle that followed has been well documented in a number of contemporary and subsequent works. There is little doubt that the British and Indian troops who took part were courageous, disciplined and determined, sustaining very heavy losses whilst continuing to press on into the Pashtun position, but there are almost no analyses of the tribesmen's actions. First, and most importantly, the new Pashtun deployments had compelled Lockhart to change his plan to bypass Dargai. Second, the tribesmen knew that the British were coming and what route they would take. The ground had been carefully selected and channelled them into a specific killing zone. Almost all the British casualties occurred in one small area that could be swept by small-arms fire. The tribesmen opened a long-range fire at about 09.30, but it was not until 11.00 that the first wave of Gurkhas was in a position to assault the heights. As they tried to cross in small groups, 'each clump of men that dashed forward melted away under the converging and accurate fire, and after a time affairs practically came to standstill'.[53] The British attack was completely held up, the baggage was at a standstill and there were concerns that 'a check at this early stage might have disastrous results'.[54] The Gurkhas were pinned down for three hours and two other British regiments fared little better. A fresh wave of two regiments nevertheless carried the whole mass forward. Interestingly, when the British made the final ascent, they found that the tribesmen had already abandoned the *sangars* along the crest. Large numbers of them were seen retreating down into the Khanki Valley. Several explanations were offered for this, including the effect of artillery and the psychological effect of the sudden rush of the Gordons and Sikhs. However, it seems clear that, whilst these contributed to the Pashtun decision to fall back, their lack of ammunition also had a part to play. The tribesmen had commenced firing at 09.30 and had held the Gurkhas, Dorsets and Derbyshires under sustained fire between 11.30 and 15.00. The Gordons and Sikhs' final assault went in just after 15.00. It is quite conceivable that the weight of fire was beginning to slacken at this point for want of ammunition. The British had suffered 200 casualties, and, whilst the tribesmen were forced to abandon the Dargai position at the end, they could claim satisfaction at their achievements if not outright victory. The British force had been held up, they had managed to escape with their own forces largely intact and they had carried away most of their own dead and wounded.

The British established their first camp in the Khanki Valley at Khangarbur on a plateau, having cleared a village of Afridi marksmen with artillery fire. After two days of accumulating supplies (caused by the absence of sufficient transport animals and the difficult terrain), the British were aware that they were in danger of losing momentum. Colonel Hutchinson regretted that in the eyes of the tribesmen the delay would be put down to 'hesitation and fear, and, in proportion to the timidity which we (in their estimation) display, do[es] their own courage and confidence increase, and their numbers too'.[55] The Afridi tribesmen used the opportunity to improve the defences of the Sampagha Pass with 'sangars to command all likely approaches, [while] digging trenches and rifle pits'.[56] Former sappers of the Indian Army who had rejoined their tribesmen at the end of their service were said to be prominent in directing the engineering.[57]

It was estimated that up to 12,000 tribesmen had concentrated from the various valleys to confront the single British column. On 23 October, foraging parties were attacked by large numbers of tribesmen and a series of small attacks were mounted against the British camp. All the hilltop picquets came under fire between dusk and midnight. Pashtun casualties were found within 30 yards of the camp's perimeter. However, there was not a concerted attempt to overrun the camp, as had been attempted at Wana three years before by the Waziris, and it is likely that the Pashtuns were more interested in raiding to acquire rifles, trophies and loot from the extensive lines of baggage.

There was then a relatively quiet day perhaps for Jirgas and then a more determined attempt to destroy foraging parties that were detached from the main
body. Each of these parties had to be protected by strong escorts of infantry
and some mountain guns. Even so, as they withdrew, they came under the fire
of tribesmen who pursued them closely. Ambushes were frequent. One favoured
tactic was to wait until the British crested a ridge where they were thus silhouetted against the skyline. A single volley from the tribesmen at 1,000 yards had
the effect of 'invariably knocking someone over'.[58] One of the greatest hazards
for British forces, though, was sniping into the camp after dark. Casualties
could amount to twenty every night, and the steady attrition caused significant problems, not least in the morale of the camp followers. Security of plans
was also a challenge. The presence of so many camp followers, and the fact that
a number were Pashtuns from the Peshawar and Kohat areas, must have created opportunities for the tribesmen, just as it did for the British who wished
to gather more intelligence on the defences at Sampagha. A party of five Afridis who tendered their surrender on 24 October, for example, were treated
with great suspicion despite the fact that all had previously served in the Indian
Army. It seemed unlikely that the tribesmen would have let them reach the
camp unmolested, and they may have been planning to rejoin their fellow
tribesmen having reconnoitred the British forces.

The British advanced towards the Sampagha Pass, hoping that the Pashtuns
would attempt a stand like that of the Orakzais at Dargai, simply because they
wanted to bring them to battle and inflict a decisive defeat rather than having
to endure the steady sniping and guerrilla attacks. At Gundaki, the British surprised the tribesmen by a sudden movement at dawn, and the snipers who were
still sleeping after a night of shooting were almost captured. In fact, the tribesmen had a routine for their sniping: they would observe the British camp and
its picquets or sentry posts closely before dusk so as to have a clear idea of the
targets to engage that night. Shooting went on between dusk and midnight,
and the tribesmen generally retired after that time, but resumed their fire after
daybreak.

As the British advanced towards the Sampagha, there was almost no opposition because the ground did not lend itself to defence. Wide valley floors and
low hills did not afford much protection. At Sampagha itself, it was soon clear
that the tribesmen did not wish to fight there either. As early as 07.00, the
clansmen began to abandon their forward positions and few had much appetite to endure the concentrated shellfire of thirty-six mountain guns and four
hours of bombardment. Although it was estimated that twelve standards had

been seen, it likely that a token force held the pass itself. About twenty clansmen held a *sangar* in the centre of the position, but after being shelled for twenty minutes they ran back over the pass, and it seems that a good many fighters were in fact herding their flocks, shepherding their families into the hills or burying their grain to the north.

It was a similar story at the Arhanga Pass, with British artillery driving off a token defence force that was estimated at no more than 1,000.[59] Whilst Lockhart had achieved his objective of penetrating into the heart of the Tirah Maidan, which had long been considered inviolate by the Afridis, there must have been some unease that they had been deprived of their decisive battle. The villages and compounds they marched past were deserted, although the haste of their departure was evident in the sheer volume of grain, walnuts and potatoes that had been left behind. The Pashtuns had dispersed into the hills and side valleys.

The clansmen were not inactive though. On two successive nights the Zakka Khel Afridis raided the baggage columns that had been overtaken by darkness before they reached the British camp. Several soldiers and drivers were killed and 11,000 rounds of rifle ammunition were seized as well as other military equipment. The raids had a disproportionate and negative effect on the morale of the baggage personnel. The Pashtuns regarded the British as raiders too. The foraging parties that went out every day into the villages of the Tirah Maidan recovered great quantities of food, such that each man of the invasion force could be provided with two full days' rations from just one small area. A few other souvenirs were taken: *jezails*, swords, daggers and handwritten Qur'ans were much prized. Bagh was of particular interest. The Musjid was left untouched but searches revealed letters between Pashtun tribal leaders and the Afghan Amir. Elsewhere General Lockhart selected the targets for his operations carefully. Where there was resistance, houses from which fighters had fired were burned down and towers were dynamited or shelled. However, on the whole, he refrained from wholesale destruction. Tribal elders were summoned to hear the terms that Lockhart would offer for their surrender, but there was little appreciable difference to the amount of fighting taking place every day. Sniping into the British camp occurred each night, and there were two incidents where British forces that were withdrawing got into difficulties and sustained significant casualties.

Over a period of ten days, while the British paused to await the outcome of the *jirgas*' deliberations and bring in their fines, every forage party was fired upon. The telegraph wire, which extended back over the passes, was cut every night and 'a mile or two of it carried off'. The Pashtuns knew that these communications were important to the British for both logistical and operational decisions, and they also knew that parties who came to fix the line could be attacked. Foraging parties were frequently surprised and occasionally knife-wielding attackers attempted to get into hand-to-hand combat. Yet it was perhaps the now constant sniping that had the most demoralizing effect. Nor were these random single shots: Pashtun marksmen would crawl into position below the picquets in groups of three or four using the natural folds in the ground and '"brown" the camp with forty or fifty shots before they [could] be dislodged'.[60] Casualties began to mount steadily with one or two killed or wounded each day.[61]

It was during this period that the British observed small groups of tribesmen carrying away the grain and stores from buildings within a few miles of the British camp. This may indicate that the tribesmen were short of supplies in the hills, as they tended to carry very little with them when fighting. Certainly letters the British intercepted earlier in the year mentioned that they were 'waiting for the summer to pass as common folk cannot afford to arrange for the necessities of Jihad. It is difficult for them to fight in summer'.[62] It made sense that they should recover the food they had buried as they needed it. To forestall the effort, the British mounted an operation on 9 November 1897 to the Saran Sar, a feature that stood amidst the Zaka Khel country where they intended to destroy houses and towers and thus induce surrender. The advance was barely opposed but, as the troops turned to withdraw at 14.00 hours, the Pashtuns 'appeared as if by magic'. They pressed hard on the heels of the British units causing 'at once many casualties'. The need to retrieve the wounded and the dead, to avoid mutilation of the bodies, encumbered the soldiers and meant they had difficulty in maintaining effective fire during the withdrawal. A company of Northamptons tried to pull back through a defile with their casualties but were attacked from above and suffered severe losses.[63] The survivors formed a small defensive ring in some buildings and spent the night there. The Afridis, having taken advantage of the British in the defile, decided not to try to pursue the British any further in case the small garrison was reinforced from the camp nearby.

On 12 November, after a lull in fighting for three days, representatives of the Orakzais were brought to the camp. It is noticeable that those who arrived were all 'graybeards'. Whilst these men accepted the fines and submission of rifles as compensation in principle, the speed at which these could be arranged would be slow. The elders were probably concerned that the British might be tempted to stay for good, or at least prolong their 'pacification' measures and destroy more crops and property, but their faces were inscrutable as they listened to the British terms. The lull in fighting nevertheless suggests that there was some unanimity about seeing an early British withdrawal. Curiously, they asked the British Political Officers to assist them in apportioning the fines across each of the clans and sections because, they said, they would 'quarrel' if left to themselves. General Lockhart immediately put an end to the destruction of property of the Orakzais and even decreed that the British would pay for any supplies they subsequently requisitioned. Nevertheless fighting continued, particularly as almost all of the Afridis were still defiant. The Afridis may have been hoping that, as the British supply situation became more acute and the winter weather threatened their already attenuated lines of communication, they could hold out.[64] The British therefore continued their punitive measures against the Afridis, destroying their houses, including that of Mullah Sayid Akbar, Aka Khel, whom they assumed was the 'leader' of the revolt. As usual, the Afridis carried out night-time sniping, and, whilst giving way before any advance, pursued any party that was withdrawing.

When General Kempster attempted to withdraw his brigade from the Waran Valley on 16 November 1897, the Afridis attacked the rearguard in large numbers. Once again, wounded men delayed the withdrawal and the Afridis tried to work around the flanks of the British force as it neared a pass. Wooded and precipitous country provided a screen for this movement, which brought them to within a few hundred yards of the 15th Sikhs. Having already inflicted a number of casualties with rifle fire throughout the afternoon, some of the clansmen were eager to close with the Indian troops in hand-to-hand fighting. However, as they emerged from the woods, the Sikhs formed a skirmish line and opened fire at close range. The effect was devastating, and later estimates claimed that 200 fighters were shot down in a few minutes.[65] Yet this did not deter the Afridis at all. As the troops began to run low on ammunition and darkness gathered, they found that a group of clansmen had again worked around their flank and positioned themselves in a cluster of small burnt-out buildings directly on their line of withdrawal. The British charged them and bayoneted or shot the clansmen and then established a hasty defensive perimeter. One half company was isolated by a *nullah* some 400 yards away, and it was clear that the Afridis meant to occupy it so as to enfilade the defenders of the main position. As they swept out of the cover of the *nullah*, they were surprised to find it occupied already and were forced to pull back. After that, the Afridis made no attempt to try to rush the defenders, who were in most cases protected by low walls or embankments. Such an attack, even at night, would have been costly. Instead, they fired into the buildings until 23.00 hrs, hurled threats at the Pashtun servant of one of the British officers, and then drew off.[66] However, they were satisfied that, for a second time, they had also managed to ambush a British half company in a ravine. A party of Dorsets had mistakenly marched into the defile in the darkness, and when attacked they had formed small groups.[67] Here the fighting was at close quarters and eleven officers and soldiers were killed. The number of casualties amongst the clansmen was unknown since they recovered all their dead and wounded before dawn.

After the incident, General Lockhart consoled his men by reminding them they were 'opposed to perhaps the best skirmishers and the best natural shots in the world, and the country they inhabit is the most difficult on the face of the globe'.[68] Colonel Hutchinson wrote that in the daily skirmishes and rearguard actions, 'the tribesmen have often got the best of it'.[69] He noted that the Zaka-Khels have 'held their own against us with quite a fair measure of success' and they continued to influence other tribal groups such as the Kuki-Khels. In terms of casualties, he estimated that 'it will not be very much in our favour'. He continued: 'And when we consider, in addition, the rifles and ammunition we have lost, the baggage that has been raided, and the transport animals that have been carried off, then it becomes obvious, and outside argument, that we are at a great disadvantage compared with our savage foe'.[70] Lieutenant Cowie of the Dorsets echoed the frustrations of many officers and men with having to remain stationary and wait for a submission of surrender by the clans when it was clear that, by their actions, they did not consider themselves defeated at all.[71] Lockhart and other authors claimed that the British had demonstrated their ability to penetrate every part of the Tirah with impunity and they possessed the means to destroy the very fabric of the Pashtun agrarian economy.[72] However, from a Pashtun perspective, some felt the occupation, whilst irksome, could be contested and that they were honour-bound to sustain the resistance as long as the British remained there.

However, the fragmented nature of Pashtun society was beginning to have an effect. On 21 November 1897, the *jirgas* of the Malikdin Khel, Kambar-Khel, Adam-Khel and the Aka-Khel offered to accept the British terms, namely a fine, the restitution of property, the surrender of 800 rifles and a formal act of submission. Interestingly, the British Political Officers also used the opportunity to dispel the rumours which they felt had given rise to the unrest and to interrogate the clansmen as to the reasons for the revolt. The tribesmen took the opportunity of blaming the mullahs, and this seemed to corroborate the idea of a conspiracy in the letters discovered in the house of Mullah Sayid Akbar. Sir Robert Warburton, an experienced Political Officer who later wrote about the 'Pathan Revolt', pointed to 'the fifteen hundred mullahs from Ningrahar'.[73] However, Robert Bruce, another frontier Political Officer, rejected the idea of conspiracy and suggested that the interrogations revealed local grievances had been more important.[74] The British were apt to see the determination of the resistance and the self-sacrificial nature of the fighters as evidence of 'fanaticism', but their millenarianism was in fact an impassioned reaction to the changes they could see taking place around them as the British advanced into their territory, or eroded their traditional way of life.[75]

On 22 November, Lockhart set out to punish the Kuki-Khels and marched into their valley of Dwatoi. Again, the chief problem was sniping. The tribesmen clung to the high ground and withdrew if troops came too close. At night, they were able to fire into the British camp, and there were attacks on survey parties and against any formations that were withdrawing. Unusually, on one occasion the British prevented the tribesmen from carrying away their dead and even captured some of their weapons. Then, there were further British successes. A party of 1st Gurkhas ambushed a group of Afridis who were lying in wait for a convoy near Unai. Five days later, a relief force cornered a group of over 200 tribesmen and inflicted severe losses on them. Despite the defiant written response of the Massozais in the upper Khanki Valley, they capitulated readily when a British column arrived in their lands. The only stubborn resistance was offered by a group that held a *sangar* on a ridge above the valley, who refused to withdraw and were killed during an infantry assault by the Queen's Regiment. Why these men chose to stay and perish, rather than fight as guerrillas, has not been ascertained, but it seems possible that they had chosen to die in the defence of their tribal homeland with the certainty of becoming martyrs. The Chamkanis, at the westernmost edge of the region and situated at the northern head of the Kurram Valley, also refused to surrender. They fought from ridgeline to ridgeline, pursued by the Gurkhas, until their leaders, Mirak Shah (Malik of the Khani Khels), Mahmud and Saidu, were killed. The clansmen's fortifications at Thabi were destroyed and the Gurkhas withdrew without opposition. The collapse of resistance here suggests that local leadership was important.

The onset of bad weather indicated that the Tirah Field Force would have to withdraw, but it was decided they would march through the Bara and Waran Valleys in order to force the Zaka-Khels, the last group to defy Lockhart, to surrender or face a wave of destruction. It was hoped that the Zaka-Khels would not risk having their lands laid waste so close to winter, but since the valleys were largely abandoned in the winter months in favour of lower pastures anyway, these expectations seem unrealistic. In the first week of December, the British began their descent in separate divisions, but the Afridis pressed the rearguards and flanks of the 2nd Division in the Bara Valley harder each day. Clearly they believed that the British were now retreating, and unlikely to make a significant counter-attack. For the Pashtuns, who had often given way before each attack and then pursued the British, this was the opportunity they had been waiting for to inflict as many casualties as possible and avenge their losses. The cold weather and the fact that the column in the Bara Valley had constantly to cross and re-cross the frozen river had a detrimental effect on morale. Colonel Hutchinson noted that the camp followers suffered the most: 'many unhappy followers, frozen by the cold, and terrified by the bullets whistling overhead, collapsed and died by the way, in spite of the efforts of the escorts to keep them all together, and bring them safely along'.[76] The transport animals, which had not been in the best of health before the expedition and which had been worked hard for weeks, also let the British down. The snail's pace of their movement meant that the rearguard was under greater pressure to hold on longer than they would have wished. Wounded men had to be carried by their comrades from the firing line because the *Dhoolie* (stretcher) bearers were exhausted. 'The wretched *kahars*', wrote Hutchinson, 'hardly able to carry the *dhoolies* when empty, seemed quite unable to bear them when loaded with the weight of a wounded man'.[77] The troops were tired by constant fighting. On 11 December, the Gordons, for example, were in action continuously from dawn until well after dark. The rearguard of 350 men under Major Downman was cut off and had to be relieved by two battalions and a battery of guns the following morning. They had suffered fifty casualties. The bad weather and temporary loss of the rearguard had caused the death of an unspecified number of followers, along with stores and baggage animals. The withdrawal was proving far more difficult than anticipated.[78]

Heavy rain, sleet and the first dusting of snow added to the misery of the troops. As they established their picquets up to a mile on either side of the main column, they had to fight for each position. The clansmen would watch them throwing up *sangars*, and then build some of their own in order to shoot at them through the night. An officer of the King's Own Scottish Borderers related how the Pashtuns grew more confident and tried to rush some of these posts in the dark.[79] When this failed, tribesmen would engage the soldiers at close range, shout abuse and even throw rocks into their positions. These seem to have been an attempt to induce the soldiers to show themselves. Another tactic was to crawl up to a sentry and, as he lunged over his parapet to bayonet the assailant, a pre-positioned marksman would shoot the soldier. The camp established every night was also under constant rifle fire, and the tribesmen hoped there would be more opportunities to acquire some of the baggage, rifles and stores. Every clan of the Afridis was, it seems, represented, and only a sustained barrage by mountain guns forced the tribesmen to break off their attack. Nevertheless sniping continued from a range of 2,000 yards into the camp. On 13 December, after a halt to reorganize, the withdrawal recommenced and almost immediately the Afridis made a series of attacks. The clansmen kept up by running parallel to the British axis and sought the most favourable positions from which to skirmish. The flanks and rear were always under pressure, and, while the British estimated that the Pashtuns had lost 300, their own casualties that day were about seventy-six, not including camp followers and drivers. The baggage train became an 'uncontrollable mass' and the fighting was at such close quarters that medical officers marching alongside the wounded 'became combatants in hand-to-hand struggles'.[80] Two days later, the British column reached the edge of tribal territory and the harassment died away abruptly.

Ironically, the other division made its way out of the mountains virtually unopposed, suggesting that the Afridis had made a conscious decision to concentrate their forces in one place. This seems to be confirmed by the fact that the British also sent a column to re-enter the Khyber Pass and for some days it was barely opposed at all. When two brigades entered the Bazar Valley, they were nevertheless engaged in constant fighting, the greatest resistance being offered to troops as they withdrew.[81] By 30 December, troops in the Khyber were under attack and a picquet of the Oxfordshire Light Infantry was badly mauled as it tried to withdraw at the end of the day's observation. The growing threat, with clansmen now clearly being diverted from the Bara Valley area, forced General Lockhart to send another brigade to the Khyber Pass. On 29 January, a force at Bara, which had set out to intercept the clansmen who were sheltering a large number of their animals in a hidden valley, failed to trap their prey. Instead, as they withdrew, they were subjected to an attack by several hundred Afridis.[82] The premature withdrawal of a picquet allowed the tribesmen to gain a vantage point and the position had to be retaken by the King's Own Yorkshire Light Infantry. However, as soon as they regained the high ground, they found themselves overlooked by another ridge and were subjected to an increasingly intense fire from a range of 150 yards. With a number of the new picquet party wounded, it was impossible for them to pull back and they had to hold their ground, suffering more losses, whilst reinforcements were summoned. This incident indicates that, throughout the winter, the Afridis remained defiant and in possession of their own territory. Indeed, 'desultory and indecisive fighting continued as before–the two most recalcitrant maliks, Khwas Khan and Wali Muhammed Khan, from the safe haven of Afghanistan, [that is, within the Pashtun tribal belt beyond the British 'Line'], exhorting [the clansmen] to stand firm and to continue to resist'.[83]

The British later explained the subsequent offer to submit to terms as evidence that the tribesmen were afraid of 'another invasion in the spring'.[84] It was claimed they had suffered 'a blow to their prestige, material losses and hardships'. Yet, from a Pashtun perspective, there was no obvious loss of prestige. They had inflicted considerable losses on the British and exchanged blow for blow in a manner that would accrue them honour and credit. Individuals who had survived the campaign would have been recognized as having demonstrated courage in defence of their lands, peoples and religion. Physical destruction could be repaired. Crops and livestock could be replaced. The chance of another invasion was, to be sure, a concern to be taken seriously, but the Pashtuns would no doubt have assumed that, if they negotiated at the end of the winter, they were doing so from a position of strength. By April, all the tribes had come in to submit to the British terms.[85]

The sense that the Pashtuns had actually enjoyed the campaign because it had offered them a chance to enhance their honour was confirmed by a bizarre epilogue to the Tirah Campaign. When General Lockhart set off to leave India in April 1898, a crowd of 500 Afridis including Zaka-Khels mobbed him with cheers and insisted on pulling his carriage to the station. Some vowed to fight alongside the British in the future and promised eternal friendship. To the Pashtuns, this campaign had not been a British victory but a draw, and, more importantly, honour had been preserved for both sides. One officer noted that, during the months immediately succeeding the close of the campaign, 'enlistment of Pathans, and especially of Afridis, into the regiments of the Indian Army, had never been brisker'.[86] If the Afridis wanted British pay, then the British certainly wanted the Afridis in their ranks. The India Office concurred with Lord Curzon's thoughts on the need for a change of policy in tribal territories: '–it has always been an axiom that the goodwill of the tribesmen affords the best guarantee for the success of a frontier policy–the friendly attitude of the frontier tribes would be of much greater moment than the absolute safety of any single pass, however important'.[87]

Conclusion: the Frontier Pashtun Way of War

The Tirah Campaign that took place during the 'Pathan Revolt' of 1897–8 offers a fascinating case study of fighting on the North West Frontier and the Pashtun 'way of war' in this period. In terms of the causes of the fighting, rumours, beliefs and myths combined to mobilize the population already fearful about British encroachments. The Afridi–Orakzai revolt certainly needs to be seen in the context of the 1893 Durand Line agreement and the British Forward Policy, but it also needs to be understood as a specific local reaction to a world that was changing around them. That reaction suggests their *pashtunwali* was not fixed and immutable, despite the strength of its obligations, but permitted interpretation depending on the level of threat and crisis. Consequently, clans responded differently to the revolt of 1897 and not all of them followed their charismatic mullahs blindly. Indeed, the clansmen proved themselves capable of great tactical prowess in mountain warfare and an eminently pragmatic strategy.[88] It appears that the Pashtun clans' objectives were limited to the defence of their immediate territories. Their tactics and their overall strategies indicated an attempt to delay and check the British by the utilization of the terrain and their relative strengths. It was not just a Jihad that would drive out the infidels from the entire region, although the idea of 'Islam in danger' coincided with local anxieties and acted as a unifying rhetoric to mobilize the otherwise divided clans.

Afghanistan's non-intervention was important, and some Afghan Pashtuns were prevented from joining the rising, but this simply empowered local leaders all the more. Clansmen were quick to blame the mullahs for 'forcing' them to fight, and it seems that few of them wanted to run the risk of being the only individual to defy their religious authorities. A collective pressure created a momentum that was hard to resist.

In the light of the Tirah campaign, some British officers felt that the fighting on the North West Frontier had cost too much for results gained. Reflecting on future operations, Captain Nevill wrote: 'To compel the surrender of guerrillas, such as the frontier tribes of India, by the usual process of breaking down the means of defence would entail operations so prolonged and costly as to be out of all proportion to the interests at stake. Other means therefore, must be found to achieve the same result, such as the destruction of villages and personal property, which has always been the only effective way of dealing with the elusive tribesmen'.[89] The financial cost of the Tirah campaign was £2.4 million, the same as the two-year-long operations in the Sudan against the Khalifa's revolt, but when combined with the other operations on the North

West Frontier, it represented a considerable burden on the Government of India's revenue. The cost in lives had also been high. The rank and file per company had been reduced by combat and sickness to just twenty men in some battalions.[90] The total British losses were 1,150 of which 287 were killed. No figures were kept for the number of camp followers killed and wounded, and it is not known how many clansmen became casualties.

The 'Pathan Revolt' is a specific historical illustration of the nature of the Pashtun region astride the Durand Line, but it is one that has been hitherto dominated by Western interpretations. To the Pashtuns, the border line laid down by the British with Kabul's compliance did not exist and they saw no objection to an appeal to the Amir of Afghanistan when hard pressed. Whilst the causes of the revolt were attributed to fanaticism, a conspiracy of mullahs, or resistance to British encroachments, the sources of resistance appear to be evidence of the internal dynamics of a society confronted by change and seeking to exclude foreign influences. It interpreted the solutions to a foreign threat and a sense of crisis in religious terms and according to the guidance of their tribal code, but the Pashtuns pursued a more practical strategy. There was some pressure to respond to the crisis in a collective way, despite the fragmentary nature of their society, but some of these fissures were not entirely closed. Some clans opted to remain neutral and others were rather half-hearted. The Zakka-Khels by contrast believed their honour was at stake and they fought determinedly throughout the campaign. The Tirah campaign was an illustration of how the Pashtuns fought at the end of the nineteenth century, but does not prove there was an unchanging 'way of war'. Although it is possible to see tactics common to other eras, we should be cautious about attributing this to a distinct military culture. Instead, we might conclude that the Pashtuns at this time had evolved the most appropriate form of mountain warfare best suited to the technology and tactics of their enemies. The best tributes to the Pashtuns came from their British adversaries, and the last word on the campaign surely belongs to one of those who took part in the Tirah operations:

We are too much accustomed to think of the tribes on our frontier as an undisciplined rabble to be treated with contempt, and brushed aside with ease, whenever we choose to advance against them in a lordly fashion. We have learned now that the conditions no longer exist which warranted such a belief. We have seen that the Afridis and Orakzais are as practically well armed as ourselves;–that they can shoot as straight as our own men; that they can skirmish a great deal better than most of them; and that they are enterprising and bold, and thoroughly understand how to make the best use of the natural advantages which their woods and mountains and rocky defiles give them. Such a foe is to be treated with respect.[91]

5

FRONTIER WARS

THIRD ANGLO–AFGHAN WAR, 1919,
AND WAZIRISTAN, 1936

The *Official History of the Third Afghan War of 1919* assessed the Pashtuns and
the Afghans as 'expert in guerrilla warfare', noting:

They seldom await an assault, but follow up a retirement relentlessly and with the
utmost boldness. They show great skill in cutting off detachments and laying ambushes
for isolated bodies of troops. They are, however, deficient in some important military
qualities. They lack steadfastness in adversity and lose heart when subjected to reverses.
They have little cohesion and concerted action on their part cannot be expected. Their
forces (*lashkars*) are brought to, and kept in, the field by the exertions of their religious
leaders, and each man fights as he pleases. Time is lost owing to lengthy discussions
which often precede military action or declaration of policy. Mutual jealousies or blood
feuds, which are sunk on occasions of fanatical outbursts, are apt to reappear during
prolonged operations.[1]

The *Official History* went on to describe various groups of the North West
Frontier with the observation that 'Among the Mahsuds and Wazirs the headmen have very little authority, and every man is a law unto himself'. This meant
that 'Among all these tribes, religious leaders (i.e. *mullahs*) arise who sweep
aside the authority of the headmen and drag the mass of the people after them
by appeals to their fanaticism'.[2] As far as the Afghans were concerned, the report
concluded, the 'real military strength of Afghanistan depends on the armed
population rather than on the regular forces', and the latter were there only in
a 'stiffening' role.[3] The irregulars 'rarely fight at any great distance from their

homes', not least because they were dependent on their villages for food supply. The report also noted, in a rather quaint way, that a small supply of flour that Afghan irregulars generally carried 'is frequently spoiled by the action of rain or perspiration and is apt to become full of maggots' which forced the fighter to go home again to get some more.

Afghanistan's strategic dilemma remained unchanged between 1880 and 1914, in that it was a mere buffer zone inside the sphere of British influence, hemmed in between the Russian Empire and the Raj. Dynastic survival depended on the ability to retain good relations with the Government of India, in order to procure arms and essential revenue. However, Afghan Amirs could neither be seen to be too closely associated with the British by their own population, nor could they risk too many concessions, since there was a real risk that Britain would try to assert its control more fully, which might in turn encourage the Russians to seize territory in Afghan Turkestan. Abdur Rahman's successor, Amir Habibullah, maintained the same finely balanced relationship with the British as his father, although he looked for opportunities to improve the quality of the Afghan Army and he made no secret of his satisfaction with the defeat of Russia in the Russo–Japanese War (1904–5). Habibullah renewed the existing treaty terms with the British in 1905. However, the settlement of the Anglo–Russian Convention two years later, which formalized Russia's recognition of Afghanistan as a state within the British sphere, caused deep resentment in Kabul. The terms of the Convention actually guaranteed that British forces would not occupy Afghanistan, and the Afghan Amir had already accepted that all foreign relations would be directed through the British.[4] What irritated the Afghans was the feeling that they had not been consulted about their own status and destiny.

Afghanistan's strategic situation altered in 1915 when a Turco–German military mission arrived during the First World War. While officially neutral, Amir Habibullah was aware that anti-British sentiment in the country was a threat to relations with the Government of India and to his authority.[5] The Turco–German military mission was thus delayed deliberately in Kabul and it failed to ignite a Jihad against the British Raj as planned. However, nationalist sympathizers were not immune to the ideas the Germans and Turks put forward, and Habibullah felt compelled to give an outward show of support by signing a treaty with the German envoy.[6] By its terms, Afghanistan agreed to support an invasion of British India but only on condition that a Turkish army arrived first, and that this force supplied the Afghans with 50,000 rifles, modern artillery and £20 million in gold. As enthusiasm for a forthcoming war developed, the Amir summoned the *khans* and elders, and reminded them that a Jihad could only be waged with the proper authority. He pointed out that he had not yet given this authority. Meanwhile he ensured that loyalists were rewarded handsomely and fuelled discord amongst his critics. In Habibullah's mind, his calculation was that any war against the British would result in another occupation and the demise of his power and that of the Barakzais. By 1917 it was clear that Germany and Turkey had less hope of victory, particularly when both Jerusalem and Baghdad fell to the British. What Habibullah expected was a generous reward from the Government of India when the war was over. In fact, the British discouraged Habibullah from sending an independent delegation to the Versailles conference and were soon preoccupied by unrest in the Punjab, and therefore the Government of India did not consider Afghanistan to be a priority. However, the Viceroy, Lord Chelmsford, was sympathetic to the Amir's request that British control of foreign affairs should be relinquished.[7] After all, it had been impossible to prevent German and Turkish emissaries reaching Kabul or a treaty being signed with two countries with which Britain was actually at war. For the sake of better future relations, Chelmsford thought that removing an irksome clause might be safer. The calculation came too late. Amir Habibullah was murdered on 20 February 1919.

Habibullah's brother, Nasrullah Khan, claimed the throne as Amir and ensured that Habibullah's eldest son and heir apparent, Inyatullah, submitted to him. The announcement was greeted with enthusiasm by the *ulema* and by the Ghilzais.[8] However, Amanullah, the third son of the late Amir, refused to accept Nasrullah's accession. His command of the military garrison at Kabul proved to be decisive. To win over the army he promised to pay each soldier 20 rupees a month and not 11 rupees as offered by Nasrullah. The troops at Jalalabad, where Nasrullah had established himself, immediately declared themselves for Amanullah. Nasrullah and his allies were arrested and a colonel who was held responsible for Habibullah's assassination was executed by being bayoneted to death. The Government of India accepted the accession of Amanullah as Amir, but the mullahs of Afghanistan, although largely unaffected by the court coup, were nevertheless concerned that Nasrullah, who was known to support the interests of the *ulema*, had been arrested. As a sign of protest, the *khutba* was not read in Amanullah's name in Kandahar. Expressions of concern spread rapidly to the rest of the population and the army began to look unreliable. Amanullah needed to establish his legitimacy with the people. His long and outspoken criticism of his father's close relations with the British offered the chance to harness public support. Within days Amanullah declared a Jihad, and Britain and Afghanistan were at war.

Afghan strategy in this period is much disputed. Amir Amanullah claimed that he was responding to British aggression and that, unable to find an answer to the subsequent bombing of Kabul by the RAF and having scored a 'decisive victory' at Thal in Waziristan, he was eager for peace. At the end of the conflict, the Amir wrote to the Viceroy claiming that he had merely deployed his army to the frontier to watch for disturbances and that he had only occupied territory marked on his maps as part of Afghanistan. He claimed to have sent a Vakil to negotiate as soon as the British started the fighting and noted that 'a day had hardly elapsed after the departure of our envoy for your camp when one of your aeroplanes flew over Kabul and bombarded the royal palace, thereby causing great excitement and panic among our loyal people'. The letter continued: 'it is a matter for great regret that the throwing of bombs ... and bombardment of places of worship and sacred spots was considered a most abominable operation [in the World War] while we now see with our own eyes that such operations were a habit which is prevalent amongst all civilized people of the West'.[9] In support of this view, Amanullah and the Afghan government could point to the absence of a full mobilization and the fact that Afghan territory, at Dakka, was occupied by the British in mid May 1919 or that Spin Boldak was seized on 27 May.

However, the balance of evidence suggests that Amanullah was using a strategy of brinkmanship and proxy war to achieve domestic popularity, as well as the strategic objective of securing independence in foreign affairs from the Government of India. Prior to the outbreak of war, Amanullah had given encouragement to the frontier clans on the British side of the Durand Line to engage in a Jihad, which included the issuing of weapons. Hamilton Grant, at the India Office, noted that Amanullah had staffed his government with nationalists or those with pro-Turkish leanings. The new Commander in Chief, General Saleh Mohammed, for example, was an Anglophobe. The Amir made a clear declaration of independence for Afghanistan, and the British noted wryly that in April 1919 Amanullah had appointed a Commissary for Foreign Affairs in defiance of the treaty with the Indian government. In addition, towards the end of April, Afghan troops began to concentrate near the border and fortifications were constructed at Peiwar Kotal.

One of the documented calculations that can be identified is the Afghan assumption that the British Empire was weakened by the First World War. In March and April 1919, British authorities in India were facing serious unrest in the Punjab. One verdict was that: 'The English are distracted in mind on account of the European war, and have not the strength to attack the Afghans. The people of India too are much dissatisfied with the English on account of their tyranny and oppression. They will never hesitate to raise a revolt, if they can find the opportunity, as their hearts are bleeding at their hands'.[10] The 'Provisional Government of India', a nationalist organization that had been established in Afghanistan during the First World War by the Turco–German military mission, set up communications with activists and militants inside British India. There was a great deal of anger with the wartime restrictions of the Criminal Law Amendment Act, popularly known as the Rowlatt Acts, and there were riots in Delhi, Lahore and Amritsar. In Amritsar, Brigadier General Reginald Dyer imposed martial law, and subsequently opened fire on an unauthorized and unarmed meeting of several hundred Punjabis, killing over 300 civilians.[11]

To seize advantage of the unrest, after the initial moves at the border, the Afghan 'post master' in Peshawar, Ghulam Hayder, reported that he was prepared to 'begin a Holy War in Peshawar City'.[12] He wrote that 8,000 men, both Hindus and Muslims, were at his call with a further 2,000 from the neighbouring villages. He even claimed that 'Sikh regiments have assured Hindus that they look on Moslems as brethren and will not fire on them'. More importantly he reported, quite erroneously, that there were 'not sufficient troops in India and [the government] often moves about one regiment, consisting of 2 or 3 companies, (sic) to make a display'. He claimed that, despite efforts to get more men, none had arrived in the Peshawar area and that even 'British subjects will not supply recruits', which was perhaps a reference to the unwillingness of Territorial battalions that had served on the North West Frontier during the war (to release regulars for service in France) to stay on beyond the end of European conflict. The Post Master reported enthusiastically that there were 'disturbances throughout India' and added the pressure that, if Afghanistan did not act in favour of the people of India, the 'public will be displeased with the Amir'. He concluded, 'it is not expedient to delay and to give the English time to collect troops'.[13]

In fact the Peshawar insurrection failed almost immediately because the city was quickly cordoned with a demand that if the ringleaders of the unrest were not handed over the population would have its water supply cut off. After a few hours, the activists, including the Post Master, gave themselves up.[14] The unrest of April was also crushed by armed police while Dyer's action at Amritsar had a salutary effect on rioters elsewhere. The British, for all the talk of their war weariness, were showing that they were as determined as ever to maintain security and control of the region and they were prepared to use considerable force to do it. If the Afghan strategy had been to exploit unrest in India hoping it would tie down hundreds of British and Indian troops, then it failed even before the war got fully underway. Indeed, the official history notes that there were three distinct phases in the war: the pacification of the Punjab was completed early on; this then allowed the Army in India to concentrate against the regular Afghan forces and some of the harassing raids by irregulars; and then, in the final phase, it could deal separately with the resistance of the clans in Waziristan and the Khyber, which developed later. Had the three elements been more closely coordinated, then the British forces may have struggled to contain the problem. The Viceroy thought that the Amir may simply have acted impulsively, telling the India Office: 'You may ask why we have not had better information. I can only answer that I do not believe that Amanulla[h] himself knew until the last moment that he was going to embark on this enterprise'.[15]

The Amir made a declaration of Jihad against British injustices and claimed he had the right to intervene in India in accordance with international law. He stated that the British had inflicted injustices of all kinds, but especially against religion, honour and modesty. The same day, a detachment of 150 Afghan troops seized Kafir Kot, the high ground above the British fort at Landi Kotal in the Khyber Pass, which controlled its water supply. Zar Shah, an irregular commander, opened fire on a party of labourers and killed five of them, while Afghan *khassadars* from the Shinwaris and Mohmands assembled at Bagh. On 5 May, more Afghan regular troops arrived. However, while Afghan clans in Nangahar and the eastern provinces, and the Afridis and Mohmands on the British side of the Durand Line, supported the Amir's Jihad, there was not much enthusiasm elsewhere.[16]

Before the outbreak of war on 6 May, the Amir had organized the concentration of an Afghan division at Ghazni, another at Kandahar and another at Dakka, west of the Khyber Pass. The Afghan army of 1919 consisted of 78 infantry battalions, 21 cavalry regiments and 280 breech-loading artillery, with another 300 obsolete muzzle-loading smooth bore cannons, giving a total strength of 50,000 men. In peacetime, 35 battalions and 3 cavalry regiments were distributed around ten military districts for internal security while 23 battalions and 8 regiments of cavalry garrisoned positions along the Persian and Russian borders. A reserve was held at Kabul. There was no attempt to create formations larger than an ad hoc brigade of infantry, cavalry and artillery, and there was no staff corps to manage logistics. Afghan regulars had little training, even in 'skill at arms', while 'tactical exercises were unknown'.[17] This meant that Afghan regulars were unable to manoeuvre in formation and consequently they tended to wait for an attack on them, hence the focus on defensive positions. At Thal, in 1919, this inability to manoeuvre was to have serious consequences.

Most units in the eastern provinces were given the best armaments, leaving the regiments on the other frontiers with obsolete breech-loaders. It was noted that, while issued with bayonets, the Afghan infantry tended to use them only for the execution of criminals and political prisoners.[18] Very few units reached their establishment figure in terms of numbers, so in wartime the ranks were topped up with locally recruited irregulars. The Afghan state still maintained approximately 10,000 levies in service, organized as companies of 100 men, but they usually deployed in groups of ten on internal security duties. All the Afghan cavalry tended to fight as mounted infantry, that is, dismounted, and British commentators remarked on the hardiness but general neglect of the Afghan horses. This had consequences for the artillery, which lacked mobility. Most of the Afghan artillerymen lacked training, and gunnery practice was again unknown. Nevertheless, the *topkhana* was issued with German 10 cm field howitzers, and a few Krupp pack guns of 75 mm calibre. There were a few vintage machine guns that required a crank-handle to operate, and only a handful of units carried ammunition that had smokeless powder, which was all imported or smuggled. Although a smokeless propellent factory had been established in 1912, it had been supplied with the wrong chemicals and was never used.

On the borders, the Afghan army had concentrated in four locations: in Kunar, at the head of the Khyber Pass, in Khost, and in Kandahar, while a reserve was kept at Kabul. This was a contrast to the peacetime distribution, suggesting that some sort of offensive action was planned. Moreover, the failure to announce a general mobilization in May, in favour of a Jihad, reflects the calculations of the Amir. His strategy was based on exploiting a narrow window of opportunity and achieving a rapid if limited success against British forces in the border area, in order to bolster his domestic position. Not all of his forces had got into position by the time the war broke out, and there is no doubt that prompt counter-offensives by the British disrupted the Afghan strategy. The main Afghan offensive on the 'central front' near Thal did not get underway until 26 May, by which time Afghan forces at the Khyber Pass and Kandahar had already been defeated.

Since 1901, the British had pulled back their military garrisons from the Afghan border and substituted many regular European battalions in favour of locally recruited *khassadars*. These small Pashtun units, invariably commanded by a British officer, had the advantage of causing less cultural offence or suspicions of occupation; they knew the ground and language, and they absorbed some young men who might otherwise have carried out raids on rivals or into British territory. The main problem was in their reliability. Those who enlisted were keen to take the money and act as a roving militia so long as their interests did not clash with the local clans or their own families.

Behind the frontier zone, the British had a number of Territorial Army battalions and some inexperienced Indian Army regiments, stiffened with mountain artillery, armoured cars and, most importantly, aircraft of the Royal Air Force. From the outset, the RAF were envisaged as a decisive arm against the Afghans. The Afghan concentration at Dakka was one of the first objectives in the campaign. Although there were some concerns that the aircraft themselves were obsolete, the air raid on Dakka was a great success, not least because, just as the aircraft approached, the Amir's officials were in the process of distributing rifles, ammunition and food to irregulars recruited from the local area. This concentrated mass of fighters made an ideal target. Some twenty-five irregulars were killed, but the effect was psychological rather than physical. The Afghans were now at risk of air envelopment, and their only protection lay in dispersal and concealment.

Operations on the Khyber Front

At Bagh in the Khyber Pass, the Afghans occupied unexpectedly a 2,000-yard long crest, the Ash Khel, and brought up more reinforcements including artillery. However, the Afghan commander, Mohammed Anwar Khan, failed to capitalize on his initial advantage in numbers so that, within two days, the British could muster five battalions, machine guns and a battery of mountain artillery to support the nearby garrison of Landi Kotal. Aware that the British would now take offensive action, the Afghans established two belts of defences. An outpost line was thrown forward to the base of the ridge, while the main position on the crest line, a natural amphitheatre, was entrenched. Although keen to take the offensive as soon as possible, the British commander, General Crocker, was concerned that his northern flank was exposed and there was every possibility that Mohmand and Afridi irregulars would appear in large numbers from this direction. Covering this northern flank meant reducing the numbers available for the attack against the Afghan regulars. Consequently, even though the outpost line was driven back, the British and Indian troops could not get through the weight of fire from the main position. At nightfall, the British dug in on the lower slopes.[19] The Afghans believed the First Battle of Bagh was a victory, but they failed to make any counter-attack and contented themselves with harassing gunfire.

The failure to exploit the situation, coupled with the failure of the Peshawar uprising, neutralized the momentum that might have encouraged the clans on the British side of the border to join the war. The British had prevented the Afghans taking control of the Khyber Pass because of the rapid arrival of British reinforcements by motor transport vehicles and through air attacks, and it is likely that the Afghan strategy depended on the ability to open the road to Peshawar. The British also noted that the Afghans made other elementary mistakes in mountain warfare. They did not, for example, occupy some vital picquet positions through the night and so the British were able to seize a key feature known as Bright's Hill at dawn on 9 May 1919 without opposition.

The Afghans did bring forward more reinforcements, but they were unable to cope with the speed by which the British could mount operations. Despite being checked at Bagh on 9 May, the British were in a position to make a second assault just two days later.[20] This time the attack was made with six infantry battalions, twenty-two machine guns and eighteen artillery pieces and was initiated at night to maintain security. The leading units were within yards of the Afghan positions when firing broke out. The British made their attacks by hurling grenades into Afghan *sangars*, and then followed up with bayonet charges and close-range fire support. Bagh was overrun and five Afghan guns captured, and as they withdrew they were strafed by British aircraft or shot down by carefully placed cut-off groups. It was estimated that in the Second Battle of Bagh on 11 May 1919 the Afghans lost 100 killed and 300 wounded, while the British lost 8 killed and 29 wounded.

To follow up their attack, the British maintained their air bombardment of Dakka, dropped propaganda leaflets urging local clans to stay out of the fighting and pushed on westwards, across the border, with ground forces. The Amir protested, claiming he had not sought to interfere in the unrest in India, and initially there was no resistance to the British occupation of Dakka, but this was merely a result of a lack of reserves in the area rather than a deliberate policy. On 16 May, British cavalry patrols soon brought reports of Afghan regular troops and militia arriving from the west. The British encampment, which had not been well sited, was subjected to Afghan artillery fire, and it was with some difficulty that the British held on to the surrounding hills. As darkness fell, the British units were withdrawn to avoid being enveloped, but this enabled Afghan snipers to close in towards the British camp, whereupon they kept up a steady fire throughout the night.[21] Meanwhile the Afghans dragged artillery up into the hills to the west of the British camp and started shelling.

At dawn the next day, the 1/35th Sikhs and 1/9th Gurkhas were ordered to clear the heights. These inexperienced troops were ambushed as they approached the crest of the hill by concealed Afghan units, and the Sikhs retreated in disorder. The Gurkhas rallied them, but neither battalion could get through the fire sweeping the slopes and the leading platoons were pinned down just 20 yards from the summit. Once again, the Afghans made no attempt to counter-attack.[22] On a southern hill, subsequently known as Sikh Hill, the 1/35th Sikhs were also pinned down 300 yards short of the crest. British reinforcements opened fire on the Sikhs by mistake. Up to this point, the Afghan plan to envelop the British position had succeeded, but it proved impossible to hold the heights against the sustained artillery and machine-gun fire with which the British responded. Once the Gurkhas wrestled control of a hilltop position nicknamed Stonehenge, and their flanks were threatened, the Afghans withdrew, and were forced to leave behind five of their best mountain guns. There was some evidence to suggest that British howitzer fire, which could plunge shells over the razor-back ridges of the area, had some effect on the Afghans sheltering in reserve.

Despite the retreat of the Afghan regulars at Dakka, the Afridi clans in the Khyber Pass prepared to launch their own attacks on the British lines of communication. The chief agitator was thought to be Yar Mohammed, a *malik* of the Malik Din Khel Afridis, and he warned the British that he was going to strike. His men, initially numbering no more than forty, were increased by other villages and there was a concerted campaign to subvert the Khyber Rifles. The rumour was that the British intended to use the Khyber Riflemen as cannon fodder in their war against the Afghans, killing both alike with their own guns. There were outbreaks of fighting south of the Khyber Pass too, and shooting incidents in Peshawar. Road blocks and ambushes were set up in the Khyber Pass itself, and telegraph wire was cut down and stolen. Despite the existence of Jihadist propaganda, the unrest appeared to be a combination of opportunism and anger at the war being waged against the Afghans.

Although there was an attack against a detachment at Ali Masjid, the arrival of more British and Indian troops and the disbandment of the Khyber Rifles quietened the area. Moreover, when a small Afghan force crossed the border north of the Khyber Pass into Mohmand country, the local clans were unwilling to assist them. The Afghan Wardaki Battalion was particularly criticized for its arrogant conduct. The main reason for their hostile reception was that their demands for supplies affected local communities who had been blockaded by the British in 1915. They remembered the difficulties associated with being short of food, and were unwilling to hand over what little they had to the Afghan Army.[23]

The Southern Front

The weak point in Afghanistan's defences against the British in the previous Anglo–Afghan wars had been the Bolan Pass and the route to Kandahar. Twice the British had outflanked the bulk of the Afghan forces, which had concentrated around the Khyber, by moving against Kandahar. To meet this threat in 1919, the Amir had despatched the chief minister, Abdul Qudus, to take command in the south personally. The forces deployed around Kandahar consisted of 5 infantry battalions, 1 cavalry regiment and 25 guns, with a further 2 battalions at Qalat and 2 en route from Kabul. The British decided to make a surprise counter-offensive against Kandahar to prevent the Afghans from stirring the Baluchis of British India to resistance, but also to put pressure on the Afghan government and draw reserves away from the northern theatre of operations.

The result was the defeat of the garrison at Spin Boldak by a British force of 4 battalions, 1 machine gun company and 12 guns, supported by aircraft.[24] The Afghan defences were based on the perimeter of the fortress built by Abdur Rahman, but its thick mud walls provided protection only against small-arms fire. The positions tended to provide the British with clear targets for their artillery and bombers, and, while some of the garrison fled before the attack got underway, the remaining defenders mounted a determined resistance. Of a force of 600 men, over 170 were killed, an unknown number were wounded, and 176 taken prisoner. The official history noted that the attack had come as a complete surprise and the ignorance of the garrison had made them 'trust their stone walls'.[25] Nevertheless, although pounded with gunfire, the Afghans had managed to pin down one assault. The British had had to fight their way into the fortress using grenades and then fight a battle at close quarters. The British praised the Afghan defenders, stating: 'It is impossible not to admire the courage with which they fought to the end without a thought of surrender' but felt that they should have attempted to break through a cordon of British cavalry and made their escape to Kandahar instead of withstanding the fire of British guns.[26]

The British did not make an advance on Kandahar since the objective had been to provide better security for the Bolan Pass. There can be little doubt this was interpreted by the Afghans as an opportunity to recover the situation. Despite digging trenches and setting up barbed wire obstacles, the British position at Spin Boldak was dependent on water supplies beyond the perimeter they had established. This led to a curious epilogue to the war, for, despite the signing of the armistice at the beginning of June, Afghan troops continued to occupy positions close to the British defences, including those at New Chaman, and from time to time opened fire on working parties and small detachments. On 12 June, a British cavalry patrol approached Murgha Chaman to investigate why water was no longer reaching Spin Boldak. The village compounds were found to be occupied by 3,000 Afghan troops and irregulars. The Afghans made attempts to envelop the cavalry but sent forward a negotiating officer, who promised to restore the water and restrain his men. Yet, when the water did not resume and sniping continued, the decision was taken to avoid further clashes and withdraw. The Afghans believed this showed that the British were demoralized.[27] Although requests were made to resume operations, the Government of India refused and for some weeks, during the negotiations at Dakka, Achakzais made raids on the British forces at New Chaman, Spin Boldak and on the Khojak Tunnel, although, when peace was finally re-established, the raids ceased abruptly.[28]

Operations on the Central Front

The main Afghan offensive was on the Central Front into Waziristan, perhaps in the hope that the Waziris, who had shown support for the Amir's Jihadist declarations like the Afridis, would accompany the Afghan Army as it advanced through British territory. The fact that an offensive did not get underway until the end of May, and the existence of entrenchments that had been started in late April, suggest that the initial Afghan strategy had been to remain on the defensive in this sector but that events at Dakka had compelled them to seek to relieve the pressure in the north. They believed that an offensive towards Kohat and Bannu, and ultimately Peshawar, might force the British to abandon any hope of reaching Kabul. The offensive was to use overwhelming force, with two axes of advance via Kurram and Matun converging at Thal, consisting of fourteen battalions of infantry and 48 guns, augmented by irregulars. The British, aware of the build-up, had reinforced their posts at Parachinar, near the Peiwar Kotal Pass, and at Thal, but there were too few troops to cover the Matun axis, and the decision to evacuate the area caused the local *khassadars* to desert or open fire on their British officers. The news of this unrest spread quickly and the North Waziristan and South Waziristan militias melted away. When General Nadir Khan commenced his offensive on 27 May, there were almost no forces left in Waziristan to resist him.

The Afghan artillery, consisting of nine German mountain guns, was packed onto mules and elephants in order to make the crossing of the difficult terrain into the Kurram Valley, and with an advance guard of 3,000 regulars and approximately the same number of irregulars, Nadir Khan advanced on Thal. Occupying the high ground around the settlement, he was able to cover three sides of the hastily dug British defences. The Afghan guns managed to destroy ration trucks in the railway siding, a petrol dump, a store of animal fodder and a wireless transmitting station on the first day. Moreover, the frontier constabulary, which had been guarding the water pumping station, deserted, and this vital position fell into Afghan hands. The small British garrison, numbering just ninety men, were able to resist a number of probing attacks, but it was clear that, without supplies, they could not hold for long. As a result, Nadir Khan decided not to risk heavy casualties with a direct assault on the shallow British trenches. He believed that clans to the east would delay any British reinforcements sufficiently, and that the advance could be resumed in any direction once he had captured Thal. However, Nadir Khan squandered his initial advantage and handed the initiative to the British. Brigadier General Dyer assembled a relief force at Kohat and implemented a deception plan, whereby he assembled dummy artillery from logs and used brushwood on the mud flaps of his motor vehicles, which raised great clouds of dust, to give the impression that a large force was approaching. It is alleged that Nadir Khan fell for the ruse, stating: 'In the name of God, we have the whole artillery of India coming against us'.[29] Dyer made a forced march with his composite force and arrived on 31 May, covering the last 18 miles in just 12 hours.

The Afghan position consisted of two wings held by irregulars while the centre, on hills to the west of the town, was held by the Afghan Army, now reinforced to 19,000 men. Dyer launched another deception plan by shelling the northern wing, but making an attack with all his forces against the southern hills.[30] These heights were held by 4,000 clansmen from Khost under the command of Babrak. After several hours of fighting, Babrak's men were dispersed. Nadir Khan sent a message to Dyer arguing that an armistice had been concluded and he asked that hostilities be suspended while negotiations were underway. Dyer was right to suspect that Nadir Khan intended to withdraw the bulk of his force without engaging the British and was hoping to buy time. The rapid defeat of the Khost irregulars had clearly unsettled his troops, and there was already a withdrawal underway when Dyer gave the terse response: 'My guns will give an immediate reply'. Nadir Khan managed to put 3 miles between the bulk of his forces and the British by the time the British started to mount their bombardment, but the assault on the outpost line of Afghan Army almost caused the collapse of the Nadir's forces. Stores and equipment were abandoned in the retreat, and the whole position was looted by local clans.

The RAF had assisted in the harassment of Nadir Khan's forces, but perhaps their most important contribution was the bombing of Kabul and Jalalabad. Just over a ton of explosives were dropped on Jalalabad in one day, which caused panic. The temporary collapse of order encouraged rural clans to descend on the city and loot it. In Kabul, the effect of the bombing was no less profound and was mentioned by Amanullah's negotiators as a key factor in their calculation to sue for peace. The first requests for a ceasefire were issued on 14 May, but it was not until 2 June that the British accepted the majority of the Afghan proposals. The British insisted that the Afghan troops withdraw 20 miles from British units and that the clans were to be informed that all hostilities had ceased.

The consequences of the war

Amanullah tried to rescue himself from the débâcle he had created by insisting on full independence, while claiming that he had not started the war. Invoking the memory of the two previous Anglo–Afghan wars, he reminded the British that: 'The Afghan nation had repeatedly been a cause of destruction and ruination to any foreign power on its sacred soil...'[31] He continued that every foreign intervention, despite the defeats, had caused a 'national regeneration'. Amanullah may have realized that he could still convert military defeat into political success at home by emphasizing the defence of Afghanistan. He told the British dramatically that 'Afghans would rather die than submit to a foreign government' and argued that 'Afghanistan was a nation in arms, the people were the army', and therefore he could not withdraw the army without evicting the people from their land. The negotiations continued throughout June and July, with the Afghan delegation threatening to pull out of talks on several occasions. Each time they returned, particularly when there was a prospect of further air attacks or occupation.

The Afghans possessed no effective counter-measures against air attacks, although concentrations of irregulars adapted their tactics by concealment, standing still or lying under cover as aircraft approached. They managed to shoot down aircraft with a slow climb rate from the highest mountains, but there was really no adequate response to this development in warfare. Nadir Khan tried to maintain his own pressure on the British by encouraging irregulars astride the Durand Line to fire on British camps. Indeed, the prolonged presence of British garrisons created fears of a permanent occupation, just as it had in the 1890s. Yet Afghanistan and its clans remained as divided as ever. Not all Pashtuns joined the resistance, and Abdul Qudus hinted that he would be willing to make a separate peace if Amanullah proved unwilling to compromise and the British would assist him to take power.[32] Amanullah may have been delaying his negotiations in the hope of getting material support from the new Soviet regime, and it was certainly in British calculations that an early peace would avoid the risk of Afghanistan moving closer to Moscow's sphere.[33]

In the negotiations at Rawalpindi in July, the Afghans played on the prospect of a Soviet threat and argued, therefore, that the British should offer concessions, but the British response was that an Afghan monarchy was incompatible with communism and therefore the Afghans would need to side with the British. The negotiators eventually agreed that regicides were to be condemned, that wealth should not be redistributed as communists advocated and there could be no 'nationalization of women', a reference to the status of Afghan women as property. Tempers flared over the issue of British bombing and the subsidy paid annually to the Amirs. But on 1 August, exasperated with the obstructions, the Government of India issued an ultimatum: if a settlement was not reached, the war would resume. The terms were that Indian nationalists and Bolsheviks were to be expelled from Afghanistan, intrigues with the Pashtuns beyond the Durand Line should cease, the frontier line should be accepted without revision and, in return, Britain would relinquish control of Afghanistan's foreign affairs. These were generous terms, but the Afghans refused in the hope of getting an amnesty for the clans involved in the fighting on the British side of the border, and they wanted any war guilt responsibility expunged from the treaty. The latter the British could accept, but, with operations still underway in frontier areas, they could not accept the former. The India Office felt that the Viceroy's staff had given away too much and not capitalized on the victory, but the unrest taking place in other imperial stations, including Egypt and Iraq, and a desire to get back to 'normalcy' had encouraged a spirit of compromise.[34]

The Amir claimed victory despite his battlefield defeats by emphasizing the strategic achievement of full independence. A victory monument was con-

structed in Kabul and an independence day announced. Nadir Khan was proclaimed the hero of Thal. His nationalist credentials established, Amanullah
tried, equally unsuccessfully, to champion the Basmachi cause against the Soviets in Central Asia. General Frunze, the Soviet commander, crushed the Islamist
fighters and the government in Moscow pressured Amanullah to abandon his
war by proxy. The Afghans then shifted their strategy to embrace the communists. Throughout the 1920s, Amanullah attempted to modernize his armed
forces, establishing the first Afghan Air Force with Soviet trainers, pilots and
aircraft. Yet, for Amanullah and many Afghan officers, there was initially more
enthusiasm for the achievements of Kemal Ataturk in Turkey.[35] The modernization and nationalism of the Turkish army, their series of victories against the
Greeks in Smyrna, and a successful confrontation with Britain over the Chanak
Straits all seemed to indicate the direction for Afghanistan. In June 1920, some
18,000 Muslims in British India attempted to emigrate to Afghanistan in the
hope of being the vanguard of a new *Khalifat* (Caliphate), but Ataturk's destruction of the old Ottoman system and Amanuallh's unwillingness to lead a *ghaza*
to restore the Caliphate, or even accommodate the *Khalifat* emigrants, caused
the movement to collapse.[36]

Nevertheless, Amanullah's preference for secularization, and his decision to
pension off many senior Afghan officers in favour of Turkish military advisors,
soon caused deep resentment in the army. Moreover, junior officers were
alarmed by the whirlwind of proposed reforms that was generating resistance
amongst the *ulema* and conservative rural *khans* and elders. The new Administrative Code, drafted by Turkish advisors and which ended the practice by
which women and daughters were treated as goods, was condemned by the
ulema as a foreign intervention, and there was a great deal of anxiety about the
arrival of foreign doctors. In March 1924 a serious revolt broke out in Khost,
led by mullahs and *maliks*, and Afghan Army units were unable to defeat the
rebels.[37] In October 1924 one military detachment was destroyed, and there
seemed a chance that the rebels would gather more support and march on
Kabul. However, Shinwaris, transborder Pashtuns including Waziris, and Hazaras were enticed to enlist as irregular fighters in defence of Afghanistan with
generous subsidies, and members of the *ulema* were persuaded by similar means
to condemn the rebels, and even declared a Jihad against them.

The government's irregular forces swarmed over Khost and sacked the province. In January 1925 the leader of the revolt, the 'lame mullah', was captured
and executed along with his family. However, the rebellion had cost the Afghan
government the equivalent of £5 million in state revenue and had demoralized

the army. The most important contributions had come from the irregulars, and also from the British who supplied Lewis guns (a light machine gun), rifles, ammunition and two aircraft, piloted by Germans. British assistance was nevertheless condemned because a son of the former Amir Yakub Khan, Abdul Karim, had arrived from British territory in Khost at the height of the rebellion to claim the throne. The suspicion was that Britain had encouraged the revolt as revenge for the Third Anglo–Afghan War, but it was necessary for the Amir to distance himself from any association with the British in order to maintain his legitimacy.

The Afghan Army deteriorated in quality after the Khost rebellion, despite the purchase of some new technologies.[38] Pay for the soldiers became erratic and wages were so low that many could hardly feed themselves. There were still no regular training packages, and no medical support services. Equipment was in poor repair. That said, young officers were sent on exchanges with foreign forces and were enthusiastic about new techniques. These 'upstart' young officers were resented by the senior commanders, although often older clan rivalries underpinned the recriminations. The result was that internal security was being weakened precisely when Amanullah needed it most. He could not afford both a strong army and a package of modernizing reforms, and hoped that the reforms would create efficiencies which would generate more revenue in the long term. Britain had ceased paying its generous subsidies when Amanullah had insisted on independence.[39]

In November 1928 unrest developed into serious outbreaks of fighting.[40] By December rebel forces reached Kabul, and the British mission there was fired on. On 14 January 1929 Amanulllah abdicated in favour of his elder brother, but Inyatullah held on for only three days and had to be evacuated on a British aircraft. Amanullah tried to regain the throne by assembling a force of 5,000 Durranis outside Qalat to retake Kabul, but, despite inflicting serious losses on the Suleiman Khels, he was defeated by more Ghilzais who had concentrated at Ghazni and he was forced into exile. Kabul was then taken over by the Tajik Habibullah II backed by 10,000 Kohistanis, until General Nadir Khan, who had resigned as Commander in Chief in 1926, returned in March 1929, raised an army and, after a series of protracted operations, secured Kabul in October that year.

Interestingly Amanullah had relied on the Afghan artillery to hold the city of Kabul when many of his troops, who had not been paid, deserted. Amanullah capitulated only when he found that he had no troops left to defend the city. Habibullah had started his campaign to take the capital by sniping into the city at night, and did not launch an attack until he had gathered sufficient numbers to overwhelm the defenders.[41] He was initially unable to pay his followers or the soldiers who had joined him and resorted to extortion of Kabuli merchants. Yet, to popularize the regime he abolished conscription, and he appealed to the clans of Khost who harboured great resentment of Amanullah and the Ghilzais after their contribution to the crushing of the Khost rebellion in 1924.

The country soon began to fragment along familiar lines. The Ghilzais believed that Nadir Khan might provide an opportunity for looting and offered him support. Durrani Pashtuns took control of Kandahar, making it autonomous. Meanwhile, Ghulam Nabi Khan, son of Abdur Rahman's Commander in Chief, recruited Uzbeks and Turcoman Afghans, and seized Mazar-i Sharif for a time. Nadir Khan tried to advance on Ghazni but was attacked by the Ghilzai leader, Ghaus ud-din, and forced to withdraw to Gardez in June. A second offensive into Logar also failed on 10 July 1929. Habibullah drove his opponents away from Kabul and captured Kandahar, executing Ali Ahmad Jan for attempting to assert his independence there. Nadir Khan concentrated on propaganda and enlisted the Kabul Khel Waziris as his principal allies, appealing for support from Pashtuns on the British side of the border. With these forces, he mounted a third offensive in August 1929 which retook Gardez at the end of that month. At almost the same time, the Hazaras inflicted two defeats on Habibullah's army at Sirchashma near Kabul. Habibullah's detachment in Kandahar was also defeated, although they held the citadel. Habibullah then attempted to disarm clan fighters in the vicinity of Kabul, but this aroused more resentment.

Nadir Khan was able to advance on the capital soon after via the Logar Valley and emerged at Charasiab on 6 October. Here Habibullah's men were entrenched. Thinking they had driven off Nadir's assaulting forces, they set off in pursuit. To their astonishment, the Waziri *lashkar* had feigned its withdrawal deliberately and Habibullah's men found themselves in a killing zone. They attempted to retreat to the trenches, but the pursuit was so rapid that all cohesion was lost. The trenches were overrun and Nadir Khan marched into Kabul the same afternoon. It took a further three days of bombardment to force the Bala Hissar to surrender.

To claim legitimacy Nadir Khan declared himself Nadir Shah, the Padshah (king) of Afghanistan.[42] Young Shinwari Ghilzais refused to accept the new dispensation and revolted in 1930 in favour of Amanullah, but their elders refused to support their rebellion. In July that year, Kohistanis, fearing retaliation, also revolted but they were crushed and eleven leaders were executed.[43] Herat, which had broken away in 1929, was recovered in 1931. However, only two years later Nadir Shah was assassinated in a blood feud and replaced with his son, Zahir Shah. The Khostwals subsequently revolted but Afghan troops at Matun quickly defeated the clansmen and prevented widespread unrest.

Resistance by the Pashtuns under British Administration, 1919–24

In 1919, at the height of the Third Anglo–Afghan War, it had taken some time to mobilize Pashtun resistance to the British. This time lag may be explained by the fact that many clans were in receipt of subsidies and had enjoyed a long period without any British presence in the area beyond the infrequent visits of Political Officers and their *khassadars*. However, fear of occupation, the opportunity of loot offered by the vulnerable lines of communication that threaded their way through the mountains, and the appeal of joining the Afghans in a war against the British all acted as incentives to action. The collapse of the Waziristan militias in British service and the pursuit of their British officers added to a sense of momentum.

The militiamen and those Pashtuns who had served in the Indian Army during the First World War brought with them new tactics and techniques, including the coordination of fire and movement by small bodies of riflemen. When organized, the fighters could lay down withering suppressive fire while others dashed closer to the British lines.[44] Modern breech-loaders and magazines also meant that they could maintain a great weight of accurate fire while their ammunition lasted. Sniping at long range also became possible with new 'weapons of precision'. Furthermore, the best shots were far more proficient than the young and inexperienced Indian soldiers who faced them. The result was that Pashtuns no longer had to get to close quarters with long Khyber knives, but could engage in the same fire tactics as the Army in India.

In the summer of 1919, the Tochi Valley and the Khyber Pass were recaptured, but resistance continued within the North West Frontier Province and it was decided to send a punitive expedition, the Dejerat column (DERACOL), into Mahsud territory that winter. An attempt to establish picquets on a feature known as Mandana Hill on the first day, 18 December, was a disaster for the British. Two detachments of Indian troops were sent up the slopes but were ambushed as they crested the hill. Their retreat was so dramatic that British officers laconically described the event as 'Derby day', since each unit appeared to be in a race to reach the base of the hill first. The next day the exercise was repeated, and morale amongst the Indian soldiers was badly shaken. On the third day, the units were dispatched to another uncontested feature known as Tarakai or Black Hill. The operation seemed to be a success and *sangars* were constructed, but, before they were finished, the Mahsuds moved a substantial *lashkar* stealthily up the far side of the hill, and then made a sudden assault over the last few yards. The plan was to pursue this time and to overrun the British encampment below. Most of the Indian troops fled, but a detachment of 3/24th Sikh Pioneers held off a series of attacks on the summit until their ammunition ran out. Their delaying action, and artillery fire from the valley floor, were sufficient to persuade the Mahsuds to abandon the main attack.[45]

The British commander, General Andrew Skeen, opted for a 'steamroller' method and used artillery, aircraft and his more reliable infantry in close cooperation. His system of building protected picquets on the heights and massed machine-gun fire to suppress any resistance proved effective. The Mahsuds therefore adapted their own tactics, operating in smaller groups and at night, keeping a watchful eye for the opportunity to ambush any unsupported detachment as it ascended or descended a hill. Rushing picquets at night was preferred until the British developed barbed wire defences and lay artillery or machine guns on fixed lines for night firing.[46] On 2 January 1920, one Mahsud party was caught and fought hand to hand with a unit of the 4/39th Garwhal Rifles, and was destroyed. Nevertheless, the best opportunity for resistance appeared to be the Ahnai Tangi Gorge: the Mahsuds scored a significant success when the first British attempt to establish a picquet nearby was defeated. The British force suffered a loss of 170 killed and wounded. General Skeen responded by making a night march, believing the Mahsuds would be reluctant to hold exposed positions at night in bad weather.[47] His calculation proved correct and two brigades managed to cross high ridges without loss. The Mahsuds, realizing the danger they were now in, made an assault on the Gurkha picquet at Flathead Left and some of the fighting was at close quarters. Losses were heavy on both sides as the Mahsuds made repeated attempts to retake the hill. Three supporting aircraft were shot down by Pashtun small-arms fire.

The failure to hold Ahnai Tangi Gorge meant that the Mahsuds fell back on the Barai Tangi defile, and here a new innovation was attempted. Light artillery, provided by the Afghans, opened up in defence of their positions, but the weight of British artillery fire and strafes by aircraft silenced them. As the weather deteriorated and there seemed to be no way to halt Skeen's 'steamroller', Mahsud resistance began to fade.

The Waziristan Campaign, 1936–7

The long-running security problem for the British on the North West Frontier and in Baluchistan, and particularly the unrest caused by the Faqir of Ipi in Waziristan in the years 1936–9, resulted in protracted military operations, but, fortunately for the British, the frontier had been relatively quiet during the First World War. Political agitation by the Pashtun movement that allied itself with Congress, the Khudai Khidmatgar or 'Redshirts' of Abdul Gaffar Khan, occasionally turned violent, but its period of protest was short-lived and it was easily contained.[48] In the period when one would have expected the Afghans and Pashtuns to have taken advantage of the weakened British security apparatus there was no coordinated action. Although the Quit India campaign, the Indian National Congress struggle towards independence, and British political machinations have been well-charted in previous scholarship, and while the performance of the British and Indian Armies have been scrutinized, there have been fewer attempts in relative terms to examine Afghan or Pashtun calculations in the 1930s beyond references to the Faqir of Ipi. The Waziristan Campaign, which was the last major operation on the North West Frontier before the Second World War, highlights particularly well the changing character of Afghan–Pashtun methods of war.

In Waziristan, Mirza Ali Khan, a pious Tori Khel Wazir, stirred agitation against the British when the verdict of a high-profile legal case involving a young girl was announced. The agitation led to a wave of raids, arson and murder.[49] Mirza Ali Khan, or the Faqir of Ipi as he became known, was able to draw on existing grievances and fears about British encroachments detrimental to traditional ways of life to lend credibility to his cause. His claim that Allah made him immune from the British seemed more persuasive when the colonial authorities initially failed to take action against him.[50] With volunteers flocking to his cause, he implored the clans to fight a Jihad against the British. When the Political Officers of the frontier asked the local elders and *maliks* to expel him, they refused, since this would have been a breach of *melmastia*.[51] The British therefore decided to 'show the flag', that is, to impress the tribesmen with the force at their disposal, and they sent two columns ('Razcol' and 'Tocol') up the Khaisora Valley in November 1936. However, far from over-awing the tribesmen, the troops provided a focus of resistance.[52] 'Razcol' was ambushed by the Faqir of Ipi's followers on 25 November, resulting in fourteen killed and forty-three wounded by the day's end.

Post-operational analyses stated that the situation had been the result of insufficient artillery, too little route security by picqueting caused by the imperative to link up both columns, and a lack of experience amongst the units involved. However, it also revealed a fatal miscalculation about the psychology of the Pashtuns: the advance of the British columns seemed to confirm the Faqir of Ipi's assertions that roads and new garrisons were but a prelude to the full occupation of the tribal areas, the destruction of Islam and the expropriation of their lands.[53]

The British reinforced their area with a brigade of the 11th Light Tank Company, armoured cars, artillery and a further two infantry battalions. Their objectives were to forestall the trouble spreading, punish the Tori Khels, and construct a road through the Khaisora Valley to facilitate future pacification. To unify the direction of operations, General Sir John Coleridge was given the command of all the military forces, Civil Armed Forces and the RAF assets. Having provoked the fighting and faced armed resistance, at this stage the British saw the solution in entirely military terms. The road was built in just two months whilst the *qalas* of known insurgent leaders were destroyed. The whole region was saturated with troops to concentrate force, but air operations were limited to an area 5 miles ahead and either side of the subsequent advance by 'Khaicol', another well-armed column. The headquarters compound of the Faqir at Arsal Kot was destroyed and Afghan volunteers, who had come to the aid of the Waziris, were driven off. British civilian control was then re-established when the Tori Khel submitted, but not until a total of 166 casualties had been sustained.[54]

However, the fighting was far from over; the Faqir kept on the move and did his best to encourage further resistance. In northern Waziristan in the spring of 1937, hostile parties attacked villages in the settled area of Derajat. Political Officers negotiated with local clans and demanded their submission. There were limited punitive air operations, but these had no effect.[55] A low intensity campaign manifest itself in the form of sniping at picquets, or attacks on bridges, culverts and telephone lines. A further two British brigades were sent to reinforce the garrison of North Waziristan, but the local *Khassadars* looked unreliable and so regular troops were soon tied down in route protection. To improve road security, permanent picquets were established, and sweeps conducted to open the road every day. Avoiding a direct confrontation, the Faqir's men continued to make isolated and intermittent attacks, although some were far more serious. At Damdil on 20 March 1937, for example, a determined night attack was made on 1/6th Gurkhas' camp picquet.[56] Swordsmen, supported by riflemen laying suppressive fire, rushed the Gurkhas' *sangars*, flinging hand grenades as they approached. The attacks were beaten off, and, with daylight, the machine-gun fire of armoured cars, artillery and strafing by aircraft compelled them to withdraw.

However, as so often in an insurgency, their losses were replaced, and, over the summer of 1937, the Faqir's *lashkar* strength increased to approximately 4,000 men. There were further raids into settled areas, with more attacks on bridges, culverts and picquets along the new road. Sniping against patrols was also frequent. The most successful and audacious ambush for the tribesmen occurred at Shahur Tangi on 9 April 1937.[57] A mixed Mahsud and Bhittani force, numbering somewhere between 100 and 300 men, knocked out the vehicle at the head of the column, and then the last vehicle, which hemmed in the rest. The armoured cars couldn't elevate their guns and the Indian escort was subjected to intense fire, losing approximately eighty men in the action. As a result, the British ceased all road traffic unless it was traversing a protected route, or where permanent picquets surrounded by barbed wire entanglements were established on high ground above the roads.

On 22 April, a new drive by British forces took place in the Khaisora and Shaktu areas, operating where it was relatively easy for armour and for aircraft to coordinate with ground attacks, but the *lashkars* carefully avoided fighting the full might of the Indian Army. Instead, the tribesmen waited for the opportunity to inflict heavier losses. To deter any further encroachments into their territory, they made a determined night attack on an encampment. Nevertheless, two days later, the same *lashkar* was caught in the open by artillery fire and air attack. On 30 April, another group of 100 clansmen was surprised as they tried to move between ambush positions. By the beginning of May, the clans around Khaisora had suffered significant losses. To administer the *coup de grâce*, 'WazDiv' (Waziristan Division), the formation based at Dosalli, intended to strike against the Tori Khels in Shaktu, the Faqir's stronghold. On 11 May the column made an unorthodox overnight advance over the Iblanke Range led by the Tochi Scouts.[58] Another brigade advanced in a converging arc, and, after a brief fire fight, the *lashkar* was cut down by aircraft as it tried to escape across the Sham Plain.

Although the Faqir escaped, the accumulated losses ensured that many fighters gave up the campaign at this point and a proportion of the Afghan volunteers left the Faqir's cause. In fact, the majority of the Tori Khels had obeyed their *maliks*, under the pressure of the British Political Officers, to keep out of the fighting. This was evidence of the weakness of the Faqir's cause and exemplified the importance for the British of a political effort alongside the military one. Moreover, when his base at Arsal Kot was taken, and his cave complex destroyed, the Faqir's prestige and credibility were further reduced.[59] Many of his promises that the British would be turned back had been proven false, and, although he maintained a small group of acolytes, the worst of the fighting was over. A new circular road was constructed during the summer and autumn of 1937 and mopping up operations were carried out against the remaining hostile clansmen, with a column making its way through Bhittani country following raids on settled areas. Small ambushes, the cutting of telephone lines, and the destruction of bridges and culverts continued, but these were regarded as a nuisance rather than events of any significance. In November 1937, British and Indian troops again swept through the Khaisora. The Faqir had to keep on the move to avoid capture, making it harder for him to maintain resistance and the momentum of support, and, as a result, raiding fell off to practically nil by the year's end.

The Waziristan campaign had been fought by only a few thousand tribesmen but it had required 61,000 troops to suppress it, a ratio not uncommon in other insurgencies.[60] The Indian Army had lost 245 killed and 684 wounded, with a further 73 deaths from diseases, despite its status as a 'low-intensity' conflict. From a military point of view, the Indian Army was able to assert control of the area of operations and to limit the mobility of the insurgents to some extent. They were able to inflict substantial casualties, despite their opponent's guerrilla tactics, because the fighters were determined to fight every physical manifestation of the occupation and that made them 'visible'. However, the greater strength and fire power of the Indian Army made the insurgents more reluctant to expose themselves to battle. It is for this reason that they resorted to sniping and night ambushes wherever possible in the latter stages of the campaign.

The principle of letting local forces lead where possible, in order to reduce costs, to make full use of their knowledge, and to avoid the antagonism created by the presence of 'foreigners', was well understood by the British authorities. The Tochi Scouts, who were about 5,000 strong, had proved useful when deployed alongside regulars or on independent pursuits. They were mobile, had local knowledge, and could operate on the flanks and rear against insurgents' attacks, although they were too lightly armed for sustained battles. It was even suggested that the Indian Army should recreate a specialized frontier unit which would be made up almost entirely of this sort of light infantry. However, the idea was rejected as impractical, on the grounds that the army needed to be prepared to fight in Afghanistan primarily against regular forces, although concerns about the reliability of the existing locally recruited auxiliaries in certain cases also played a part in the decision.[61]

The Indian Army had been restricted in its prosecution of the campaign by new political considerations. Rules of engagement were considered irksome, and John Masters, a subaltern in the 4th Gurkhas, believed 'we fought with one hand tied behind our backs'. The area of operations was strictly limited to a defined 'proscribed area'. Outside of this zone, they could not fire unless shot at. Within the zone they could only engage groups of more than ten men if they were armed and not on a path. Given that clansmen dressed the same as the inhabitants and could conceal their weapons, and that the nature of the country defied any neat definition of the term 'path', Masters admitted that the rules were not adhered to if 'there was no Political [Officer] around'.[62] Inexperienced units inflicted their own punitive measures against those closest to routes where hostile action had occurred. The local fighters would often mine roads and construct booby traps with grenades, but the clansmen's practice of mutilating the dead or wounded elicited the strongest reactions. In one incident, the troops retaliated by refusing to take prisoners.[63]

Masters parodied the rules of engagement with other military maxims. In response to the traditional idea to 'shoot first, shoot fastest, shoot last and shoot to kill', he wrote that the new rules implied: 'Do not shoot unless you have been shot at, and then try not to hurt anyone, there's a good chap!' And furthermore, to the maxim: 'Mystify, mislead and surprise your enemy, then never leave him a moment to gather himself again, but fall on him like a thunderclap and pursue him to his utter destruction, regardless of fatigue, casualties or cost', Masters wrote: 'Announce your intentions to the enemy, in order that he may have time to remove his women and children to a place of safety—and time to counter your plan. At all events, stop what you are doing as soon as he pretends to have had enough, so that he may gather again somewhere else'.[64]

However, the most controversial rules governed the use of air power. The older *Manual of Operations on the NWF of India* was eventually replaced in November 1938 by *Frontier Warfare (Army and RAF) 1939*, but the publication was delayed because of sensitivity about the issue of bombing, especially of villages.[65] Warnings were issued by dropping leaflets prior to a bombing run on property, usually twice; although in certain circumstances it might only be once. The length of time between warnings and a bombing was determined by how long it would take for a village to convene, discuss and then present a response or submission, but it was never less than 24 hours. The warnings had to specify which tribe and section were affected, and an outline of the circumstances that led to the threat. Clear instructions, including the precise course they had to follow, and the place and date where a submission was to be made, were also to be included. The final leaflet drop was printed on red paper, which included the same details and the explicit reason why air action was about to be taken against them, and a description of the nearest place of refuge. To avoid the risk that civilians would not get the warnings, ground messages were also delivered if possible. After the action, white leaflets were dropped, and efforts would be made to destroy any unexploded ordnance because local clans tried to make use of them as road mines.[66]

In subsequent interviews, older tribesmen recalled that not all got the warnings in time because they were widely dispersed across the hills. The effects of bombing on a marginal community in mid-winter were clearly far-reaching. One remarked: 'When we saw the aeroplanes appear without warning in the sky–we would hide in caves, gorges, in the undergrowth and wherever we could find shelter. Some dug trenches and hid in them'.[67] Another recalled: 'We had to leave most of the food behind in the villages. Many people died of hunger. People had to leave their homes at night and that wasn't easy, especially for the elderly, the women and children. Some of them died on the way to the mountains; many children died due to the cold and the harsh weather. Hunger was a big problem. The food we had was only enough to last us for two or three days. The children suffered the most'. Reflecting on the duration of the effects, he continued: 'The difficulties were limitless for everyone. The hardship went on for years'. As with all oral history, chronology is uncertain and it is not entirely certain whether these descriptions refer to the 1930s or the Soviet era.

Although major operations had ceased in 1937, the Faqir of Ipi remained at large, and between 1938 and 1939 'irreconcilable tribesmen' continued to snipe at troops and posts, attack roads, rob traffic and cut telephone lines.[68] Villages in Derajat were raided and special defensive arrangements had to be made. Troops were called in and a line of communication established to provide platforms of observation using the regulars, Tochi Scouts and aircraft patrols. However, the various divisions of the Masud and Waziri clans did not necessarily recognize any settlement made by their neighbours and continued their resistance independently, leading to a fragmented peace, whilst some simply resumed their fighting once the pressure was off. On 23 July 1938 there was a serious raid on Bannu, in which several civilians were killed and properties burned.[69] Many fighters were killed and 20 were captured, but the rest stayed in the hills nearby and hundreds of civilians left their homes in fear of further violence.

Throughout operations in Waziristan, the British had kept a close eye on the Afghans. Referring to all Pashtuns, a military handbook was published in

1933 and advised: 'They appreciate justice, an open hand, firmness and patience, good humour and the English disposition to punish and be friends again', but there was also a warning that the Pashtuns and Afghans were a mass of contradictions.[70] Amongst the lessons of past wars for officers to remember when fighting the Afghans came the advice: 'Never surrender when you are in a tight corner', which might result in a barbarous death; it was thought to be better to die fighting and preserve one's honour. British officers were advised to conduct a 'vigorous offensive' since 'Afghans are easily discouraged'. The emphasis was on 'resolute fighting' with an attack timed for the right moment to cause a loss of confidence. In negotiations, officers were warned: 'Never trust an Afghan', since 'firmness combined with bold and vigorous action' was the safest way to deal with Afghan 'guile and chichanery'. British troops were cautioned 'never relax precautions', since the Afghans were 'observant' and 'will spot weaknesses' since 'even a small tactical success has an extraordinarily stimulating effect on the Afghan'. British and Indian infantry were thought to be best employed in 'dashing offensive action' with armoured vehicles and cavalry used boldly and rapidly in pursuit.

The British military handbook illustrated the characteristics of regular armies operating in mountain warfare, highlighting the importance of the need to picquet heights on a route, well-sited perimeter camps, and recommended movements along spurs and not vulnerable *nalas*. There was always a need for the careful coordination of rearguards, advice to 'get settled before dark by proper calculation of time and space', the avoidance of weak detachments, and an emphasis on leaving strong camps and depots. The guide suggested that, against Afghans, commanders should 'never hesitate or remain inactive' and that speed and energy were required. The handbook noted that, since 'fanaticism' impels sudden charges by Afghans, troops should be prepared at all times for these rushes, and, referring to British firepower, suggested they 'will dissolve if resolutely met'. In defence, it was suggested that 'Afghans will hold a position with utmost determination until their front is penetrated or flank turned' then they make 'a sudden retreat in disorder'.

To counter the guerrilla-style low intensity conflict in the mountains, officers were told to 'Do unto the Afghans as they do unto you', namely 'lay ambushes, especially in withdrawal; use night marches; dawn attacks and frequent surprises, especially in winter' when their supplies were more vulnerable. There was advice to 'never make terms with the Afghans, unless they can be compelled to observe those terms', and 'never attempt to conceal military weakness by the payment of subsidies or bribes', although this was a practice familiar to Political Officers. Readers were advised to 'pay cash on delivery—never in advance' for their locally procured supplies because the locals could not be trusted to engage in honest commerce. Infringements of all kinds were to be punished in a way that was 'stern and drastic' since 'half measures are worse than useless'. When fighting had broken out, officers were urged to take offensive action which should be 'planned to inflict the heaviest casualties', followed by a 'relentless pursuit'. Tribunals that attempted to carry out a trial and an execution of individual guerrillas were not advised since they 'just exasperate and fuel resentment'. The handbook concluded with an awareness of the patience that Afghans exhibit and the importance of regaining a sense of honour, noting that 'Afghans will often wait for hours if compelled to abandon a position, and pursue [British forces] as a means to regain honour'. There was also a suggestion that Afghans would try to conceal their weaknesses for the sake of honour, for, when forced to retreat: 'They invariably contend they were merely luring an enemy into a trap'.

The Frontier during the Second World War

At the outbreak of the Second World War in 1939, there were forty-eight British and Indian battalions on the North West Frontier, which represented 38 per cent of the army in India's peacetime strength and gave some indication of how seriously the colonial authorities took the threat and manpower demands of guerrilla warfare. With the Faqir of Ipi still raiding Derajat, in December 1940 it was decided to build frontier posts in Waziristan. However, intelligence that the Faqir of Ipi was the object of some interest to German and Italian envoys in Afghanistan, and the success of the *Wehrmacht* against Russia in 1941, caused concern.[71] In an unwitting form of flattery for the Pashtuns, it was suggested that the Indian Army would stop the Axis forces in Afghanistan's mountains using Pashtun tactics and mountain warfare techniques: 'The Army in India starts with having studied the Pathan and his ways and having acquaintance with the conditions, tactical and administrative, of fighting in the mountains. It should be able to adapt the Pathan's harassing tactic to worrying a more stereotyped opponent both near the battlefront and on the L[ine] of C[ommunication]'.[72]

By 1943, there were fifty-seven British and Indian infantry battalions and four armoured car regiments committed to the North West Frontier, although, by then, it was the threat of invasion on the north-eastern border that was absorbing the lion's share of the wartime expansion of the Indian Army. The

NWFP governor's fortnightly intelligence reports provide an interesting assessment of the falling away of Pashtun resistance during the conflict and the clans' interest in the war. Initially, the Faqir of Ipi and the insurgents kept up their routine of raids and 'outrages'.[73] By February 1942, the situation had changed and the Governor wrote: 'I believe that the efforts we have been making for some time to influence the Faqir through two or three important mullahs are bearing some fruit'.[74] In August 1942, it was estimated there had been 57 incidents for the year to date, which compared with 59 incidents in 1941, and 176 in 1940.[75] The steady decline in violence continued so that by 1944–5 the frontier was relatively quiet.

There were multiple explanations for this trend. The Governor admitted that during the war 'we have a large number of local people of influence, including many of the best known mullahs, working for us'.[76] Newspapers were carefully monitored for signs of propaganda.[77] Recruiting was also more problematic for both the Indian Army and the Faqir during the late summer when labour was needed for wheat cutting, but this also absorbed the numbers of young raiders. The Governor noted that: 'In all the country through which I have toured the paucity of young men of military age is now very noticeable'. The decline in raids may also have been in response to the British themselves assuming a defensive posture.

A confidential report in December noted that in Kurram and Dera Ismail Khan, 'the general attitude of the people [was] excellent'.[78] The same report noted that at all the *jirgas*, the tribesmen expressed pleasure in the Allied victories in North Africa and Stalingrad, whilst the Indian National Congress (INC) was 'rarely mentioned'. They were 'far more interested in their own small problems of irrigation' and the rising cost of foodstuffs, but the report noted that it was remarkable how well informed the average villager was regarding the general trend of the war. Swabi Tehsil in Mardan district was one of the 'bad spots' in 1930, and the report stated: 'It is difficult to picture it as ever having been in that condition. It is a great recruiting area, and has a very fine record during this war. One village which has produced 550 recruits in the last three years has got a war memorial of the last war which shows only 112 were enlisted between 1914 and 1918'.[79] In the *Review of Frontier Defence* in 1944, in a tacit acknowledgement that forward garrisons tended to encourage resistance, there was a recommendation to revert to Curzon's policy of 1901, namely to withdraw the Indian Army from its garrisons inside tribal areas and place them with smaller bodies of frontier Armed Civil Forces. It was a policy decision that Pakistan itself adopted in 1948.

The Faqir of Ipi remained at large until 1960, but his campaign of resistance was never as effective as it had been, briefly, in 1936. After the war, the British returned to their policy of maintaining local auxiliaries in the frontier province while keeping larger regular garrisons further back inside British territory. The British, nevertheless, were soon to leave South Asia and the NWFP was incorporated into Pakistan. Relations between Afghanistan and Pakistan were tense periodically, but, despite calls for a revision of the border, there were no major conflicts, not least because Pakistan's focus was on fighting India and contesting the sovereignty of Kashmir. Afghanistan would not be troubled by a serious conflict until the domestic unrest of the 1970s.

6

THE SOVIET WAR

THE MUJAHIDEEN, IDEOLOGY
AND GUERRILLA WAR, 1978–89

Resistance to the Afghan communist government and the subsequent Soviet military intervention changed profoundly the manner in which the Afghans conducted war. This was, in essence, a civil war into which foreign forces of the 'Soviet Limited Contingent' were committed, but which also drew in Pakistan, the United States and, in a more limited way, Iran and a number of Gulf States. Foreign intervention changed the character of the war dramatically and affected the lives of every Afghan more comprehensively than previous conflicts, but this was also an intensely ideological war which had long-term effects on the country and on the region. The resistance groups found themselves in an asymmetrical conflict which required new approaches to warfare, and a whole generation was schooled in the arts of guerrilla operations and political warfare, with varying degrees of success.

After the Soviet withdrawal, the civil war continued and new approaches to fighting emerged in the form of conventional operations. These were conducted using former communist government and Soviet equipment or arms and munitions supplied by Pakistan, although for some it proved difficult to shake off the guerrilla style of fighting. This preference, the sheer number of factions and the parity of strength between them led to a protracted conflict. In this period Afghan force structures also changed. The most dramatic development was the gradual disintegration of the Afghan regular army and the emergence of militias led by paramilitary freebooters popularly styled as 'warlords'. Yet there were some themes of consistency, and older cultural traditions influenced the conduct of operations during the Soviet War. Indeed, it is striking how the conflict was interpreted through the traditional Afghan cultural lens. Nevertheless, in almost every aspect of the way the war was fought, even in the realm of negotiations, there was a great deal of change.

In the 1960s, Prime Minister Daud Mohammd Khan had championed the creation of 'Pashtunistan' which would wrest the North West Frontier Province from Pakistan, fulfil an irredentist dream of recovering lost territory, and create a powerful, Ghilzai-dominated bloc in Afghan politics. The Afghan government extended support to the mullahs of the Federally Administered Tribal Area and even appeared complicit in a 1960 uprising of 15,000 Pashtuns who crossed the Durand Line, with the Afghan Army closely behind them.[1] Yet all was not as it seemed. Daoud, a Durrani Muhammadzai Pashtun, appeared to favour a separatist movement but was in fact keen to exploit a nationalist-ethnic issue in order to popularize his position at home. The Pakistan government also found it useful to criticize Afghanistan for 'encouraging' the separatists for its own domestic ends. But the result was far-reaching. The severance of relations between Pakistan and Afghanistan meant that Afghanistan was forced firmly into the arms of the Soviet Union as an outlet for its goods and therefore its customs revenue. With Pakistan and Iran in the American sphere, Afghanistan provided the Soviets with a useful partner in the region.[2]

For years, Afghanistan was courted by both the United States and the Soviet Union in their Cold War rivalry, but by the 1970s, the number of Soviet advisors increased. The Afghan Marxist party, the PDPA (People's Democratic Party of Afghanistan) gained support in urban areas, particularly amongst students and intellectuals. The party was nevertheless divided into two rival factions, Parcham (banner) and Khalq (masses), which, like most Afghan politics, were dominated by rival clans or confederations. King Zahir Shah's brief experiment with a limited democracy between 1963 and 1973 merely intensified rivalry between these radical factions, which, in turn, alienated the religious conservatives. The more traditionalist elements of society were also offended by Western influences, the growth of narco-corruption and by increasing numbers of foreign advisors. Despite the growth of radical politics in urban areas, much of rural Afghanistan would have been recognizable to Babur of the sixteenth century. It was the unchanging nature of religion, agricultural life and tribal culture that now seemed under threat from 'modernity'. Nepotism in government, a declining state revenue and resentment at Soviet influence brought matters to a head. Daoud seized power in 1973 in what he called the

Inquilab (Revolution), a title designed to earn support from his Soviet neighbours. The Russians responded: financial aid increased to $1.25 billion by 1979 and in 1977 General Secretary Brezhnev appeared to give the Soviet seal of approval in a state visit. The Afghan Army and Air Force were equipped with Soviet weapons, vehicles and aircraft. To all appearances, Afghanistan looked like another Soviet bloc state.

In fact, Daoud wore his communist credentials lightly and would have preferred to make Afghanistan a non-aligned nation. He resented Brezhnev's demands and the influx of yet more Soviet advisors. His attempts to achieve a rapprochement with Pakistan, an ally of the United States, increased Soviet suspicions that Daoud might be insincere in his politics. The death of a Parcham official under suspicious circumstances soon generated fears of a purge of the entire PDPA. Given Daoud's true allegiances, this fear had some grounds. The result was that the Parcham and Khalqi factions, led respectively by Barbak Karmal and Mohammed Nor Taraki, launched a *coup d'état* against Daoud on 27 April 1978, an event subsequently edified as the Saur Revolution. During the mêlée, Daoud was murdered along with his family. In the aftermath, thousands of alleged 'bourgeoisie', a euphemism for all enemies of the communist state, were arrested. Led by young Marxist officers, troops of the 4th Brigade, a commando unit and elements of the air force had taken part in the coup, while only 1,800 troops had stayed loyal to Daoud, and this made it clear that control of the armed forces would be vital to the success of any political action. Khalq had already set up a secret 'United Front of Afghan Communists' amongst the officer corps to facilitate their control of the armed forces before they took power. Nevertheless, the coup was hardly swift: the operation had begun in the morning at Kabul airport, but it was not until 16.00 hrs that resistance at Daoud's palace was crushed, and the aircraft appear to have been called in because of the strength of the defences.[3]

The Khalqis, the dominant faction of the PDPA, could command no consensus. They issued decrees but imposed them with coercion. They demanded land reform and called for women's equality, outraging rural, conservative opinion. Opposition was met with brutality and murder. The infamous Pul-i-Charki prison began to take political prisoners and torture them. Then Hafizullah Amin took over as Prime Minister. His method of restoring order was to inflict yet more terror and coercion. He executed his rivals, including Taraki. He sent his secret police to suppress, arrest or murder all opposition. Villages which supported the embryonic resistance were razed and the inhabitants butchered. An attempt by protestors to seize the centre of Kabul was betrayed and the activists were arrested or killed. On 15 March 1979, Khalqi officials and their Soviet advisors were attacked by a mob in Herat chanting Islamic slogans.[4] Anxiety about an Islamist movement destabilizing the southern USSR grew in Moscow.

Afghanistan had descended into civil war. It is striking that the period between April 1978 and December 1979 is so often overshadowed by the subsequent Soviet intervention. Nevertheless, this was a critical period in Afghanistan's politics, generating violent and widespread opposition to the government in Kabul to such an extent that, as soon as Soviet forces arrived, they were confronted by armed and increasingly organized resistance.

With Iran in turmoil in 1979, and the West deploying medium-range nuclear missiles in Europe, Moscow felt it had to act to restore order and influence along its vulnerable southern flank, not least because an Islamist revolt threatened to engulf the Central Asian Soviet Republics. With Hungary (1956) and the Prague Spring (1968) in mind, the Soviet Union launched an air mobile *coup de main* on Kabul. Amin was caught and killed by the KGB. Simultaneously a motor rifle division thrust southwards from Termez and Kushka. Within days, the Soviets controlled the main corridors of communication and the urban centres, and had installed Barbak Karmal in power. Karmal was informed that his role was to reunify the political parties, modernize the army, popularize the regime, extend the government's remit and carry out economic development.

However, the USSR's intervention was seen by the embittered Afghan people as another form of coercion, and Karmal was regarded as little more than the puppet of a foreign power. Worse, the reform agenda of the government confirmed fears that the regime intended to restructure Afghanistan completely. The opposition to the Afghan government and its Soviet military support therefore assumed the character of a struggle for liberation from foreign ideologues in defence of Islam. The resistance believed they were defending the people and the very fabric of their life in a people's war. One fighter remarked to a journalist: 'Why do you differentiate between fighters and old men, women and children? If you have courage and treasure freedom, you are mujahed. We are all mujahedeen'.[5]

The Soviet troops made little attempt to win the 'hearts and minds' of the Afghan population. Since the resistance fighters were dressed in civilian clothes, and attacks against Soviet forces normally took the form of ambushes, the Soviet troops often assumed that all the Afghans opposed them. A culture of systematic bullying, *dedovshchina* (the grandfather system), within the Soviet forces also encouraged a similar attitude of punishment towards Afghan civilians.[6]

The only experience the Soviets could draw upon for their intervention in Afghanistan and the suppression of political opposition was the example of Hungary or Czechoslovakia. In these cases, Soviet forces had moved directly to the main urban centres and, largely by their presence alone or by the support of secret police and Special Forces, they had quelled popular protests. However, in Afghanistan, while they had initially treated the campaign as one of quelling civil unrest, the character of the war that developed did not suit the doctrine of the Soviet army. Their tactical approach, designed for the European theatre, dictated that armoured and motor rifle forces would thrust along narrow axes, securing lines of communication and destroying utterly any location of resistance by combined armour-infantry-air assault. The Soviet Army had little experience or training in a protracted counterinsurgency role. This explains their techniques of 'clearance', where they sought to control certain areas of ground by destroying property and fighters in their path, and of driving out the population. Edward Giradet, a journalist who covered the war, believed that 'the occupation forces unleashed a deliberate policy of "rubblisation" aimed at emptying the border regions and turning them into a no-man's land devoid of human habitation except for pro-government enclaves and garrisons'.[7] This was a calculated strategy to apply maximum force to deprive the embryonic resistance of any local popular support. To escape destruction some 800,000 Afghans had fled across the border to Pakistan by May 1980.

The overall strategy was initially to deny the resistance of popular support, but when this failed the Soviets turned to severing the means by which the insurgents could be supplied. This meant not only stripping areas of civilians or of persuading them, through destruction, that it was too costly to support the resistance, but also of interdicting supply routes from outside the country. The bulk of the insurgents' war material came over the Pakistan border. A series of operations were mounted to clear particular nests of support and to cut these lines of communications, but the steady attrition through ambushes and mines meant that, between 1980 and 1985, the Soviet 40th Army lost 9,175 killed in action.

To wean the Afghan population from the resistance, the Soviets continued with their pre-war development work and initiated new projects. Road building, well digging and urban development projects were common. At Jalalabad, a major irrigation project had produced six large state farms, producing citrus fruit, vegetable oils, dairy products and meat. The work had included the construction of a dam and a canal, a hydroelectric power station, a workshop, a timber yard and a jam factory. Soviet civilian advisors, numbering over 2,800 men and women, continued to operate as best they could, although most were armed or protected. Not all advisors were civilian. There were between 1,600 and 1,800 Soviet military advisers in Afghanistan by the end of 1980, some of whom had served in the country before the intervention. The Soviets retained most influence at senior levels. There were at least 60 generals, and the rest were distributed at a ratio of 11 officers to each Afghan Army division, 4 to each regiment and 4 to every battalion, each of which had one or more interpreters.[8] Of the aid budget, a significant amount went to the Afghan Army. The total aid to the Afghan military and the Soviet Limited Contingent was 1,578.5 million roubles in 1984, increasing to Rs 2,623.8 in 1985, Rs 3,197.4 in 1986, and Rs 4,116 in 1987. This equates to $7.5 billion over four years.[9] While the resistance did their best to seize the assets of development work to fund the insurgency, there was often a struggle with local interests who benefited. When the Soviets inserted taps on the fuel pipelines along the Salang Highway to enable locals to obtain free fuel, for example attempts by the resistance to destroy the line led to opposition.[10]

The Soviets were faced by several problems in trying to crush the insurgency. They found it impossible to seal off the eastern border with Pakistan, across which trickled the arms, ammunition and personnel to sustain the resistance. Detachments of Special Forces did eliminate certain groups of fighters, but their own units could be isolated and wiped out. The general configuration of the ground, with its complex of mountains, valleys and caves, provided the Mujahideen resistance with a large arena for guerrilla operations and plenty of places for concealment. Indeed, the Mujahideen had a number of criteria considered essential by theorists for a successful insurgency, a fact recognized by their backers in the Pakistan intelligence service, the ISI.[11] Brigadier Mohammad Yousaf, who directed Mujahideen operations from within Pakistan, believed that the Afghan resistance enjoyed the support of the people, who, at great risk to themselves, would 'supply shelter, food, recruits and information'. He felt that guerrillas need to 'believe implicitly' in their cause and 'be willing to sacrifice himself completely to achieve victory'. Yousaf concluded: 'The Afghans had Islam. They fought a Jihad, they fought to protect their homes and families'. Yet Yousaf did not acknowledge that he was referring only to 'his' Afghans. The defence of the country against foreign influences was also the motivating factor for the government forces. He referred to the requirement for inhospitable terrain and a safe haven, acknowledging that Pakistan provided 'a secure base to which the guerrilla could withdraw to rest and refit without fear of attack'. The most important element of any resistance though, he concluded, was external backing, and he acknowledged that Pakistan provided access to international councils and funds.

Yousaf knew that there could be no conventional operations against the logistical chain from the Soviet frontier to the major urban centres, and much as he would have preferred to 'turn their flank' and sever their line of communications, he had to orchestrate a campaign of a thousand cuts: 'The better strategy would be the raid, the ambush, the stand-off attack, but made with such frequency and ferocity that the loss of blood from these multiple cuts would seriously weaken the enemy's ability to continue'. He believed in 'the added benefit of compelling the Soviets to tie down an ever higher proportion of their men in static security duties'.[12] He estimated that perhaps nine out of every 10 troops were committed to these tasks and was eager for the Mujahideen to retain the initiative.[13] The assessment is accurate but perhaps attributes rather too much credit to the Pakistani ISI. The fact is that the Mujahideen, even without the higher direction of the ISI, were already inflicting a number of losses on the Democratic Republic of Afghanistan (DRA) and Soviet forces, and the operations of the northern factions, largely cut off from the Pakistani sources of supply, underscores this fact.[14]

The ISI believed that pressure had to be brought to bear on Kabul, which they believed was the centre of gravity of the campaign. General Akhtar, as head of the service, believed that the capital should be subjected to 'every type of assault and harassment' in order to 'gain a political and psychological edge in the international press and media'.[15] This effort to popularize the Mujahideen cause through broadcasting the actions of the resistance was fraught with risks. If a direct association was made with Pakistan, then there could be retaliation by the Soviets. Moreover, terrorist operations could even backfire on the resistance as civilian casualties would be the inevitable consequence of such a campaign. The most important factor, which Yousaf and the ISI played down somewhat, was the Cold War. The opportunity to challenge and inflict losses on the Soviets was far more attractive for Westerners than championing the Mujahideen as an Islamic resistance movement. Comparisons might be drawn with American indifference, even hostility towards contemporary organizations like the PLO to prove the point.

The Soviets developed their tactics in response to the guerrilla operations of the Mujahideen. Seizing the high ground with paratrooper units and heliborne lifts in a form of vertical envelopment replaced a purely armour-infantry doctrine, although the extensive use of firepower, including artillery and mortar concentrations, tended to squander the element of surprise. Airstrikes and carpet bombing were particularly important throughout the campaign. Colonel Aleksandr Rutskoi of the Soviet air force told the Russian parliament after the war that air power had been effective in neutralizing resistance: 'A *kishlak* fires at us and kills someone. I send up a couple of planes and there is nothing left of the *kishlak*. After I've burned a couple of *kishlaks* they stop shooting'.[16] Jet aircraft could only be used to neutralize area targets, such as villages that might harbour gunmen, and more precise targeting was dependent on close air support from helicopter gunships, especially the notorious Hind M1–24 with its array of 12.7 mm cannon, 57 mm rockets, high explosive bombs, white phosphorous, incendiaries, cluster bombs and scatterable mines. Air attacks were used to cover movement, for deception, to neutralize positions offering resistance and to exact reprisals after a successful Mujahideen ambush.[17]

Entire populations migrated to the cities to get food, and to avoid the bombing of many thousands more left the country and were housed in refugee camps. One Kabuli businessman remarked that 'the resistance must go on, but we must also feed our families. There are no jobs left to speak of in the countryside, so we have no choice but to move to the cities'.[18] Although many internally displaced people who migrated to the urban areas were PDPA or their families, a significant proportion supported the Mujahideen and, while they took jobs with the government to survive, they sent remittances to the resistance. Some tried to continue to farm the land in rural areas; the rest lived outside the country. By the end of the war it was estimated there were 5 million Afghan refugees in Iran and Pakistan out of a population of 19.5 million.[19]

Soviet ground forces raided villages where resistance fighters were thought to be based, advanced into the mountains to destroy Mujahideen bases, mounted ambushes and perfected counter-ambush drills, and mined routes which they suspected the resistance used. In contrast to the fluid, lightly-equipped resistance, many Afghan and Soviet troops were pinned to the defence of roads, settlements and communications. More than a third were tied up in this way and it is estimated that combat troops, that is those who took part in regular, offensive operations, amounted to only 20 per cent of the total strength of the 40th Army. Only 51 battalions were engaged in frequent operations out of the 133 battalions in the 40th Army, and, of these, some battalion commanders complained that it was almost impossible to get all the men to take part in combat.[20] The sheer effort of getting ammunition and combat supplies into the country by road and air absorbed much of the Soviet 40th Army and the Afghan forces. By far the most useful counter-insurgent troops were the Special Forces units.[21] They could operate deep in the mountains to ambush the guerrillas, and they were particularly adept at intercepting the routes taken by the Mujahideen caravans. In one operation in May 1987 they destroyed a large Mujahideen column, killing 187 fighters and capturing large quantities of ammunition and equipment. Nevertheless, the Soviets themselves believed they only succeeded in intercepting some 15–20 per cent of all the caravans.

While regular motor rifle formations were the most numerous forces in all major operations, and some reached high levels of efficiency and competency in mountain warfare, the Mujahideen reserved the greatest respect for the elite *Spetznaz*, parachute units, and reconnaissance elements of the Motor Rifle Regiments. All units were capable of mounting ambushes. In July 1983 the Mujahideen had not observed the necessary security precaution of varying their route, and they were subjected to an ambush where the Soviets had dug in tanks and infantry on two sides of a valley with a stop group to close off the exit. The ambush resulted in the killing of over 100 fighters and drivers.[22] The Soviets established a Special Forces Group in 1985 to coordinate their operations, consisting of 2 brigades, each of 8 battalions, an independent company, an independent reconnaissance battalion, 4 regimental reconnaissance companies and 9 reconnaissance platoons, with supporting assets. The military personnel totalled 3,000 men, and attached to them for specific operations were members of the intelligence agencies.

The defence of urban areas and keeping open routes were fundamental parts of the Soviet strategy, which absorbed much of the Afghan government forces and more than 20,000 soldiers of 40th Army. A network of over 800 blockhouses (*zastavas*) were placed at regular intervals around major cities, airports, power stations, along roads and pipelines, and on strategically important high ground. Each one had the ability to call in an airstrike or artillery barrage in a FPF (final protective fire) plan. The remote posts, particularly those near the border, were manned by Afghan troops less than enthusiastic about their duties. While some *zastavo* were attacked, other garrisons exercised a 'live and let live' system. Giradet visited one in 1982 and found 'a group of bored conscripts, ... kicking an empty can about. We met several soldiers hauling water from a nearby desert well. We shook hands and they watched as dozens of guerrillas marched by, leading strings of pack mules loaded with arms, ammunition and other supplies'.[23] Information, guides, routes through minefields and safe conduct passes were exchanged.

The Afghan Army, which was supposed to support the Soviets, was plagued by desertions, defections, informers, ghost pay rolling and even murdered some of its Russian officers. Many battalions were unwilling to engage in combat. In theory the army of 1979 consisted of 10 divisions, armed with modern Soviet weapons, with its own integral aircraft, armour and artillery.[24] By 1989 the army had expanded to 12 divisions, with several specialized brigades and support services. However, Afghan units were often understrength. A division might only be able to muster 1,000 men. Entire units defected. Two brigades of the 9th Division in Kunar, a brigade in Badakhshan and another brigade of the 11th Division at Jalalabad abandoned the army and either went home or joined the resistance. The Afghan Air Force had 7 air regiments, with 30 fast jets, over 70 fighter-bombers, 50 bombers, 76 helicopters and 40 transport aircraft. Many of the officers, pilots and ground crew spoke Russian and had received their specialist training inside the Soviet Union.[25] But many officers of the army and air force were not trusted by their own government or by the Soviets. Amin and then Karmal had sacked, arrested or executed officers for disloyalty. Some defected and their expertise was invaluable to the Mujahideen.

The desertions reached epidemic proportions by 1980, with the losing a quarter of their strength. The government lowered the age of conscription from 18 to 15, forced villages to provide manpower at gunpoint, increased service to a three-year term and mobilized reservists up to the age of 39, although sometimes men of 55 were still serving.[26] After their first three-year stint, soldiers were granted two years' leave, and then they were required to serve a further three or four years. The only exemption was if soldiers married and had children. The measures succeeded in stemming the flood, although attrition was never resolved. The available pool of manpower was also drained by clearance operations. Those who refused to enlist were given a four-year gaol sentence. Absenteeism without authorization could carry a sentence of five years. Desertion could carry a penalty of fifteen years or execution.[27] Ultimately, conscription was extended to four years during the conflict, a measure which provoked mutinies in some battalions. Eventually the army increased to 40,000 by 1982 and, theoretically, to 150,000 by 1989.[28] However, each of the divisions rarely exceeded 5,000 men.[29] Possibly as many as 50 per cent of the conscripts deserted and most of them absconded with their weapons. Not all joined the resistance, and there were reports of some soldiers changing sides up to seven times. Money was often the determining factor. Traditions of low pay in the army were never improved upon, and soldiers earned 200 *afghanis* a month, the equivalent of $2. In combat, Soviet commanders could not be sure whether the Afghan troops would either sit out the whole action or else simply run off. Garrisons were at least hemmed in by their own barbed wire and mines. By early 1984, attempts to conscript at gunpoint were failing even in permissive areas, as elders tried to spirit the young men away to the hills in order to preserve precious agricultural manpower.[30]

Afghan officers began to complain that they were being used for all the most dangerous missions, while the Soviets preserved their manpower. There were clearly tensions when Afghan personnel felt as if they were treated as second-class citizens in their own country. General Kutsenko, a senior military advisor to the Afghan Army, concluded: 'The Soviet military [officers] served only two years and were then replaced. Few of them learned the customs of the local tribes. But the Afghan commanders had been fighting for 5 to 8 years and they well understood the psychology of their people'.[31] Believing that the Soviets should have allowed Afghan units to conduct their own operations, he observed a lack of cooperation between Afghan and Soviet commanders and a general deterioration in morale: '... Soviet officers began to say that if the Afghan forces did not want to fight the *mujahedin*, why should they be doing so?'

This attitude led to unofficial understandings between government troops and the resistance. Major Izmailov, a Muslim in the Soviet 40th Army, took the view that the Afghans needed to be treated courteously, recommending that convoys drove through villages at very low speeds to avoid accidents, stopping to help if there were accidents, and crucially talking to the village elders prior to moves. If there were some incident, Izmailov argued, the Afghans would take payment in kind in compensation, even for a death. Conversely, if the Russians refused to accept responsibility or give compensation then the Afghans assert *badal*, mining the routes and setting up ambushes. The Mujahideen claimed that their intelligence was so good they could identify column commanders. Izmailov related how one Soviet colonel who refused to treat the locals well had his column ambushed in February 1987 and the colonel was killed.[32]

The Soviet army was often deprived of vital intelligence. Since the resistance did not always use radios, the Soviets needed human intelligence. The KGB *Kaskad*, later known as *Omega*, and Interior Ministry *Kobalt* teams were only able to provide a limited amount of information.[33] For all its coercion, the infamous KhAD (*Khadamat-e Etela'at-e Dawlati*, the State Information Agency or secret police) was often equally constrained. The Soviet teams set out to construct a web of agents among the Mujahideen, to study the 'Human Terrain' of clan networks in their area of operations, and to identify the locations of Mujahideen bases, main supply routes and weapons caches. The Afghan and Soviet agencies were supposed to facilitate defections by Mujahideen commanders and reconcile them to the government. They practised 'Psyops' and attempted to fuel the rivalry between clans to the point where Mujahideen groups would fight each other. Intelligence teams were also expected to conduct covert operations: to kill or capture foreign advisors attached to the resistance. Nevertheless, there were serious problems with counter-intelligence. The resistance maintained a number of sympathetic personnel within the ranks of the Afghan Army or the *Tsrandoi* (gendarmerie). In May 1985 the head of the Military Intelligence Department of the Afghan General Staff, General Khalil, was arrested with ten of his officers. He was charged with supplying intelligence to Ahmad Shah Masud, the Afghan–Tajik Mujahideen commander in the Panjshir Valley.[34]

Intelligence agencies could also act as the first interlocutors in negotiations between the resistance and the Soviets and Afghan government, but for the communists all talks were just part of a package of counterinsurgency measures. Throughout the campaign the Soviets reinforced their presence in Afghanistan, bringing in more men and resources, eventually fielding 108,800 personnel. Nuclei projects were also designed to bring about rural development and engage the local *ulema* in them.[35] In some cases, locals were made responsible for the security of development projects. Hasan Khan Kharokhel, an elder from Sarobi, was paid and given weapons to protect hydro-electric power pylons that ran through his lands. The Mujahideen eventually threatened the elder, an ultimatum being delivered by Abdul Haq in August 1984 to the effect that he must 'choose sides'. Fearing retaliation, the elder and 300 related families abandoned Sarobi and resettled in Pakistan. Soon after, the pylons were blown up, causing black-outs in Kabul. In many development projects, the small detachments of Afghan troops that were sent to guard them were overrun by resistance fighters, and the Soviet representatives in nuclei projects often lacked the authority to respond quickly or effectively to the demands of the rural population. By 1985–6, the emphasis was on reaching agreement with local elders or leaders and large-scale Soviet operations had become rare. The most significant step was the agreement to set up self-defence units.[36] There were, as a result, fewer attacks on government forces in Pashtun areas in the eastern border regions where these militias existed.

Meanwhile, the Afghan Army continued to be strengthened: discipline was tightened and desertion curtailed. To ameliorate the feelings of the population, freedom of religion was declared and mullahs were incorporated into the Afghan Army's administration. However, the Mujahideen did their best to spread their influence within the army and try to prevent an end to combat operations. Thus the protracted character of the war continued. There were occasional operations led by the Afghan Army and supported by Soviet firepower, but the Russians began their withdrawal in 1987. That year, aside from Operation Majistral in Khost and Operation Typhoon in the Panjshir, Soviet forces remained largely on the defensive.

The Mujahideen

Jon Lee Anderson, who travelled with the Afghan resistance, observed:

Just as they can be harsh when deciding the fate of other people's lives, they can also be stoic when it comes to their own. This stoicism comes out of their culture, in which war enjoys an exalted status, and from their faith in the Islamic idea that after death, a better life awaits. If they are to die, so be it, as long as they do well in battle in the eyes of God. They are mujahedin, holy warriors. They live to make holy war, to kill the enemy, and if necessary be martyred themselves. These are facts they accept. Most of them would have it no other way.[37]

The Mujahideen was a highly motivated movement. They combined religious devotion and personal values of honour and courage with loyalties to their clan and community which also extended to the level of supporting the principle of national liberation. Some were former army personnel with military skills who had turned against the government because of its coerciveness and their own conscience. There were some who emphasized the religious nature of the struggle. Others put the focus on a desire for revenge because of indiscriminate bombing or the death of a relative. There were some who felt it was simply their duty to resist the government in the belief that they had never been governed by outsiders. Some fought for money. Others fought to recover their homes and lands because the only alternative was to languish in a refugee camp. Mohammed Hamid, who was captured and interrogated by the Soviets, stated: 'In general nobody was happy with the arrival of foreign forces, or with the government which they had put in place. I personally saw what the *shuravi* (Soviets) got up to in the provinces: they would wipe out whole villages in retaliation for one rifle shot'. He continued, explaining why Afghans fought so bitterly:

I had to fight, not with my tongue but with a machine gun. People who wanted to cut off heads went ahead and did it. People who didn't want to didn't do it. Incidentally torture and the cutting off heads is not some kind of special regime thought up especially for Soviet soldiers. Any infidel can end up without his head, including an Afghan. Everybody has his own view of the world. Some people cut off heads, others don't. I prefer to sell my enemy for cash to people who are willing to buy, rather than to torture him. I saw that in the province of Logar. In the region of Sorkhab we destroyed a column and took several Soviet prisoners. They cut off the heads of the soldiers but they sold the officers. Prisoners were mostly sold to Germany where they were brought by various human rights bodies who paid good money for them.[38]

Afghan resistance fighters prided themselves on their toughness. They travelled light, with just a weapon, a blanket or scarf, ammunition and a minimal amount of food.[39] Nan bread and tea were the items of their staple diet, wrapped up in cloth. Where the civilian population could not house them, they slept rough. Their blanket was especially important, acting as bedding, camouflage from helicopter gunships, prayer mat, improvised rope, makeshift stretcher, or shroud. Physical courage was idealized and expected of all. Mohammad Yousaf noted that, for an Afghan, 'to be without courage is abhorrent; such a person is despised'.[40] But Afghans were just as capable as anyone else of being frightened and terrorized. They preferred to fight using hit-and-run tactics in order to stay alive and fight again, and were far from suicidal, although they were just as capable of pressing home an attack as regular soldiers.

For some, death was in the hands of Allah and would mean access to Paradise, but recklessness tended to be an attitude more acceptable to the Arab volunteers. Indeed, some Arab fighters who joined the conflict with 'a murderous hatred of non-Muslim Westerners' favoured a deliberately self-sacrificial approach to combat and were criticized by Afghans.[41] However, Afghans favoured a heroic death and there was veneration for *ghazis* who showed exemplary courage when inspired by religious obligation. That said, few wanted to risk crossing minefields which might result in mutilation. They preferred a 'clean' death which would mean their body would enter Paradise intact, but there were other more pragmatic anxieties. Yousaf noted: 'I found that most were afraid of mines, and were hesitant to attack posts closely protected by minefields. Their concern was living the life of a cripple, in a society where physical stamina and hardiness is indispensible'.

Nevertheless Islam became the justification for all military activities, and was a convenient means to motivate the resistance fighters. It was even said, citing the Prophet, that 'the Mujahid who spends one night on guard duty has performed equally with the ordinary man who prays for a thousand nights'.[42] Such values were essential to motivate any society at war. Just as important was the ability to play on concepts of personal honour. Many sought to emulate the bravest of their comrades or those who had already killed as a means to acquire social prestige.

The Mujahideen fighters were rarely able to articulate a concept of strategy or victory, emphasizing instead that they had to endure and continue the struggle as an obligation, and they focused on repeated tactical engagements. The Mujahideen knew their own local territory and they felt compelled to fight for it, but the war gave certain individuals a new and important status as fighters and areas of responsibility for particular commanders expanded. This enabled the Mujahideen to develop from a purely localized resistance into a national insurgency. There was some encouragement in the fact that outsiders, especially the Arabs, had come to fight on their behalf. Most significantly, there was an elevation in the status of the mullahs, who provided the ideological justification for the fighting and sustained the resistance psychologically. In times of crisis, the *ulema* had always assumed a more prominent position, and the protracted character of the war made this change of status more permanent. *Jirgas* also had a renaissance as elders organized the establishment of surveillance teams, guides to Mujahideen groups that were in transit, and local security.[43]

In Afghanistan, terrain has been the enduring theme which determines the 'way of war'. Mountainous areas provided the best areas for resistance and to secure supplies, but most of the population lived in the plains or along narrow river valleys.[44] In the cultivated areas, 'green zones' of close vegetation and irrigation ditches gave the fighters some cover in the summer months, and traditional large compounds could house large numbers of fighters at any time. Careless Soviet commanders could be ambushed within villages and *zelenka* (green zones) and suffered heavy casualties, the fighters escaping through predesignated routes, protected by booby traps.[45] When the Soviets devastated populated areas, the Mujahideen were forced to carry more food and ammunition, which affected their mobility. Moreover, there were limits to their ability to operate through the winter months on minimal supplies. The tempo of operations tended to tail off as the bad weather approached and resume when spring foliage provided cover.

However, there were significant technological developments which once again forced the Afghans to adapt their 'way of war'. The helicopter and the anti-personnel mine were particularly important in hindering their traditional methods of guerrilla resistance to outsiders, just as aircraft had done in 1919 and 'precision strike' was to do in 2001. In the 1980s, the Mujahideen were forced to adapt their techniques although they never acquired a solution to the new weapons. Some managed to bring down even heavily armoured assault helicopters with curtains of heavy machine guns, and there were even attempts to lure aircraft into pre-designated canyon killing zones.[46] The Stinger surface to air missile was able, in turn, to alter Soviet air tactics but it was not, contrary to popular belief, a 'war winner'.[47] Most resistance fighters were armed with small arms, and, despite the ubiquity of the Kalashnikov assault rifle, many Mujahideen preferred the range and accuracy afforded by the British Lee Enfield 0.303 bolt-action rifle. The Lee Enfield was ideal for sniping, and its rounds could penetrate Soviet flak jackets, causing acute fear amongst Soviet conscripts.[48] The other most common weapon for the resistance was the RPG-7, the shoulder-launched Rocket Propelled Grenade. The drawback of the RPG was its short range, and the relative inaccuracy of the weapon at longer ranges.

To increase their reach, the Mujahideen tried to acquire heavier weapons including heavy machine guns, MBRLs (multi-barrelled rocket launchers), an improvised single-barrelled version, mortars, anti-tank recoil-less rifles, and even tanks and anti-aircraft guns.[49] However, each of these heavy weapons limited mobility and tended to be confined to the protection of bases or very deliberate operations where weapons could be dug in. Occasionally, heavy weapons appeared in compounds of *kishlaks*, but on a number of occasions these weapons had to be abandoned in order for fighters to escape.

In terms of tactics, the Mujahideen proved adept at ambush and the pursuit of small detachments. However, at times there was a tendency to want direct engagements rather than more clandestine and operationally effective targeting: 'They wanted noise, excitement, personal glory and the spoils of war'.[50] The ISI struggled to get them to sabotage or destroy installations like oil pipelines because they preferred assaults on security posts.[51] They were very predictable in the selection of ambush sites or places from which to launch missiles, habitually using the same locations, which made them vulnerable to counter-ambush. Battlefield security was often neglected.

Guerrilla forces rarely hold ground, and it is in the nature of guerrillas to remain elusive and sacrifice space for time. However, all guerrilla forces need space to manoeuvre. If cornered, the Mujahideen could not survive. By the mid 1980s, the Mujahideen were able to move over 85 per cent of the country. What they could not do, however, was establish a permanent presence. Every valley and district could only be held temporarily. Major urban areas remained outside their control, even though they could transit through them and conduct operations within them. Although they made attempts to capture towns, they had not the means to hold them, and Soviet retaliation was inevitable. Large-scale attacks, especially in the early years, were often costly and ineffective. One Western intelligence officer remarked that, if concentrated and giving the government "'a whiff of the old Jihad", they got a bloody taste of cannon fire and napalm from the air'.[52] Nevertheless, some attacks were audacious and ambitious. In the summer of 1980 a Mujahideen group based only 4 miles from Kabul bombarded the headquarters of the 40th Army in the capital with rockets. They attacked Soviet and Afghan air bases, destroying a number of aircraft in the process. In their first use of Stinger SAMs, on 26 September 1986, a Soviet-trained engineer called Ghaffur shot down three Mi-24 helicopters that were coming in to land at Jalalabad.[53]

The frequency of small-scale attacks was impressive and acted as a wearing-out strategy. The head of Soviet Military Intelligence in Afghanistan reported in 1980 that 'If in April this year there were 38 terrorist acts, and 63 people killed, then in May there were 112 terrorist attacks, killing 201 people. In a directive of the Islamic Party of Afghanistan ... the rebels are instructed to continue to avoid direct armed confrontation with regular forces, and to camouflage themselves among the civilian population'.[54] Attacks against Soviet and Afghan Army road columns were the most common, and it is estimated that 11,000 vehicles were destroyed in this way.[55] The standard procedure was to destroy the lead vehicle and then the last vehicle in a convoy, and then destroy the rest more systematically. On the Salang Pass on 16 October 1986, in broad daylight, a column of Soviet oil tankers, more than a mile long, was attacked by several hundred of Ahmad Shah Masoud's fighters. A BTR-60 (armoured personnel carrier) escorting the column was knocked out in the first salvo of mortar bombs. The tankers were set on fire one after the other and a QRF (Quick Reaction Force), although arriving promptly after the ambush, was unable to prevent the destruction of the column. Even regular units could be attacked with the same comprehensive results. On 30 April 1984, the 2nd Battalion of the 682nd Motor Rifle Regiment was destroyed after it advanced into a ravine leading off the main Panjshir valley without first securing the heights above. Initially the battalion was offered no resistance and was lured into a better ambush site. Then they were hit from three sides, the Mujahideen firing down into the valley floor. The Soviet battalion lost 53 dead, including 12 officers, and 58 wounded.[56]

Attacks were also made whenever Soviet units started to withdraw at the end of a set-piece operation. Sergeant Sergei Morozov of the 56th Air Assault Brigade recalled:

This was the first operation where we met major resistance. There were ambushes [and] the roads were blown up ... On the way back along the mountain path, my battalion was ambushed. Thirteen men were killed in the leading platoon. My own platoon had been in the lead on the way out, and so we were in the rearguard on the way back. We stopped for the night, and had to beat off a number of Mujahideen attacks: their weapons in those days were simple, many of them home made. They didn't get mortars until later. The numbers opposing us were very small—perhaps only a few dozen.[57]

But the Mujahideen would also establish their retreat routes in advance. Abdul Salam Zaeef, operating near Kandahar, remembered:

If the Russians drew too close or if the mujahideen sustained too many casualties, they withdrew towards Arghandab, Sansigar or Zangiabad, and if they came under pressure in Arghandab they then withdrew towards Mahalajat, Shah Wali Kot and Panjwayi'. He then added: 'Later, when the Russians removed their forces, the mujahideen would return to their original positions.[58]

The fighters were often ill-disciplined, disorganized and lacked coordination in their operations. They were better at raiding and when operating at night, but their fire discipline was bad: at times, large quantities of ammunition were expended for no effect. Mujahideen were averse to digging trenches, although they built well-sited and camouflaged *sangars* and built or extended tunnel complexes as bases, the latter mainly for shelter and respite. Brigadier Yousaf of the ISI at one site confessed to feeling 'exasperated' by the lack of entrenching taking place: 'Trenches had not been dug, gun positions were exposed without proper camouflage, tents were conspicuously pitched close to forward positions and overhead protection was lacking everywhere'.[59] He explained that tunnels had been built with enthusiasm, using bulldozers and explosives, and at Zhawar near the Pakistan border they included a mosque, garage, armourer's workshop, small medical aid post, radio station, kitchen, guest houses and stores. He noted 'it was even possible to watch video films at the base', but noted that tunnel building 'always had priority over the tactical defences facing the enemy'. Yousaf explained this 'indiscipline' as the result of party leaders and commanders wanting to have a showpiece base to show off to visitors, but there was 'a false sense of security' pervading the complex. These observations, and the habit of adopting the same locations or routes, cast some doubt on the Mujahideen's ability to assimilate and adopt new techniques, or 'tactical learning' as the Western armies describe it.

The ISI offered training to the Mujahideen as a means of getting influence over the operations of the resistance. The offer of weapons and ammunition, as well as money and supplies, created competition amongst Mujahideen commanders as they vied for Pakistan's support. In return, the Mujahideen were expected to carry out operations designed by the ISI. Allegedly, there were occasions when the Mujahideen commanders claimed to have fulfilled operations in order to obtain more weapons and supplies, but in reality no operation had taken place. The training, particularly on prestige weapons, was much sought after, but not all training was a success. Experiments with the Blowpipe SAM were a failure, and Cordovez and Harrison estimated that only half of all Stinger launches hit their target.[60] Mohammad Yousaf claimed that in the first year of its deployment, from 1986 to the middle of 1987, the Mujahideen had a 75 per cent hit rate with their Stingers.[61] During 1987 the Soviet and Afghan air forces lost 150–200 aircraft, but in 1988 the losses fell to less than 50. About 100 aircraft were lost in 1986, before the deployment of Stingers, to small-arms fire and other SAM weapons which either suggests the effectiveness of Stingers was exaggerated, or that the Soviets altered their air tactics accordingly. Certainly the Soviets tried to buy Stingers from the resistance and offered US $3,000 for each one.[62] For all the inadequacies of the Mujahideen, many of those from rural backgrounds were excellent shots, having been brought up with weapons from an early age. President Zia, when observing Afghans in a rifle range in an ISI camp, is said to have remarked: 'I only wish our army had half this standard of shooting'.[63] Zaeef tells a very different story of inaccurate shooting, and Yousaf repeatedly referred to his frustration with the inflexibility of the Afghans and the fact that they frequently politely ignored his advice over training issues.[64]

The prevalence of mines was a common feature of the conflict and hindered mobility and resupply for both sides. The largest mines destroyed vehicles, including armoured personnel carriers and tanks, but routes could be cleared, and the greatest fear was of the smaller anti-personnel mines that could blow off a foot. The Soviets believed these were more effective, as a wounded fighter needed up to eight comrades to get him off the battlefield, thus absorbing the Mujahideen's manpower. All minefields were supposed to be recorded, but maps were sometimes inaccurate and tactical considerations often took precedence. Helicopters that scattered mines, including the 'butterfly' type, were not able to make accurate records. Consequently, Soviet and Afghan Army troops were sometimes blown up by their own mines, and civilians frequently blundered into them. Both sides used booby traps, configuring explosives into random objects to cause wounds rather than death.[65] Mujahideen would breach known minefields with captured vehicles, hurling rocks, firing recoil-less rifles along a path, and even drive flocks of sheep into the minefield. These methods were sometimes successful.[66] When the Soviets lost a number of pylons to saboteurs, they took to laying anti-personnel mines at the base of replacement structures. The Mujahideen used the 'rock method' to clear these and then destroyed the pylons again.[67]

The Mujahideen resistance would have struggled without the influx of foreign weaponry, expertise and money. The Americans allocated $2 billion to the Mujahideen, dwarfing the contribution of the Arab countries. They also provided weapons, often purchased from developing countries, to avoid being traced back to the United States. Yet the assisting agencies of the United States, in common with other foreign donors, had their own agendas, which did not always coincide with the Mujahideen's plans. Saudi Arabia, for example, saw the war as an opportunity to contain the Shias in Iran by setting up a Sunni, pro-Wahhabi regime in Kabul. The United States was keen to support the resistance as part of the Cold War effort to undermine the Soviet Union, but the Americans effectively abandoned Afghanistan once the Cold War came to an end, and the perception that they boasted about their aid effort caused much resentment. Afghans believed that the donor loses face in such circumstances.[68] Iran supported Shia resistance groups as a means to forestall Soviet influence in the Gulf region. Pakistan saw an opportunity to eliminate the Pashtunistan proposal, by aligning itself with the Pashtuns against the Soviets. Under General Zia, the armed forces were 'Islamicized' as part of a policy of gaining popular support across Pakistan and uniting the country just eight years after the independence of Bangladesh. The war in Afghanistan provided the perfect backdrop to advocate a 'holy war', but only insofar as it served Pakistan's interests. China, Pakistan's ally, assisted in weapons sales too. These conflicting foreign interests fuelled the underlying divisive and clannish nature of the Afghan resistance.

There was a regular traffic of weapons and supplies across the Afghanistan–Pakistan border. Edward Giradet noted that merchants would transit goods out of Afghanistan and then ship weapons and ammunition back on the return journey, charging money for the service. Old smuggling routes with storage facilities were also invaluable. Transport included buses, jeeps, trucks, motorbikes and mules.[69] Supplies had to be moved in the spring, summer and autumn, as the winter snows tended to close most of the passes. Pre-dumping enough ammunition and rations to last through to the following spring was essential.[70] Even so, sustaining Mujahideen units in the field in the winter weather proved very problematic. They found it difficult to march through snow, sleep rough and mount ambushes without specialist equipment and clothing. Although the Mujahideen could occupy hills near Kabul in 1984, they were driven back in the winter months in 1985 and again in 1986.[71] The Soviets established blockhouses and minefields to prevent the Mujahideen reoccupying these positions when the good weather returned.

The Mujahideen also tried raising money locally from the population in order to sustain their resistance. Some units set up their own 'shadow' taxation system, expropriating the traditional *zakat* and *ushr* for the war effort. Some of the funds paid for their own levies of part-time fighters.[72] Vehicle checkpoints were established to collect road tolls in much the same way their ancestors had done. Refusal to pay usually invited the confiscation of a vehicle and its goods, or violence. Records were kept and forms issued, and a regular fee of between 50 and 100 *afghanis* was charged for each journey. The Kabul–Khyber route was said to be the most lucrative for local fighters, much as it had been for generations. In Panjshir, the Mujahideen imposed a tax of 5 per cent on all salaries, and farmers were expected to pay 10 per cent on all produce sold. The lapis lazuli mines continued to function during the war, and gems were sold to fund the resistance. Protection rackets also thrived, especially in urban areas. Afghan officials working for the government were willing to pay for their own survival. The widespread nature of these practices made it easier for certain groups to make profits that had little to do with the war. Gangs posing as Mujahideen occasionally robbed the traffic, and clans in the mountain passes imposed traditional levies.[73] Even within clans, old rivalries could turn violent if the distribution of wealth was not perceived to be fair. Opium, a crop grown in Afghanistan for generations, was grown in larger quantities too.

The ISI were frustrated that, amongst the Mujahideen, there appeared to be little logistical planning. There was 'no discernible pattern to their activities; they fought when they saw an opportunity or they needed loot, and when the time suited them'.[74] In Khost, the Mujahideen insisted on moving into neighbouring Urgan when it seemed likely that it might fall to the resistance: they did not wish to miss out on the spoils if it did so. Yousaf condemned this 'typical tribal fighting' which had 'no higher strategic objective'.[75]

There was also a patient attitude towards time. Supplies could often only be delivered at the pace of a mule, and fighters could only reach positions at the speed of a brisk walk. It took twelve weeks for one team to make it from Pakistan to the Koh-i Safi near the Soviet air base at Bagram, and it took a further three weeks to mount an attack. The total time to make one deliberate attack was four months and the ISI considered this to be 'about average'.[76] When winter intervened or the Soviets harassed the build-up, the time taken for operations to be staged was longer. The failure to capitalize on time as a resource caused a strategic failure of some importance. Yousaf argued that the Mujahideen should have won the war in 1980 when the Soviet 40th Army was not yet trained in counterinsurgency techniques and the Afghan Army had virtually collapsed. He attributed the Mujahideen's failure to the inability to 'combine quickly to take advantage of their enemy's weakness'. By 1983 the Soviet and Afghan forces had recovered their balance and the opportunity was lost. Yousaf's verdict can be criticized, but his identification of the failure to make use of the window of opportunity is sound. The recent and oft-repeated slogan that 'The Americans have all the watches and the Afghans have all the time' is one of those simplistic and convenient expressions that is seriously misleading. In the case of the Soviet War, the Afghan Mujahideen were forced into a more costly and protracted conflict in which they focused on tactics at the expense of strategy. Two examples may illustrate the issues.

The Battle of Khost

Khost lies 10 miles from the border with Pakistan and is linked by a mountain road, vulnerable to ambush, to Gardez and Kabul. The most critical section crosses the 10,000 foot Satykandav Pass. The guerrilla force in the area was led by Jalaluddin Haqqani who was supported by the ISI.[77] The Mujahideen base at Zhawar consisted of a complex of tunnels, manned by 500 fighters, and they were armed with a D30 122mm howitzer, MBRL rocket launchers, nine anti-aircraft guns, and two T-55 tanks they had captured from the Afghan Army in 1983.[78] From this base Haqqani was able to keep Khost under attack, although he later emphasized that the role of the base was primarily to supply fronts elsewhere.[79] However, in 1985 the front commanders near Khost decided they wanted to try to take the city. The ISI advised against it, pointing out that any attack against entrenched Afghan Army forces would end in disaster. However, eager to maintain the relationship, ISI agreed to provide heavy weapons and to facilitate the cooperation of various commanders. Brigadier Yousaf advised that a night assault on the Torgah heights, held by the Afghan government troops, should precede any offensive, but he was dismayed by Haqqani's insistence on a daylight attack.[80] The offensive was scheduled to commence at 10.00 hrs but through delays did not get underway until midday. The result was inevitable. Mujahideen fighters were cut down by concentrated machine-gun fire as they tried to rush the nearest trenches. They managed to get a lodgement on the slopes after dark, and a couple of bunkers were seized, but the position could not be held and they withdrew at midnight.[81] Haqqani wanted to try a second assault a fortnight later, but by then the Afghan Army had strengthened its trenches on Torgah. The Soviets planned to relieve pressure on Khost by mounting a counter-offensive in September that would sweep the area along the border from Khost, northwards to Ali Khel, near the Peiwar Kotal Pass, and also southwards towards the Mujahideen base at Zhawar.

The Second Battle of Zhawar

The Soviets and Afghan Army had made a brief attempt to neutralize the resistance around Zhawar in 1983, but the offensive which began on 20 August 1985 was a far larger and more elaborate operation. The Mujahideen, who had failed to observe basic security precautions, were taken by surprise when a combined infantry and artillery attack began to the north-east of the base.[82] To delay the advance of Afghan Army forces, eighty men were established as a block group on the eastern slopes of the Moghulai Mountains. The Afghan Army ran into this stop group at night, lost two APCs and withdrew to Khost. The second axis of the Afghan Army's advance was from the north-west, from the town of Tani. An outpost line of Mujahideen fighters was forced back, but a twenty strong group took up a position on the Manay Kandow Pass.[83] They used a rock overhang as shelter from artillery bombardment and started to excavate shallow trenches so as to be able to crawl up to firing positions once the shelling ceased. As Afghan infantry advanced, the Mujahideen group opened fire and drove them off. The artillery resumed its bombardment, accompanied by air strikes. The pattern was repeated several times for ten days until the Soviets delivered such a heavy air raid on 14 September 1985 that the rock overhang began to collapse. The position was therefore abandoned. Crucially, they had bought time for defences in depth to be improved.

With the high ground secure, the DRA troops began to direct air strikes against Mujahideen positions further back, and they were able to bring more forces through the Manay Kandow Pass. Anti-aircraft guns and small arms were unable to arrest the government offensive at this point. When the DRA troops took Tor Kamar, a prominent peak, it put them within half a mile of the Zhawar base. However, Alam Jam and Muhammad Salim, two Mujahideen commanders, deployed their tanks out of the cave complex and opened fire on the hill top *sangars*. The first round destroyed an artillery OP, and after several attempts a second OP was neutralized. This encouraged the Afghan Army troops to withdraw other exposed posts and fall back. For five days more deliberate operations were mounted, but they failed to take any of the Mujahideen positions. The entire offensive was terminated after forty-two days of almost continuous fighting. The Mujahideen had lost 106 killed and 321 wounded. The Soviet offensive postponed Mujahideen attacks on Khost and caused some serious concern in Pakistan. The ISI believed the fall of the base would have proved catastrophic to the resistance because it was such an important logistics hub.[84]

The Third Battle of Zhawar

The Mujahideen strengthened the Zhawar base prior to the next Soviet offensive in 1986. Anti-aircraft defences were pushed out to 7 kilometres from the base itself and a series of defences constructed in depth. All the likely approaches were mined and covered by small arms, RPGs, mortars and recoil-less rifles.[85] Field telephones and radios linked the various outposts. For the offensive, the Soviets deployed one air assault regiment and 12,000 Afghan Army personnel. Two waves of helicopters preceded the advance which alerted the 800 Mujahideen defenders to an attack—although it is important to note that this was the first idea they had of a major offensive, their intelligence within the ranks of the DRA having failed. Soon after, air strikes and artillery concentrations began falling on some likely Mujahideen positions.

At 07.00 hrs the first heliborne troops began to deploy in a series of dispersed landing zones around Zhawar, including the eastern side of the base, close to the Pakistan border. Although two helicopters were destroyed at these landing sites, the Mujahideen had no effective means to defeat the aircraft that supported them and air strikes destroyed several Mujahideen positions.[86] A single precision attack killed 18 fighters. Another bomb detonated at the entrance to a cave and trapped 150 fighters inside, including Haqqani.[87] Ironically, subsequent carpet bombing destroyed the debris blocking the cave and released its captives. In order to compensate for the air attacks, the Mujahideen decided to 'hug' the Soviets and prevent further air attacks: they overran four landing zones in a close-quarter battle and claimed to have captured 500 Soviet soldiers.[88] One of the Soviet detachments held out for three days before being defeated. However, the Mujahideen accounts made little mention of the fact that their positions overlooked the landing zones. As they landed, the 37 Commando Brigade had come under intense fire from machine guns and RPGs. Soviet tactics were subsequently altered to avoid landing right on the enemy positions.

The Afghan Army made a series of attempts to push through the Manay Kandow Pass and was held up in a repeat of the operation of the previous year. A flanking column unhinged the defence and forced the Mujahideen to fall back. As more troops poured into the Zhawar area, the Mujahideen decided not to contest the base any longer and dispersed. Rumours that Haqqani was dead had a profound effect on the fighters' morale at this point.[89]

The DRA troops held Zhawar for only five hours and did not linger to seize the stores and ammunition within. Attempts to destroy the caves were half-hearted, and, while a few seismic mines claimed casualties when the Mujahideen returned, the rest of their arms and equipment remained intact. The Mujahideen rallied enough men to launch some rockets at the withdrawing DRA troops, signalling their defiance. Although the government in Kabul heralded the battle as a victory, the base was fully operational again just weeks after its capture. The Mujahideen had lost 281 killed and 363 wounded, but DRA casualties were also significant.[90] Of the prisoners, all the officers were executed. The captured soldiers were compelled to do two years' manual labour in the logistics areas for the Mujahideen and then offered an amnesty. Having fixed themselves to the defence of a base, the Mujahideen were forced to endure the might of Soviet and DRA firepower. A guerrilla strategy would ordinarily have meant that the base should be abandoned and the strength of the resistance preserved. Indeed, neither side could claim to have succeeded, while tactical skills on both sides can be severely criticized.

The Mujahideen reassessed

In the history of the war, many have tended to overlook the weaknesses of the Mujahideen resistance. One of the most serious structural problems was in command and control because of deep divisions amongst the resistance. The Mujahideen was never a homogeneous organization, but a patchwork of competing factions.[91] Individual leaders, who formed coteries of fighters in varying numbers, were effectively rivals and sometimes represented distinct ethnic groups or ideologies: Gailani, Mojadidi, Mohammedi and Khalis were Islamists; Hekmatyar was the protégé of Pakistan; Rabbani and Sayyat were pro-Saudi; Behesti, Mazari, Akbari and Mohseni led Shia factions (until Iran insisted on the formation of a united Hezb-e-Wahdat in 1990); whilst Ahmed Shah Masoud, Maulawi Haggai and Ismail Khan were more 'secular' warlords. The first attempt to unite the seven major groups in a single *jirga* in 1981 failed, forcing their foreign backers to deal with each group in turn.[92] Rival groups did their best to exclude others from resources and there were violent clashes. There were over 300 separate 'fronts', and not all were aligned with recognized parties or leaders.[93] Their effectiveness and the tempo of their operations varied enormously.

The ISI were critical of the Mujahideen commanders' 'rigidity, resistance to change and proud inflexibility', which caused 'serious problems in the tactical field'. There was 'endless bickering' and sometimes a point-blank refusal to cooperate with other parties of commanders.[94] Mohammad Yousaf stated that 'personal rivalries, prejudices and hatreds ... often clouded their views and dictated their actions'.[95] He estimated that 75 per cent of General Akhtar's time, as chief of the ISI, was spent in resolving disputes between factions. Commanders of the same area would sometimes join different parties, which led to conflicts over the right to tax the local population and how much support they could enjoy. Each Mujahideen commander tended to behave as if he was a 'king in his area'.[96] Exclusive control of any zone meant that commanders could monopolize income streams and recruits, and there could be violence if a rival commander tried to manage the same base location. The commanders therefore remained very local in outlook and often refused to run the risk of operating in another's area of influence.

Uzbek and Tajik groups got less support from the Pakistani ISI, partly because of the distance from the Durand Line border, but also because of deliberate obstruction by rival Afghan groups.[97] Indeed, even without the conflict between the Mujahideen and the government troops, most of the violence in the 1980s was Afghan against Afghan.[98] After DRA operations at Barikot in Kunar in January 1985, in which resistance had been weak and a number of bases were overrun, despite a spirited show of force, the ISI tried to ascertain why the Mujahideen had been surprised and defeated. It transpired that local Mujahideen commanders, even those from the same party under the leadership of Khalis, had not cooperated. Haji Mir Zaman, one of the commanders, had failed to mine the approaches to Barikot, arguing that he needed the road open in order to carry out raids that would furnish his men with food and other loot.[99]

One of the most notorious individuals was a former captain of the Afghan Army called Asmat, an Achakzai Pashtun who controlled the trans-border area on the basis of clan relationships.[100] He had defected in 1981 and made a personal fortune through gun running, extortion and robbery. He attempted to attack Mujahideen convoys and the resistance began to cooperate against him, but after some sustained but inconclusive fighting a deal was arranged. It was not long before Asmat started to harass Pakistani officials, but after complaints he realized he could make more money by cooperating with the ISI and he was rewarded with arms and cash. It then appeared that he was working for KhAD, but when the ISI attempted to move against him, the Pakistan Military Intelligence branch refused to sanction the arrest, arguing that Asmat was providing them with vital information. In the confusion, Asmat fled to Kabul and later returned to Kandahar where he survived a series of assassination attempts. His insubordination with Soviet officers led to his recall, but he attempted to rejoin the Mujahideen in return for large sums of money and weapons. The ISI rejected the freebooter as unreliable.

The rivalry between commanders was often ruthless. Syed Jamal, one of Gulbuddin Hakmatyr's senior front leaders, murdered thirty-six of Ahmad Shah Masoud's men in an ambush in 1989.[101] The dispute arose because Masoud's and Hekmatyar's factions had seized and cleared Taloqan in 1988, and the town had been divided up between them. Despite a binding agreement, Jamal set up an ambush in the Tangi Fakhar gorge. Those not killed immediately were tortured and executed. Masoud issued an order for the capture of the participants and a bounty of 1 million *afghanis* was offered for Jamal. He was eventually betrayed and seized. Hekmatyar was suspected of having ordered the massacre at Fakhar and he certainly earned few friends. Despite receiving the lion's share of arms and munitions from Pakistan, and controlling much of the south of Afghanistan, subordinate commanders refused to accept his edicts and they set up a new organization under Mohammad Khan.[102] This new organization preyed upon caravans destined for Hekmatyar's men, and there were revenge attacks by one of Hekmatyar's local commanders, Janbaz. The fighting escalated near the Pakistan border and involved 2,000 Mujahideen fighters; attempts by the Pakistanis to stop the conflict failed. To augment their incomes opium smuggling was expanded, but, despite all the cash and arms lavished on Hekmatyar by the ISI, he failed to defeat Mohammad Khan.

The one group free of the internecine faction fighting of the Mujahideen was the Shi'ite Hazaras. Traditionally ostracized by Pashtuns and occupying the central mountain belt of the country, the Hazaras elected their own president, Sayed Ali Behesti, and military commander, Sayed Mohammad Hussein, known by his *nom de guerre* as Djendral. The Shia party, *Mardaz-e Wahdat* or the Centre of Unity, came to dominate all political activity in the Hazarajat. The fighters stated that their aim was to fight the Soviets, but, in an echo of Iranian revolutionary rhetoric, they aimed for liberation 'for the whole world' against oppression, by which they also meant the Pashtuns.[103] Areas of operations were aligned to *wilyats* (provinces) under the political leadership of a *wali*, a *sayyid* or a mullah. In areas closer to Kabul, military commanders tended to run the provinces. The Afghan government attempted to blockade the area

to deprive the insurgents of food, and there were occasional air raids, but Mujahideen groups were reluctantly forced to concede that the Hazaras enjoyed the
most unified and effective 'shadow government' in the country. Nevertheless
there were still disputes between the Maoist-style *Sholai-e Jaweid*, who were
led by intellectuals, and the *ulema*, who were inspired by Iran.

The Hazara method was to sustain a guerrilla army of 20,000 men aged
twenty-two, each of whom was required to provide one year's service. Those
Hazaras in other countries, including inside Iran, were expected to contrib-
ute a tax in lieu of their absence. Each group of ten families was expected to
pay for the costs of maintaining a conscript fighter in the field, including his
rations and a small salary. Given the hardships that most families faced, this
demand was unpopular and hard to meet. Each Hazara fighter received a
month's training from former Afghan Army officers before being sent to a
local *japha*, or front. The fighters served up to eleven months in the field, covering strategic entry points into the mountains. Regular telephone communications linked the centres of resistance and the fronts, which gave the Hazaras
the ability to mobilize large numbers in an emergency. During a sudden Soviet
assault near Ghazni in December 1980, fighters poured in from outlying
areas.[104] Nevertheless, the Hazaras were careful to avoid operating outside their
own area. There were a few isolated fronts amongst Shia minorities in Balkh
and Samangan, and there, through necessity, the Hazaras cooperated with
other factions. In the Panjshir, for example, Shia fighters worked with Masoud's
Afghan–Tajiks.

No single leader emerged to lead the Mujahideen, although there was a suggestion that King Zahir Shah might serve as a figurehead. In 1984, at a meeting in Peshawar, Hekmatyar's representative argued: 'The people of Afghanistan
need a leader. Everybody wants Zahir Shah because he is all we have'.[105] Others maintained that 'he has not suffered with us' and therefore rejected him.
Real leadership was still exercised by independent field commanders. Through
sheer necessity, rivalries might be suspended and some cooperation established.[106] In time this cooperation became a form of comradeship, and once
again Islam provided the explanation or justification. In 1984, Edward Giradet noticed that incidents of different factions 'rushing in to help besieged
guerrilla fronts' and 'joint assaults involving several different fronts at a time'
were increasing.[107] While *jirgas* continued to insist on majority verdicts, commanders could make independent judgements in a crisis.[108] The ISI acknowledged there was 'no real unity among leaders' and parties would still refuse to
allow supply caravans through areas held by Ahmad Shah Masoud, but they

did manage to persuade some front commanders to undertake diversionary operations on Kabul, at Bagram and near the Pakistan border that year.[109]

Ahmad Shah Masoud, the 'Lion of the Panjshir', was one of the most celebrated Mujahideen commanders in the West, but he was not always supported by the majority of Afghans. He nevertheless commanded the grudging respect of many Pashtun leaders. Several stated that, while they would never serve under him, they would cooperate with him as an equal.[110] Masoud's legendary status was derived not only from his ability to sustain an effective resistance, often in the teeth of deliberate Soviet–Afghan army offensives like Operation Typhoon, but also from his desire to maintain the support of the Afghan–Tajiks who lived in the region in which he fought. A student of Mao, Masoud noted that the greatest risk was not keeping the Afghan people on side as the 'sea' for his 'fish'. He stated:

Unfortunately we are in danger of losing our people. This is where the Soviets may succeed. Failing to crush us by force, as they have said they would with each offensive, they have turned their wrath on defenceless people, killing old men, women and children, destroying houses and burning crops. They are doing everything possible to drive our people away.[111]

Masoud believed that the Soviets had failed to achieve their objectives militarily and that his fighters had managed to elude the attackers by withdrawing deeper into the mountains. Once the Soviets were drawn in after them, 'we hit them from all sides'. He acknowledged that the heliborne 'commandos' had learned a great deal about mountain guerrilla warfare but 'we have learned to cope with them'. The leitmotif of Masoud's operations was to gather intelligence on forthcoming attacks through his agents within the Afghan Army, consult with local elders on the most effective ways to protect the population, assist with their evacuation and then prepare for the attack. Manpower was carefully selected and a balance struck between the numbers who were in service as fighters and the requirements of administration and agriculture. Less dominated by clan councils, the Panjshiris were willing to accept Masoud as their overall commander, and his early successes elevated his status amongst the people.

It had not always been that way. He had been exiled after Daoud's coup in 1973 with other Islamist militants under Rabbani.[112] He returned two years later to participate in an abortive uprising in the Panjshir. He returned again in 1978 in the aftermath of the Saur Revolution. He was joined by about 200 fighters, took control of two valleys and forced out the local government official from Rukha, the provincial centre.[113] They prepared defences at the mouth of the valleys, but they were outnumbered by government troops and forced to escape into the mountains. These two setbacks taught Ahmad Shah Masoud of the importance of sufficient training, weapons and organization. He rebuilt the resistance, not with Islamist idealists, but engineers, farmers, drivers and students. He trained small units as a nucleus for the recruitment of others, passing on their skills and creating new groups. As they spread their influence down the Panjshir, their numbers began to grow. By January 1980, the entire region was in Masoud's hands. There were two major Soviet offensives every year, except during the truce, and in 1982 and in 1984 the valley was overrun, but sporadic resistance was maintained.[114]

The Panjshir was divided into seven military districts, and two Mujahideen forces were created: the *moutariks* were mobile teams of 75 men who could reinforce a threatened zone and mount hasty operations; the *sabbets* were local defence teams about 50 strong who served under one of 25 *karegars*, field commanders, who lived in the valley. *Moutariks* were paid a salary and given allowances of cigarettes and *naswah* (rations). Their families were supported by a resistance committee and payments given if fighters were killed in action. Between defensive operations, Masoud was able to deploy the *moutariks* as raiders against the Salang Highway, attacking Soviet columns and raiding others to procure supplies that were returned as a commonwealth for the Panjshiri resistance as a whole. On 25 April 1982, the *moutariks* made a significant raid against Bagram airbase. Storming the perimeter wire, they broke into the base and destroyed or damaged 23 helicopters and aircraft. They opened fire with mortars on barracks and a hospital, killing and wounding a number of Soviet troops.

In May 1982, in retaliation, the Soviets launched an offensive into the Panjshir with 12,000 troops and all the accompanying assets of armour, artillery and air power. The preliminary bombardment, systematically destroying one village after another, lasted a week. Heliborne troops seized the highest ground and valley junctions. On 17 May, after three days of fighting, the southern portion of the valley was overrun and a northern pincer completed the occupation. Reinforcements were then brought in to relieve the heliborne units at the northern end of the valley after Masoud's men targeted the most isolated detachments. The guerrillas had fallen back as the Soviet and Afghan Army approached, and they concealed themselves in pre-designated positions, replete with rations, ammunition and other stores.[115] During the occupation they carried out sniping, laid mines, made sudden mortar bombardments and night raids. The heliborne units were under such pressure that they had to withdraw from the exposed peaks, and communications within the valley itself were constantly threatened. Masoud's men expressed admiration for the courage of the Soviet paras, but they noted: 'As soon as they came down and took losses, they evacuated'.[116] The contest for the peaks had been a close-quarter battle which resulted in significant casualties on both sides. The Mujahideen observed that much of the Soviet bombing was ineffective and some ordnance failed to detonate. Masoud's men had their own artillery: they dynamited the valley sides and caused rock avalanches to block routes. They also managed to persuade a number of Afghan Army personnel to defect to their side in the early stages of the operation.

With the exception of Masoud and the Hazaras, welfare of the local population was, perhaps surprisingly, low on the list of priorities of the Mujahideen. There were only a handful of schools, literacy programmes, medical dispensaries or sources of economic support, in contrast to many other global insurgency movements. Masoud purposely established twenty-eight schools in the Panjshir Valley, a hospital and a prison. He sent representatives to Pakistan to obtain regular supplies and to ensure that his faction was represented in any resistance alliance.[117] Most Mujahideen groups in the south relied on local communities helping themselves, although individual personnel clearly prioritized the safety of their own families. Political or ideological education was nevertheless constantly reinforced in every discourse, through poetry and songs. Masoud's team stated: 'We try to teach the people the history behind the rise of communism and the Russian takeover in Afghanistan as well as to explain the concepts of democracy and Islamic revolution'.[118] This was a new departure for the Afghan 'way of war'. Propaganda was emerging as a vital tool to sustain the morale of the fighters and the population on whom they depended.

Gulbuddin Hekmatyar placed considerable emphasis on propaganda. As early as 1979 he established a radio station to broadcast the existence of his Hezb movement, its aims and achievements.[119] Hezb stated that it had 300,000 fighters, a grossly exaggerated number, and often claimed victories over Soviet or Afghan government forces. Western journalists were attracted to the war zone and were invited to photograph or film Mujahideen attacks. Hezb claimed that it was killing thousands of Soviets every month and had lost only a handful of 'martyrs'. Such inflated statements may have had more effect on a largely illiterate public, but Western journalists and the ISI questioned these accounts. *Shabnama* (night letters) were used by the Mujahideen just as they had as a means of silent protest from the 1960s, but there were new attempts to reach the public. Tape recorders were left on rooftops at night to urge resistance, praise the Mujahideen, repeat Islamic slogans, condemn the Soviet occupation and even parody Karmal's name as '*karghal*' (thieving). Loudspeakers were used by the Mujahideen when conducting ambushes or approaching Afghan Army bases, either calling for the Muslim soldiers to desert the Russians, or to intimidate with threats. Even the muezzin could be used to register a subtle defiance of the Soviets.[120]

Megaphones were also used for battlefield communications because of the shortage of radios. Runners were employed and, in a tradition going back centuries to the *harcarra* or *cossids*, young men were able to carry messages across Afghanistan and over the border to Pakistan.[121] Mujahideen commanders would often add their own messages of encouragement and solidarity as the messengers flitted across the country. These links helped establish the idea of a national resistance, even where real unity of effort was lacking in practice.

Recruitment to the cause was relatively simple for the Mujahideen. In most cases recruits were members of the family or clan, serving under a local leader. The leaders themselves often felt obliged to show solidarity with the cause. Entire communities could be swayed to join either the government or the resistance in this way. Some young men joined for the chance to prove themselves or for the thrill of adventure. Abdul Salam Zaeef admitted that the first group he joined did not fulfil his expectations so he went looking for a team with a more formidable reputation for action.[122]

The Mujahideen recruited individuals, including children, to carry out surveillance in villages close to their own and to the Soviet or Afghan Army bases, to report on troop movements. The Afghan Army and *Tsarandoi* were penetrated by agents of the Mujahideen to the extent that the Soviets, to preserve operational security, only issued the objectives of joint operations just before a move or an offensive was about to begin, and sometimes not until after the operation had already begun.

The Mujahideen would argue that age was of no consequence in the struggle. 'Boys of 13 or 14 and men in their sixties with snow white beards', noted Yousaf, 'frequently fought side by side'.[123] Lee Anderson recalled seeing a group of boys set up their own home-made rocket battery in a village compound and fire a few rounds at the Afghan government forces. The only effect of these rockets was 'to attract the enemy's attention', and soon after tank rounds were fired in their direction followed by an air strike.[124] Anderson recalled how, in another exchange, a boy was shot in the head and died, but despite the evident grief of his family and immediate friends, the death was used to galvanize the community to resistance. He wrote: 'In the memories of his comrades and family, he will be honoured as a brave mujahed, a holy warrior. They will not pity him, because he has achieved martyrdom and is now in the paradise that awaits them all. They have lost a friend, a brother, but they have gained strength and pride in the struggle, for now they have a death to vindicate. In a holy war, death becomes a combustive element, a means to an end in itself'.[125]

All too often, the Mujahideen were not able to save their wounded from death. Infection was the biggest killer. Relief agencies estimated that one in five of those with thoraco-abdominal injuries died before reaching assistance.[126] Consequently around 90 per cent of those who made it to surgery in Pakistan had limb injuries. Many of those had already developed gangrene by the time they got there. Zaeef estimated that it took an average of ten to fifteen days for men in his unit near Kandahar to get to a doctor or medic.[127] The Soviet tactic of cordoning Mujahideen bases prior to operations made it impossible to spirit out the casualties. Wounded Mujahideen would be crowded into small rooms of compounds until it became possible to move them.

The difficulty of moving across country applied to prisoners as much as to the wounded Mujahideen, and it was not uncommon for prisoners to be executed.[128] Mullah Naqib, a Pashtun Mujahideen commander near Kandahar, gleefully explained that he preferred to execute all communists: 'we kill them all', he said.[129] The Mujahideen were unaware of the Geneva Convention and argued that, since the Soviets destroyed their villages and killed their people, they were justified in taking *badal*. Prisoner executions were brutal: in January 1984, the 860th Motor Rifle Regiment had briefly captured the village of Karamugul near Faizabad but, in the withdrawal, a section was left behind. While some of the Soviet soldiers escaped, Pashanin, a senior soldier, was captured. Afghan agents later informed the Soviets that he had been castrated and a ring put through his nose. He had then been dragged naked through local villages, and shot dead a month later.[130] When Soviet troops found their comrades' corpses pinned out, flayed, beheaded or with their throats slit, some took reprisals. Mujahideen prisoners were also shot and some were run over by tanks.[131]

The Mujahideen were sometimes unable to punish all those they suspected of collaboration. Loyalty to the *qawm* could take precedence. Olivier Roy, who visited the Mujahideen in Ghor province, related how the resistance were prevented from assassinating their suspect: 'his *qawm* made it known that his death in combat would not be considered an offence, but that his execution on his home territory would, on the other hand, provoke a duty of vengeance leading to one of those vendettas which the resistance was trying to avoid at all costs'.[132] The man was not killed. On the whole, the Mujahideen were intolerant of collaborators or those who did not support the Jihad. In the refugee camps in Pakistan, Islamist groups threatened Afghan women who did not cover themselves in the *burqa*, assassinated rivals, and tortured or executed those they suspected of collaboration with the government.[133] They summarily shot 'collaborators' and 'spies' inside Afghanistan, and sometimes their families.[134]

Poverty could drive families to send sons into both the Mujahideen and the Afghan Army or police, in order to get enough money to live.[135] Pashtuns in Pakistan also had a 'foot in both camps'. Thousands who supported the Mujahideen were eager to profit from the sale of goods and supplies to the Afghan Army and even the Soviets. Selling fresh food to the border posts was particularly popular.[136] Some border guards even bartered weapons and ammunition for items that would augment their rations or make their concrete bunkers more comfortable. The Afghan Army hired buses and trucks from the clans astride the border in order to move around and move their supplies. Even KhAD agents were not above selling arms in the bazaars of Pakistan's North West Frontier Province. Many families needed their menfolk as breadwinners and so, even when some had served in the Mujahideen on tours lasting three or four months, they might terminate their active service in order to return home and tend to the domestic economy. Often, another relative would be found as a replacement, but Mujahideen teams would fluctuate in strength. Mujahideen commanders were not accommodating to the needs of civilians, and were particularly indifferent towards civilian casualties they might inflict in their rocket attacks on major cities. Abdul Haq, who bombarded Kabul, stated: 'their target [our fighters] is not the civilians... but if I hit them I don't care... If my family lived near the Soviet Embassy I would still hit it. I wouldn't care about them. If am prepared to die, my son has to die for it, and my wife has to die for it'.[137]

The Afghan communist government was just as indifferent to civilian casualties, and the brutality of Karmal's secret service was unbridled. The 30,000 men and women of KhAD continued to carry out their duties of counter-insurgency, surveillance and intelligence gathering with considerable violence. Businesses that participated in strikes were threatened with being shut down permanently. Suspects were beaten up or hauled into prisons, where torture was routine.[138] The effect of this was to encourage subsequent regimes that lacked popular consensus, including that of Najibullah and the Taliban, to resort to the same repressive techniques. Karmal's attempts to popularize the regime failed. He tried to make the regime appear more 'Islamic', called for a war of liberation against Pashtuns, and restyled the PDPA as the 'National Fatherland Front'. The word 'democracy' was also associated with Soviet propaganda and government oppression.[139] The Soviet army launched more offensives, but there was no lessening of the resistance. In the mid 1980s, Soviet leader Mikhail Gorbachev could see that the war could not be won using the old techniques. Describing Afghanistan as a 'bleeding wound', he 'retired' Karmal and began to explore ways of 'Afghanizing' the war effort. Perhaps even more important was the cost: feeding the urban populations and the troops, supplying the army of occupation and buying off Afghans was costing an estimated $12 million a day.[140]

The Soviets chose Dr Najibullah, a Parcham member of the PDPA, to improve their situation. He created militias to take over the control of road and urban area protection. At the end of the war the Mujahideen grew bolder: there were major attacks on Kabul, Qalat and Kunduz. However, in the latter there was an ominous outcome. The Mujahideen acted in a heavy-handed way towards the civilian population, costing them their previous popularity. They were in danger of being seen as ruthless brigands, no better than the Najibullah regime itself.

Najibullah resorted to buying support and abandoned his attempts to reunite the PDPA. He continued the policy of coercion and ignored the Soviet Union's calls to initiate a policy of reconciliation. Gorbachev had urged the Afghan communists to: 'Widen your social base. Learn, at last, to lead a dialogue with the tribes, use the particularities [of the situation]. Try to get the support of the *ulema*. Give up the leftist bend in economics. Learn to organize the support of the private sector...'[141] In the end, it was money, and fear of the consequences of surrender, that kept the regime going.

Negotiating with the Soviets

The Soviet military intervention in Afghanistan was not, as contemporary Western observers suggested, part of the 'onward march of socialism' in Asia, but an attempt to shore up an increasingly unpopular and divided Afghan communist regime under the PDPA. Publicly, the Soviets were confident of victory on behalf of Afghan socialism because they believed their historically progressive ideology opposed an Asiatic backwardness that was doomed to extinction. However, there were real concerns that the Islamist nature of the unrest in Herat, much of which had been directed against Soviet advisors and their families, might herald an Islamic revolution in Soviet Central Asia, or provide the opportunity for Western intelligence to exploit the vulnerable southern flank of the USSR. The combined fears and ideological position of the Soviets, with the angry reaction of the opposition in Afghanistan, made any negotiations unlikely, and therefore the two sides would be difficult to reconcile. However, what made any rapprochement even more unlikely was the brutal heavy-handedness of the government and its secret service, the KhAD. The inability of the PDPA to reconcile divisions within its own ranks, particularly between the Parcham and Khalqi branches of the party (which themselves reflected ethnic or *qawm* fracture lines as well as ideological splits), meant that Soviet intervention was likely.

The Soviets had regarded Afghanistan as a potential protégé from the 1930s, but the Revolution by Mohammed Daoud in 1973 and its apparently pro-communist character cemented the Soviet alignment. When Soviet forces failed to totally extinguish resistance by their sheer presence, they applied overwhelming force. The 'stick' was accompanied by the 'carrot' of reforms designed to bring about modernization in agriculture and bureaucracy, and there were active campaigns to recruit collaborators as a means to achieve victory. However, since these changes appeared to herald a process of social engineering, they generated fears that the religion and way of life of Afghans was about to be overthrown and local resistance stiffened. The Soviets maintained that their objective was the resolution of civil conflict, but they wanted the installation of a government more acceptable to the USSR that could ensure stability. However, the invasion earned international condemnation, provoking intervention.

For the resistance, there was a general unwillingness to compromise. Although there was no national movement, the Soviets were viewed by rural populations as foreign unbelievers set on occupation and destruction of traditional ways. However, some, including urban and educated Afghans, chose to collaborate and negotiated their future under occupation or as local communist participants. Yet, in the conduct of military operations the Afghans remained subordinate, which caused a corresponding slump in morale. In political terms, the Soviets selected their surrogate leaders, but neither these, nor the Soviet forces, could find a solution to the military impasse developing. Stalemate in the ground conditions did not produce a desire to negotiate on either side, and the war continued.

By 1985 the conflict in Afghanistan appeared to be intractable.[142] General Secretaries Chernyenko and Andropov were too elderly or ill to exercise much leadership, and the Central Committee selected a younger, more energetic leader in Mikhail Gorbachev to find a solution. The Chief of the General Staff, Akhromeev, explained to him the dire military situation:

In the past seven years Soviet soldiers have had their boots on the ground in every square kilometre of the country. But as soon as they left, the enemy returned and restored everything the way it was before. We have lost this war. The majority of the Afghan people support the counter-revolution. We have lost the peasantry, who have got nothing from the revolution. 80% of the country is in the hands of the counterrevolution. And the position of the peasants there is better than it is on the territory controlled by the government.[143]

Within a year, Gorbachev was looking for an exit strategy that would help in improving relations with the West and allow more urgent and substantive reforms at home. The emphasis switched to creating or employing more local forces to 'Afghanize' security, although such was the unreliability of the Afghan Army that the bulk of operations were still carried out by Soviet troops and their security personnel. Moreover, the surrogate communist government in Kabul proved unable to deliver on reforms. By 1986, the Soviets' objective had changed to a desire to exit Afghanistan with honour. Ultimately the UN was seen as the 'third party' that could open and conclude negotiations between the Pakistanis (and by extension the Americans) and the Afghan government (and therefore the Soviets). There was no desire to negotiate with the Afghan resistance at all, since it was generally assumed the Mujahideen were dependent on the Pakistanis and Americans. The Geneva Accords (1988) finally gave the USSR the opportunity to depart in 1989, leaving a surrogate regime well equipped and well funded to continue to face down the resistance. Meanwhile a United Front was formed in Pakistan by negotiation amongst most of the Mujahideen factions, although the prominent exceptions included many Pashtun groups.

Beneath these international actions, the Soviets were, like the British, eager to conclude local deals that divided the resistance. They attempted to employ militias, and there was an acceptance of local truces that seemed to ensure Soviet control of rural areas.[144] One example illustrates the contours of the Afghan decision to negotiate or collaborate. The Ismailis in the Kayan Valley of Baghlan province responded positively to the call of Najibullah, for a militia, because they were a marginalized group. Surrounded by sectarian or ethnic rivals, they were eager to defend themselves. When the Tajiks and Pashtuns near the Salang Tunnel aligned their groups either with Jamiat or with the Jihadist Hizbi-i Islami, Sayyed Mansur Naderi of Kaihan, brother of the *pir* (spiritual head) of the Ismailis, organized his community to arm and defend their lands and the road between Kabul and the Soviet border. By 1989, Naderi had 13,000 troops organized in the '80th Division' under the command of his son, Jaffar, and a place in the local government council.

Informal truces and deals could be made by more junior officers. The situation was often fluid and Afghans could change their minds depending on the behaviour of Russian or DRA troops or changes in the local security situation. Fighting alternated with negotiation. Both sides might observe a mutual local ceasefire as part of a continuum of violence and communication. Locals might be willing to barter with Soviet troops if they turned a blind eye to smuggling. Blockhouse garrisons were particularly vulnerable and maintained a trade with Afghans to ensure their survival. Goods exchanged included canned food, sugar, cigarettes, soap, kerosene, matches, used clothing and shoes. Soldiers even handed over magazines but took care to 'cook' their ammunition in boiling water so that the cartridges could not be used against them.

Mutual destruction could also create an equilibrium. Alexander Kartsev commanded a blockhouse detachment but got on well with locals, using his pre-war medical skills to treat their illnesses. When Afghan government officials arrived to negotiate with the local Mujahideen commander, they were taken prisoner and the Mujahideen threatened to kill them. Colonel Wahid, commanding the local KhAD, asked Kartsev to negotiate the release of the men and their armoured vehicles. Kartsev was told that the Mujahideen would release the vehicles but not the prisoners, who were scheduled to be executed as 'allies of the enemies of Islam'. Kartsev was reassured that, as a gesture, the prisoners would not be tortured. Kartsev argued that if the officials who were acting as envoys in negotiations were killed, the Soviets were bound to take reprisals against the local villagers and their crops. Many would be killed. After a *jirga* amongst the Mujahideen, the prisoners and their vehicles were released.[145]

Another Soviet soldier, Feliks Rakhmonov, a Tajik, developed an affinity with local Afghans at Shindad airbase. The Afghan civilians would bring in individual soldiers who had been taken prisoner. One group brought three soldiers in a donkey cart, and Rakhmonov exchanged the prisoners for flour and diesel. A precedent had been set and soon a number of Soviet soldiers were being brought in for exchange.[146]

To improve security, the Afghan Army engaged in negotiations with the aim of establishing territorial units amongst local leaders who had been former resistance. These groups were essentially co-opted to regular units or given regular army designations. The local communities decided who would serve, and only one third would have to be on duty at any one time, the rest being able to remain at home in civilian employment. The system worked as long as the funds continued to flow in, but allegiances were never guaranteed and many changed sides the moment the Soviets withdrew.

In all cases, the Soviets were prepared to negotiate only to ensure the success of their mission and to bring about a local pacification of the population. However, the Afghans were just as capable of making truces to suit their own designs. The most significant of these was Ahmad Shah Masoud's truce in the Panjshir Valley in 1982. As already noted, the Afghan–Tajik warlord leader had mounted a successful guerrilla campaign astride the strategic Route 1 from Kunduz, Mazar-e Sahrif and Kabul, and his men enjoyed some successes against the Soviets around the Salang Tunnel area. The Soviets therefore launched an offensive in May 1982 and stepped out their counter-measures between August and September, which kept Masoud on the defensive. To buy time for his exhausted forces to regroup and to break out to the Tajik homelands to the north-east, Masoud concluded a truce with the Soviets which lasted from December 1982 to April 1984.[147] Harsh winter weather was certainly a factor that prolonged the truce, but the primary purpose appeared to be to gain time to get the bulk of his forces out of the area to fight another day.[148] Masoud spent a great deal of time negotiating with elders within his own area, and was particularly adept at moving populations prior to significant operations in order to reduce civilian casualties; the fate of the civilian population was uppermost in his mind when he opted for a ceasefire. The Soviet view was that they could demonstrate the material gains which could be made by coming to some accommodation with the Karmal regime and that, given time, the local population would want to stay at peace and not resume violence in favour of the resistance.[149] By demonstrating that a key warlord leader was prepared to talk with them, the Soviets also hoped to send a signal that others were free to arrange truces too. Yet it was the Soviets, or rather the Kabul government, who also broke the truce with a new operation against the Panjshir Valley in 1984 as reprisals for guerrilla activity elsewhere.

The Soviet reconciliation policy had several stages in its evolution. Soon after the invasion it had placed local leaders in positions of power at provincial level through the Afghan government in Kabul, but on 9 January 1987 it announced the establishment of a national reconciliation commission based on several more permissive provinces. In March, the commission stated that it had achieved a number of successes in Kabul, the north-east and some central provinces. By June of that year, there were 1,800 sub-commissions and the following month this had risen to 2,498. It was alleged that 90,000 had reconciled themselves to the government and a further 51,000 had laid down their arms while 93,000 were in talks. By the end of the year, the Politburo reported that it had had some success with joint governance at provincial level in Afghanistan. In fact, the statistics were utterly misleading. There were strikes in major urban areas and public condemnation of reconciliation efforts. Hafi Mohammed Aman, the chairman of the reconciliation commission in Kandahar, was assassinated.

In terms of reconciliation, it was the Mujahideen who enjoyed the greatest success. Towards the end of the war they found it was possible to take tactical positions by negotiation with their garrisons rather than launching attacks. The only problem for the more senior front commanders was that, having secured local control, some Mujahideen groups lost interest in the struggle and refused to operate out of their local area.

The most significant element of the negotiations that brought to an end the Soviet occupation of Afghanistan was the Geneva Accords brokered by the United Nations. The Soviet Union had the ability to veto any condemnation of its initial invasion as a permanent member of the Security Council, but this also meant that it could treat the UN as a third party when it came to negotiating a settlement with at least some of its adversaries. The UN, unable to implement Chapter VII against the Soviets, could at least try to initiate a withdrawal through its 'Good Offices' and some shuttle diplomacy. Article 99 of the UN Charter gave the Secretary General the authorization to initiate negotiations unilaterally in order to prevent or resolve 'any matter which may threaten the maintenance of international peace and security'. The Secretary General can also call upon the Secretariat to provide personnel to assist him in his negotiations, and he is able to appoint Special Representatives or Personal Representatives to maintain the momentum of negotiations. These representatives have the ability to act directly for the Secretary General and not on behalf of the Security Council. Nevertheless, initially the Soviet Union was not content to see the UN play any role and preferred to get the Karmal regime in Kabul to negotiate directly with General Zia ul Haq in Pakistan. Brezhnev was suspicious that the UN might only act on behalf of anti-Afghan and anti-Soviet powers.[150]

The Soviets maintained that a political solution had to be found to the conflict, a view it had broadcast from 1980, but for several years few in the UN believed that the Soviets were interested in a peaceful solution.[151] Nevertheless, the UN made attempts to reach an agreement from 1982 onwards, with the first communications established between Kabul and Islamabad from April

1981 thanks to the work of Javier Pérez de Cuéllar (who subsequently became UN Secretary General the following year). Shuttle talks were continued through 1982 and 1983 by Diego Cordovez, the Under-Secretary General for Special Political Affairs. By 1984, proximity talks had been established with the negotiating parties occupying different suites in the Palais des Nations in Geneva. Pakistan nevertheless refused to recognize the Karmal regime in Kabul, and this prevented any direct talks from taking place. Nevertheless, the UN envisaged the withdrawal of foreign forces, non-interference in the internal affairs of Afghanistan, international guarantees of Afghanistan's integrity and the repatriation of refugees, the latter having risen to a staggering five million, a fifth of the population, by the end of the war.

Although the Soviets were effectively in control of Afghanistan's destiny, the Afghan communist delegation frequently defied their Moscow masters, particularly when it was clear that the Soviet forces were being withdrawn.[152] Pakistani officials also distrusted the United States, who was the leading paymaster of the Mujahideen, and feared American interests would not coincide with Pakistan's in the long term. Iran was also not directly involved in the talks, but took a keen interest in the process. Changes of government added further delay and disruption, and often raised false expectations of a sudden breakthrough. The appointment of Andropov as Soviet leader was expected to produce more progress, but Herschberg has shown that this was a Western illusion.[153] Andropov was using negotiations to buy time, hoping that a more vigorous military counterinsurgency strategy would bear fruit. He also hoped to divide the Afghan resistance, and to sow discord among the Western powers and Pakistan.

Misunderstandings plagued the negotiations as far as the Americans and Soviets were concerned. President Reagan was eager to punish the USSR in Afghanistan and inflict a Vietnam-style defeat on what he termed an 'Evil Empire'. He was therefore surprised that his own negotiating team had agreed to stop all financial assistance to the Afghan Mujahideen at the point when the Soviets agreed to withdraw, even though Soviet military and financial assistance would continue to support the Karmal regime. Reagan felt that would give the Soviets a decisive advantage and perhaps enable them to crush the Afghan resistance. His repudiation of any deal of this nature in December 1987 came after Gorbachev's announcement that the Soviet forces would withdraw, and there was a risk the talks would collapse entirely. The Americans clarified the US position that it would discontinue its support if the Soviet Union continued to exercise restraint.[154] Pakistan was concerned that the Afghan regime, which it had consistently refused to recognize, might simply gain legitimacy by default. Moreover, the absence of the Afghan resistance in the negotiations meant that Pakistan's favoured factions, including that of the austere Islamist Gulbuddin Hekmatyar, might be excluded from power. Nevertheless, the Accords were signed on 14 April 1988, leaving significant areas unresolved but at least agreeing on the Soviet departure.

The Accords provided for four elements of a peace settlement. The first assured Afghanistan and Pakistan of mutual non-interference and non-intervention, covering territorial integrity, sovereignty and economic stability. Article II (8) spelled out that there should be no 'training, equipping, financing and recruiting of mercenaries from whatever origin for the purpose of hostile activities, sending of such mercenaries into the territory [of each country] – and accordingly deny facilities including the financing of training, equipping and transit of such mercenaries'. Article II (12) was even more specific in its requirements to deny bases, support or training to any group which aimed to disrupt the other country. This element of the Accords gave Afghanistan a free hand to tackle its own insurgency and removed the threat of intervention.

The second element of the Accords dealt with international guarantees from the United States and Soviet Union not to interfere or intervene in the internal affairs of Afghanistan, and obliged them to support the bilateral agreement set out in the first element. The third part of the Accords provided for the voluntary repatriation of refugees from Pakistan with assistance offered by the UN. The fourth and final element of the Accords stated that there should be a 'settlement of the situation' in Afghanistan, and stated that the troops of the Soviet Union would begin a phased withdrawal, starting on 15 May 1988 and concluded nine months later.

The Accords were a good example of how limited objectives, persistence in negotiation and realistic expectations could produce a settlement.[155] It has been suggested that the exclusion of the Mujahideen was an advantage because it avoided having to conclude separate deals with rival groups, which would have prolonged the war and caused intense in-fighting between rival factions.[156] However, whilst the Accords undoubtedly paved the way for the withdrawal of the Soviets, enabling them to argue that they had conceded to international requests, there was no guarantee that the civil war, which had effectively started in 1978, could be brought to an end. Indeed, even in 1989 there was every indication that the war would continue. The USSR perpetuated its financing of the Najibullah regime, and ensured that even when it did pull out it left behind a massive arsenal of weapons and ammunition; Najibullah had also shown that he was prepared to use force to reassert himself as President. The Soviet withdrawal was not opposed by the resistance, because each faction was gathering its strength to bid for exclusive power over Afghanistan.

The exclusion of the Mujahideen parties may have made the process easier for the states involved, and prevented Pakistan from using them as a lever for advantage in the talks, but in every civil war those that have done the fighting expect to have a significant voice in the outcome. As William Maley points out, the failure to address who would govern in Kabul and the nature of that government, which had caused the unrest in the 1970s, was not addressed.[157] There was also no discussion of how the Afghan government would carry out the process of conflict resolution and reconstruction. Trust-building measures, the repair of infrastructure, the distribution of power, the management of force and the rehabilitation of the resistance were all conspicuously absent. Unsurprisingly, therefore, the war continued.

The further deterioration of the stability of the Afghan state was exemplified by the attempted coup by General Tenai in 1990. His failure led to an erosion of confidence in the regular security forces. The government, unable to rely on the Afghan Army and looking to achieve consensus with rural leaders, formed larger militias to replace the regular troops. These forces were soon so large that they were unaccountable to their local areas, in contrast to traditional *lashkars*. When the funding stopped abruptly with the collapse of the USSR, the militias abandoned the government. The most powerful commanders became 'warlords' with personal fiefdoms across the country, but there were multitudes of small-scale groups which attempted to control smaller zones. Thus a new and perhaps even more lethal phase of the civil war had begun.

The Geneva Accords can be criticized on the basis of excluding the key warring parties of the resistance, and similar charges have been made against the Bonn Agreement in 2002 which did not include the Taliban leadership. It is a reminder that negotiation with the enemy, however fractured their structures, is a prolonged but necessary element of the process. Moreover, as Walter argues, keeping sight of the long-term security guarantees, as well as addressing the root cause of conflict, is essential. The Geneva Accords served the interests of the USSR and, to a lesser extent, the communist government in Kabul. Pakistan may have had the reassurance of non-intervention, but there were no guarantees of greater stability on its western border. The continuation of the civil war practically compelled Pakistan to take a more proactive approach to resolving the conflict by backing its most favoured factions. Similar calculations were made by Iran and the Central Asian republics after 1992.

7

THE CIVIL WAR, THE TALIBAN
AND THE INSURGENCY, 1990–2011

Some 15,000 Soviet soldiers died in the Afghan war, and the number of Afghan civilian casualties has been estimated to be between 600,000 and 2.5 million.[1] Violence did not lessen after the Soviet withdrawal, deterring reconstruction agencies and the return of 5 million refugees who had fled across the borders. Moscow continued to fund and arm Najibullah's regime which kept the war going. Yet there were key vulnerabilities for the regime. Najibullah authorized the printing of more money and became dependent on the militias and their warlord leaders, especially those drawn from the minorities. Eventually 100,000 former insurgents were in government service. The 17th Division in Herat, for example, was made up of 3,400 regular troops and 14,000 militiamen. When the Soviet Union withdrew, many assumed that the Najibullah regime would disappear, but, propped up with cash, mercenary militias and soviet weaponry, and faced with a faction-ridden resistance, it survived for a further two years.

The ISI calculated that the fall of Jalalabad would open the way to Kabul where they expected Hekmatyar to take power. As soon as the Soviet 40th Army had left, fighting escalated around the city.[2] The offensive began in earnest in March 1989, although the first outpost was captured rather undramatically by bribing the officer in charge.[3] The Mujahideen then tried to seize the airport, but they were repulsed with heavy losses. Mujahideen commanders denounced rival factions angrily for the failure, arguing that while they made attacks, other factions were asleep. The fact that each offensive was uncoordinated allowed the garrison to defeat each thrust in turn. Arab volunteers, who massacred prisoners as a matter of course, discouraged any further defections from the Afghan Army and reinforced their determination to fight on.

The Afghan government forces made extensive use of air power to pound Mujahideen positions around the city, and they even deployed Scud missiles. Fired ballistically, Scuds gave no warning. General Greshnov believed the Mujahideen 'were psychologically unable to cope when these rockets were employed against them'. He summed up the operations in terms that the Soviets would have understood: 'Losses among the civilian population could be counted in thousands, and the battle itself acquired such a massive and brutal character that it could be compared in military terms perhaps only with the battle for Stalingrad'.[4] The battle for Jalalabad, which lasted five months, cost the Mujahideen over 3,000 killed and wounded. Ismail Khan, then a guerrilla commander, believed that 'the battle of Jalalabad lost us the credit won in ten years of fighting'. Brigadier Yousaf gave a similar verdict: 'The Jihad has never recovered from Jalalabad'.[5]

Hekmatyar, aware that the war might be swinging against him, offered to switch sides and join Najibullah in an attempt to gain political power. In his own *volte face*, Najibullah tried to recruit Pashtun militias into government service, but the fall of Mazar-i Sharif to General Dostum, on whom he had previously depended to control the north, spelt the final end of the government. As the various factions converged on the capital, there was a brief period of hope for a compromise. Initially there was euphoria as the resistance claimed victory over the communists. Looking back in 2002, Rabbani stated:

We forced the communists out of our country; we can force all invaders out of holy Afghanistan–Had it not been for the Jihad, the whole world would still be in the communist grip. The Berlin Wall fell because of the wounds which we inflicted on the Soviet Union and the inspiration we gave all oppressed people. We broke the Soviet Union up into fifteen parts. We liberated people from communism. Jihad led to a free world. We saved the world because communism met its grave here in Afghanistan![6]

Afghanistan may have been liberated, but if the resistance had fought to preserve the Afghan way of life then it had failed: Afghanistan had been totally transformed and the civil war accelerated the social changes which the Islamic purists had most feared. Moreover, by February 1993 the capital had become a battlefield between five major competing organizations.

The Afghan Civil War (1993–6) led to the collapse of any unified authority, and Pakistan is the nation that Afghans blame most for the war. Abdul Salam Zaeef argued that Pakistan was treacherous towards everyone and subsequently betrayed the Taliban.[7] But Afghans were already bitterly divided. As Soviet involvement came to an end, and the communist regime collapsed, so the Afghans lost their common enemy. At Kandahar, Mujahideen factions had been prevented from taking control of the city by militias, such as the Jawzjani of General Dostum. Their habit of looting earned them the sobriquet 'the carpet stealers' from the Kandaharis. When the government funds ran out in 1992, the Jawzjani withdrew, and the Mujahideen factions were involved in a chaotic takeover. Mullah Naqib and his followers seized the old Afghan Army base; Amir Lalai took control of the commercial district; Haji Ahmad held the airport; Uztaz Abdul Aleem took possession of the police headquarters and prison, and Haji Sarkateb held Bagh-e Pul. When it was clear that the city could no longer support these fighting units, the Mujahideen commanders turned to robbery. Within a month, the city had been systematically looted and there was barely anything left to sell. Tanks were sold to the Tajik–Afghans in the north and even the hospital was stripped of its beds. When the city had been sacked, the Mujahideen turned to banditry on the highways. The lawlessness generated a great deal of anger amongst southern Pashtun clans.

Pakistan and Iran were the only two external players left trying to influence the chaotic division of the country. However, Hekmatyar, Pakistan's favoured candidate to lead the country, was initially excluded from the Afghan negotiations for a new government. His response was to make rocket attacks on the city. Rabbani, then heading the interim government, decided to offer Hekmatyar a government post, but this failed. Hekmatyar's militia then clashed with the fighters who belonged to the Shura-i-Nazar (Council of the North), a coalition of minority groups. As a result, the capital was the arena of violent faction fighting. In the north of the city were the fighters of Masoud. In the centre was the Jumbesh-e Meli Islami, the faction of General Dostum. To the west were the Hezb-e Wahdat Shia fighters of Mazari and also the rival Ittehad-e Islami, the Saudi-backed Sunnis. Outside the city was Hekmatyar. In 1993, Wahdat attacked Ittehad whilst Hekmatyar launched an offensive against Masoud's men. Masoud and Ittehad then united to fight Wahdat, and Dostum joined them, thus creating the 'United Front'. In the fighting there were massacres of civilians, and it is estimated that as many as 10,000 were killed. Looting was widespread. Sectarianism, which had always been a feature of the conflict, worsened with a particularly notorious massacre of Shias at Afshar in February 1993.

In 1995, there was a brief interlude of peace when Ittehad and Masoud's Shura-i-Nazar gained control of Kabul, but a new force now entered the conflict. It was ironic that, just as there was a possibility of order being restored, a new faction backed by Pakistan deepened the war. The Taliban, disaffected former resistance fighters from the Soviet War and younger Pashtuns recruited from the refugee camps and religious schools of tribal north-west Pakistan, were armed and supplied by the ISI.[8] Initially they had done no more than set up their own vehicle checkpoints between Kandahar and the districts of Maiwand and Panjwayi.[9] However, they were aware that Kandahar, like many cities, had been reduced to rubble by constant fighting between former Mujahideen commanders.[10] The Taliban ambushed several of the most notorious of these commanders, and when they captured them they executed them and displayed their corpses on gibbets, with banknotes stuffed in their mouths. They then drove the embittered warlords first out of Spin Boldak and then Kandahar itself.[11] To avoid destruction, many former Mujahideen joined them. The Taliban now had some momentum and, with gifts of cash to aid the flow, or offers simply to end the faction fighting by acting as third-party negotiators, the movement spread quickly across the south.

Hekmatyar, now out of favour with Pakistan, finally accepted a government post as Prime Minister, but the withdrawal of his men from the outskirts of Kabul occurred at just the moment when the Taliban were preparing for a major offensive. Masoud mined the approaches to the city and took up a defensive position at Sarobi.[12] There were rumours that the Taliban, led by Mullah Bor Jan, drove vehicles into the minefield, one after another, to detonate the mines and clear a path. Some of the vehicles were said to be carrying a number of Taliban volunteers carrying flags and chanting Islamist slogans. Even by Afghan standards of devotion, this behaviour, if it indeed took place, was shocking and indicated that a new ideological motivation had gripped some of the faction fighters. The Taliban proclaimed that their objective was simply to impose Sharia law across the country in order to assert justice and end the conflict. Yet they had already decided that they would act as judge and jury, and inflict severe punishments on all they considered guilty.

Aware that Hekmatyar was prepared to resist more stubbornly, the Taliban had initially bypassed his stronghold at Ghazni, but Hekmatyar had struck against them in a counter-offensive on 19 January 1995. While the fighting escalated, the governor of the city defected to the Taliban and the city itself fell without a struggle. Hekmatyar tried to launch a new thrust against Ghazni soon after his rival Rabbani sided with the Taliban to help defeat the offensive. Hundreds of Hekmatyar's men were killed in the outskirts, and they were forced to fall back to their headquarters at Charasiab.[13] Hekmatyar's entrenchments around his headquarters did not fall to the Taliban's direct assault at Maiden Sheher in February 1995, but were cut off from their line of communications to Jalalabad. The eventual capture of this stronghold, with some 200 killed on each side, caused Hekmatyar's militia to begin to break up.

However, the Taliban's aura of invincibility was shattered by the fiasco of their offensive against Herat. As they advanced towards the city, they were strafed by General Ismail Khan's private air force, and, following a Herati request for help, a *lashkar* of 1,000 Tajik experienced fighters from Masoud's command were airlifted in. Although the Taliban dug in around Dilaram, 200 miles south of Herat, they were thrown into confusion when their commander, Mullah Mohammed, was killed. In August they were being driven out by Ismail Khan's forces and harried all the way to the Helmand River.[14] The Kandaharis were mobilized, and rallied with the warning that a Tajik and Shia army was on its way. Funds and vehicles were provided to stem the advance, and an army numbering almost 10,000 was assembled along the Helmand. After a short but close-quarter battle at Gereshk, the Taliban returned to the offensive and the front line stabilized again at Dilaram. Beyond this, Herati strongpoints centred on dug-in tanks were systematically overrun with costly light infantry assaults. The momentum of these broke the morale of the Tajik and Herati forces, and the retreating troops fled through Shindand airbase without even trying to hold it. Some fifty-two Mig-21 aircraft, 60 field guns and several helicopters fell into Taliban hands. By stretching their control up to the border of Iran, Herat was effectively cut off. Despite a series of battles, the Heratis were too demoralized to continue resistance and sought a settlement. Similar sentiments affected Khost, Jalalabad and towns south of the capital. At Sarobi, a three-pronged Taliban offensive by waves of fighters, seemingly fearless of death, caused the defenders to crack. The Kabul militias were so shaken that they chose not to resist the force of 30,000 that was assembling around the city.[15]

The Taliban briefly allied themselves to the Shia Wahdat, but this unholy alliance of Sunni and Shia was brought to an abrupt end by a skirmish outside the capital. The Taliban then seized and executed the Wahdat leader, Mazari. Dostum had pulled out of Kabul to reinforce his control of the north-west, which left the forces of Masoud to face the Taliban onslaught alone. With the Taliban backed by Pakistan's weaponry, fuel, aircraft, funds, intelligence and abundant supplies, Masoud knew that his own men might well be trapped in the capital. He therefore withdrew to conduct a campaign from the Afghan–Tajik heartland in the Panjshir and the north-east. Consequently, the capital fell to the Taliban with very little resistance. Najibullah, who had sheltered in a UN compound in Kabul, was one of those unceremoniously accused of treachery and crimes against Islam. He was tortured, murdered and dismembered.[16]

However, resistance was not extinguished. Masoud and Dostum defeated the Taliban on the Hindu Kush in 1996 and again in 1997, and there was a rebellion in Kunar under the leadership of Haji Abdul Qadeer, the former governor of Nangrahar, in February 1997.

Pakistan lost control of its Taliban partners. Islamabad had hoped that the Taliban would provide Pakistan with 'strategic depth', a secure hinterland, a ready supply of Pashtun volunteers, and potentially oil resources from the north of the country (and perhaps from post-Soviet Central Asia too) so as to be able to conclude the Kashmir question with India.[17] The Taliban was not, however, a purely Pashtun phenomenon. It attracted many foreign idealists and religious dogmatists. It was a movement of militant and militarist thinkers and a magnet for many who felt angry at the outcome of the war against the Soviets, the chaos of the civil war, and the arbitrary rule of the warlords. Some idealists railed against the world order, not least the weak position of the Muslim world compared with the West. The strict discipline and the rigidity of thinking attracted those who were either poor, without families or just eager to play their part in the restructuring of the world. Many young Afghans had grown up in an environment where irregulars were able to command the loyalty of others by their armed strength, coerce the reluctant and punish those who stood in their way. It was a militarization of Afghan society, overturning old traditional models of social relations. Power was now exercised, as Mao once put it, from the barrel of a gun.

Mullah Omar, who had emerged as the leader of the movement, stage-managed the idea that Afghanistan was the model Islamic state. He claimed that since Allah's power was not divisible, there could be no democracy in Afghanistan. He and his Taliban confederates idealized the past; they claimed that it was they who had driven out the communists and destroyed the Soviet Union. Osama bin Laden, who had been compelled to abandon his base in Sudan, soon found refuge in the new Afghanistan. Memories of his construction of hostelries for foreign fighters and funding of their families during the Soviet occupation were refreshed. He reciprocated the hospitality of the Taliban by praising their efforts, but he was focused on more distant objectives. He saw the Taliban's regime as a platform for the training of legions of Mujahideen who would fight the 'Jews and Crusaders' who controlled the Middle East. Like the leader of the Egyptian Islamic Jihad, Ayman al-Zawahiri, he was particularly eager to recruit men who would engage in covert operations against the West. He wanted to harness the idealism of the Taliban and take it beyond Afghanistan into a global Jihad against all unbelievers. If the Mujahideen had defeated the Soviet Union, he reasoned, why not the United States too?

Their ideological doctrines, and continuing armed resistance, convinced the Taliban that Afghan society needed security and protection. In 1996, Masoud was still defiant in the north-east and acted as leader of the United Islamic Front for the Salvation of Afghanistan, known to the West as the Northern Alliance.[18] The Hazaras in the central-western region and Dostum in Mazar-i Sharif also kept up resistance. During a major offensive against Mazar-i Sharif, they persuaded the faction of Malik Pahlavan to abandon Dostum's command and align with the Taliban. This gave them control of the city. However, fighting broke out between Pahlavan's men and the Taliban soon after and there were massacres on both sides.[19] As the Taliban reeled from the city and rallied to re-enter it, Dostum's forces arrived and drove them back. In 1998 the Taliban made a third attempt to seize the city, and this time they succeeded. In three days of killing, the Taliban and their Arab allies (led by Mullah Abdul Manan Niazi) slaughtered hundreds. In the Mazar hospital, thirty patients were killed in their beds. There were grotesque episodes of torture: some victims were asphyxiated or boiled alive in the sun's heat by being locked inside metal containers. They ordered that corpses were to be left in the streets: no one was permitted to bury them as a mark of shame. Eyewitnesses reported seeing dogs feeding on the carrion flesh. The Taliban were just as furious in their assault on Bamian in 1998, massacring the inhabitants. At Yakaolong in the Hazarajat, 300 were killed when people were herded into a mosque and rockets were fired into it. Despite pleas for clemency from Shia elders, the Taliban regarded the Hazaras as sectarian and ethnic enemies of such low status as to render them apostates or *kufr* (without faith). Elsewhere the Taliban engaged in ethnic cleansing, and razed crops and villages.

In 2000 serious fighting flared up again, with the most effective resistance in the north-east. The Taliban used tanks and aircraft against Masoud, who, despite being increasingly short of equipment and supplies, was able to beat them off. Taliban tactics left much to be desired. There were no elements of organization which typify regular armies: there were no combat estimates or appreciations, no fire plan, and no assembly areas. Instead, rockets or light artillery were 'fired in the general direction' of the enemy, accompanied by a 'hail of bullets from automatic weapons' whereupon 'hopefully the rival militia surrenders'.[20] If there was any sort of resistance, a hastily organized attack was mounted. If very stubborn resistance was encountered, the Taliban simply assembled more men, sometimes upwards of 1,000 fighters. Ordinarily Taliban units rarely exceeded 500, which reflected the guerrilla structure of their forces and the problem of obtaining large volumes of supplies in an impoverished country. Guerrilla tactics, of hit and run or a short rocket fusillade without any actual attack by foot soldiers to follow it up, were common. Air attacks from the limited air assets available often amounted to a single strike. The need to avoid anti-aircraft fire meant that bombing runs were usually hopelessly inaccurate. Yet, fighting against Pashtun groups was rare. The usual process was to halt and send forward a mullah under the white Taliban flag with its green *Kalima* and entreat the opposition to lay down their arms because the Taliban had come to end all fighting in the country. Their aim was to gain support by consensus, to appear to be a neutral force, and to avoid taking sides in inter-clan fighting.

The Taliban's fear of uprisings and resistance led to fierce repression. Afghans often refer to the Taliban years in power as *wahshat* (terror). The Amir-e bil Marouf Wa Nahi Anil Munkar, the Department for the Preservation of Virtue and Elimination of Vice, banned the private ownership of televisions and radios and claimed to want Afghanistan to be 'weapons free' (except, of course, their own).[21] Moderate Afghans who opposed them were assassinated and there were public executions for dissent. The Taliban also tried to ensure compliance with their rule by imposing cultural and social disciplines. There was to be no music, dancing or drumming which might encourage impure thoughts. Ironically idealist mullahs and *qazis* had tried to prevent music during the struggle against the Soviets, but many Mujahideen had refused to accept the *ulemas'* rulings.[22] There was to be no visual representation of living beings, which resulted in the vandalizing of the Kabul Museum, the Bamian Buddhas and other structures. Women were denied employment, which led to the deaths of some war widows through starvation. Stoning was introduced for women accused of adultery. Women had to remain entirely covered in public, and there were sentences of capital punishment for a variety of offences involving female 'dishonour'. In May 2001, all non-Muslims had to wear a yellow patch to identify them to Taliban 'security'. The Taliban were thus eager to assert not just physical security for Afghans, but a moral security too.

The defeat of the Taliban

The greatest error of the Taliban was allowing Osama bin Laden to establish his training camps in Afghanistan for his global Jihad. The Taliban leadership soon lost control of those they hosted. Abdul Salam Zaeef, a former member of the Taliban, believed that allowing al Qaeda to operate from Afghan soil was likely to have repercussions, but Mullah Omar allegedly felt obliged to honour those who had fought the Soviets with him.[23] From its nerve centre near Kandahar, in 1998 al Qaeda carried out attacks in Kenya and Tanzania in the vicinity of American embassies.[24] The coordinated attacks were designed to cause mass casualties, the 'signature' of the movement. The Americans responded with cruise missile attacks into Afghanistan, which killed some of the fighters in their bases, but not Osama bin Laden. The Taliban knew that the United States had a 'global reach', but they remained defiant and refused to hand over bin Laden and his associates, despite American calls to do so.

The decision to harbour Osama bin Laden was not an easy one, since relations were somewhat strained and al Qaeda was as much an ideology as a movement. It represented the aspiration to create a unified Muslim world, purged of its modern-Western 'impurities', corruption and immorality. Its objective was not just spiritual but territorial in the sense that it aimed to recreate the Arab empire of the eighth century. The means to this end was the waging of total war. In 1996 bin Laden issued a fatwa, without authority, which argued that since Western civilians voted for their governments they shared the responsibility for the 'crimes' of the West, and therefore killing them, wherever they could be found, was 'justified'. Indeed, the death of Westerners was to be considered the duty of every Muslim. This world view was intolerant of sectarianism in the Islamic world, since there would be no room in their future for the Shia, Sufi and other branches of the faith. It was also an ideology that implied exterminism and grandiose dreams of a single caliphate, despite the historical failure of every similar enterprise from the Umyyads onwards. In fact, al Qaeda simply lacked the capacity to mobilize the fractured Muslim world, and their dreams of empire concealed their sense of humiliation that Islam, which they regarded as the superior way of life, was weak in comparison with the modern, wealthy and militarily powerful West.

Some of the Taliban resented bin Laden's fatwas and the Arab hubris, calling their Arab brethren 'camels', although it is also true that some embraced the global idealism of al Qaeda. A Taliban fighter known as Haqqani believed: 'We gave those camels free run of our country, and they brought us face to face with disaster. We knew the Americans would attack us in revenge'.[25] Mullah Omar stubbornly maintained that, according to the tribal tradition of Pashtunwali, he had to be seen to offer hospitality to a former fighter of the Soviet war. He was also eager to continue the stream of funding the Saudi had brought with him and his alliance against Masoud's resistance in the north. Indeed, al Qaeda carried out a suicide bombing and killed Masoud on 9 September 2001 when two 'journalists', allegedly Moroccans, detonated a bomb concealed in a video camera. Two days later, al Qaeda attacked New York and Washington, killing 2,893 in the cities and a further 233 on Flight 93. It was the world's worst terrorist atrocity, and, as Abdul Salam Zaeef had predicted, it was bound to evoke a military response from the United States.

The Global War on Terror announced by the administration of President George W. Bush appeared to be a vague expression of strategic objectives, and it was unclear just how America's overwhelming military power would be deployed against terrorist organizations, which tended to be concealed within civilian populations. In fact, the 'war on terror' coincided with wider American concerns about failed or rogue states, the state sponsorship of terrorism and the transfer of Weapons of Mass Destruction. In the pursuit of their goals it seemed likely that the United States would launch air strikes into Afghanistan and perhaps use ground operations to neutralize al Qaeda's training camps, along with its command and control structures. Bush gave an ultimatum to General Pervez Musharaf, the Pakistani head of state who had hitherto asked for 'understanding' towards the Taliban, that Pakistan would have to terminate support for the Taliban or face American financial and perhaps even military action. The Pakistan president complied. Uzbekistan, eager to gain American approval, also opened up its air space to the Americans.

Operation Enduring Freedom consisted of a rapid air campaign in support of 'Northern Alliance' militias. Teams of Special Forces, primarily from the United States and the United Kingdom, were inserted alongside the Northern Alliance while independent units carried out reconnaissance deep in the interior, hunting for al Qaeda. They enlisted a number of local clan militias to assist them. Under a heavy air bombardment, the Taliban were decimated and many chose to switch sides. The Taliban withered under the air bombardment in which some 12,000 bombs were dropped and 6,700 guided munitions were used. AC130 gunships strafed Taliban positions and cruise missiles destroyed the training camps and infrastructure. One Taliban fighter called Akhunzada recalled: 'When the bombing started, I was commanding some 400 fighters on the front lines near Mazar-i Sharif. The bombs cut down our men like a reaper harvesting wheat. Bodies were dismembered. Dazed fighters were bleeding from the ears and nose from the bombs' concussions. We couldn't bury the dead. Our reinforcements died in their trenches'.[26] He and his surviving comrades were unable to use the roads and took to the hills: 'We walked four days in the deep snow without food or water. Kids started shooting at us from the hilltops, hunting us like wild animals'.[27] The operations were so swift that the Taliban had no chance to reinforce their positions or regroup. They lost 12,000 personnel, with 20,000 wounded and another 7,000 captured. Some of the prisoners put up a last-ditch defence in Qala-i Jangi prison in Mazar-i Sharif, but their uprising was crushed. It was a hopeless act of resistance. In the aftermath, Abdurrashid Dostum took no chances and allegedly massacred the prisoners under his jurisdiction.

After three weeks of resistance, the Taliban had collapsed. Their remnants were soon being pursued southwards and eastwards, some making for the sanctuary of Pakistan's North West Frontier Province where they could rely on fellow militants for support. The rest, aware of the power of American forces, melted back into the rural areas and urban centres and looked to join any new government.

Meanwhile, in the far south, the Taliban tried to move 1,000 fighters in Toyota pick-up trucks to Tarin Kot, the provincial capital and concentration point for resistance in the mountains of Uruzgan. Of the 100 vehicles in the column, 30 were destroyed in a single air strike mission. The destruction of this Taliban formation at Tarin Kot and the fall of the small Taliban garrison of Kunduz on 26 November 2001 concluded a very one-sided campaign. Only on the eastern border of Afghanistan, where the mountainous terrain made pursuit more difficult, was there any sign of further resistance. Al Qaeda fighters and their allies were making use of extensive cave systems at Tora Bora to protect themselves from air attack and tried to hold out for some time, but they were driven into Pakistan where the international border gave them sanctuary.

The Karzai government and Afghanistan after 2001

At the Bonn Conference on 3 December, six neighbouring states, Russia and the United States agreed that Afghanistan should have a multi-ethnic, freely elected government, and a number of Afghan factions were consulted on the shape of a future administration.[28] The problem was that the Taliban and some of the warlords, including Dostum, were not involved in the negotiations. An interim administration was nevertheless accepted. The 'Emergency Loya Jirga' was led by a moderate Popolzai Durrani Pashtun who belonged to no political party, Hamid Karzai, and he was therefore a useful compromise candidate. However, there was some suspicion amongst Afghans that the United States could use Karzai as their surrogate leader and deprive Afghanistan of its sovereignty. That said, Karzai embodied a widespread dissatisfaction with the Taliban and the consequences of civil wars. In 2001, amidst high expectations, Karzai was eager to establish a more permanent political authority. He, his foreign partners and the Loya Jirga quickly moved to establish a currency, a Supreme Court, UN support for refugee repatriation and reconstruction, and a human rights commission. Afghanistan also obtained the military backing of the International Security and Assistance Force (ISAF), under the command of the British Major General John McColl. This force, whilst initially small, provided a vital deterrent to warlords who might be tempted, as in 1993, to seize the capital. Kabulis expressed satisfaction with the security that the British military presence brought to the capital.

There was some disquiet amongst Afghans that government and opposition candidates had not been prosecuted for their alleged war crimes. The loyalty of the warlords to the regime was very much in doubt.[29] When Jawed Ludin, the Chief of Staff of the Afghan National Army, announced that he was considering arming the militias to augment the small police and state military forces in June 2006, there was anger and fear in southern Afghanistan. Habibullah Jan, a former militia commander who became an MP for Kandahar, predicted it would create a lawless group of 'thieves and looters' just as it did under the Soviets. International observers were also concerned that reconstituting militias would strengthen the warlords at the expense of the central government. But the Afghan army and police had to be raised from scratch, and unsurprisingly barely trained personnel could be defeated, bribed or encouraged to desert for better pay to particular leaders.

As corruption flourished amongst government officials and their security forces, the Taliban's argument that they aimed to root this out as well as driving out the foreigners gained greater currency and fuelled their resurgence. The badly paid ANP used extortion to maintain their influence, and brigandage became common in rural areas.

After 2001 there was a severe shortage in the manpower requirement for the security of Afghanistan, not least when US forces were reallocated to conduct operations in Iraq in 2003. The Americans encouraged other NATO partners to assist in the security of the country in 2006, as the recovery of the Taliban became more evident. However, the restrictions against operational flexibility by troops of some European countries, caused by their governments' aversion to risk, affected the security envelope that could be achieved. Each nation had a different interpretation of what a military force or a provincial reconstruction team could do, resulting in patches of insecurity and uneven development.

In the south, British forces were not given permission to tackle the opium fields which they believed funded the insurgency, since this, they were told, was the remit of the Afghan government. Moreover, their mission of extending the authority of the government antagonized many local power brokers, including those ostensibly allied to the Kabul government but deeply implicated in narcotics, and created grievances that were exploited by the insurgents.

In January 2003 a force of eighty Taliban fighters was intercepted at Spin Boldak by an American patrol. Unlike guerrillas, this Taliban detachment fought for twelve hours and was practically destroyed when the Americans called in air support. In the same period, American patrol bases in Regional Command East were subjected to rocket attack and aid workers were assassinated. These incidents illustrated the new direction the Taliban were taking. They believed that foreigners would only be driven out by inflicting significant losses on them, the assumption being that Westerners cannot sustain casualties for political-strategic reasons. The attack at Spin Boldak nevertheless showed that the Taliban was tactically inept. Trying to defeat an isolated patrol in such a large grouping invited destruction from American airpower, just as had occurred two years before. The enthusiasm for their ideological struggle seemed to have taken precedence over the need to engage in a more clandestine campaign.

The Taliban of the North West Frontier

Operating from Miranshah in Waziristan, Jalaluddin Haqqani, the former Taliban Minister for Tribal Affairs, was said to be a member of the Ruhbari ('Quetta') Shura but also close to Osama bin Laden. His methods were characteristically more ruthless and extreme than the 'old' Taliban, especially against Pashtun *maliks* of the North West Frontier Province and eastern Afghanistan, and they exemplify another change in the Afghan way of war.[30] One Taliban fighter attributes Haqqani's involvement as a crucial turning point in the insurgency in Afghanistan:

Jalaluddin Haqqani's tribal fighters came actively back to our side because the Americans and the Pakistanis had arrested his brother and other relatives. He appointed his son, Sirajuddin, to lead the resistance. That was a real turning point. Until then villagers in Paktia, Paktika, and Khost thought the Taliban was defeated and finished. They had started joining the militias formed by the Americans and local warlords, and were informing on us and working against us. But with the support of Haqqani's men we began capturing, judging, and beheading some of those Afghans who worked with the

Americans and Karzai. Terrorized, their families and relatives left the villages and moved to the towns, even to Kabul. Our control was slowly being restored.[31]

It is alleged that the network has been able to muster 12,000 fighters, but this figure may be an inflation of the actual numbers, and almost certainly far fewer were ever on operations at the same time. Their strength and objectives may nevertheless reflect the practices that evolved in the Soviet War. Siraj looked to emulate his father's executive role in the Hezb faction, to repeat the seizure of Khost and Urgan from communists, and to re-establish links with the ISI. Jalaluddin's Arab wife certainly offered better access to donors and fighters from outside Afghanistan, but the connection meant the adoption of more ruthless tactics and brutal intimidation of Afghan civilians. There were also alleged links between Haqqani, Lashkar-e Taiba in Pakistan and al Qaeda. In 2008, the Haqqani network escalated the fighting against the Americans in eastern Afghanistan, but this only elicited a stronger reaction. By 2010, Haqqani was scaling back its operations amid suggestions that it was waiting for the American withdrawal announced by President Obama.

During the Soviet War, the Pakistani ISI had armed and equipped men from the largely Pashtun refugee population when they escaped the ravages of war in Afghanistan. Fearful of Pashtun nationalism, not least because the refugees were accommodated amongst Pakistan's Pashtun population, which had conducted an insurgency to obtain an independent Pashtunistan only a few years before, the ISI emphasized religious solidarity between the Pakistan state and the Pashtuns in order to mobilize the population against the Soviets. The ISI had maintained discipline by controlling supplies to selected leaders, and this tended to elevate Pashtun commanders in wealth, status and military power.[32] The war 'accelerated this process of ethnic crystallisation, and brought about a sort of political awareness of ethnic identity'.[33]

Nevertheless, the unequal distribution of military power between Pashtuns and the ingress of more radical, Pakistan-inspired religious doctrine created divisions amongst Afghan Pashtuns and forced non-Pashtuns to redefine themselves, as Olivier Roy noted: 'the Sunni Persian speakers did not previously use the word "Tajik", applied to them by both Soviet and Western ethnologists', but rivalry pushed them to 'define themselves as an ethnic group'.[34] Ahmed Shah Masoud became one of the 'heroes for the Tajik: military efficiency is no more seen as a Pashtun prerogative'.[35] In the same way, 'war brought an ethnic reassertion among the formerly despised Shi'a Hazara, who have liberated their own area and benefit from political support, if nothing more, from Iran'.[36] The traditional Durrani–Ghilzai split had weakened the Pashtun cause further.

Hekmatyar's call for a centralized Islamic state was opposed by other groups that did not wish to lose their autonomy to a centralized polity and a single leader. Even though Afghan Pashtuns looked to the Pakistani Pashtuns for support, they could not overcome rivalries here either.[37] The dynamic was changed further by the rise of the front commanders at the expense of the traditional community authorities: 'Now the *mullah* and the *malik* have no role in the village, everything is done by the commander, and he knows only money'.[38] Front commanders of the Mujahideen exercised their 'influence through networks of [other] commanders'.[39]

A youngster in Waziristan named Younas remembered the aftermath of the American destruction of the Taliban regime in Afghanistan:

I watched as wounded, disabled, and defeated Taliban fighters straggled into Wana and the surrounding villages, along with Arabs, Chechens, and Uzbeks. Every morning as I went to school I could see them wandering around town, almost like homeless beggars. Little by little, the tribal people started helping them, giving them food. Some people even took them into their houses; at first these once proud jihadis survived, thanks to the people's charity.[40]

A former Taliban fighter tried to rehabilitate himself having fled over the Pakistan border:

Once proud Taliban mullahs and fighters changed the way they dressed so they wouldn't be recognized. No one wanted to be identified as a *Talib*. Friends and relatives who had respected me while I was a commander now turned away. I had no money or job. I moved my family to a village in Punjab, far from Afghanistan, to become a day labourer, but I was a failure at it. I couldn't speak the local language, and no one would hire me. So I returned to Peshawar and started selling vegetables from a basket in the market.[41]

The 'Arab Afghans' took the view that the NWFP was merely a refuge to continue the struggle. Younas, who had not been through the devastating bombing of 2001, was attracted to the neo-Taliban:

At first I didn't hear the Afghans talking about going back to fight. But the Arabs did, and they encouraged the Afghans and the local tribal people not to give up. Nothing much happened for the first year or so, but then the Arabs started organizing some training camps. The first one I heard about was at Shin Warsak village, near Wana. When I had some time off from school, I decided to visit. I was really impressed. There was more than one camp. One was run by Arabs, and another by Chechens and Uzbeks– Nek Mohammad Wazir [killed June 2004] gave the Arabs places to train and access to weapons and other supplies. They moved openly on the main roads and in the towns and villages, showing no concern about security. I decided to leave my studies and join their resistance.[42]

Mohammed, a young Waziri *imam*, also felt compelled to enlist:

Some of the worshipers asked me outright why I hadn't fought in the jihad like these men. I needed to make up for not joining the fight. I started asking around if the mujahedin were still active, but no one could give me a real answer. Then one day I heard about a young Afghan named Azizullah who had been in the resistance [who pointed me to a training camp near Wana].

A former fighter, Haqqani, described the moment when the Taliban was reconstituted in early 2003:

The Taliban's defence minister, Mullah Obaidullah, came to see me—the first senior Taliban leader I had seen since our collapse. He was travelling around Pakistan to rally our dispersed forces. Half the Taliban leadership was back in touch with each other, he said, and they were determined to start a resistance movement to expel the Americans. I didn't think it was possible–Obaidullah told me: 'We don't need you as a deputy minister or bureaucrat. We want you to bring as many fighters as you can into the field.'[43]

The former Talib fighter Akhundzada also re-enlisted after a personal visit by a former senior commander: 'I was sent to Quetta, where survivors from my unit had settled. There had been 400 fighters under my command. In Quetta I found 15 of them. They embraced me and the idea of returning to free our land of the American invaders. In North Waziristan we trained, re-equipped, recruited more men, and got ready to return to Afghanistan.'[44]

A former Taliban fighter, Mohammed, described the training regime for the renewed Jihad in 2003:

The first thing I learned was to shoot, field-strip, and maintain an AK-47. Then we did ambush and guerrilla-war exercises day and night in the hills. The Arabs taught us how to make an IED [Improvised Explosive Device] by mixing nitrate fertilizer and diesel fuel, and how to pack plastic explosives and to connect them to detonators and remote-control devices like mobile phones. We learned how to do this blindfolded so we could safely plant IEDs in the dark.

He continued:

Discipline was strict. Any trainee who broke the rules could get a severe beating. You had to wake up before dawn every morning for physical exercises and to run in the mountains. Recruits were awakened at all hours of the night so they would learn to be alert in an emergency–After two months of hard training, we graduated. There were 200 of us: about 160 local tribals, a few Punjabis, and about 40 Afghans like me. We were divided up into 10 groups [and sent to different provinces in Afghanistan]. Each had two or three Arabs assigned to it as commanders and instructors.[45]

The steady stream of dead and wounded acted as an incentive for more to join the fighting in Afghanistan. Younas, on his way back from an operation against an American base, noted: 'We carried the stiff and bloodied bodies of our martyrs back to Wana. Thousands of locals attended their funerals, saying it was an honour to witness the burial of these martyrs. People brought flowers, ribbons, coloured cloth, and flags to decorate their graves. As the news travelled, a lot of former Taliban began returning to Wana to join us.'[46]

Inter-clan warfare and the Taliban in Helmand

Brigadier Ed Butler, commander of the small British task force deployed to Helmand, wanted to extend the sphere of Afghan government influence slowly, using the classic 'ink spot' strategy of developing a presence from a secure core, and building on the 'light footprint', a benign, minimalist presence established by American and British Special Forces with the consent of local Pashtuns. However, a combination of factors prevented Brigadier Butler and 16 Air Assault Brigade from ever realizing this strategy. Many have sought to blame Afghan politics and the desire by many government officials to reduce the power of Sher Mohammed Akhundzada, a warlord figure who effectively controlled the province as a personal fiefdom. Akhundzada was eager to protect his narcotics profits and to maintain his personal militia. The Akhundzada clan had profited from the Soviet War when a number of *khans* in Helmand had been killed and their lands seized. Other Alizai leaders resented the Akhundzadas' domination, and opposition developed under the leadership of Mullah Abdul Wahid, known as 'Rais-e Baghrani', and Abdul Rahman, a Khan Khel who joined Hezb-i Gulbuddin. Abdul Rahman was defeated at Gereshk but Mullah Abdul Wahid obtained the support of the Taliban in 1994. Together they drove Sher Mohammed Akhundzada out in January 1995. When the Coalition defeated the Taliban, Sher Mohammed Akhundzada took advantage of the absence of governance in Helmand to re-establish himself. He gained the support of Dad Mohammed Khan, the National Directorate of Security (NDS) Chief for Helmand, who controlled a private militia, and together they imposed an arbitrary and exploitative rule. Meanwhile the governor of Kandahar, Sherzai, was eager to break narco syndicates across the region using government and ISAF forces. The Ishaqzai of upper Sangin in Helmand were particularly keen to protect their share of the narcotics industry, and, perhaps unsurprisingly, they turned to the resurgent Taliban in 2003 for help.

The Taliban, who were gearing up for an offensive in 2003, were able to present the idea to the Helmandis that the British were coming to occupy their land, to break up their livelihoods with a counter-narcotics programme, back the warlords and to 'get their revenge for the Battle of Maiwand'. The British were asked by the Provincial Governor to establish small posts around the province that would signal that the government of Afghanistan was the only legitimate authority. Because their doctrine directed them to follow the host-nation government's lead, the British were obliged to construct posts at Musa Qala, Now Zad and Sangin, and to protect the dam at Kajaki. These had the advantage of being close to areas of population and therefore held out the opportunity to meet with and perhaps win over the local communities, protect the local bazaar and its economic activity, and control routes. However, it soon became apparent that some of the local police were in league with the Taliban, and no sooner had the bases been established than they came under attack. The sight of the Forward Operating Bases being constructed seemed to prove to the local Helmandis that Akhundzada's warnings were true. The Taliban rushed to encourage resistance and threw their own forces into action.

The British in northern Helmand were surprised by the ferocity of these initial assaults. There were almost 100 days of continuous combat at Now Zad. Small detachments of the brigade were forced to fight for days as the Taliban enveloped their positions. The Taliban and their local allies knew that the small garrisons of 'Platoon Houses' were relatively isolated and might be overrun. Every effort was made to engage with small arms, RPGs fired in volleys, sniper rifles and mortars. The fighters often got to close quarters. However, not one of the small garrisons was defeated or overrun. Backed by airpower, plenty of ammunition and sheer determination, the British detachments held every attack at bay. Some Taliban would adopt a 'shoot and scoot' tactic, trying to ambush a foot patrol or fire on a base and then disappear, just to exhaust the British troops. As the British tried to send out patrols to engage the population, they were ambushed and attacked. As soon as the British patrols fell back, the insurgents would swarm after them. From the cover of the Forward Operating Bases (FOBs) milan and Javelin missiles were used alongside small arms and medium machine-gun fire. Longer-range weapons, and air power, proved invaluable in the destruction of buildings that provided the insurgents with cover or which concealed their assembly areas. The firefights lasted into the night, with individual Taliban fighters trying to work their way closer. Some firefights took place within yards of the patrol base walls. Taliban and local Helmandi casualties were heavy, and it is estimated that 1,800 of them were killed between April and July 2006.[47]

After some weeks of continuous fighting, the British had to decide whether they were achieving their mission or simply incurring great risks for no strategic results. The chance that a helicopter might be lost seemed particularly acute when, at this early stage of the campaign, there were so few of them. There was an alarming rise in the number of 'mine-strikes' (number of mines detonated) by vehicle patrols, and so helicopters were becoming the preferred mode of transport to get ammunition and food in, and the wounded out. The British calculated it was perhaps only a matter of time before the Taliban deployed Surface to Air missiles against the limited airlift capability the British possessed.

The situation seemed even more acute when there appeared to be a step change in the skills and abilities of the insurgents. The British suspected that a sudden improvement in accuracy of mortar fire, RPGs and sharp shooting was the result of external support. The insurgents were improving in their accuracy, as trained Taliban personnel came up, while new equipment and weapons, including night vision gear and sniper rifles, began to make themselves felt. Some evidence suggests that Pakistan was being used as a conduit for these specialist tools and personnel. However, insurgent losses deterred further direct assaults. In 2007, the attempts to overrun the British posts were abandoned.

In light of the initial battles in Helmand, the British changed their force structures and tactics. FOBs were consolidated and reinforced, and more troops were deployed, although still far short of the numbers required to cover the entire province. There were still too few men to give the brigade commanders a reserve for manoeuvre. This led to innovation. When the Royal Marine Commandos were deployed in 2006–7, they took advantage of the traditional winter lull to take the fight to the enemy, and, treating the open areas of *dasht* (desert) like the open sea, they established a more aggressive patrol pattern that gave them back their mobility through MOGs (Mobile Operating Groups). New efforts were also made to win the support of local leaders and farmers, but violence in Helmand remained at a higher level than any other province of the country. The insurgents tried to counter the Marines' mobility with more improvised mines or ambushes from the broken terrain around the more densely populated 'Green Zone'.

By 2009 American Marines had joined the British, and they began to secure the north, west and southern 'green zone' (known as the 'Fish Hook'), allowing the British to concentrate their forces in the centre around the provincial capital of Lashkargah. There was therefore a chance to carry out a traditional counterinsurgency strategy, namely to shape (influence the population), clear (drive out the insurgents), hold and build (making improvements to local infrastructure). Nevertheless, the insurgents kept up their violent disruption and intimidation.

From 2003 the Taliban made a series of attacks, the most frequent being across the Pakistan border. Younas, a young *imam* serving as a fighter, described an operation typical of the south and eastern fronts:

One night in April [2003], we crossed the border in five pickups and one larger truck. Once we were safely across, we sent the vehicles back to wait for us on the Pakistan side. Our target was a U.S. base just across the border at Machda in Paktika. We attacked at dawn. I think we really surprised them. We shelled them with 122mm rockets and mortars for about 30 minutes.

However, the chief problem was Western airpower, for which they had no answer: '—we didn't get close enough to fire our Kalashnikovs; before we could move in, American helicopters came, raining rockets and bullets on us. Terrified, I crawled and ran to escape death. Amid the noise and explosions, dust and smoke, I remember seeing six of us cut down and killed: two Arabs, three [Pakistan] tribals, and an Afghan'.[48]

Defeated in their conventional light infantry assaults in 2006–7, the Taliban returned to guerrilla techniques. Tactically, they placed the emphasis on mine warfare and the development of Improvised Explosive Devices. By studying the pattern of movements and identifying important roads, the Taliban aimed to deny the Western forces their mobility and to inflict a steady stream of casualties. This, they reasoned, would sap the strategic patience of the Western governments and compel them to withdraw. Moreover, this was a useful way to reduce their own casualties and to keep the flame of resistance alive: signalling to the Afghan people that the resistance was still able to strike at will. At first the preference was for Soviet-era mines, but increasing armour and better detection rates forced the Taliban to develop their own explosive devices that minimized metal components. Fertilizer, plastic and bombs clustered together became increasingly common on the dirt tracks that pass as roads in the south of the country. Not all are constructed expertly, and the Taliban were forced to find 'facilitators' to teach others how to manufacture and lay the devices.

Typically, Taliban teams operate in groups of 8 to 12 men, which could either concentrate into groups of 30 (or 100 in the eastern provinces) for attacks on outposts, or split into groups of 5 or pairs for smaller tasks, including laying IEDs. On election day in 2009, two IEDs intended for Western military convoys detonated prematurely in RC-South, killing the bomb layers. Nevertheless, there were 2,000 IED strikes in 2006, rising to 7,000 in 2009. The IED attacks in 2009 killed 275 ANA and Coalition troops.

The Taliban fighter Haqqani stated that it was Arab expertise which explained the improvements in tactics:

[After 2004] Arab and Iraqi *mujahideen* began visiting us, transferring the latest IED technology and suicide-bomber tactics they had learned in the Iraqi resistance during combat with U.S. forces. The American invasion of Iraq was very positive for us. It distracted the United States from Afghanistan. Until 2004 or so, we were using traditional means of fighting like we used against the Soviets: AK-47s and RPGs. But then our resistance became more lethal, with new weapons and techniques: bigger and better IEDs for roadside bombings, and suicide attacks.[49]

Suicide bombing, 'martyrdom operations', have been effective but are not necessarily the preference of most Afghans. In 2005 Mullah Obeidullah, of the Rubhari Shura, announced that he had recruited an army of fighters prepared to use suicide bombing in the war against the Afghan government and Western forces. There were 21 suicide attacks in 2005, 140 in 2006, and 239 in 2008. Yet many Afghans are troubled by the numbers of civilians killed by such attacks and, indeed, the deliberate detonations in busy bazaars or city streets where there are often no security forces. James Fergusson observes that, in contrast to the Palestinians, there are no parades, posters and hoardings celebrating the lives of suicide 'martyrs'.[50] There is evidence to show that a significant number of the suicide bombers are mentally or physically disabled, or otherwise psychologically traumatized. In Iraq, many Palestinians were recruited for these operations, but there is no conclusive evidence that this has been the practice in Afghanistan. However, there is no doubt that many of the suicide bombers have been drawn from madrassahs in Pakistan where their indoctrination could be more strictly controlled. Using Pakistanis has certainly enabled the resistance to avoid igniting blood feuds between Afghan factions. The Afghan insurgents have expressed contempt for the Pakistani 'martyrs', treating them only as a weapon.

Many Afghans expressed a readiness to fight, regardless of allies or the enemy. One SAS officer operating near Spin Boldak noted that 'killing was a way of life' for them and they 'would pick up a gun for the slightest of reasons, and fight under the flimsiest of flags'.[51] Consequently, for the Western troops, 'it was often quite impossible to tell who was who'. Afghans with feuds or grudges would condemn rival groups as 'Taliban' in the hope of getting an airstrike to kill them all and then have the blame passed to the West.[52] After a high-pro-file case in which a wedding party, enjoying celebratory gunfire, was obliter-ated by an airstrike after a misleading tip-off, any potential air attack against a wrong target has become known to Western forces as 'the wedding party syndrome'.

The Taliban fighter Mohammed explained how heavy-handedness by secu-rity forces changed the situation for the Jihadists:

[In 2004] The Afghan Taliban were weak and disorganized. But slowly the situation began to change. American operations that harassed villagers, bombings that killed civilians, and Karzai's corrupt police and officials were alienating villagers and turning them in our favour. Soon we didn't have to hide so much on our raids. We came openly. When they saw us, villagers started preparing green tea and food for us. The tables were turning. Karzai's police and officials mostly hid in their district compounds like prisoners.[53]

Insurgent strategy

It is difficult to ascertain a single conception of the insurgent strategy, not least because of the sheer variety of armed organizations fighting in Afghanistan. Many seem to have only a vague idea of what constitutes victory. One Taliban fighter expressed the view that: 'One year, a hundred years, a million years, ten million years—it is not important, we will never stop fighting'.[54] More typi-cally, Taliban fighters express a desire to impose the Sharia throughout Afghan-istan and aim to drive all foreigners out.

Higher up the chain of command, there is a more coherent conception of planning. There have been significant attempts to mount strategic offensives. In 2006, the offensives through the Helmand Valley and the Arghandab were defeated, and the latter was particularly costly. The Arghandab was a major base being prepared for operations against Kandahar, but a Canadian-led coun-ter-offensive concluded with a major battle at Pashmul and the dispersal of the Taliban. In 2007, the Taliban announced Operation *Kamin* (Ambush), which focused on increasing the number of tactical, guerrilla attacks but which scaled back the large-scale light infantry attacks which had proved costly in Helmand and the eastern provinces. Heavy casualties amongst the commanders seriously disrupted this offensive.

In March 2008, the Taliban launched Operation *Ebrat* (Lesson), which aimed to sever provincial security and destroy the development work of the Provincial Reconstruction Teams; consolidate the Taliban's grip on areas near

Lashkargah and Gesreshk; and intimidate the population by targeted assassinations of recalcitrant *khans* and government officials. Mobile phone broadcasting towers were also targeted, because of concerns that mobiles were being used by those loyal to the government to warn of Taliban movements.

In 2009, there was clear intent to make attacks on the capital not only for its symbolic effect but also in an attempt to ring the city and gradually tighten a blockade. Part of the plan involved attacking convoys of supplies destined for the insurgency further south. Indeed, during major Western-led operations in Regional Command-South (and, since the subdivision of the south in 2010, Regional Command-South West), the Taliban felt compelled to make attacks on Kabul in retaliation and to divert resources back to the north. Operation *Nasrat* (Victory) in Helmand in the spring of 2009 continued its focus on attacking convoys with IEDs, trying to inflict casualties on ISAF personnel and all government officials or their contractors. However, it was also notable that, having withdrawn some senior Taliban leaders due to more accurate ISAF targeting the previous year, the Taliban felt compelled to push new leaders back into the province and across the south. Throughout 2009 and 2010, however, the steady attrition of field commanders was a serious problem for the insurgents.

The Taliban were forced to recalibrate their plans several times between 2003 and 2010. When the British were beginning their deployment to Helmand in 2006, the Taliban were preparing for what they believed was their 'final offensive'. They had been gearing up for three years, and assumed that the Iraq War, which had tied down thousands of Western troops, would keep the Coalition forces in a weakened state in Afghanistan. There had been months of booby traps, IEDs, assassinations and widespread intimidation. Local Afghans who refused to assist the Taliban were threatened, 'disciplined' and eventually shot. The Taliban were determined to ruin Western development projects and burned down schools, threatened Non-Governmental Organizations, or kidnapped family members of wealthier families to exact a ransom. The Taliban had targeted disgruntled communities, and offered to support them in return for loyalty to their cause. The Taliban felt they could call upon thousands of volunteers, including enthusiasts from militant Pakistani madrassahs, to launch an offensive that would overwhelm the poorly trained Afghan security forces, and persuade the West to abandon Kabul.

However, the Taliban's success was not so much in their military operations but their ability to align, integrate and accommodate local clan dynamics. The treatment of civilians, casualties and the continuing conflict were particularly important in recruiting rural Afghans into the insurgency. Nazar Mohammed, a farmer, blamed foreign occupation forces for the violence on his property near Kandahar: 'It's very obvious. Right now we see foreigners with tanks driving through our fields. They destroy people's orchards... they break through walls and just drive across. When they take up positions in the village like this, nobody can co-operate with them'.[55] Similar anger with government officials, including Afghan National Police who were eager to demand bribes from farmers or road users, increased the appeal of the insurgents. The Taliban have exploited every opportunity, looking for the most aggrieved sections of society. They have tried to make the locals identify their own problems with the higher need to resist the government and its foreign backers. Mohammed Anif, a spokesman for the Taliban, argued: 'We rose up and saved almost the whole country from the evils of corruption and corrupt commanders ... that's why the people are supporting the Taliban again now'.[56]

According to one journalist, many of the younger Taliban were men who 'had never set foot in Afghanistan and therefore had only vague conceptions of what Afghanistan was like before the war'.[57] The Taliban claimed to be defending 'village identity' in contrast to government officials, who were 'products of Kabul University or had worked for state-sponsored institutions'. This seemed an effective tactic because they were putting themselves on a par with the people whose support they had to enlist.[58] Among the Pashtuns, the Taliban 'brought back collective memories of Pashtun uprisings ... that were well enshrined in oral culture' but they were also eager to create a new foundation for a pan-Pashtun identity that transcended tribe and village.[59] Yet the Taliban had numerous enemies in Afghanistan, including independent, self-financing bands that thrived on banditry, taxing traffic, smuggling and small-scale poppy production; networks of patronage belonging to clan leaders, the Afghan government, and *qawm* confederations. Each of these possesses firepower as well as resilience and cohesion. It is not just the ISAF forces that pose a threat to the Taliban but many interests and traditionalists too.[60]

The Taliban obtained support by sequentially engaging patronage networks in order to undermine their rivals and seek supporters. In terms of recruitment, the Taliban understood that Pashtuns are less interested in what interlocutors say compared with what they do, as they are masters of 'a dynamic process-based approach' to social relations.[61] As a *modus operandi*, the Taliban first sent a small group to determine the local clan structure and power dynamics, and then they began to build relationships that would allow them to operate within a given area.[62] These reconnaissance teams were responsible for identifying villages, elders and sympathizers who could be relied upon for support. Traditionally, the Taliban approached those weakest in the local hierarchy of power who had the most to gain from political change. In addition, they contacted the clients of the most powerful local leaders, to see if they could undermine their support for them.[63] Leaders without a reputation for brutality and corruption would be encouraged to join the Taliban. Those who could not be co-opted would be forced to disband their own militias or killed.[64]

Night letters were used to make more general statements to the local population.[65] Gauging from individuals' reactions, they saw who could be trusted to provide intelligence, shelter, and supplies.[66] The Taliban then developed a local network to provide logistics, safe houses and bases. Some properties of trusted individuals were more suited to concealing 'heavier weaponry such as 12.7mm machine guns, recoilless guns, and mortars and ammunition', allowing fighters to be free of cumbersome equipment and ensuring a high degree of mobility and a 'capacity to move large numbers of fighters in small amount of time.'[67]

Eating meals and sleeping in different villages, the Taliban used the traditional social structure as their physical protection and also as the means to spread their 'presence'. The Taliban fighters pride themselves on the minimal equipment and supplies they require, their austerity in such matters being considered a virtue. Prayer times are strictly observed if not engaged in operations, but every effort is made to fit in with the population and to ally those fighters who belong to a community. Movement through villages was possible even in areas where support for the Taliban is negligible because of *melmastia*. As one aid worker put it: 'They turn up in the villages of the tribesmen and ask for shelter, and what can they do? Custom decrees they cannot refuse'. It made little sense for local tribes to risk conflict with the Taliban, particularly when there was no corresponding government presence.[68] With time, large strongholds were established, including 'training centres [and] facilities for large scale operations'.[69] Increasingly, a shadow government was established, with few ministers or governors but with military commanders and *qazis* whose responsibilities were to establish Sharia and control spaces with military force, backed, wherever possible, with local consent and support. The *qazis* were designed to provide a provisional judiciary in places where there was a local demand due to the corruption or absence of a government judicial system.[70] There have also been attempts by the Taliban to establish health clinics run by kidnapped doctors.[71]

Mullah Abdul Salam, an Alizai, defected from the Taliban in October 2007 having fought the British presence at Musa Qala. In a local deal with the town's *maliks*, the British had agreed to withdraw while a militia promised to drive out the Taliban. In February 2007, that militia were routed and the Taliban were back. Mullah Salam's defection encouraged ISAF to retake the town and exploit differences between the clans within the Taliban. It took three months and 2,000 troops to secure the settlement. In December 2008, the Taliban tried to assassinate Mullah Salam by attacking his house, twenty policemen were killed in the operation, but the Talibans' target was not even present at the time. In February 2009, they made another attempt with an IED against his vehicle column. However, the overall strategy was not to try to retake the Musa Qala but to render the space 'insecure' and to try to undermine his 500-strong militia.

To win hearts and minds, the Taliban learned to be more protective of local communities, warning villages of planned attacks on Coalition forces in a process of 'losing tactical surprise, but gaining solidarity'.[72] Suicide attacks are generally avoided in villages because of the danger of civilian casualties, although, if fighting breaks out, then civilian losses are accepted as part of the fortunes of war. For some time, senior Taliban commanders were concerned about the violence and intimidation that their men were exercising and which was costing support. It was necessary to issue a handbook on conduct, the *Laheya*, and to increase the strictures to avoid 'harassing innocents, searching houses, and confiscating weaponry without permission of senior commanders'.[73]

Throughout the crisis of the civil war, and every occupation, Afghans 'operate as members of networks [since] a salary does not just feed your immediate family, it supports an entire group of people to whom you have obligations'. Understanding, respecting and guarding these relationships has been crucial to success in rural areas.[74] The Taliban also know that striking a deal with opponents who cannot be defeated is a more effective way of neutralizing them in the short term, and offers the chance to wait for a better opportunity. In the Hazarajat in 1998, in exchange for disarmament, the Hazaras of Jaghori district received a Taliban promise 'not to commit atrocities and not to interfere in cultural affairs' even to the extent of allowing the continuation of women's education.[75] Such deals allowed the Taliban to present themselves as the best available guarantee of security. However, such arrangements have proven less effective where clans were 'on good terms with one another and the tribal elites were able to govern effectively' as in Paktia and Khost.[76] Here, the Taliban turned to assassinations in an attempt to destabilize and intimidate the local clans into submission.[77]

Most importantly, it is moral and physical security on which the Taliban base their appeal. Their vehicle checkpoints and 'protection rackets' allow them to extract taxes for safe passage, generating additional revenue. Levying *ushr* on farmers, especially opium crops, is particularly lucrative. By guaranteeing the flow of trade and economic activity, the Taliban are seen as being supportive of the livelihoods of ordinary people.

After the chaos of Mujahideen fighting, the exhausted Afghan populace, according to David Edwards, welcomed the 'reputation for keeping security [which] preceded them into each new area'.[78] In contrast to the Mujahideen, 'which could never surmount their individual political interests when given the opportunity to rule', the Taliban successfully formed a government with a unified purpose and direction.[79] In the regions under their control, the roads were relatively safe from the predation of the militias, allowing people to move around without fear of being searched at checkpoints, and traders were able to carry goods without having to pay exorbitant road taxes.[80] In the 1990s, the Taliban were careful to cultivate and maintain this image. They made it a policy to create an 'anticharismatic movement' with the emphasis 'not on leaders and their promises but on the movement itself and its supposed rootedness in an idealized sort of ordinary village existence that had been absent for twenty years and that was longed for all the more for that reason'.[81]

Afghanistan's counterinsurgency

In contrast, the government of Afghanistan struggled to be accepted by the Afghan population. David Kilcullen, the counterinsurgency specialist, argued that the Kabuli government was simply being 'out-governed' by the Taliban.[82] It is difficult to conceive of a legitimate government when its reach into rural areas seemed so limited and it was backed by foreign forces. The budget for his personal security was over $20 million in 2009, perhaps the same value by which the Taliban ran its entire campaign that year.[83] Indeed, the contrast between the government and the insurgents has been so great that Abdulkader Sinno believes the only 'tools left at U.S. disposal are the use of brute force and patronage, both of which have proven self-defeating in the past'.[84] However, these were not the only tools the United States either used or possessed.

To augment the number of counter-insurgents in Afghanistan, and to pave the way for the Afghan government to take control of its own security, the Americans launched an ambitious plan to increase the size of the Afghan National Army (ANA) to 100,000 by 2011 and eventually to 250,000, to build a fully functioning Afghan National Police (ANP) force of 82,000, and to expand the National Afghan Air Corps. The much publicized 'surge' was not only about Western forces, but involved a growth in the ANA from under 79,000 in 2008 to 95,000 in February 2009, and the final scale of the Afghan National Security Forces (ANSF) was planned to be 400,000. The rapid growth of the ANSF was to be matched by a corresponding improvement in quality and professionalism, measured by 'Capability Milestones'. In July 2009 it was claimed that 47 per cent of ANA units had reached CM1, the 'ability to operate independently'. However, only 24 police units had reached this total in the same period, while 447 remained at CM4, 'formed but not yet capable of conducting operations', reflecting the slower rate of development of the police in Afghanistan more generally. These improvements in quality were considered essential when police abuses and army heavy-handedness were blamed for antagonizing the population, thereby fuelling the insurgency.

However, building an army in the midst of a war has been a challenging undertaking. ANA recruits were young, three in ten were drug addicts, nine out of ten were illiterate and 25 per cent per year were prone to desertion.[85] Amongst the embedded training teams (the OMLTs or CTTs), few Western military advisors believed that Afghan units were capable of fighting the insurgents without Western forces being present. One veteran Afghan major told this author that if the West left Afghanistan, his feeling was the ANA would last only two days. Others are not so pessimistic and point to the domination of non-Pashtun ethnic groups in the ranks of the ANA, which would provide a trained bulwark to any Taliban offensive. Pashtuns in the south believe the ANA is a Tajik–Afghan militia designed to oppress them.[86] In fact, 40 per cent of the rank and file and 70 per cent of the officer corps is Tajik, which reflects the legacy of the Northern Alliance victory and the relationship of the north with the Karzai government, rather than conspiracy.

Afghan recruits were not untypical in finding it hard to adjust to life in barracks and a timetable that planned their day from dawn until dusk. 'Some were mystified by the socks that came with their uniforms. Like soldiers around the world, they complain particularly about the food'.[87] The training programme had to turn a raw recruit into a soldier, capable of reacting to ambushes, shooting, marching, maintaining battlefield discipline, and calling in fire missions in just eighteen weeks. One American Staff Sergeant noted that: 'The hardest lesson is getting through the idea of "one target, one shot". They tend to go blacko on ammo'. Other military trainers called it the 'spray and pray' school of target practice.

Because of the relative inexperience, the insurgents preferred to target ANSF rather than ISAF, but it was also a question of firepower. The ANA had fewer armoured vehicles and found it more difficult to call for air support. It is difficult to call in an air strike if one cannot read, or navigate a map. Crucially, the insurgents' targeting resulted in a rising casualty toll that affected recruiting. Colonel Karimullah, the officer in command of army recruiting in Kabul remarked: 'The boys themselves are not afraid, but it is their parents who make the decisions to let them join, and when they see all this on TV, they don't think it's worth it'.[88] Recruitment rates rose from 600 to 2,000 a month in 2007 because of attractive rates of pay, but re-enlistment remained a problem. Only half the soldiers renewed their contracts once their three-year terms of service expired. Some soldiers reported that their $100 monthly salaries were less than what they could make growing poppies or smuggling.

In 2001, the United Nations was keen to see a comprehensive process of nation-building get underway and it insisted that the occupying powers assist in extending the writ of the Afghan government in Kabul over the whole country. In the south, particularly in Helmand, narcotics had long been the mainstay of the local economy. In the 1990s and 2000s, Afghanistan became the chief exporter of opium, supplying 90 per cent of the world's addiction to heroin. Poppy production rose by 169 per cent between 2005 and 2006, and locals and narco-traffickers were eager to protect their income. In 2010 opium production generated $2.3 billion, and in some places it has been far more lucrative than other types of farming. This drug money was being used by narco-leaders to run protection groups, ensure patronage and buy off their enemies. It was often unclear whether these narco-leaders were also members of the Taliban or simply cooperating with them. When the British Army was tasked with the support of a counter-narcotics programme and the extension of the Afghan government's jurisdiction in Helmand in 2006, the centre of drug production, it put them on a collision course with a number of vested interests.

In fact, although the British did not realize it at the time, drug money was being used by the lower echelons of the government to buy positions and patronage too. Local police forces were also getting pay-outs from the drug barons, indulged in clan rivalries or were so badly paid by the government that they simply robbed local citizens.[89] The civilian casualties that have resulted from ISAF airstrikes, or snatching suspected Taliban leaders in night raids, have caused anger amongst Afghans. When properties are destroyed and people killed, it was hard to appreciate that the West had come to carry out reconstruction or defeat the scourge of drugs. When Governor Asadullah Wafa planned a counter-narcotics eradication programme at Bolan in Helmand in

2008, a number of local people assumed that the government was there to make life even worse for them and they supported Mullah Mohammed Qasim, the local Taliban commander who offered protection. While some senior Taliban propagate international idealism, many Taliban fighters are no more than a local 'coalition of the angry'.[90]

Nevertheless, trying to protect narco-production and trafficking has been costly for the Taliban: when British and Afghan forces seized Loy Charahai Bazaar, a major weapons and narcotics hub, the Taliban brought up reinforcements from as far as Pakistan to fight back and drive the British out. They lost 47 men, 100 tons in drugs and a number of 'IED factories'. Nevertheless, the Taliban recognized the importance of opium to the Afghan livelihood and have been careful to frame support for the trade against government control or eradication. They have offered financial recompense for those whose fields were being eradicated, in exchange for support against the government.[91] The labour-intensive nature of the harvesting means that a surplus of often migrant labour is at hand at the end of the season. There has been a noticeable spike in violence in Helmand at these times, suggesting that migrant workers were being recruited into the insurgents' ranks.

In parts of rural Afghanistan, where the wage rates traditionally equate to $1–$2 a day, opium labourers have been paid at least $3 a day, and as much as $6 a day during harvest time.[92] It has been suggested that Taliban fighters receive $3–$5 a day with commanders earning twice that amount. In 2009, ISAF headquarters suggested that most insurgents were 'ten-dollar-a-day Taliban', motivated not by ideological convictions but by unemployment. Unemployment did indeed plague the south, with sections of the population apparently susceptible to becoming 'tier three Taliban', led on by the wealthier and 'irreconcilable' 'tier one' leadership.[93]

Taliban finances have not been limited to narcotics and roadside taxation. Fund-raising for operations has been organized centrally by the senior command based in Pakistan.[94] Field commanders have limited means or authority to raise money, and this makes them dependent financially on the central leadership. The network of Taliban fund-raising has included 'contacts in Pakistan and the Gulf, Karachi businessmen, Peshawar goldsmiths, Saudi oil men, Kuwaiti traders, Pakistani Islamic militants, and jihadi sympathizers within the Pakistani military and intelligence ranks'.[95] This global network used many of the same relationships that were set up to finance the war against the Soviets in the 1980s, but the process has relied on the system of trust, most notably the *hawala* system, in which funds are remotely transferred through networks. Such a system has become a 'mainstay of the economy' due to the collapse of the formal banking system.[96] Resources, including weapons, money, motor transport and other logistical necessities, are funnelled to the field commanders via Pakistan and, to a lesser extent, Iran.[97]

Insurgents' command and control

It was not until June 2003 that Mullah Omar reconstituted his 'shadow government' in the form of the Quetta Shura, but military command and control for the Taliban have been at the lowest possible level in order to exploit local clan relations and ground conditions. The Taliban created a centralized network in which each field commander creates sub-networks in order to generate revenue, attract recruits and accommodate local interests in line with the Taliban's higher objectives. These sub-networks are operationally independent from the Taliban senior command, but are reliant on them for munitions and larger funds. Decision-making in operations has been devolved to the local commanders. Competency is valued over prestige: field leaders often 'exercise considerable power despite being from a region where age and experience are valued'.[98] This has been effective because it allowed the Taliban to partner with individuals and organizations beyond the Pashtun south. Decentralization was an innovation introduced in 2006 following the heavy casualties incurred by Mullah Akhtar Osmani and Mullah Mansur Dadullah against Coalition Forces.[99]

Nevertheless, charismatic leadership, which had always been important in Afghanistan's military history, was still evident in the insurgency after 2006. A fighter called Akhundzada was in thrall of Mullah Mansur Dadullah, a leader who, ironically, was not that popular with other senior Taliban. Akhundzada stated: '...we lacked weapons and money. So I visited Mullah Dadullah. He had gone into Helmand province in early 2006 with thirty people. When he returned months later, he had organized 300 sub-commanders who each had dozens of troops. He had also signed up and was training hundreds of suicide-bomb volunteers. His return was like the arrival of rain after five years of drought'. Akhundzada recalled that he gave him a list of his military needs: 'he called me, took a page out of a notebook, wrote something on it, and gave it to me'. The note said to go and present the list to a comrade. Back in Pakistan, he found the man who promptly 'kissed Dadullah's letter. After two weeks this man had provided me with all the guns, weapons, and supplies I had requested'.[100] But some Taliban fighters, like Haqqani, maintain: '[While] I admit Taliban commanders are being captured and killed–that hasn't stopped us, and it won't. Our Jihad is more solid and deep than individual commanders and fighters—and we are not dependent on foreigners, on the ISI, or al Qaeda. We can no longer allow these camels to roam freely without bridles and control'.[101]

Taliban command systems have often been thrown into turmoil by the death of a leader at a critical point. Although details are still classified at the time of writing, the identification, location and surgical elimination of certain Taliban commanders in Regional Command South threw several cells into confusion on the eve of a major ISAF offensive in 2009. Indeed, given the need to consult certain groups and to gain the assent of the senior leadership for command appointments, Coalition forces were able to predict with some accuracy when groups would become operational again.

The Taliban commanders also showed that they could regenerate, adapt and respond. In December 2008, ISAF had launched Operation Sond Chara and cleared parts of Nad-e Ali in Helmand after Taliban re-infiltration earlier that year. A large number of weapons and communications equipment had been seized. Similar American operations at Garmsir were producing the same results. To recover the initiative, the Taliban conceived a bold and daring plan to make a four-pronged assault on Lashkargah. The aim was to divert Western troops from their offensives, to get into the urban space to engage in a close-quarter battle which would neutralize Western air power, and to score a propaganda victory akin to the Tet Offensive in Vietnam. On 11 October, 200 Taliban fighters were detected advancing on the provincial capital, with an eastern group attempting to set itself up as a blocking force to cut off reinforcements. Apache helicopter gunships and air strikes broke up the attacking columns in a firefight lasting four hours. The Taliban are thought to have suffered more than sixty casualties, but they had failed to pierce the perimeter. On 14 October the Taliban made a second attempt, seeking to wipe out ANP posts on the city's outskirts. Another 18 Taliban were killed in the assault. Yet, they claimed they had created insecurity in the provincial capital and showed that they could attack when they chose to do so.

In April 2009 there was another attempt to assault Lashkargah. The aim was to move Taliban volunteers from Waziristan up their concealed routes and to deploy pre-positioned four ZPU-1 anti-aircraft guns to assault Marjah before pushing on to the provincial capital. There were delays to the operation caused by the poppy harvest, the death of a local clan elder and an ANA assault on Marjah in which sixty Taliban were killed. A much smaller offensive was therefore planned for 15 May 2009, but this was hit by airstrikes as Taliban fighters concentrated, which resulted in twenty-two killed including six commanders. The only operation that could be mounted in the end was an eight-man assault on a police post and some opportunity attacks, including IEDs.

Insurgent tactics

To add to these setbacks, the Taliban were finding that ambushes against mobile patrols and columns were becoming less effective. ISAF were detecting more IEDs than could be detonated, and columns invariably outgunned the smaller Taliban detachments. Battles with dismounted patrols were more effective in inflicting losses on ISAF but Taliban casualties were also inevitably that much higher, especially when the Coalition brought in air support. Feints, secondary attacks from a second axis and a main assault from a third axis, have sought to confuse and disorientate the ISAF troops. As a result of the setbacks, however, the Taliban have tried to focus on re-infiltration amongst the population, as they managed in March 2009 in Spin Masjid and Amin Kalay in Helmand. They have also used motorbike-borne suicide attacks, individual vehicle bombs and even attempted a swarm-attack using a number of suicide bombers, styled *Fedayeen*, armed with assault rifles and grenades.

The Taliban have struggled to maintain high tempo resistance with a very insecure supply system, but they have shown a determination to learn from their mistakes. One fighter, Khan, stated:

By the end of 2005 the Taliban's ranks in Ghazni were increasing. There were new recruits like me and more former Taliban returning home from Pakistan. At the same time, we started receiving shipments of RPGs, rockets, mines, and bombs, most of which were old and rusty. My group only had three RPG launchers and only one mortar tube, and a few rounds for each. We had a few rusty Russian mines that only worked about 30 percent of the time. So we could only carry out very quick and limited attacks on convoys, construction crews, and district compounds. At first we didn't have much success. But we were learning.[102]

Khan noted improvements in other areas in 2008:

Our men are watching American bases 24 hours a day. They inform us of American movements. We used to hit the Americans with roadside bombs and then disappear. Now when we explode an IED, we follow that with AK and RPG fire. We now have more destructive IEDs, mostly ammonium-nitrate bombs that we mix with aluminium shards. We get regular deliveries of these fertilizers, explosives, fuses, detonators, and remote controls.[103]

The Taliban have continued to evolve their tactics, mostly in response to Western air power. Taliban fighter Masiuddin related an attack on an isolated American and ANA post:

Then American helicopters arrived, firing rockets and machine guns. We fought [from just before dawn] until sunset. We lost 12 Taliban to martyrdom, largely to the helicopter fire that comes down like heavy rain. We cannot compare our military strength to that of the Americans. But we have learned how to stay protected behind rocks and mountains. Even with all their advanced technology, we forced them to withdraw.[104]

The insurgents have set out to discredit and undermine the administration of Karzai, which they describe as the 'government of slavery'. This requires them not only to maintain resistance, but also to reduce confidence in the government and to generate insecurity and instability nationally. The majority of fighters are nevertheless concerned with local issues on their own fronts. Most insurgents enjoy a fairly devolved command structure and determine their own area of operations. In these zones the insurgents are able to move relatively freely, which means that fighters can organize their own operations, attack with impunity and rotate out of the campaign every few weeks, for rest and recuperation. During this period of rest it is believed that groups of commanders and fighters share their exploits and discuss their successes and failures, resulting in a transfer of knowledge. They make acute observations of ISAF and ANSF tactics and routines, and plan to exploit any patterns and weaknesses on their next rotation. Inside the fighting areas, when under pressure, insurgents will cache their weapons and equipment, and, since they are dressed in the same way as locals, they will try to blend into normal rural life. At best the insurgents benefit from the unequivocal support of sections of the Afghan population, and at worst they can achieve support through intimidation. There are very few examples of Afghan civilians challenging insurgents directly. Many provide information, food, an ideal firing point, or accommodation, and they often remain reluctant to talk with Coalition forces for fear of reprisal. This explicit or implicit support provides fundamental assistance to the insurgents. Moreover, some locals, including children, have provided early warning of the presence of Coalition forces and ANSF, using radios, flags, messengers on motorbikes, smoke signals, kites and mirrors. Insurgents depend on this information and will not engage unless they are confident that they know where all their enemy units are and that their escape route is not cut off.

However, this does not mean that all Afghans welcome the insurgents, and many are resentful of the constant fighting. It is not unknown for Afghans to applaud when ISAF troops drive the insurgents out of a village. Part of this can be explained by the insurgents' arbitrary punishment of alleged collaborators. Propaganda is accompanied by physical and psychological coercion to ensure compliance. Moreover, they do not observe the law of armed conflict and will actively seek to exploit the more restrictive rules of engagement of the Western forces. For example, during an engagement, if events turn against them, the fighter will conceal his weapon and emerge unarmed, knowing that ISAF troops will not attack him. Firers will arrange to have supporters change their clothes after a shooting incident in order to escape recognition. Reconnaissance missions are conducted and rehearsed without weapons to avoid arrest. Women or children are sometimes used as shields in compounds, and in some cases are encouraged to crowd around a firer so that ISAF will not return fire. In one instance in Nad-e Ali in Helmand, insurgent casualties were transported in minibuses with women to prevent their capture.

The insurgents believe that, following a skirmish with Western forces, the most likely course of action is that ISAF ground troops will withdraw to a nearby base. Insurgents therefore initiate battles at the forward edge of a contested area with sufficient force to discourage ISAF from moving deeper into insurgent-held territory without a significantly larger force. Many of the ISAF and ANSF patrol bases are limited in their ability to free troops for offensive operations, and manpower considerations have often restricted the area that can be brought under government control. By default, this has given the insurgent greater freedom of movement. Moreover, insurgents will often initiate an ambush as the ISAF troops are returning to base, knowing that the patrol will have been out for a long time and therefore is more likely to break off the engagement. The insurgents then use this in their propaganda as evidence that ISAF have been driven off.

Despite the apparent alignment of physical resistance with 'information operations', the insurgents still lack the ability to coordinate their actions effectively, and there are frequent disagreements about operational priorities or the ways in which local Afghans should be treated. There are patterns to their behaviour, too, that ISAF forces are able to exploit. Soldiers observe that insurgents are often creatures of habit, frequently re-using the same sites as firing points or the same choke points for IEDs. It has been noted that insurgents will rarely operate at night and only move into position after dawn. Given the time taken to get into position, the need to rest during the hottest part of the day, and their desire to break off engagements a few hours after dark, Coalition forces can predict the 'battle rhythm' of the insurgents. ISAF troops have often surprised the insurgent teams by their night operations.

It is reported that insurgents have been particularly fearful of attack helicopters which they call 'wasps'. When helicopters have been airborne, insurgents have attempted to get under cover and not move. The helicopters' ability to hover, loiter and strike with precision results in insurgents remaining stationary, and this effect has been exploited by some units to fix insurgents in place and guide ground teams towards their position. However, insurgents recognized that if they ceased activity while helicopters were in close proximity, they only needed to do so for a limited period as the helicopters tended not to remain in position for long periods.

Many Afghans, including the insurgents, lack education about modern weapons. In Helmand, a malfunction in an unmanned aerial vehicle led to a patrol being tasked to recover it, whereupon a local farmer explained he had tied the aircraft to a tree because he 'didn't want the bird to fly away'. There were also rumours amongst the population that insurgents thought the ISAF was training mice to fly the smallest unmanned aerial vehicles. It is clear that the insurgents have consistently underestimated the comprehensiveness of Western surveillance capabilities.

Insurgents' prestige weapons have been scarce and valuable, and have only been utilized when they assessed it was safe to do so without immediate interdiction. As in the Soviet war, the further from the border areas the insurgents are, the more difficult it has been to supply the heavier weapons and the ammunition required. Rocket attacks, even on fixed positions, have been problematic because of the logistics burden of the ammunition, the difficulty of avoiding detection in transit, and the risk to the firer from remaining in position long enough to ensure accuracy. However, sharpshooting attacks are much less risky for the insurgents in this regard. It is far easier to conceal a single firer and screen the firing point than it is to set up cumbersome and less accurate indirect fire weapons. A sharpshooter also conserves ammunition, needing only a few rounds to inflict a casualty, although multiple attacks have been common. In one incident near Char Coucha in Nad-e Ali in Helmand on 25 October 2010, a patrol was attacked by sharpshooters having been distracted by a more general attack from small-arms fire. Some members of the patrol became casualties, and, as they attempted to extract their colleagues, a command wire IED was detonated. It is possible that insurgents in this area had, probably more through accident than design, shaped the tactics of the local patrols because, until that attack, they had previously used short-ranged grenade attacks from compounds. This had forced ISAF troops to use more open terrain in an attempt to mitigate the threat, but that had allowed the insurgents to use longer-ranged, accurate sharpshooters. The sudden change in the technique of attacks enabled insurgents to cause multiple casualties. It was also ascertained that the fields in the area had been flooded deliberately in order that ISAF would be forced to use the tracks or particular ground.

After the initial offensives of 2006, the insurgents have not been able to mass and coordinate large numbers for a major assault. The majority of insurgents are not prepared to die unnecessarily and they will seek to carry out operations in which they have a good chance of remaining alive to fight another day. They have not sought martyrdom at the expense of an operation's success. Where there were determined assaults against ISAF patrol bases in 2006, by 2009 the emphasis was instead on breaching these defences using ANP turncoats or allies within the perimeter. Moreover, the insurgents have preferred to strike against weaker government forces or their militias rather than take on the full might of the Western Coalition. Nevertheless, they believe the ability to over-run a police post and raise the Taliban flag provides them with a propaganda opportunity as powerful as inflicting casualties on foreigners.

It appears that the insurgents' willingness to fight has been undermined by perceptions that they are outflanked, that the ability to extract casualties or a withdrawal route is blocked, or that they cannot locate where all counter-insurgent forces are and may therefore be surprised. The principles for engagement have been to understand the layout of their enemy forces before an attack; to initiate an attack, with surprise, from multiple positions, each of which is protected by obstacles; to use deception and create confusion in order to overload ISAF or ANSF communications; to maintain security and secrecy of identity, and to change position frequently and at speed to outrun any pursuit or avoid being fixed by the enemy's greater firepower.

Insurgents have retreated when pursued and they have gone into hiding to avoid detection. However, they have been willing to take risks, to assault a position which they assess they can overrun, and they have not been averse to an exchange of fire from close range. Harassing fire from a safe distance has been their first preference, and they have used linear features to guide their aim. This fire has also been used to cover moves elsewhere, or has acted as a deception measure to draw attention away from where logistics were being assembled or IEDs laid. It has been common for them to try to use a screening feature, such as a line of trees or compounds, to obscure firing points and to delay any ground forces that pursue them. There has been a development in shooting, not only towards the use of sharpshooters, but also in close-range engagements from 'murder holes', namely concealed apertures in thick compound walls, from which they then make a rapid escape. Like many insurgent attacks, they have rarely inflicted many casualties, but they have been very carefully prepared and rehearsed and have looked to guarantee inflicting just one or two losses on their adversaries. Insurgents have even, on occasion, dug trenches with overhead protection to take on Coalition or ANSF patrols.

Digging is much more common in the placement of IEDs. In Nahr-e Saraj in Helmand in July 2010, a local farmer indicated to the neighbouring ISAF forces that a number of IEDs and booby traps had been entrenched close to a patrol base and in an area that helicopters were likely to use. No fewer than four large devices were uncovered, with a command wire running along an irrigation ditch to a firing point about 200 metres away. It is not certain when the preparation took place and it could have occurred during the day or night, but the fact that insurgents had managed to emplace these devices without detection demonstrates their audacity. Moreover, insurgents have created IEDs with increasing skill. This has been due, in part, to external supporters, but also reflects a natural evolution in insurgent tactics through trial and error.

Digging in was also a feature of the insurgents' approaches to constructing defences. At Kajaki Olya in Sangin, an area considered to be their safe haven, there were multiple layers of IED belts, bunkers and firing points. A screen of scouts constantly monitored the approaches. However, the insurgents were powerless to prevent a night-time infiltration by ISAF forces and were taken by surprise. Unable to mount resistance as they had planned, the insurgents fled on motorcycles or on foot. It is clear that in this example the insurgents' system of signalling had failed. In another example in October 2010, it was noted that a Taliban white flag was flying on a pole outside a compound. Several days later, after an operation in which ISAF successfully pushed the insurgents back, the flag had also moved back into 'Taliban territory'. The position of the flag here indicated the loss of a compound, but the use of flags has also been an indicator for the loss of a route into a particular area, to indicate the arrival of foreign insurgents into unfamiliar territory, an attempt to indicate local sympathies or as a warning by the Taliban to locals about their presence which should not be defied. White flags have sometimes been used to mark the limits of insurgent influence and to warn locals of where a front line was located.

The localized nature of the insurgency means that insurgent commanders have the freedom to make decisions about what to do in their own area. Insurgent commanders will, for example, tailor levels of intimidation specific to local conditions and levels of support. An insurgent presence is established by vehicle checkpoints, by targeted threats and beatings, or by clandestine messaging. One journalist in Qalat in 2009 known to the author received threats that should he continue to operate in the local area after two warnings, he would be killed. After the second threat, he and his family moved hurriedly to Kabul. *Shabnama* (night letters) have been pinned to the doors of mosques or left at compounds by insurgents moving through villages after dark, giving warnings about talking with ISAF or issuing orders such as curfews.[105] Night letters have had a significant psychological effect, as they have demonstrated the hidden insurgent presence and enhanced the perception of insecurity. The night letters have often been read aloud to the village by a *khan* or mullah because literacy levels are low, but this has, in fact, provided the perception of legitimating the insurgents' desire.

The Battle of Wanat

A serious assault was made at Wanat at dawn on 13 July 2008 when the Taliban attacked an American outpost in Kunar province close to the Pakistan border in Regional Command East. It was a short, sharp battle that left nine Americans and more than thirty insurgent fighters dead, using tactics that were intended to neutralize American air power and their response times, but it also demonstrated the continued asymmetry of the conflict. The US troops were drawn from 2nd Platoon, Chosen Company, 2nd Battalion, 503rd Infantry Regiment. This force of forty-five men had begun building a patrol base in the Waygul Valley, close to the village of Wanat. Three US Marines had joined the outpost in order to continue the training of a dozen Afghan National Army soldiers. As the work progressed, successive days of bad weather prevented any American air cover, which gave the insurgents the opportunity to approach the base undetected, concentrating from distant hide-outs via side valleys and nearby gullies. As the insurgent fighters reached their final assembly area, they opened an irrigation dam, so the sound of rushing water would cover the noise of their footsteps and whispers. Some Taliban fighters managed to locate the Claymore directional mines on the approaches to the base, and turned them around. Others used previous reconnaissance intelligence to point out the location of American heavy weapons.

Just before the commencement of the battle, the American base was still far from complete. There had not been time to build entrenched observation posts on high ground around the base. The base itself lacked construction materials and, because of the high Afghan summer temperatures and intense work required, the garrison had almost run out of water. However, a more dangerous situation had developed with the local Afghans. In an attempt to win hearts and minds, the Americans had been talking to village elders for several weeks, trying to persuade them to let a base be built in Wanat. However, it seems that the Taliban knew of the discussions, and used the negotiation time to prepare a major attack before the base was fully operational. The Americans were eager to find and arm local tribesmen who would work with them in order to increase the allied forces available, but this eroded rather than enhanced their security. There simply weren't enough American troops to cover every valley and protect every community in Kunar from Taliban fighters, who could slip across the Afghan–Pakistan border with relative ease.

Hitherto, American forces in the province had frequently engaged in firefights and battled for their survival. The shortage of manpower and the nature of the fighting meant that base security had to be provided by the same troops engaged in construction. This meant round-the-clock labouring for tired men, and it also implied that it was impossible to mount enough patrols beyond the new base to dominate the ground and deter attacks.

At 04.20 hrs on 13 July 2008, volleys of rocket-propelled grenades began to land on the half-constructed base. This was the preliminary bombardment to an assault by between 100 and 200 Taliban fighters. The first salvoes concentrated on the Americans' heavy weapons, namely a 120 mm mortar, a TOW missile system, and a 0.50 calibre machine gun. One soldier described the barrage as feeling like 'a thousand RPGs at once'.

With the heavy weapons knocked out, the Taliban rushed forward to fight at close quarters in order to make it impossible for the Americans to call in air strikes. Just like their forefathers, the Taliban threw rocks into the Americans' trenches, hoping they would mistake them for grenades and jump out, whereupon they could be killed. The Taliban closed in from several directions, bringing as much fire to bear as possible. The Americans were simply unable to move because of the weight of fire on their positions.

One soldier described the intensity of the battle: 'I continued to lay suppressive fire with the 240 [machine gun] but it was difficult because I was unable to stand due to wounds in both legs and my left arm'. When this soldier ran out of ammunition he realized he was the only one still alive in his corner of the patrol base. The Taliban were so close he could hear them talking. As the Taliban tried to move right into the base, they were forced to leave their cover, or were silhouetted against the sky. Here they presented a clear target. The Americans were thus able to cut down the Taliban as they tried to swarm over the base perimeter. The 0.50 calibre machine gun had also survived the initial barrage and engaged the Taliban fighters at relatively short range.

The Taliban knew it would take at least thirty minutes before American air support was available, although the battle lasted an hour before the fighters withdrew with their wounded and dead. The exhausted defenders were too preoccupied with identifying who was still alive and tending to the wounded to pursue them. Some 9 Americans were killed and another 27 were wounded, representing 75 per cent of the initial strength of the post, but the Taliban also took heavy losses: it was estimated that between 21 and 52 fighters were killed by the defenders. The final toll could not be verified. The Taliban had failed to complete their objective. Even with the element of surprise, greater numbers and all the intelligence they needed, they had been unable to overrun the Americans.

Misconceptions of the insurgency

The insurgents also struggle to maintain the fighting fronts when terrain or weather conditions are unfavourable. A Taliban fighter, Masiuddin, noted:

[In June 2008] we began carefully planning an attack. One of our men said that the mission would be hard even if the Americans only threw stones at us, as we'd be attacking up a steep mountain. Everyone laughed at him, but we knew there was some truth in what he said. I asked for volunteers, and everyone signed up. As usual we prepared a medical team, including donkeys and stretchers to evacuate our wounded. But as I divided up weapons, ammunition, explosives, and communications gear, it started to rain heavily. The Americans have heavy boots and other mountain equipment that allows them to move up and down the steep rocks. But our men mostly wear leather sandals that don't give us any grip. So we postponed the attack for two weeks.[106]

The insurgency that developed in 2003 has been characterized by a number of misperceptions on both sides. Much criticism has been levelled at the Western government and armies for failing to 'understand' Afghanistan and its 'Human Terrain'. However, the Coalition's enemies are often equally misguided and believe deeply in selected national myths. A professor of Pashtun history at Kabul University could be guilty of the same misunderstandings. Reflecting on a series of invasions, he stated:

Then you British came, 150 years ago. You had 60,000 troops and the best artillery, but it was *Pashtuns* who surrounded Kabul and killed 17,000 of you as you tried to escape. The rulers of your empire thought this was an accident: they couldn't accept such a defeat, so they attacked again, in 1880. We killed 12,000 of you that time, at Maiwand. The same with the Soviets in 1979: most of their original army was destroyed. What makes you think it will be any different for America this time?

Apart from the obvious errors in statistics here, the final analogy is perhaps the most revealing. America is not an 'imperial' power but part of an internationally-backed, UN-sanctioned Coalition acting on behalf of the sovereign Afghan government. As General Sir David Richards, a British officer who commanded ISAF in Afghanistan recently, put it: 'It is true that, in Afghan military history, the Afghans have always won, but, this time, we are fighting on the same side as the Afghans'.[107]

During the insurgency in the 2000s, a number of Afghan zealots on both sides have exercised great brutality, like the pro-Soviet regimes and the Mujahideen factions of the civil war before them, even though this was counterproductive and contradicted their aims, namely, to bring about consensus, security and order. The Taliban have practised the very crimes they claimed they had come to stop. Security and protection of 'Islamic culture' (as they interpreted it), at the expense of human rights and free expression, condemned the country to stagnation in the 1990s. They failed to see that the values of civil liberty were not Western 'evils' but universal ones, essential to any society. The Taliban feared difference and they were in denial of the global linkages of the world in terms of ideas and economics, and this often explains their desire to avoid negotiations and dialogue. The 'do or die' philosophy of the hardliners, however motivating in their own ranks, was evidence of their weakness as much as their strength. Like the authoritarian regimes of the twentieth century, they demanded of their followers a self-sacrificial, total war mentality to make up for their evident material deficiencies. The heroic fantasy of fighting for a liberated emirate and doing battle with the overbearing West gave them the prestige they lacked in the real world, but ignored the fact that, in essence, they were still waging a war on fellow Afghans. For the rest of them, the less ideological, their wars have been about clan rivalries, battles over land ownership, slights to prestige, a share of profits, and old feuds. After more than twenty years of civil war, fuelled by the availability of weapons and military forces, foreign influences and extremist ideologies, it was violence, rather than dialogue and negotiation, that became the means to settle disputes. Yet, negotiations may still be a viable means to end conflict, as they form an integral part of Afghan warfare.

Negotiations and reconciliation after 2001

The process of negotiation with an enemy tends to follow a pattern. First, there is the decision to negotiate; second, there are calculations about the ground conditions prevailing; third, the terms are offered and the process of negotiation gets underway; fourth, terms are implemented; and finally, there is the realization of perceived or desired outcomes. The latter will often determine the ability of the belligerents to trust the other party, and to make decisions about the advantages and disadvantages, risks and opportunities that might arise from ending a military campaign. However, the process is often asymmetrical, and the location of power (including the possession of military force) is far more important than any apparently cultural considerations, although Afghan identities and values permeate the decision-making process.

In the First Afghan War, ground conditions (namely a significant shift in power in Kabul after a successful revolt and a military victory at Beymaru Ridge) opened the way for negotiations, but attempts to subvert the process and the failure to guarantee the Afghans' preferred outcome led to a resumption of fighting. The fractured nature of the Afghan groups made a unified and coordinated response very difficult, especially when trust in the negotiating process was broken and the opportunity to inflict a crushing defeat and loot the British garrison was presented. In the case of the Soviet War, a third party was far more important to Soviet interests than to Afghan ones. Indeed, only the Communist puppet regime was engaged in the process of negotiation, and it seems that the Karmal delegation at Geneva was acutely aware that Afghan interests were unlikely to be well served by the Accords. The Mujahideen were not engaged in the process and thus continued the war against the regime of Najibullah until 1992. Failure to create a united resistance during the period of the Accords was a major factor in the subsequent division of factions, civil war and warlordism that followed.

During the various conflicts in Afghanistan, local truces, bargaining and negotiations between bouts of violence were the norm. The fractured nature of Afghan society meant that such arrangements were pragmatic and necessary. The nature of the insurgency in Afghanistan after 2001 bears similar hallmarks, but it is interesting to note that the Afghan government and the Western military forces have so far preferred to negotiate only on terms of reconciliation with the Karzai regime in Kabul.[108] The insurgents feel that they were excluded from the Bonn Agreement (although there is no evidence to suggest they would have offered to negotiate anyway) and that the Karzai government could not be trusted even if fighters did give up the campaign. Criticisms of this nature feature prominently in Abdul Salam Zaeef's recent critique.[109]

The Afghan Pashtun expression 'Mizh der Beitabora khalki-i' (we are a very untrustworthy people) would reinforce the more critical historical judgements that can be found in Western historical sources, but apportioning blame to the Afghans without any contextual reading of the situation is a gross over-simplification. The Afghans have frequently been confronted with adversaries who are equally difficult to trust and who often possessed greater military power. Wit and cunning were needed to survive such encounters. Lying during negotiations to outmanoeuvre a foreigner or a rival, *al-Taqiyya*, was admired if it was successful. Inflations of land ownership, of the numbers of men under the command of a particular leader, or other criteria that measured honour, were the response of people long accustomed to the need to survive instead of a failure in some moral integrity. Unbreakable bonds of trust between relatives and friends can be cited as evidence of the fidelity of Afghans, and are all the more impressive when one considers that such trust can be a life or death matter. Afghans have been remarkable in their willingness to die as a point of honour for a bond, for the promise they have given to protect others, and for their faith.

Western perspectives tend to focus on reconciling Afghans to the government in Kabul, but it is not clear whether the emphasis should have been on traditionalists, in order to reconstruct the political and social system that existed before 1973; on the new generation, who envisage more radical change and progressive politics; or on the aggrieved, specifically those who have lost land, status or political power. There has been a division of opinion on how to approach the insurgents, but broadly the categories are: the local fighters, who might have been persuaded to lay down their arms; the 'Tier 2 Taliban', who may have needed a mixture of coercion and incentive to end their conflict; and the 'irreconcilables', who, for ideological reasons, were not expected to negotiate at all.

There have been significant obstacles to reconciliation efforts. Few Western official sources acknowledge that reconciling to the regime in Kabul has been itself the key problem, although there are many references to the corruption of the administration, the fact that it has been staffed with former warlord leaders with murderous pasts to a senior level, and that narco-dollars and patronage have distorted the machinery and policies of the government. Ethnic rivalries have prevented reconciliation too. Some Tajik–Afghans have been concerned that peace with the Pashtuns would mean reunification and the empowerment of their old enemies. Mindful of the brief period of Tajik–Afghan ascendancy in 1929 and the bitter repression of the Taliban in the 1990s, it has perhaps been in Tajik–Afghan interests to keep the Pashtuns divided. Cutting across the ethnic boundaries, many in the government's service have been keen to sustain the conflict. Poorly paid Afghan National Police officers have been criticized, for example, for augmenting their income with protection money, arrests for cash returns, bribes and even kidnapping for ransom. Former Taliban in the government administration have been keen to keep those who would take revenge at arm's length, while some in the Wolesi Jirga sympathized with the Taliban. Those Taliban in the field who wish to end the fighting feared they would be betrayed and assassinated by fifth columnists. Some Taliban fighters expressed fear of their comrades, of the 'Quetta Shura' headquarters and even of the ISI, if they tried to turn themselves in.

Afghans are aware, like any other community, that information is power. Negotiations and offers are unlikely to stay secret for long if any individual or group feels that it would profit or lose out in any negotiations. The egalitarian ideals of the Pashtuns have made this especially problematic, as no individual feels he can truly be represented by someone else. Moreover, even the idea of reconciliation, however secret, can be perceived as treachery by another party. Abdul Haq, a former Mujahideen leader, was eager to reconcile members of the Taliban, but his secret plan was revealed by the freelance journalists known as the Ritchie brothers in late 2001. As a result, Abdul Haq was kidnapped, tortured and murdered and his body was strung up in Kabul.

In 2007, James Semple and Mervyn Patterson were ordered out of Afghanistan by the Karzai government on the charge that they had been secretly doing deals with the 'irreconcilable' Taliban in a way that was detrimental to the interests of the administration in Kabul. These men, acting on behalf of the British, had some experience of 'back channels' negotiations in Northern Ireland, with the Ulster Volunteer Force, and in Anbar province in Iraq. Semple had also worked with NGOs in Afghanistan and spoke Pashto. He believed that the insurgency was very localized in Helmand, and, observing that the 'Taliban' tended to follow local leaders, he set out to open a dialogue with them. Governor Wafa aroused the suspicions of the government, fuelled perhaps by rival former Taliban in the Kabul administration, and Semple and Patterson were ordered out in December that year. Assadullah Khalid, governor of Kandahar province, alleged that the British were offering money; 'it was a business deal', he said, although the fact that Britain and not the Afghan government appeared to be in the lead was the main cause of concern.[110]

The Semple–Patterson case also illustrates another aspect of negotiations in Afghanistan. Semple was led to believe that Mansur Dadullah (also known as Bakht Mohammed) was a local Helmandi leader, but in fact he was a Kakar Baluchi whose brother had been killed that year and who was part of the external Taliban apparatus. The confusion may have arisen because Dadullah, nick-named the 'Lame Englishman' (previously wounded, his epithet as Englishman denoted his lack of trustworthiness), was demoted by Mullah Omar and his headquarters. Selection of the right negotiating partners was evidently critical, but so too was the process of engaging the Afghan government.

The Americans had driven the agenda on negotiations with the Taliban on their own terms in 2001. As Karzai led a force south towards Kandahar, when the Taliban forces collapsed and fled under the American bombardment, he had allowed the Taliban fighters to return home to avoid defeat and destruction. Taliban leaders, including Mullah Obeidullah and Mullah Naqib of the Alikozai, accepted the arrangement and they joined forces with Hajj Basher Noorzai to keep order in the city. The Americans nevertheless overturned this decision, and Obeidullah fled to Pakistan where he joined the insurgency.

There were further errors in the case surrounding Wakil Ahmad Mutawakil, the former Taliban Foreign Minister who was traced to Kandahar in 2002. The Afghan government had planned to reconcile him to the regime, not least because his brother had been killed by the Taliban, but American troops arrested him and took him to Bagram where he was held for three years. When he was released he joined the Afghan Wolesi Jirga, but an opportunity had been lost for him to speak out against the neo-Taliban and to promote the merits of reconciliation. The Americans were eager to track down any associates of Mullah Omar and Osama bin Laden, but the tactical success was allowed to obscure the greater strategic advantage that could have been gained.

In negotiations, tangible benefits in the long term are required and assurances reinforced during the process of dialogue. In 2005, Abdul Wahid Rais al-Baghrani, an influential figure amongst the Khalozais of the Alizai, was deterred from cooperation with the Afghan government by the lack of any evident benefits or security guarantees. In 2004, he had urged the Khalozai to participate in parliamentary elections, and, having fought alongside Rabbani and the Tajiks in the Soviet War, he was eager to see the country reunited. After consulting his people, he called for reconciliation with the government in a public meeting in Kabul in 2005; but when he returned to the south, he had nothing to show for his efforts. Suspicions grew, and the expectation that development aid might flow into his area as a result of his announcement remained unfulfilled. In 2006, his people were engulfed by fighting in the south between insurgents and the Coalition. The fate of al-Baghrani and his people suggests that the allocation of development aid needed strategic direction. Much development money appears to have had little effect on loyalties, and there is criticism that Western development funds often ended up in the hands of the insurgents or just one or two influential pro-government clans. Concentration of funds into areas actually controlled by the government would appear to be a far better way of incentivising cooperation and peaceful reconciliation.

The existence of List 1267 has also been seen as a significant obstacle to successful negotiations. The list, named after UN Resolution 1267, details Taliban and al Qaeda leaders subject to travel bans, frozen assets and embargos against the carrying of weapons. About 250 names were thought to be included, but the list soon became subject to myth.[111] Many former Taliban assumed that they were on this inventory of 'irreconcilables'. The death or capture of former Taliban has led many to believe that the government has made all former fighters permanent outlaws. The list also made no reference to the neo-Taliban, members of the Haqqani network or Hizb-i-Gulbuddin (HIG), which have been behind insurgent activity across the country. Nevertheless, the Americans remain strongly committed to the capture of members of al Qaeda responsible for or connected to any attacks on American interests.

The Afghan government wants to remain in charge of all negotiations with the insurgents, but its own efforts are not trusted by other parties. The United Kingdom has assisted the reconciliation effort by funding the Program Tahkife Solh (PTS), which was headed initially by Sibghatullah Mojaddidi, but neither the British nor Mojaddidi were trusted by the Taliban. Mojaddidi was widely respected as a peacemaker, but he was also seen by many Pashtuns as the man who had effectively handed over power in 2001 to the Tajik factions without a fight. The British believed that the PTS should have an Afghan Special Co-ordinator with a committee of Afghans drawn from a wide variety of communities and UN officials. They also wanted a programme that took account of returnees. The process of reconciliation involves initial contacts, checks on their links to extremists, the issue of a certificate and then the allocation of a job, land or a place to live. However, the continuing harassment by Western Special Forces or ANP, the lack of security for reconciled personnel, and the feeling that the British were behind attempts to alter the country or provide the coercive backing to a corrupt and greedy government in Kabul destroyed any faith in the system. In Musa Qala in 2006, the British had favoured the reinstatement of Mullah Salam, an ex-Taliban leader who could be persuaded to work with Task Force Helmand. Salam claimed he received no support from the British, a fact underscored by the death of his son, and he argued that he felt safer under the Taliban. The British tried to establish a deal to hand over the town to the local elders and withdraw an otherwise irksome presence, but the plan foundered when the Taliban reoccupied Musa Qala, and a subsequent operation had to be mounted to retake the settlement a second time in 2007. The lack of any development activity during the period of British occupation was remarked upon by those who joined the insurgency. Mahmud Khan, an insurgent leader, commented: 'we gained our freedom from Britain 160 years ago, and should remain free. We don't accept their claim that they are here to rebuild our country. They have done nothing for us'.[112] Reconciliation was not the objective of the Taliban, but simply an end to foreign domination. Afghans have often wondered why development, if that is indeed the West's aim, needs a military occupation at all.

The year 2006 marked a turning point for negotiations in Afghanistan. There was a general shift in Afghan public opinion away from the Karzai regime, an intensification of the insurgency and increased numbers of civilian casualties. ISAF attempted to extend the writ of the Afghan government just as the Taliban prepared a major offensive to overrun the south. Neither side had significant channels open for dialogue at this stage, and, since the insurgency developed as a result of the weaknesses of the Afghan government, the Taliban, who wanted to overthrow the Karzai regime, had no incentive to talk.[113] Moreover, rising levels of violence deterred wavering members of the Taliban from any idea of reconciliation. When Pashtun witnessed the death of relatives and clansmen, or destruction of their local areas, they were more inclined to join the resistance against Western interventionist forces. Other Afghans were simply opportunistic. Some saw profit in providing security to Taliban or to narco-transit routes. Afghan security forces personnel sometimes assisted the same narco-leaders for their own personal profit, to buy allegiances or to pay their commanders. Negotiation for peace was all too often sacrificed for profit.

The UN is unlikely to be able to act as a third party in any future insurgent-government negotiations, because the Islamist factions regard the UN as a tool of the Western powers. The UN offered its 'good offices' under Resolution 1868 (23 March 2009), but the results of its meetings in 2006 with the Taliban were not encouraging.[114] Foreigners were simply not trusted and the Afghan government was regarded as too weak to offer binding agreements, which were subject to foreign approval anyway. But UNAMA remains optimistic that reconciliation is a social norm in Afghanistan; that the long duration of the conflict lends itself to negotiation for peace; and that there are lessons from past failures that can now be applied. However, the UN is aware that its own offices and the ISAF forces are effectively operating under the same remit, namely Resolution 1868, which compromises its independence in negotiations. The failure of ISAF to be entirely selective in its targeting and the Taliban's ruthless punishment of those it suspects of treachery and apostasy have increased levels of bitterness on all sides. Afghan civilians are increasingly of the view that foreign occupation is prolonging the fighting.[115] When the Americans announced that there would be a surge in troop numbers into Afghanistan in 2008, many Afghans saw any Western efforts at building peace as insincere. Equally, setting a timetable for withdrawal in 2014 increased the feeling that the West would soon depart and the Karzai government would collapse. The Obama administration added to suspicions by stating that it would only talk to moderate elements and not to hard-line fighters, but since this definition would be determined arbitrarily by the Americans themselves, few insurgents were prepared to take the risk.[116] Moreover, when Qayum Karzai, the President's elder brother, led the government delegation on reconciliation, the Taliban felt that this was merely an attempt to consolidate a dynastic regime.

The Organisation of the Islamic Conference or one of the prominent Gulf States might offer a viable alternative. Equally, the uncompromising values of many of the insurgents mean that their demands are unlikely to be acceptable to the Karzai administration or the Western powers, but a diplomatic offensive by leading Islamic scholars and authorities could be effective if presented alongside a package of practical measures. That said, in 2010, after many delays, Karzai initiated the 'peace *jirga*' concept, and talks have continued for some time with various groups and leaders. Some of these have agreed to end their campaign, but other previously neutral elements have taken up arms against Kabul. The only terms likely to be acceptable to the insurgent groups, particularly the Taliban and Hezb-i Gulbuddin, are some sort of power-sharing and new legislation that strengthens the role of the *ulema*, the Sharia and social controls (particularly with regard to women). The fate of former anti-Taliban 'warlords', rival *qawms* and families who have fought each other will not be easily resolved but are likely to be key concerns for the negotiators. Ethnic differences between the Tajiks, Hazara and Pashtuns will underlie most of the process too.

Intervention to enforce a peace in Afghanistan will be extremely difficult, and it is unlikely that any states will be willing to assume the mantle of the Western military that has borne the burden of security for ten years. As a result, it is difficult to see how trust-building measures and enforcement of the negotiation process can be achieved. Accusations of betrayal and reprisals of the type seen in the First Afghan War seem likely. Any process that fails to engage

THE AFGHAN WAY OF WAR

the actual belligerents, like the Geneva Accords, would appear to be doomed. Successful negotiations would therefore need to emerge from the Afghan factions with the lead taken by the Karzai administration or its successors. Emphasis on reconciliation as equals, based on the precepts of the Qur'an and the Hadith and supervised by relevant external authorities, might assist the process. Significant benefits available at the end of conflict might also hold out a sufficient incentive to each of the belligerents. As historical examples show, shifts in ground conditions can alter the prospects for negotiation dramatically, and even then the process is likely to be very protracted, interrupted by episodes of renewed violence and lacking in any guarantees. Indeed, the tensions of violence and negotiation have always been a feature of Afghanistan's history. Where once the traditional values of rural society provided a check or balance, increasingly this role will be demanded from the state. But until the Afghan state is accepted by the people, the civil war will almost certainly endure.

8

LESSONS LEARNED?

The recent neo-Taliban resistance since 2003 has followed the pattern of many historic insurgencies, although it is overlaid with new challenges for the Western and Afghan government security forces who oppose it. There have also been many distinctive features of this conflict which differentiate it from previous foreign interventions in Afghanistan, and it is interesting to note the frequency with which commentators have tried to draw lessons from previous wars, or even suggest that the conflict which began in 2001 is a repeat of historic struggles. Much is made of the iconic episodes of history, especially the British retreat from Kabul in 1842, the battle of Maiwand in 1880, the murder of Envoys, or the immutable Afghan Mujahideen guerrillas operating from the inviolate hills and mountains. In the attempt to make these direct comparisons, history is selected and reduced to stereotype: Afghanistan is rendered simply as 'the graveyard of empires' and therefore, by definition, a hopeless, irredeemable place of perpetual conflict. The implication of this attribution is that Afghanistan is not worth the West's effort and is doomed to failure.

Alongside the key events and traits, the Afghans themselves are reduced to manageable categories and attributed with timeless characteristics. Afghans are still deemed to be 'cold-blooded, treacherous', 'cruel and avaricious', 'ferocious and fanatical'. The protracted character of the conflict of 2001 has perhaps enhanced the temptation for policy-makers and commentators to see Afghans at war as unchanging, although this is not an assumption of the soldiers, marines and police forces who fight the insurgents. They are all too aware of the insurgents' ability to adapt and change. A search for greater understanding of the Afghan population and the techniques of the Taliban fighters is required by counter-insurgent forces in order to drive a wedge between the Taliban and the civilian population and apply practical solutions. This is especially problematic when so many 'Taliban' are local nationals fighting to protect their livelihoods, property and territory, or when rural Afghans look to gunmen to ward off predatory policemen and favour the quick and rough justice offered by the Taliban's itinerant *qazis* (judges) over the state's dysfunctional criminal justice system. There are multiple problems associated with revisiting Afghanistan's history. The chief difficulty is applying historical lessons to entirely new situations in the present. The campaign in Afghanistan has been plagued by a mismatch between the policy requirements in the West and its doctrines of counterinsurgency on one side, and the actual character of the fighting and other demands of the situation on the other. The urgent search for solutions has produced a tendency to reach for simple templates in many Western fora, whereas those 'on the ground' know all too well that in Afghanistan things take time and the 'friction' of war means that things never quite fit the comprehensive plan.

Many scholars have tried to identify national ways of war or military cultures. However, others have criticized the tendency to perceive caricatured, and rather unchanging war-fighting characteristics. The British and Indian Army's military manual on Afghanistan of the 1930s advised British officers to conduct vigorous offensives because Afghans are 'easily discouraged', and noted that the tribesmen were patient, always watching for an opportunity to strike. Small successes were said to animate them 'extraordinarily'. In mountain warfare, British soldiers were advised to watch for sudden 'swarm' attacks especially against isolated posts, to secure heights and routes and maintain tight security. Inactivity was discouraged and troops were told to 'do as the Afghans do' by setting ambushes, conducting night operations and carrying out deception. Afghans were able to hold a position with determination unless flanked, and they were likely to pursue any withdrawing force as a matter of honour. The 1933 Manual also advised British officers to punish Afghans collectively with 'stern and drastic measures' and to avoid trials or tribunals which, it was claimed, Afghans did not respect. Equally, British troops were told to avoid surrendering to an Afghan when in a tight corner because of the likely 'barbarous' mistreatment of prisoners. Soldiers were informed that it was better to fight it out to the death to preserve their honour.

Many would be tempted to look for direct similarities with the Taliban insurgents today, and it is understandable that there should be a search for patterns of behaviour. Rather than there being unchanging characteristics, it would be more accurate to say that Afghans adapt to the forces and tactics used against them, through time and contingent upon the situation. Moreover, the problem with these historical assessments is that they convey values that have since been discredited in the West, and troops today would not be permitted to breach the Geneva Convention and international law in this way. Equally, new weapons and techniques, including sniper rifles and IEDs, and new forms of justification, including militant, violent ideological interpretations of Islam, now prevail and have altered the environment. The asymmetrical stance of Afghan insurgents after 2003 is a direct result of being too weak to confront Western and Afghan security forces in any other manner. An emphasis on information operations by the Taliban leadership reflects the need to subvert the more effective physical security the West can install and the West's vulnerability to 'public opinion' and open communications. In other words, we should be extremely circumspect of the historical record as a means to glean lessons for current operations. That said, aside from the enduring influences of climate and topography two areas of warfare in Afghanistan are perhaps still worthy of consideration: the use of Islam in war and the character of guerrilla warfare.

Islam and war in Afghanistan

Islam is used selectively by Afghans to justify and legitimize a variety of actions in war. Islam can motivate but does not determine how or why Afghans fight. The anxiety for many Afghans is that prolonged contact with non-Islamic ways can threaten the Afghan–Muslim way of life, and therefore foreign, Western influences have to be held at arm's length or opposed. But the reality is also that Islam often provides the only unifying element between Afghans of such diverse and embittered backgrounds. It is not surprising that Taliban leaders, eager to overcome clan and *qawm* divisions that threaten unit cohesion, not only stress Islamic justifications for waging war but often claim to be mullahs in order to advance their own legitimacy and credentials with their fighters.

Islam can provide a unifying bond for some fighters, but equally it is the line of division for many Hazaras and Pashtuns, and, in the civil war that has effectively lasted from 1978, fractures in Afghan society on political, ideological, ethnic and generational lines are often far more important than any unity that Islam might have fostered. The conflict that has plagued Afghanistan since 2001 is a continuation of an Afghan civil war that has rent the country asunder. From a grand strategic perspective, the Afghans were surrounded by hostile states and often failed to secure allies, even amongst their Muslim neighbours, the exception being the period after 1980. Nevertheless, Afghanistan has found that those it considered allies, including Muslim ones, can all too quickly become forces of malign influence or of occupation. Inherent weaknesses in Afghanistan's conventional forces, for all the Islamic rhetoric, meant the Afghans were invariably defeated, leading towards localized, low-intensity, guerrilla operations.

Islam is much more recognizable as a motivating feature of war, but hard cash has been just as influential. A reassessment of Afghanistan's military history illustrates the strategic role of money in determining the actions of Afghan factions, a feature often overlooked or downplayed in standard histories.

Guerrilla warfare

The terrain remains a more predictable constraint in Afghanistan, altering tactics, force structures and equipment, as well as channelling and limiting all operations. Britain's experience of fighting irregular opponents in its colonial wars in the late nineteenth century prompted Charles Callwell, the author of the famous *Small Wars*, to admit that guerrilla wars in difficult terrain, like those conducted against the Afghans and frontier Pashtuns, were 'the most unfavourable–for regular troops'.[1] When the enemy engaged in hit-and-run tactics from the mountains, Callwell argued that the destruction of property, crops and livestock, measures that would 'shock the humanitarian', would invariably tempt them into battle where force could be concentrated against them and a decisive result achieved: 'which will probably bring the war most rapidly to a conclusion'. The object of pacification was to 'inflict punishment on those who had taken up arms', so as to leave the refractory subjects 'chastised and subdued'. Moreover, decisive and destructive action was, he argued, more likely to forestall any chance of long-term resistance. However, he warned against unlimited devastation and violence, suggesting that the purpose was to 'ensure a lasting peace' and not the 'exasperation of the enemy'. He concluded that a 'moral effect was often far more important than material success' and he drew a clear distinction between civilized European theatres and 'savage' enemies in the application of his theory. In actual operations, Callwell highlighted the importance of intelligence, the use of local auxiliaries and the need for mobility.

The fighting against Afghan irregulars and on the North West Frontier of India went through several phases of development and variations in British policy, but there were consistent characteristics involving advances into the hills to carry out a punitive destruction of elusive tribal *lashkars* or their villages and crops, known as 'butcher and bolt', subsequently followed by more extensive deliberate operations that required a short-term occupation of a large area and the imposition of fines or restrictions.[2] These were invariably in response to 'outrages' of raiding, kidnapping and murder by the clans. By the Inter-War Years, the Army in India could use methods of 'air policing' to augment their columns on the ground, although the terrain meant that there were limits to the use of air power alone. The topography also hampered the use of heavy artillery and tanks. Movement through the valleys still meant that infantrymen had to 'crown the heights' to protect the logistics chain below. The lack of infrastructure meant that pack mules and light machine guns or mountain artillery were essential, although roads were used for wheeled transport whenever they were available. Despite the greater firepower available to the Army in India of the 1930s and 1940s, it was confronted by the same problems that had plagued their forebears.[3] Severe logistical problems were created by the vast distances. Heat, the mountainous or arid nature of the ground, and fatigue limited the troops' mobility still further. Guerrillas, in small dispersed bands, with knowledge of the terrain, made it difficult for regular troops to concentrate against them and harassed lines of communication with raids.[4]

Guerrilla warfare operations in Afghanistan appear to fit the classic model. The Afghans appear to have a mastery of war by a 'thousand cuts', using ambushes amidst broken terrain, trading space for time, cutting logistics, while adding costs and sapping the strategic patience of the occupiers. The Afghans have often tried to cut off the supplies of their enemies, gradually strengthening a ring of steel around cities, severing routes and conducting passive resistance in rural areas. However, disunity, a lack of coordination, the temptation to seek personal or collective gain through collaboration, and the need to conduct conflicts against rival groups inside Afghanistan rather than against an occupation force have all tempered their success. Indeed, historically, occupation forces have not been driven out, but make a strategic judgement to depart on their own terms. Moreover, occupations have been followed by civil wars as Afghan factions attempt to assert themselves. Resistance by guerrillas has also been problematic and ended in victory for government forces as often as it did for the resistance.

Too often Western officers overlook the problems that confront the Afghan resistance. Their command and control is often chaotic, and disunity remains a constant threat. Disloyalty, changing sides and clan rivalries can only be overcome with strict discipline and shared hardships on campaign. The leaders are vulnerable to assassination and their logistics are often limited, which places further constraints on the timing and location of their operations.

In periods of civil war, internal divisions, specifically the ethnic, *qawm*, sectarian and clan fissures of Afghan society, were deepened and became more embittered. The British and the Soviets struggled to exploit these divisions (hoping instead for a unified, stable state modelled on either colonial or Soviet lines), but through them Afghan leaders like Dost Mohammed, Abdur Rahman and Najibullah were able to remain in power.

In the Soviet case, external support to the various Afghan factions was also critical. The injection of money, munitions and arms, and the availability of training and external advisors, prevented the Soviets from buying off resistance groups or being able to suppress them effectively. The Mujahideen groups learned to disperse and concentrate rapidly, to conduct complex ambushes from multiple firing points, and to lure motor rifle formations into a battle in depth (which ended in prepared positions). However, they frequently suffered crippling casualties, exaggerated their successes, and failed to defeat Soviet forces tactically. Crucially, they remained divided despite the existence of 'foreign' occupation.

During the civil war of the 1990s, guerrilla forces were no more successful than before. The militia armies of the warlords and the Taliban in the 1990s had to hold ground and provide internal security in their own territories. This necessitated the development of mobile, light infantry force structures, and it was these that provided obvious targets for the Western air forces in 2001.

The regrouping of the Taliban and the emergence of new insurgent groups since 2003 have been motivated by the idea of resistance to foreign occupation and the rhetoric of a more hard-line version of Islam. Yet insurgents are still opportunists and look for the chance to extend their power and prestige, their esteem amongst their peers, to acquire experience and therefore greater respect, and to justify their presence as protectors of the people, articulated through women, land, livelihood and law. They also wish to protect their narco-profits in the south-west against their rivals within the state apparatus of government of Afghanistan. Many Taliban aspire to be an Afghan Hezbollah, with jurisdiction over schools, clinics and security. The majority of Afghans, however, are 'hedging', waiting to see which side is the most likely to win. It is worth noting, therefore, that the insurgents of the 2010s are still plagued by the problems they have always faced: the shortage of skilled advisors and facilitators, disloyalty and disunity, logistical weaknesses and heavy casualties amongst commanders and comrades.

Money and power continue to affect the course of the conflict in Afghanistan. The insurgents play a critical role in Afghan economic relations as a guarantor of secure trading routes, essential in an economy that imports far more than it exports. Guerrillas are able to align incentives effectively and efficiently for many rural Afghans. The Taliban embodies a modern transformation and reconciliation of traditional and modern forms of legitimacy, creating an identity that is a potent nexus between pan-Pashtun identity, the traditional role of neutral Islamic mediators, and the legacy of an Afghan national sovereignty, but it does so on the basis of guarantees about the moral and material future of Afghans. The Taliban also has an effective strategy of building local capacity through social networks, creating what could best be characterized as a robust network-state grounded in local relationships and a sense of security. However, this sense of material security is contested by the Afghan government and the West. The offer of development aid, alternative livelihoods and work creation schemes that absorb unemployment; the creation of physical security at village level, the control of routes, access and economic conditions; and the evolution of improved communications through mobile phone technology, all point to the possible withering of the appeal of the insurgents. Material gain, moral security and evident military power will, ultimately, determine the loyalty of the majority of Afghans.

Assumed characteristics are misleading generalizations. Afghans are not culturally determined in their actions, but are reactive and adaptive. Their operations are shaped and influenced by a cultural 'lens', but they are also pragmatic. *Pashtunwali*, for example, is an ideal type of behaviour for Pashtuns that can be adapted and sometimes abandoned altogether. They will assess new situations and act accordingly. Non-Pashtun Afghans share this sense of pragmatism, adaptability and opportunism. We should be sceptical of over-arching theories about behaviour and character, and guard against the temptation to look for patterns while ignoring diversity. Above all, we should be conscious that Afghans adapt and change, even if their interpretations and their cultural lens appear to be immutable. This book has attempted to reassesse the Afghan wars, including those fought by Britain, Afghanistan's civil wars, the Soviet war and the recent insurgency, to examine Afghan strategy and operational planning, motivation, force structures, leadership, command and control, tactics, and attitudes towards negotiations. What emerges is a catalogue of consistent problems and constant change. Ultimately, war is still about friction, perception and human will, and, like humans, war remains a specimen beyond absolute scientific classification. Thus, it is well to be reminded of the Pashtun Warrior's Farewell:[5]

> Beloved, on a parchment white
> With my heart's blood to thee I write;

THE AFGHAN WAY OF WAR

My pen a dagger, sharp and clean
Inlaid with golden damascene,
Which I have used, and not in vain,
To keep my honour free from stain.

Now, when our house its mourning wears,
Do not thyself give way to tears:
Instruct our eldest son that I
Was ever anxious thus to die,
For when death comes, the brave are free
So in thy dreams remember me.

NOTES

PREFACE AND ACKNOWLEDGEMENTS

1. Cited by Olaf Caroe, *The Pathans* (Oxford: Oxford University Press, 1958), p. 526.

1. INTRODUCTION: A CONTESTED HISTORY

1. The question of who the Pashtuns are is not easily resolved. The British used the term Pathan, a corruption of the Indian pronunciation of Pay'than, to describe the frontier tribes from the Khyber to South Waziristan, but there was also an acknowledgement that these peoples were linked to the Pashtu-speaking groups in southern Afghanistan. Some of the problems of definition are dealt with later in this chapter, including origin myths.

2. Without doubt the best analysis of the operations on the North West Frontier from the British perspective is T. R. Moreman, *The Army in India and the Development of Frontier Warfare, 1849–1947* (London: Macmillan, 1998). See especially chapters 2 and 3.

3. Military culture has been much debated as a concept: see Theo Farrell and Terry Terriff, *The Sources of Military Change: Culture, Politics, Technology* (Boulder, CO.: Westview, 2002), pp. 3–21; Theo Farrell, 'Culture and Military Power', *Review of International Studies*, 24 (1998), pp. 407–16; Ann Swidler, 'Culture in Action: Symbols and Strategies', *American Sociological Review*, 51, 2 (April 1986); Peter Wilson, 'Defining Military Culture', *Journal of Military History*, 71, 1 (2008), pp. 11–43.

4. Patrick Porter, *Military Orientalism* (London: Hurst & Co., 2009).

5. George Crile's *Charlie Wilson's War* (London: Atlantic, 2007) has been made into a film, and features the same degree of fantasy and escapism as *Rambo III*, which was also set in the Soviet-Afghan War.

6. Lawrence Sondhaus, *Strategic Culture and Ways of War* (London: Routledge, 2006), p. 1.

7. B. H. Liddell-Hart, *The British Way in Warfare* (London: Faber and Faber, 1932); Alex Danchev, 'Liddell-Hart and the Indirect Approach', *Journal of Military History*, 63 (1999), p. 317.

8. See, for example, Brian M. Linn; Russell F. Weigley, 'The "American Way of War" Revisited', *Journal of Military History*, 66, 2 (April 2002), pp. 501–33.

9. Jeremy Black, 'Determinisms and Other Issues', *Journal of Military History*, 68 (2004), pp. 122–7; Jeremy Black, *Rethinking Military History* (London: Routledge, 2004), p. 142.

10. F. A. Kierman and J. K. Fairbank (eds), *Chinese Ways in Warfare* (Cambridge: Harvard University Press, 1974); W. P. Baxter, *The Soviet Way of War* (London: Brassey's, 1986); E. Jordaan, 'The South African Way of War: Operational Strategy and SANDF', paper presented at the Military Academy, Saldanha, September 2000; G. D. Bakshi, *The Indian Art of War: The Mahabharata Paradigm* (Delhi: Sharada, 2002); P. Layton, 'The New Arab Way of War, *US Naval Institute Proceedings*, 129/3 (March 2003), pp. 62–5.

11. Victor David Hanson, *The Soul of Battle: from Ancient Times to the Present Day* (New York: Free Press, 1999).

12. John A. Lynn, *Battle: A History of Combat and Culture from Ancient Greece to Modern America* (Boulder, CO.: Westview Press, 2003).

13. Ken Booth, *Strategy and Ethno-centrism* (New York: Holmes and Meier, 1979).

14. Ken Booth, 'The Concept of Strategic Culture Affirmed' in C. G. Jacobsen (ed.), *Strategic Power: USA-USSR* (New York: St Martin's Press, 1990), p. 121.

15. Booth, 'The Concept of Strategic Culture Affirmed', pp. 125–6.

16. Michael W. Doyle, *Ways of War and Peace: Realism, Liberalism and Socialism* (New York: W. W. Norton and Co., 1997), pp. 19–20.

17. Paul W. Schroeder, 'Historical Reality vs Neo-realist Theory', *International Security*, 19, 1 (1994), pp. 119 and 129.

18. Alastair Iain Johnston, 'Strategic Cultures Revisited: A Reply to Colin Gray', *Review of International Studies*, 25 (1999), pp. 522–3.

19. Colin S. Gray, 'Strategic Culture as Context: The First Generation of Theory Strikes Back', *Review of International Studies*, 25, 1 (1999), p. 60.

20. See, for example, Craig Cameron, *American Samurai: Myth, Imagination and the Conduct of Battle in the First Marine Division, 1941–1951* (Cambridge: Cambridge University Press, 1994); Gautam Chakravarty, *The Indian Mutiny in the British Imagination* (Cambridge: Cambridge University Press, 2005).

21. Porter, *Military Orientalism*, p. 193.

22. Joseph P. Ferrier, *History of the Afghans* (London: John Murray, 1858), p. 285.

23. John William Kaye, *History of the War in Afghanistan* (London: Richard Bentley, 1857), p. 145.

24. Patrick Macrory, *Signal Catastrophe* (London: Longman, 1969), p. 45.

25. Archibald Forbes, *The Afghan Wars, 1839–42 and 1878–80* (London: Seely & Co., 1892), p. 107.

26. Keith Stanski, '"So these folks are aggressive": An Orientalist Reading of "Afghan Warlords"', *Security Dialogue*, 40, 73 (2009), p. 88.

27. Hew Strachan, 'The British Way in Warfare' in David Chandler (ed.), *The Oxford History of the British Army* (Oxford: Oxford University Press, 1994), pp. 417–34.
28. Geoffrey Parker, *The Grand Strategy of Philip II* (New Haven, CT.: Yale University Press, 1998), p. 12.
29. Geoffrey Parker, *The Cambridge Illustrated History of Warfare: The Triumph of the West* (Cambridge: Cambridge University Press, 2000); Jeremy Black, *Rethinking Military History* (London: Routledge, 2004), p. 142.
30. Parker, *The Cambridge Illustrated History of Warfare*, p. 6.
31. Colin S. Gray, *Recognizing and Understanding Revolutionary Change in Warfare: The Sovereignty of Context* (Carlisle Barracks, PA., Strategic Studies Institute, 2006). See also MacGregor Knox and Williamson Murray (eds), *The Dynamics of Military Revolution* (Cambridge: Cambridge University Press, 2001), p. 12.
32. Brian Robson, *The Road to Kabul: The Second Afghan War, 1879–81* (London: Arms and Armour Press, 1986), pp. 15–21.
33. Sir Lawrence Freedman, 'Creating Power', Changing Character of War Annual Lecture, November 2010, Oxford University.
34. See Fred Donner, 'The Sources of Islamic Conceptions of War' in John Kelsay and James Turner Johnson (eds), *Just War and Jihad: Historical and Theoretical perspectives on War and Peace in Western and Islamic Traditions* (New York: Greenwood, 1991).
35. Alia Brahimi, *Jihad and Just War in the War on Terror* (Oxford: Oxford University Press, 2010), pp. 2 and 13.
36. Brahimi, *Jihad and Just War*, ch.4.
37. For an example of the militant justification, see http://abuqutaybah.blogspot.com/2006/10/fard-ayn.html Accessed November 2008.
38. Qur'an 8:60.
39. For Muslims, men and women are led astray by *Iblis* on the basis of rebellion against Allah, pride (Qur'an 2:34) or deception (Qur'an 20–22). Spiritual defence is possible through *ibadat* (devotions), the guidance of *Madhab* (path) jurisprudence and *jihad* (struggle). These general ideas are also intrinsic to Afghan rural culture.
40. Qur'an 32:5.
41. Qur'an 4:76.
42. Qur'an 60:8.
43. Linda T. Darling, 'Contested Territory: Ottoman Holy War in Comparative Context', *Studia Islamica*, 91 (2000), p. 140.
44. Darling, 'Contested Territory', p. 142.
45. E. Bosworth, *The Medieval History of Iran, Afghanistan and Central Asia* (London: Valorium Reprints, 1977).
46. Al-Utbi, *Kitab-i Yamini*, trans. James Reynolds (London: Oriental Translation Fund, 1858), pp. 335–6, 363 and 450.
47. Zia al-Din Barani, 'Tarikh-i Firoz Shahi' in H.M. Elliot and John Dowson (eds),

The History of India as Told by its Own Historians, vol 3 (London: Truebner and Co., 1869), p. 226.

48. Darling, 'Contested Territory', p. 161.
49. Donald L. Horrowitz, *Ethnic Groups in Conflict* (Berkeley, CA.: University of California Press, 1985); Steven Grosby, 'The Verdict of History: the inexpungable tie of primordiality—A response to Eller and Coughlan', *Ethnic and Racial Studies*, 17, 1 (1994), p. 168.
50. Roy Licklider, 'The Consequences of Negotiated Settlements in Civil Wars, 1945–1993', *American Political Science Review*, 89, 3 (1995), p. 685.
51. James D. Fearon and David D. Laitin, 'Ethnicity, Insurgency and Civil War', *American Political Science Review*, 97, 1 (February 2003), pp. 78 and 88. See also Charles King, 'The Myth of Ethnic Warfare', http://www.foreignaffairs.com/articles/57435/charles-king/the-myth-of-ethnic-warfare Accessed July 2010.
52. Anthony Smith, *Nationalism: Theory, Ideology, History* (Cambridge: Polity, 2001), p. 55.
53. Stathis Kalyvas, *The Logic of Violence in Civil War* (New York and Cambridge: Cambridge University Press, 2006).
54. Monica Duffy Toft, *The Geography of Ethnic Violence: Identity, Interests and the Invisibility of Territory* (Princeton, NJ.: Princeton University Press, 2003).
55. Bruce Gilley, 'Against the Concept of Ethnic Conflict', *Third World Quarterly*, 25, 6 (2004), pp. 1155–66.
56. Jon W. Anderson, *Doing Pakhtu: Social Organization of the Ghilzai Pashtun* (Ann Arbor: University Microfilms International, 1979), p. 15; Akbar S. Ahmed, *Millennium and Charisma among Pathans* (London: Routledge and Kegan Paul, 1976), p. 6.
57. Ahmed, *Millennium and Charisma among Pathans*, p. 7.
58. Fredrik Barth, *Political Leadership Among Swat Pathans* (London: London School of Economics Monograph, 1959).
59. Anderson, *Doing Pakhtu*, p. 15.
60. Charles Lindholm, *Generosity and Jealousy* (New York: Columbia University Press, 1982).
61. Anderson, *Doing Pakhtu*, p. 37.
62. Anderson, *Doing Pakhtu*, p. 36. See also Richard Tapper, 'Who are the Kuchi? Nomad Self-Identities in Afghanistan', *Journal of the Royal Anthropological Institute*, 14, 1 (March 2008), pp. 97–116.
63. Lars-Erik Cederman, Andreas Wimmer and Brian Min, 'Why Do Ethnic Groups Rebel? New Data and Analysis', *World Politics*, 62, 1 (January 2010), p. 97.
64. Cederman, Wimmer and Min, 'Why Do Ethnic Groups Rebel?', p. 97.
65. Ibid.
66. L. Kryuchkov, *Lichnoe Delo*, I (Moscow, 1996), p. 226. The veracity of Kryuchkov's views can be challenged by J. Prados, *Safe for Democracy: The Secret Wars of the CIA* (Chicago: Ivan R. Dee, 2006), pp. 485–7.

67. Mary Kaldor, 'Is Clausewitz Still Relevant?' Lecture at the Department of Politics and International Relations, Oxford University, 2009.
68. Arno Mayer, *The Furies: Violence and Terror in the French and Russian Revolutions* (Princeton: Princeton University Press, 2000); Stathis N. Kalyvas, *The Logic of Violence in Civil War* (Cambridge: Cambridge University Press, 2006), ch. 3 and 6.
69. Joanna Bourke, *An Intimate History of Killing: Face to Face Killing in Twentieth Century Warfare* (London: Granta, 1999).
70. Robert Johnson, *Lessons in Imperial Rule: Instructions for Infantrymen on the Indian Frontier* (London: Greenhill, 2008), Introduction.
71. L. Kryuchkov, *Lichnoe Delo*, I, p. 227; see also A. Kalinovskii, *A Long Goodbye: The Politics and Diplomacy of the Soviet Withdrawal from Afghanistan, 1980–1992* (Thesis at the London School of Economics, 2009).
72. George Modelski, 'International Settlement of Internal War' in James Rosenau (ed.), *International Aspects of Civil Strife* (Princeton: Princeton University Press, 1964), p. 143; in international relations, a similar view was put forward by A. F. K. Organski in World Politics, 2nd edn, (New York: Random House, 1968). I. William Zartman has evaluated the concept of stalemate in civil wars as a precursor to negotiations in 'The Unfinished Agenda: Negotiating Internal Conflicts' in Roy Licklider (ed.), *Stopping the Killing: How Civil Wars End* (New York: New York University Press, 1993).
73. Barbara F. Walter, *Committing to Peace: The Successful Settlement of Civil Wars* (Princeton: Princeton University Press, 2002), p. 3.
74. Axelrod cited in Walter, *Committing to Peace*, p. 22.
75. Mountstuart Elphinstone, *An Account of the Kingdom of Cabaul* (Karachi, 1839), pp. 198 and 326.
76. Ibid., p. 198.
77. Cited in Hutchinson, *Tirah*, p. 106.
78. C. E. Callwell, *Tirah, 1897* (London, 1911, republished with a new Introduction by Rob Johnson, Williamsburg, VA., 2010), pp. 34–5.
79. H. D. Hutchinson, *The Campaign in Tirah, 1897–1898* (1898, reprinted New Delhi: Lancer, 2008), p. 89.
80. H. W. Bellew, *The Races of Afghanistan, being a brief Account of the Principal Nations Inhabiting that Country* (Calcutta: Thacker and Spink, 1880), p. 55. See also *Report on the Yusufzais* by Henry Bellew, (Lahore: Punjab Government, 1864). IOR L/Mil/17/13/128.
81. Christian Tripodi, 'Peacemaking through Bribes or Cultural Empathy? The Political Officer and Britain's Strategy towards the North-West Frontier, 1901–45', *Journal of Strategic Studies*, 31, 1 (February 2008), pp. 137–8.
82. R. H. Macdonald, *Sons of the Empire: The Frontier and the Boy Scout Movement, 1890–1918* (Toronto and London: University of Toronto Press, 1993), p. 5.

83. Hutchinson, *Tirah*, p. 100.

84. Sir Terence Coen, *The Indian Political Service* (London: Chatto, 1971), pp. 37 and 43.

85. Ben Hopkins, *The Making of Modern Afghanistan* (New York and Basingstoke: Palgrave Macmillan, 2008); Ronald Inden, *Imagining India* (Oxford: Basil Blackwell, 1990).

86. Tripodi, 'Peacemaking through Bribes or Cultural Empathy?', p. 127.

87. *Instructions governing the employment of armed forces in the maintenance of tribal control of the NWF of India and in Baluchistan, 1940*, Confidential (Government of India, Defence Dept) IOR L/PS/20/B308; David M. Anderson and David Killingray (eds), *Policing the Empire: Government, Authority and Control, 1830–1940* (Manchester: Manchester University Press, 1991); Tim Moreman, '"Small Wars" and "Imperial Policing": The British Army and the Theory and Practice of Colonial Warfare in the British Empire, 1919–1939' *Journal of Strategic Studies*, 19, 4 (1996), pp. 105–31.

88. G. Bobrov, *Soldatskaya Saga* (Moscow, 2007), pp. 202–3.

89. A. Greshnov, *Afganistan: Zalozhniki vremeni* (Moscow, 2006), p. 148.

90. Tom A. Peter, 'Should anthropologists help US military in Iraq, Afghanistan wars?', *Christian Science Monitor*, 11 December 2009, http://www.csmonitor.com/World/Middle-East/2009/1211/Should-anthropologists-help-US-military-in-Iraq-Afghanistan-wars

91. Louis Dupree, 'The Retreat of the British Army from Kabul to Jalalabad in 1842: History and Folklore', *Journal of the Folklore Institute*, 4, 1 (June 1967), p. 52.

92. Dupree, 'The Retreat of the British Army from Kabul', p. 72.

93. Sayyid Mohammed Qasim Rishtiya, *Afghanistan dar qarn-i nuzdah* (Afghanistan in the nineteenth century) (Kabul, 1958).

94. Pierre Centlives and Michel Centlives-Demont, *Et si on parlait de l'Afghanistan?* (Neuchatel, 1988), p. 286.

95. M. Nazif Shahrani, 'The Future of the State and the Structure of Community Governance' in William Maley (ed.), *Fundamentalism Reborn? Afghanistan and the Taliban* (London: Hurst & Co., 1998), p. 229.

96. Anthony Hyman, 'Nationalism in Afghanistan', *International Journal of Middle East Studies*, 34, 2 (May 2002), p. 310.

97. Hyman, 'Nationalism in Afghanistan', p. 311.

98. James Belich, *The New Zealand Wars and the Victorian Interpretation of Racial Conflict* (Auckland: Auckland University Press, 1987).

99. Belich, see chapter 1, pp. 102–3, 107.

100. See, for example, Louis Dupree, 'The Retreat of the British Army from Kabul to Jelalabad in 1842: History and Folklore', *Journal of the Folklore Institute*, 4, 1 (June 1967), pp. 50–74.

101. Ranajit Guha, *Subaltern Studies*, I (Delhi: Oxford University Press, 1982), p. 3.

102. Edward Said, *Orientalism* (New York: Random House, 1978).

103. P. O'Hanlon and D. Washbrook, 'After Orientalism: Culture, Criticism and Politics in the Third World', *Comparative Studies in Society and History*, 34, 1 (1992), pp. 141–67; Robert Johnson, *British Imperialism: Histories and Controversies* (London: Palgrave, 2003), pp. 91–106.

104. David B. Edwards, 'Mad Mullahs and Englishmen: Discourse in the Colonial Encounter', *Comparative Studies in Society and History*, 31, 4 (October 1989), pp. 649–70.

105. 'The Correspondence of the Mullahs', in Colonel H. D. Hutchinson, *The Campaign in Tirah, 1897–98* (London, 1898), pp. 124–5.

106. J. Comaroff and J. Comaroff, *Ethnography and Historical Imagination* (Boulder, CO.: Westview, 1992), p. 17.

107. F. Barth, *Political Leadership Among Swat Pathans* (London: Athlone, 1959).

108. Akbar S. Ahmed, *Millennium and Charisma among Pathans: A Critical Essay in Social Anthropology* (London: Routledge and Kegan Paul, 1976).

109. David Edwards, 'Pretexts of Rebellion: the Cultural Origins of Pakhtun Resistance to the Afghan State', unpub. PhD thesis, University of Michigan, 1986.

110. Mukulika Banerjee was also able to show through her study of the Khudai Kitmatgars that such responses were not always military: M. Banerjee, *The Pathan Unarmed* (Karachi and Delhi, 2000).

111. S. W. A. Shah, *Ethnicity, Islam and Nationalism: Muslim Politics in the North West Frontier Province 1937–47* (Karachi: Oxford University Press, 1999), pp. 10–11.

112. Hutchinson, *Tirah*, p. 129.

113. D. Edwards, 'Pretexts of Rebellion: The Cultural Origins of Pakhtun Resistance to the Afghan State', unpub. PhD thesis, University of Michigan (1986), p. 75.

114. The region was called 'Yaghistan', the land of rebels. A. C. Yate, 'North West Frontier Warfare', *Journal of the Royal United Services Institution* (May 1900), p. 1176.

115. Bob Woodward, *Obama's War* (New York: Simon & Schuster, 2010).

2. DYNASTIC STRUGGLES AND POPULAR RESISTANCE IN AFGHANISTAN: THE ERA OF THE FIRST ANGLO–AFGHAN WAR

1. Ganda Singh, *Ahmad Shah Durrani* (Bombay: Asia Publishing House, 1959).

2. Hasan Kawun Kakar, *Government and Society in Afghanistan: The Reign of Amir Abd'al Rahman Khan* (Austin and London: University of Texas Press, 1979), p. 93.

3. The Sadr-i-a'zam was Mir Abdul-Qasim; the two *na'ib al-sultanat* were Naib Sarwar, the governor of Herat, and Muhammad Nabi; the *na'ib al-dawla* was Sardar Ghulam Rasul, the governor of Jellalabad; and the *wazir* was Sipah Salar Charkhi.

4. Kabul Diary, 37, 25 September 1895, Section F, November 1898, 5, 147–82. National Archives of India.

5. Ghulam Mohammed Ghobar, *Afghanistan der Masir-i Tarikh* (Afghanistan on the Highway of History) (Kabul: Book Publishing Institute, 1967), p. 653.
6. Kakar, *Government and Society*, p. 111.
7. David B. Edwards, *Heroes of the Age: Moral Fault Lines on the Afghan Frontier* (Berkeley, CA.: University of California Press, 1996), p. 197.
8. Mountstuart Elphinstone, *An Account of the Kingdom of Caubul* (London: Longmans, Green & Co. 1815), p. 514.
9. Thomas Barfield, *Afghanistan: A Cultural and Political History* (Princeton and Oxford: Princeton University Press, 2010), p. 105.
10. Percy Sykes, *A History of Afghanistan*, p. 383.
11. Cited in Stephen Tanner, *Afghanistan: A Military History* (Cambridge, MA: De Capo, 2002), p. 133.
12. Joseph Ferrier, *A History of the Afghans* (London: John Murray, 1858), pp. 151–6.
13. Robert G. Watson, *A History of Persia from the Beginning of the Nineteenth Century to the Year 1858* (London: Smith and Elder, 1866), pp. 262–5.
14. Edward Allworth (ed.), *Central Asia: A Century of Russian Rule* (New York: Columbia University Press, 1967), pp. 12–24.
15. *Correspondence Relating to Persia and Afghanistan*, Dost Mohammed to Mohammed Shah, pp. 27–8. Caroe, *Pathans*, pp. 314–15.
16. Kaye, *War in Afghanistan*, pp. 269–70, 278.
17. Kaye, *War in Afghanistan*, pp. 273–6; Tanner, *Afghanistan*, p. 138.
18. *Notes of General Semineau*, cited in Ferrier, *History of the Afghans*, pp. 250–54.
19. Ferrier, *History of the Afghans*, pp. 258–9, 403–6.
20. Ibid., p. 471.
21. Charles Metcalfe MacGregor, *Central Asia*, II, *A Contribution Towards the Better Knowledge of the Topography, Ethnology, Resources and History of Afghanistan* (Calcutta: Government of India Publication, 1871), p. 72.
22. Henry Marion Durand, *The First Afghan War* (London: Longmans, Green and Co., 1879), p. 167.
23. Durand, *The First Afghan War*, p. 168.
24. Durand, *The First Afghan War*,p. 166.
25. Ibid., pp. 167–8.
26. The walls of Ghazni were 60 feet thick with towers 150 feet high, and the entire edifice reached up along a steep ridge. The British field guns were inadequate to breach walls of such magnitude. The fact that Mohan Lal could obtain a deserter suggests that movement to and from the fortress by the Afghans was still possible, unless he was captured while accompanying the neighbouring Afghan field forces.
27. Patrick Macrory, *Signal Catastrophe*, p. 99; Tanner, *Afghanistan*, p. 141.
28. Captain Henry Havelock, *Narrative of the War in Affghanistan* [sic], vol. II (London: Henry Colburn, 1840), p. 96.

29. Ibid., p. 97.

30. Robert Johnson, *Spying for Empire: The Great Game in Central and South Asia, 1757–1947* (London: Greenhill, 2006), p. 87; Peter Hopkirk, *The Great Game* (Oxford: Oxford University Press, 1990), p. 279; L/P&S/7/35 and 38. IOR.

31. Durand, *First Afghan War*, p. 211.

32. Thomas Barfield, *Afghanistan: A Cultural and Political History* (Princeton and Oxford: Princeton University Press, 2010), p. 116.

33. J. A. Norris, *The First Afghan War* (Cambridge: Cambridge University Press, 1967), p. 333.

34. Ibid., p. 333.

35. Barfield, *Afghanistan*, p. 117. The Mughal freebooter and founder of the dynasty Babur had noted these tactics in the Baburnama during his raids across the Suleiman range. See the translation by Wheeler M. Thackston, *Baburnama* (New York: Modern Library, 2002).

36. Trevor Report, 31 August 1840, Secret Letters, enclosure 73, no. 5 of no. 140, 19 December 1840; Yapp, 'Revolutions in Afghanistan', p. 339; Barfield, *Afghanistan*, p. 119.

37. In Kabul, the muster rolls indicate that in August 1839 there were 5,662 cavalrymen and in 1840 there were 5,797. Kandahar raised 1,218. The numbers were limited because they represented what Dost Mohammad, or the Kandahari leaders, could afford. In times of war, these troops were augmented by larger numbers of 'irregulars'. See also Malcolm Yapp, 'The Revolutions of 1841–1842 in Afghanistan', *Bulletin of the School of Oriental and African Studies*, 27, 2 (1964), p. 338. Allowances in land were also still allocated in lieu of cash or grain in certain areas.

38. Macnaghten's estimates are unreliable, but indicate that even the British were concerned about the effects of inflation. British officers in command of local troops also reported on the difficulties of providing supplies and equipment when prices went up. See Managhten to Maddock, 17 June 1841, encl. Secret and Political Letters, L/PS/5/79, no. 90 of no. 68, 20 August 1841. IOR.

39. Trevor Report on the Janbaz, 7 June 1841, encl. Secret and Political letters, L/PS/5/160, 79, no. 109 of no. 68, 20 August 1841. IOR.

40. Lieutenant E. Haley, Report on the Hazirbash, 12 August 1841, encl. Secret and Political letters, L/PS/5/160, 79, no. 21 of no. 88, 21 October 1841. IOR.

41. Tax revenue increased from 225,000 to 900,000 rupees per annum. Barfield, p. 120.

42. A. C. Yate, 'North West Frontier Warfare', *Journal of the Royal United Services Institution* (May 1900), p. 1177.

43. Vincent Eyre, *The Kabul Insurrection of 1841–2*, ed. G. B. Malleson, (London, 1879), pp. 68–9; Lady Florentina Sale, *A Journal of the Disasters in Affghanistan, 1841–42* (London, 1843), pp. 7–8; C. A. Macgregor to W. H. Macnaghten, October 1841, encl. Political and Secret Letters, L/PS/5/167, 86, no 38A of 14, 17 May 1842. IOR.

44. Eyre, *Operations at Kabul*, pp. 8–15; Gleig, *Sale's Brigade in Afghanistan*, pp. 105–16; A. C. Yate, 'North West Frontier Warfare', *Journal of the Royal United Services Institution* (May 1900), p. 1183.

45. Yar Mohammed is alleged to have sent 400 men to Kandahar on 9 December 1840. Rawlinson to Colvin, private correspondence, 24 December 1841, encl. Political and Secret Letters, L/PS/5/165, 84, no. 66 of no. 25, 22 March 1842. IOR.

46. Cited in Tanner, *Afghanistan*, p. 153.

47. Shah Shuja to Lord Auckland, 25 February 1842, encl. Secret and Political Letters, L/PS/5/166, 85, no. 27 of no. 3, 21 April 1842. IOR.

48. Mackeson to Maj. Gen. Pollock, 11 February 1842, encl. Secret and Political Letters, L/PS/5/165, 84, no. 6 of no. 25, 22 March 1842. IOR.

49. Gleig, *Sale's Brigade in Afghanistan*, cited in A. C. Yate, 'North West Frontier Warfare', *Journal of the Royal United Services Institution* (May 1900), p. 1184.

50. Barfield, *Afghanistan*, pp. 122–3.

51. Mohan Lal, *Life of Dost Mohammed* (London, 1846), II, p. 392.

52. Ibid., p. 412.

53. Lieutenant Haley, Report on the Hazirbash, 12 August 1841, encl. Secret and Political Letters, L/PS/5/161, 80, no. 70 of no. 88, 21 October 1841.

54. Shah Shuja to Macnaghten, undated, encl. Secret and Political Letters, L/PS/5/158, 77, no. 21 of no. 47, 9 June 1841. IOR.

55. Burnes' Memorandum, 12 July 1840, encl. Secret and Political Letters, L/PS/5/151, 70, no. 35 of no. 99, 13 September 1840. IOR.

56. Yapp, 'Revolutions', pp. 345–6.

57. Lady Florentina Sale, p. 120.

58. Tanner, *Afghanistan*, p. 163.

59. Macnaghten to Macgregor, undated, encl. Secret and Political Letters, L/PS/5/163, 86, no. 9 of no. 2, 9 January 1842. IOR.

60. A. C. Yate, 'North West Frontier Warfare', *Journal of the Royal United Services Institution* (May 1900), p. 1182.

61. Tanner, *Afghanistan*, p. 172.

62. Anon. [G. R. Elsmie], *Epitome of Correspondence Regarding Our Relations with Afghanistan and Herat* (Lahore: Government Press, 1863), p. 50ff; T. A. Heathcote, *The Afghan Wars, 1839–1919* (Oxford: Osprey, 1980), p. 56.

63. Patrick Macrory, *Signal Catastrophe* (London: Hodder and Stoughton, 1966), p. 191; Heathcote, *The Afghan Wars*, p. 56.

64. These were Mir Misjadi and Abdullah Khan Achakzai; see Mohan Lal, *Life of Amir Dost Mohammed* (Oxford: Oxford University Press, reprinted 1978), II, pp. 350, 392 and 403. Other papers relating to this allegation were lost in Kabul in November 1841, except authorizations for the assassinations by Macnaghten and Connolly. Afghan popular culture maintains that the British issued a number of assassination warrants.

65. Sayyid Mohammed Qasim Rashtiya, *Afghanistan dar qarn-i nuzdah* (Afghanistan in the Nineteenth Century), 2nd edn (Kabul: Ministry of Press and Information, 1958).
66. Yapp, 'Revolutions of 1841–42', p. 380.
67. Louis Dupree, 'The Retreat of the British Army from Kabul to Jelalabad in 1842: History and Folklore', *Journal of the Folklore Institute*, 4, 1 (June 1967), pp. 61 and 63. Afghan popular accounts often confuse the First and Second Afghan Wars and the Soviet War, mixing technology, misnaming geographical locations and making other errors in chronology or personality.
68. On the final day of the retreat from Kabul, an Afghan group that came forward to negotiate was fired upon. Dupree, 'The Retreat of the British Army from Kabul', 67; Heathcote, *The Afghan Wars*, p. 63.
69. Captain Oldfield, cited in Heathcote, *The Afghan Wars*, p. 63.
70. Kaye, *Afghan War*, II, p. 121; A. C. Yate, 'North West Frontier Warfare', *Journal of the Royal United Services Institution* (May 1900), p. 1177.
71. Cited in Heathcote, *The Afghan Wars*, p. 69.
72. Cited in Heathcote, *The Afghan Wars*, p. 72.
73. Revd J. R. Gleig, *Sale's Brigade*, pp. 114–15.
74. Mohan Lal to Colvin, 29 January 1842, encl. Secret and Political Letters, L/PS/5/167, 86, no. 30A of no. 14, 17 May 1842. IOR; John Kaye, *History of the War in Afghanistan*, III, p. 424.
75. Conolly to Macgregor, 10 March 1842, encl. Secret and Political Letters, L/PS/5/165, 84, no. 91 of no. 25, 22 March 1842. IOR and Conolly to Macgregor, 1 March 1842, encl. Secret and Political Letters, L/PS/5/166, 85, no. 24 of no. 37, 21 April 1842; Kaye, *History of the War in Afghanistan*, III, pp. 424–6.
76. Lal to Macgregor, 25 April 1842, encl. Secret and Political Letters, L/PS/5/167, 86, no. 31 of no. 14, 17 May 1842. IOR.
77. Connolly to Macgregor, undated, encl. Secret and Political Letters, L/PS/5/167, 86, no. 4 of no. 36, 13 May 1842. IOR.
78. Lal to Macgregor, 25 and 27 April 1842, encl. Secret and Political Letters, L/PS/5/167, 86, no. 31 of no. 14, 17 May 1842. IOR.
79. Mirza Agha Jan to Macgregor, undated, encl. Secret and Political Letters, L/PS/5/167, 86, no. 23 of no. 15, 8 June 1842. IOR.
80. Fath Jang toPollock, undated, encl. Secret and Political Letters, L/PS/5/167, 86, no. 28 of no. 15, 8 June 1842. IOR.
81. Lal Memorandum, 29 June 1842, encl. Secret and Political Letters, L/PS/5/169, 88, no. 24 of no. 32, 17 August 1842. IOR.
82. Fath Jang to Pollock, undated, encl. Secret and Political Letters, L/PS/5/168, 87, no. 21 of no. 22, 18 July 1842. IOR.
83. Lal to Macgregor, 25 May 1842, encl. Secret and Political Letters, L/PS/5/168, 87, no. 16 of no. 22, 18 July 1842. IOR.

84. Lal to Shakespear, 10 June 1842, encl. Secret and Political Letters, L/PS/5/168, 87, no. 35 of no. 22, 8 July 1842, and Lal to Shakespear, 30 June 1842, encl. Secret and Political Letters, L/PS/5/169, 88, no. 21 of no. 32, 17 August 1842. IOR.

85. Lal to Macgregor, 21 June 1842, encl. Secret and Political Letters, L/PS/5/169, 88, no. 6 of no. 32, 17 August 1842. IOR.

86. Lal to Shakespear, 31 July 1842, encl. Secret and Political Letters, L/PS/5/170, 89, no. 13 of no. 38, 17 September 1842. IOR.

87. Lal to Shakespear, 17 July 1842, encl. Secret and Political Letters, L/PS/5/169, 88, no. 49 of no. 32, 17 September 1842. IOR.

88. Lal to Shakespear, 26 July 1842, encl. Secret and Political Letters, L/PS/5/169, 88, no. 59 of no. 32, 17 August 1842; Peshawar and Kabul Intelligence, 26 August 1842, encl. Secret and Political Letters, L/PS/5/170, 89, no. 98 of no. 38, 17 September 1842, and no. 46 of no. 49, 19 October 1842. IOR.

89. Mir Ali Murad Khani to Pollock, 2 August 1842, encl. Secret and Political Letters, L/PS/5/170, 89, no. 25 of no. 38, 17 September 1842. IOR.

90. Papers of Maj Gen Nott, letter to General Pollock, 22 Sept 1842, no. 747, Mss Eur F439/6 IOR.

91. General A. Snesarev, *Afganistan* (Moscow, 2002, first pub. 1921), p. 199.

92. Papers of Maj. Gen. Nott, letter to General Pollock, 17 Sept 1842, Mss Eur F439/6 IOR.

93. Papers of Maj. Gen. Nott, letter to General Pollock, 27 Sept 1842, Mss Eur F439/6 IOR.

94. Rawlinson to Hammersley, private correspondence, 31 December 1841, encl. Secret and Political Letters, L/PS/5/165, 84, no. 64 of no. 25, 22 March 1842. IOR.

95. Rawlinson to Hammersley, private correspondence, 9 January 1842, encl. Secret and Political Letters, L/PS/5/165, 84, no. 67 of no. 25, 22 March 1842. IOR.

96. Letter from Qandahar, 16 January 1842, encl. Secret and Political Letters, L/PS/5/165, 84, no. 85 of no. 25, 22 March 1842. IOR; Yapp, 'Revolutions', p. 374.

97. Rawlinson, Journal, 14 January 1842, 18 February 1842 and 19 February 1842. Papers of Sir Henry Creswicke Rawlinson, Special Collection, Royal Geographical Society, London.

98. Yapp, 'Revolutions', p. 380.

99. Rawlinson to Outram, private correspondence, 3 May 1842, PRO 30/12/62, National Archives, Kew.

100. Rawlinson to McNeill, [Teheran] private correspondence, 11 December 1841, folio 329, McNeill Papers, Mss Eur D1165 IOR.

101. Rawlinson, Journal, 25 May 1842, RGS.

102. Rawlinson, Journal, 5 January 1842, RGS; Kaye, *History of the War in Afghanistan*, III, p. 135.

103. Rawlinson's explanation of the revolt in the south and its course of events can be located in Rawlinson to Maddock, 6 March 1842, encl. Political and Secret Letters, L/PS/5/166, 85, no. 32 of no. 3, 21 April 1842. IOR.

104. Rawlinson, Journal, 12 January 1842. RGS; Durand, *First Afghan War*, pp. 406–7.

105. Rawlinson, Journal, 24 February 1842.

106. Durand, *First Afghan War*, p. 409.

107. Yapp, 'Revolutions', p. 369.

108. Rawlinson, Journal, 1 April 1842 and 5 April 1842.

109. Rawlinson, Journal, 1 May 1842.

110. Rawlinson to Hammersley, private correspondence, 17 April 1842, encl. Political and Secret Letters, L/PS/5/167, 86, no. 22 of no. 10, 17 May 1842. IOR.

111. Nott to Pollock, 30 May 1842, encl. Political and Secret Letters, L/PS/5/168, 87, no. 41 of no. 22, 8 July 1842. IOR; Kaye, *History of the War in Afghanistan*, III, pp. 313–16.

112. Rawlinson, Journal, 29 January 1842. RGS.

113. Yapp, 'Revolutions', p. 379.

114. Eyre, *Operations at Kabul*, pp. 66 and 115.

115. Vincent Eyre, cited in Tanner, *Afghanistan*, p. 168.

116. Yate, 'North West Frontier Warfare', p. 1186.

117. Captain E. Peach, Indian Staff Corps, cited in A. C. Yate, 'Sixty Years of Frontier Warfare', *Journal of the Royal United Services Institute*, XLIV (March 1900), p. 245.

118. Lady Florentina Sale, cited in Tanner, *Afghanistan*, pp. 168–9.

119. Jonathan Lee, *The 'Ancient Supremacy': Bukhara, Afghanistan and the Battle for Balkh, 1731–1901* (Leiden: Brill, 1996), p. 259.

120. Major Broadfoot, *Memoirs*, p. 149.

121. Yapp, 'Revolutions of 1841–2', p. 381.

3. ASYMMETRICAL WARFARE: THE AFGHAN CIVIL WAR (1863–8) AND THE SECOND ANGLO–AFGHAN WAR (1878–81)

1. Foreign Department, 4 November 1863, no. 8, enclosing no. 3, Copy of the Wakil's Diary from 11–13 August 1863. L/PS/5/257, vol. 176, enclosures to secret letters, 1863–66. IOR.

2. Ibid.

3. Foreign Department, secret, 5 October 1864, no. 6, enclosing despatch nos.766, 575, in no. 4, 19 September 1864, Cabul Diary. L/PS/5/257, vol. 176, enclosures to secret letters, 1863–66. IOR.

4. Foreign Department, secret, 5 October 1864, no. 6, enclosing despatch nos. 766, 575, in no. 4, 2–8 September 1864, Cabul Diary. L/PS/5/257, vol. 176, enclosures to secret letters, 1863–66. IOR.

5. Foreign Department, secret, 5 October 1864, no. 7, enclosing despatch nos. 527, 791 in no. 3, 26 September 1864, Cabul Diary. L/PS/5/257, vol. 176, enclosures to secret letters, 1863–66. IOR.

6. Foreign Department, secret, 9–15 September 1864, Cabul Diary. L/PS/5/257, vol. 176, enclosures to secret letters, 1863–66. IOR.

7. Foreign Department, secret, no. 1 of 1865, no. 3, enclosing dispatch, no. 23, 23 December 1864, Cabul Diary. L/PS/5/257, vol. 176, enclosures to secret letters, 1863–66. IOR.

8. Foreign Department, no. 1 of 1865, 23 December 1864, no. 3, from Lt. Col. H. W. Green (Superintendant Upper Scinde) to Sir Bartle Frere (Governor of Bombay), L/PS/5/257, vol. 176, enclosures to secret letters, 1863–66. IOR.

9. Foreign Department, no. 47 of 1865, 15 May 1865, no. 3, 10–13 March, Cabul Diaries, L/PS/5/257, vol. 176, enclosures to secret letters, 1863–66. IOR.

10. A. P. Thornton, 'The Re-opening of the Central Asian Question', *History Journal* (1956), pp. 123–6; P. Morris, 'Russia in Central Asia', *Slavonic Review*, 53 (1975), pp. 521–38; D. MacKenzie, 'Expansion in Central Asia: St Petersburg vs the Turkestan Generals (1863–66)', *Canadian Slavonic Studies*, 3 (1969), pp. 286–311.

11. Foreign Department, A of 1 July 1865, no. 3, 26 June 1865, no. 319, 594, 13–15 June, Cabul Diaries, Appendix I, Kabul Munshee received 12 June, L/PS/5/257, vol. 176, enclosures to secret letters, 1863–66. IOR.

12. Foreign Department, A of 1 July 1865, no. 3, 26 June 1865, no. 319, 594, 13–15 June, Cabul Diaries. L/PS/5/257, vol. 176, enclosures to secret letters, 1863–66. IOR.

13. Ibid.

14. The troops had only been paid two months' salary in the previous year, and the dispute appears to have been entirely financial.

15. Foreign Department, no. 124 of 1865, 28 August 1865, no. 3, 11–14 August, Cabul Diaries, L/PS/5/257, vol. 176, enclosures to secret letters, 1863–66. IOR.

16. Foreign Department, no. 124 of 1865, 12 September 1865, no. 3, 22–24 August, Cabul Diaries, L/PS/5/257, vol. 176, enclosures to secret letters, 1863–66. IOR.

17. Ibid.

18. Foreign Department, no. 140 of 1865, 19 October 1865, no. 3, 22–25 September 1865, Cabul Diaries, L/PS/5/257, vol. 176, enclosures to secret letters, 1863–66. IOR.

19. Foreign Department, no. 136 of 1865, 16 September 1865, no. 3, 1–4 Sept 1865, Cabul Diaries, L/PS/5/257, vol. 176, enclosures to secret letters, 1863–66. IOR.

20. Foreign Department, no. 140 of 1865, 19 October 1865, no. 3, 22–25 September 1865, Cabul Diaries, L/PS/5/257, vol. 176, enclosures to secret letters, 1863–66. IOR.

21. Ibid.

22. Foreign Department, no. 163 of 1865, 24 October 1865, no. 7, 6–9 October 1865, Cabul Diaries, L/PS/5/257, vol. 176, enclosures to secret letters, 1863–66. IOR.

23. Foreign Department, no. 117 of 1865, 18 October 1865, no. 3, 29 September–2 October with no. 163 of 1865, 18 October, no. 5, Cabul Diaries, L/PS/5/257, vol. 176, enclosures to secret letters, 1863–66. IOR.

24. Foreign Department, no. 163 of 1865, 24 October 1865, no. 7, 6–9 October 1865, Cabul Diaries, L/PS/5/257, vol. 176, enclosures to secret letters, 1863–66. IOR.

25. Barfield, *Afghanistan*, p. 137.

26. Christine Noelle, *State and Tribe in Nineteenth Century Afghanistan: The Reign of Amir Dost Mohammed Khan (1826–1863)* (Richmond: Curzon Press, 1997), pp. 11–13.

27. Frere, cited in Vartan Gregorian, *The Emergence of Modern Afghanistan* (Stanford, CA.: Stanford University Press), p. 84.

28. *Strength and Distribution and Armament of the Afghan Army*, Foreign Department, Secret-F, February 1893, nos. 224–229. National Archives of India.

29. Ghulam Mohammed Ghobar, *Afghanistan dar Masir-i Tarikh* (Afghanistan along the Highway of History) (Kabul: Book Publishing Institute, 1967), p. 596.

30. Kakar, *Government and Society in Afghanistan*, p. 16.

31. Lambert, 'Statement of Revenue and Expenditure of Afghanistan, 1877–78', 6 March 1884, Foreign Department, secret-F, 1886. National Archives of India.

32. Kakar, *Government and Society in Afghanistan*, p. 96.

33. J. P. Ferrier, *History of the Afghans* (London: John Murray, 1858), pp. 312–13.

34. *Report on the Second Afghan War*, strictly confidential, Captain Oliver for Major General MacGregor, Simla, 1885–6, p. 3. L/MIL/17/14/29/1. IOR.

35. Various estimates have been offered for state expenditure in this period. Lieutenant N. F. FitzG. Chamberlain estimated that the Afghan military budget totalled 1,921, 195 Kabul rupees (Kr) and was broken down as follows: Kr 1,781,233 on pay; Kr 120,235 Kabul Arsenal; Kr 19,727 Military Clothing Department. The total Afghan budget was thought to be Kr 7,982,390. Hensman, *The Afghan War of 1879–80*, p. 320; C. M. MacGregor, *The Second Afghan War: Official Account* (London: Intelligence Branch, 1908), pp. 634–5.

36. Hasan Kakar, *A Political and Diplomatic History of Afghanistan* (Leiden, Brill, 2006), p. 22; Barfield, *Afghansitan*, p. 138.

37. See P. S. A. Berridge, *Couplings to the Khyber* (Newton Abbot: David & Charles, 1969).

38. The 'gap' was not purely technological but also involved new forms of organization and impulses to imperial possession, but, in many instances, these changes revisited older concepts and should be seen in context. See Jeremy Black, *Western Warfare, 1775–1882* (Chesham: Acumen, 2001), p. 187.

39. Hensman, *The Afghan War of 1879–80*, p. 330.

40. Cited in Brian Robson, *The Road to Kabul: The Second Afghan War, 1878–1881* (Staplehurst: Spellmount, 1996), p. 35.

41. Sir Frederick Haines, CinC India, to Lord Lytton, 'Most Likely Plan in the Event

of War with Russia', November 1876, in *Report on the Second Afghan War*, confidential (Simla, 1885), L/MIL/17/14/29/1. IOR.

42. G. J. Alder, *British India's Northern Frontier, 1865–1895* (London: Longman, 1963), p. 165.

43. MacGregor, *The Second Afghan War: Official Account*, pp. 636–8.

44. Copies of the letters were reproduced in the appendices of Lord Roberts' autobiography, *Forty-One Years in India* (London: Macmillan, 1898).

45. Lytton to Charles Girdlestone, 27 July 1876, Lytton Papers, Letters Sent, 518/1, p. 435. Mss Eur E218. IOR; J. Martineau, *Life and Correspondence of the Right Honourable Sir Bartle Frere*, 2 vols. (London, 1895); Lytton's change of tone can be traced through the Afghan Committee's *Causes of the Afghan War* (London, 1879): see, for example, Sir R. Pollock to the Amir of Kabul, 1876, p. 99.

46. Afghan Committee, *Causes of the Afghan War*, p. 116.

47. Robson, *Road to Kabul*, p. 64.

48. Hasan Kakar, *A Political and Diplomatic History of Afghanistan, 1863–1901* (Leiden: Brill, 2006), pp. 26–7.

49. Howard Hensman, *The Afghan War of 1879–80* (London, 1881, reprinted New Delhi: Lancer, 2008), p. 321; Lord Roberts, *Forty-One Years in India*, pp. 559–63.

50. Hensman, *The Afghan War of 1879–80*, p. 321.

51. Ibid., p. 316.

52. Ibid., p. 314.

53. Ibid., p. 322.

54. Loc. cit.

55. Ibid., p. 324.

56. Police Report, no. 27, 14 April 1878, in MacGregor, *The Second Afghan War: Official Account*, p. 635.

57. Hensman, *The Afghan War of 1879–80*, p. 323.

58. Ibid., p. 213.

59. A full account of the British decision-making can be found in Ian F. W. Beckett, 'Cavagnari's *Coup de Main*', *Soldiers of the Queen: Journal of the Victorian Military Society*, 82 (September 1995), p. 24.

60. MacGregor, *Official History*, p. 28.

61. Robson, *Road to Kabul*, p. 76.

62. MacGregor, *Official History*, p. 29.

63. Ibid., p. 30.

64. Robson, *Road to Kabul*, p. 77.

65. MacGregor, *Official History*, pp. 33–4.

66. *Report on the Second Afghan War*, confidential (Simla, 1885), p. 24. L/MIL/17/14/29/1. IOR.

67. The payments were divided between the clans on the invasion routes used by the

British. The Kuki Khel, Malikin Khel, Zakka Khel, Shinwaris and Sipah clan received Rs 1,300 per month, while the Kambar Khel and Kamarai received Rs 500 and Rs 250 respectively. The *khans* of the Malikin Khel and Zakka Khel also received a personal allowance to ensure their compliance. *Strictly Confidential Report on the Second Afghan War* (Simla, 1885), L/MIL/17/14/29 and Mac-Gregor, *Official History*, p. 15.

68. There was an attempt to avoid a full-scale invasion of Afghanistan, but in order to force the Amir to negotiate it was thought a limited war that demonstrated the worthlessness of the Afghan army would suffice. Robson, *Road to Kabul*, pp. 69–70.

69. Lieutenant Alexander Hubert Mason, *Record of expeditions against the tribes on the North-West Frontier* (London, 1884), L/MIL/17/13/15. IOR.

70. MacGregor, *Official History*, p. 38.

71. Ibid., p. 40.

72. Ibid., p. 44.

73. Captain H. L. Nevill, *Campaigns on the North-West Frontier* (London, 1912, reprinted Nashville: Battery Press, 1999), p. 81.

74. MacGregor, *Official History*, p. 48.

75. Ibid., p. 49.

76. Ibid., p. 58.

77. Robson, *Road to Kabul*, p. 91.

78. MacGregor, *Official History*, p. 53.

79. Loc cit.

80. Nevill, *Campaigns on the North West Frontier*, p. 84; Robson, *Road to Kabul*, p. 80. The British eventually withdrew to Gandamack at the very end of the campaign without a shot being fired. Secret, no. 194, dated 24 August 1880, in A. W. Moore, *Narrative of events in Afghanistan from August 1878 to December 1880, and connected correspondence* (in continuation of memorandum dated 30 August 1878), Political and Secret Dept, India Ofrfice, 31 December 1880. L/PS/20/Memo5/17. IOR.

81. MacGregor, *Official History*, pp. 57–8.

82. Ibid., pp. 93–4.

83. Ibid., pp. 100 and 102.

84. Robson estimates the numbers as 1,800 and later as 3,500, although the *Official History* suggests that the numbers of Afghans that withdrew across the pass in the days preceding the battle were 18,000. The *Official History* also goes on to estimate the numbers on the pass at 4,000 in three regular regiments with eighteen guns, and a mule battery of six small guns which was unable to deploy in time for the engagement. Robson, *Road to Kabul*, pp. 84 and 86; MacGregor, *Official History*, pp. 98 and 114.

85. MacGregor, *Official History*, p. 118.

86. Ibid., p. 104.

87. Ibid., p. 106. One man was subsequently hanged and several others were transported for their treachery. Some eighteen soldiers of the regiment deserted during the battle, and a Havildar attempted to steal some of the Field Force's cash. *Confidential Reports on Officers of the Kurram Force*, Roberts Papers 7101–23–148. National Army Museum, London.

88. MacGregor, *Official History*, pp. 108 and 109.

89. Ibid., p. 107.

90. Ibid., p. 111.

91. Ibid., pp. 117–18.

92. Ibid., p. 120.

93. Ibid., p. 121.

94. Ibid., pp. 124–5. Robson, *Road to Kabul*, p. 93.

95. MacGregor, *Official History*, p. 126. The issue was reported critically by a British journalist attached to Roberts' force and caused some controversy, but there was no evidence of a deliberate policy of murder.

96. Robson, *Road to Kabul*, p. 93.

97. Ibid., p. 89.

98. It is estimated that 12,000 had died in the crossing of the Bolan Pass. G. R. Elsmie, *Field Marshal Sir Donald Stewart* (London, 1903), p. 216; Robson, *Road to Kabul*, pp. 71 and 89.

99. Countess of Balfour (ed.), *The History of Lord Lytton's Indian Administration, 1876–1880* (London, 1899), p. 322.

100. Robson, *Road to Kabul*, p. 103.

101. MacGregor, *Official History*, p. 184.

102. Ibid., p. 187. A full account of the defence of the Residency can be read on pp. 188–90.

103. *Report on the Circumstances of the Attack on the British Embassy at Kabul, September 1879*, A. R. Thompson et al., Secret, L/PS/18/A28. IOR.

104. MacGregor, *Official History*, p. 191.

105. Roberts to Foreign Secretary, telegram, 17 September 1879, *Correspondence Relative to the Affairs of Afghanistan* (London: HMSO, 1880) no. 1, 55, *Parliamentary Papers*, C2457.

106. General Sir Donald Stewart to Lady Stewart, 15 September 1879, Elsmie, *Sir Donald Stewart*, p. 286.

107. MacGregor, *Official History*, pp. 194–225.

108. Ibid., pp. 228–9.

109. Captain B. A. Coombe, *Letters from Afghanistan* (London, 1880), p. 80.

110. MacGregor, *Official History*, p. 304.

111. Ibid., p. 237.

112. Ibid., pp. 292–3.

113. Ibid., pp. 296.

114. Ibid., p. 300.

115. Ibid., *Official History*, pp. 303–5.

116. MacGregor, 8 October 1879, cited in Robson, *Road to Kabul*, p. 137, n.16.

117. Lytton to Roberts, private correspondence, 9 September 1879, Lytton Papers, 518/4, pp. 732–5.

118. In the *Confidential Report on the Second Afghan War* it was claimed that eighty-seven had been executed and seventy-six released. Executions were carried out under the following charges: dishonouring bodies, attacking escorts to release prisoners, murdering camp followers or residency members and wounded soldiers, possessing property of the embassy and being armed within a 5-mile radius of the city. p. 70. L/MIL/17/14/29/2. IOR; Robson, *Road to Kabul*, pp. 142–3.

119. *Confidential Report on the Second Afghan War*, p. 60. L/MIL/17/14/29/2. IOR.

120. MacGregor, cited in Robson, *Road to Kabul*, p. 143.

121. Roberts, Dispatch no. 1027, 23 January 1879, cited in Robson, *Road to Kabul*, p. 147.

122. *Confidential Report on the Second Afghan War*, p. 75. L/MIL/17/14/29/2. IOR; Hensman, *Afghan War*, pp. 162–3.

123. Hensman, *Afghan War*, p. 154.

124. Cited in Major E. W. Sheppard, *The Ninth Queen's Royal Lancers, 1715–1936* (London, 1939), p. 167.

125. Robson, *Road to Kabul*, p. 152.

126. Robson, *Road to Kabul*, p. 156.

127. Ibid., p. 157.

128. Combe, cited in Robson, *Road to Kabul*, p. 158.

129. Robson, *Road to Kabul*, p. 178.

130. Hensman, *Afghan War*, p. 264.

131. Robson, *Road to Kabul*, p. 170.

132. Hensman, *Afghan War*, p. 252.

133. Hensman, *Afghan War*, p. 176.

134. Ibid., p. 177.

135. Ibid., p. 259.

136. Ibid., p. 278.

137. *Notes by Members of the Political Committee on Mr Lepel Griffin's Report on 7 April 1880 on the State of Affairs in Northern Afghanistan*, confidential, L/PS/18/A33. IOR.

138. Robson, *Road to Kabul*, p. 187.

139. Stephen Wheeler, *The Ameer Abdur Rahman* (London: Bliss, Sands and Foster, 1895), p. 79.

140. *Further Correspondence Relating to the Affairs of Afghanistan* (London: HMSO, 1881), no. 1, p. 13 C2776 Parlimentary Papers.

141. Elsmie, *Sir Donald Stewart*, p. 326.

142. A. C. Yate, 'North West Frontier Warfare', *Journal of the Royal United Services Institution* (May 1900), p. 1176. Yate wrote: 'The nominal odds were 5 to 1 in favour of the Afghans, but two thirds of the Afghans would appear never to have come to close quarters'.

143. General E. F. Chapman, *Blackwood's Magazine* (February 1902), p. 262.

144. Captain Elias, *RUSI Journal*, XXIV, pp. 669–70.

145. Robson, *Road to Kabul*, pp. 194–5.

146. Lieutenant G. Robertson, *Kurram, Kabul and Kandahar* (Edinburgh, 1881), p. 181.

147. Robson, *Road to Kabul*, p. 206.

148. Ibid., p. 215.

149. The structure was erected in 1959 by King Zahir Shah and has an inscription by Malalai: 'If you do not taste martyrdom today on this field of Maiwand, By Allah, you will lead a life of shame forever more'. The 1924 memorial, the *Minar-i elm wa Jahil* (Column to Knowledge and Ignorance), was commissioned by King Amanullah. King Nadir Shah also erected a monument, the *Minar-i Abdul Wakil Khan*, to commemorate a general killed in action against the Tajik leader, Habibullah.

150. James Ferguson, *Taliban* (London: Bantam, 2010), p. 133.

151. Correspondence with India, secret, encl. no. 56, in no. 251, dated 19 December 1879, Colonel St John's [British Political Officer at Kandahar] account, pp. 111–12. L/PS/7/23. IOR.

152. Correspondence with India, secret, no. 255, dated 31 December 1879. L/PS/7/23. IOR.

153. *Narrative of Events in Afghanistan, 1878–1880 and Connected Correspondence*, secret, p. 206. L/PS/18/A43. IOR.

154. Colonel St John asked him to be more specific. Government of India to Secretary of State, secret, no. 90, 7 April 1880. L/PS/7/25. IOR.

155. Actual news of Ayub's advance appeared in the Afghan Papers, presented before Parliament in 1880, no. 3, p. 3, cited in *Narrative of Events in Afghanistan, 1878–1880 and Connected Correspondence*, secret, L/PS/18/A43, p. 209, IOR. The need for reinforcements was outlined in secret, no. 219, dated 12 October 1880. The British believed they had little to fear. It was reported in early June that the intelligence of the defeat inflicted on the tribes by Sir Donald Stewart near Ghazni had produced a profound impression on the Kabuli soldiers, increasing their anxiety to return to their homes. *Narrative of Events in Afghanistan, 1878–1880*, L/PS/18/A43 p. 207. L/PS/18/A43. IOR.

156. Robson, *Road to Kabul*, p. 222; Correspondence with India, secret, no. 185, dated 17 August 1880. L/PS/7/26. IOR.

157. News of advance of the Luinab with 2,000 horse towards Zamindawar was the first verifiable intelligence the British received, Correspondence with India, secret, no. 185, 17 August 1880. L/PS/7/26. IOR.

NOTES pp. [131–135]

158. *Correspondence Relating to the Affairs of Afghanistan* (London: HMSO, 1880), no. 3, p. 6, Parliamentary Papers, C2475. *Official History*, pp. 479–80.

159. *Official History*, p. 485. See also Correspondence with India, secret, no. 175, 3 August 1880. L/PS/7/26. IOR.

160. The commander was an Alizai, and no doubt felt pressured by his clan loyalties to change sides. *Official History*, p. 488. The defeat of the mutineers is described on pp. 490–91.

161. Captain Harris, DAQMG, *Reports and Narratives of Officers who were Engaged at the Battle of Maiwand, 27 July 1880* (India Intelligence Branch, 1881), p. 19.

162. *Official History*, p. 487.

163. General Haines, cited in Robson, *Road to Kabul*, p. 227; *Official History*, p. 496.

164. *Official History*, p. 499.

165. Ibid ., pp. 502–3.

166. Ibid., p. 506.

167. Ibid., p. 508.

168. General Burrows estimated there were between 25,000 and 50,000, and the *Official History* also suggested a figure of 23,000, *Official History*, Appendix XXVIII, p. 696. Mirza Mohammed Akbar believed there were 6,000 regulars from Herat, 1,500 men who deserted from the Wali and an unknown number of irregulars. The Intelligence Branch noted that the figures cited for the number of *ghazis*, 20,000, was 'probably exaggerated'. Interestingly, Ayub Khan's army also consisted of officers from the Ghilzais, Logaris and Tajiks. Saidal Khan, brother of Ghulam Haider, commanded the regular infantry.

169. *Official History*, p. 508.

170. Robson, *Road to Kabul*, p. 233.

171. *Official History*, Appendix XXVIII, p. 697.

172. Ibid., p. 508.

173. Ibid., pp. 510 and 511.

174. Ibid., pp. 509–10.

175. Major A. C. Yate, 'Sixty Years of Frontier Warfare', *Journal of the Royal United Services Institution*, XLIV, 265 (March 1900), p. 238.

176. Major A. C. Yate, 'North West Frontier Warfare', *Journal of the Royal United Services Institution*, (May 1898), p. 1175; Vincent Eyre, *Operations at Kabul*, ch.VI; Kaye, *Afghan War*, II, pp. 245–50.

177. *Official History*, p. 513.

178. Ibid., p. 515.

179. This event was described by one of Ayub Khan's officers. *Official History*, pp. 519–20.

180. *Official History*, p. 524; Robson, *Road to Kabul*, p. 238.

181. The Persians greeted Maiwand as 'a piece of good news' according to the Meshed Agent, 7 August 1880, in Mr Thomson's no. 195 of 1880. *Narrative of Events*,

p. 211. L/PS/18/A43. IOR. However, Ayub Khan must also have been aware that he could not entirely desert his base in Herat, and the further he marched towards Kandahar the more vulnerable he became to a Persian *coup de main.*

182. Robson, *Road to Kabul*, p. 241.
183. *Official History*, p. 532; *Narrative of Events*, L/PS/18/A43, secret, p. 215. IOR. Some 12,500 were expelled. Letter from Colonel St John, 7 October 1880, cited in ibid.
184. *Official History*, p. 537.
185. Ibid., pp. 541–2.
186. The decision to send Roberts can be located in Home Correspondence, no. 658 of 1880, L/PS/3 and telegram, 3 August 1880. L/PS/7/26. IOR.
187. Hensman, *Afghan War*, p. 550. The Afghans believed that a contest with a British formation on 31 August had gone their way, and they did not realize that this was only a reconnaissance. They believed that the position they occupied could therefore be held for some time. See pp. 498 and pp. 513–14, including details of how Afghan troops were supplied.
188. Hensman, *Afghan War*, p. 505.
189. Ibid., p. 549.
190. Ibid., pp. 551–2.
191. Musa Jan, the young man proclaimed Amir in December 1879, and other fugitives from Ghazni went to Herat on 10 September but later fled to Persia, where they became known as the 'Afghan Exiles'. Letter from Herat, 26 September, in Thomson's no. 253 of 1880. Cited in *Narrative of Events*, L/PS/18/A43. IOR.
192. Robson, *Road to Kabul*, p. 267.
193. Telegram from Colonel St John, 2 December 1880 in Mr Lyall's demi-official letter, 15 December 1880. The British pondered whether to accept and perhaps arm Ayub Khan in the partition plan, but later rejected the idea. Home, no. 949 of 1880, telegram, 13 December 1880, L/PS/3.
194. Ayub Khan's strength in September 1880 was 2,000 *sowars* and some guns at Zemindawar, although he could call on a number of irregulars. The loyalty of this element of his force was the key weakness of his army. Meshed Agent, 26 September 1880, in Thomson's no. 253 of 1880. Cited in *Narrative of the War in Afghanistan*, secret, L/PS/18/A43 IOR.
195. Secretary of State to Viceroy [Lord Ripon], 31 July 1880, cited in R. A. Johnson, '"Russians at the Gates of India?" Planning the defence of India, 1885–1900', *Journal of Military History*, 67 (2003), p. 706; Kakar, *Government and Society in Afghanistan*, p. xxi.
196. Ayub Khan was reported to have mistreated Heratis, and there was a prospect of a rising by the city's inhabitants and the Aimaks against him. Secret, no. 236 in December 1880, and Home Correspondence, no. 897 of 1880, telegram, 30 November 1880. L/PS/3 IOR. Herati troops broke up an intended confedera-

tion against him. Home Correspondence, no. 949 of 1880, telegram, 17 December 1880. L/PS/3 IOR.

197. Roberts' Memorandum of 12 May 1880, secret, para. 32, in no. 208, dated 14 September 1880, *Narrative of Events*, p. 230. L/PS/18/A43 IOR.

198. *Narrative of Events*, secret, p. 231, L/PS/18/A43 IOR.

199. Colonel J. W. Ridgeway to Foreign Office, 20 December 1886, cited in Kakar, *Government and Society*, pp. 96–7.

200. Kabul Diary, 20–23 February 1892, L/PS/7/65, p. 959. IOR; Kayz Mohammed, *Saraj al-Tawarikh* (The Lamp of History) (Kabul: Afghan Government Publication, 1915), p. 642; Kakar, *Government and Society*, p. 97.

201. Newswriter in Kandahar to Government of India, Simla, telegram, 5 November 1880, no. 8, p. 1945 L/PS/7/26 IOR; Peshawar Agency Diary, 20 December 1899, no. 179. L/PS/7/119 IOR.

202. Kayz Mohammed, *Saraj al-Tawarikh*, p. 554.

203. Kakar, *Government and Society*, p. 98.

204. Peshawar Diary, 31 May 1885, p. 225, L/PS/7/44 IOR.

205. Kabul Diary, 5 August 1887, p. 1843, L/PS/7/50 IOR.

206. Kandahar Diary, 1 February 1883, p. 762, L/PS/7/35 IOR.

207. Kabul Diary, 26 March 1890, p. 1241. L/PS/7/36 IOR; Kabul Diary, 11 July 1896, Letter no. 2090-F/96. L/PS/7/87 IOR.

208. Kakar, *Government and Society*, p. 98.

209. The colonel was paid a handsome 200 kabulis, with a sliding scale of pay for each of the subordinate ranks. The second in command was the Nap or Adjtan; there were four Sil Mishar, or Ressaldars; four Parak Mishar (commander of fifty), or jemadars; one Mirza (head of admininistration); one Kotnap (Major) who ran the pay and accounts; one Landakwar (Sergeant) or 'sajan', who was in charge of rations and forage. Some sub-ranks, like Mir Akhors, were excused guard duty or given other privileges; Sowars were paid 20 *kabulis*. Lt. Col. Charles Edward Yate, *Afghan Cavalry* (Simla: Government of India, 1893), p. 1. L/MIL/17/14/19 IOR.

210. J. W. Ridgeway, *Strength of Afghan Troops in Turkestan and Badakshan*, September 1886, L/PS/18/A70 IOR; Yate, *Afghan Cavalry*, p. 4. L/MIL/17/14/19 IOR.

211. Yate, *Afghan Cavalry*, p. 2. L/MIL/17/14/19 IOR.

212. Ibid., p. 3.

213. *Military Report on Afghanistan* (Calcutta: Government of India, 1906), pp. 201–2. L/MIL/17/14/4 IOR.

214. *Military Report on Afghanistan*, p. 197. L/MIL/17/14/4 IOR.

215. David B. Edwards, *Heroes of the Age: Moral Fault Lines on the Afghan Frontier* (Berkeley, CA.: University of Califormia Press, 1996), pp. 118–19.

216. Mir Agha Sahibzada to the Peshawar Commissioner, Peshawar Diary, 8 October 1891, p. 764. L/PS/7/64 IOR.

217. Kayz Mohammed, *Saraj al-Tawarikh*, p. 527; Kakar, *Government and Society*, p. 110.

218. Kayz Mohammed, *Saraj al-Tawarikh*, p. 622.

219. *Military Report on Afghanistan*, p. 191. L/MIL/17/14/4 IOR.

220. Peshawar Diary, 29 October 1895, no. 20, L/PS/7/83 IOR; Kabul Diary, 28 April-1 May 1894, p. 757. L/PS/7/74 IOR.

221. Kabul Diary, 21–24 April 1894, p. 647. L/PS/7/74 IOR; Kabul Diary, 28 April-1 May 1894, p. 757. L/PS/7/74 IOR.

222. *The Military Resources of Afghanistan*, 23 May 1887. L/PS/18/A78 IOR. *Kitab-i Qanun-i Afghanistan* (Books on the Payment of the Army of Afghanistan), (Kabul, n.d.) cited in Kakar, *Government and Society*, p. 308.

223. Kayz Mohammed, *Saraj al-Tawarikh*, p. 1172.

224. Kabul Diary, 11 July 1896, Letter no. 2090 F (96). L/PS/7/87 IOR.

225. Kakar, *Government and Soviety*, p. 112.

226. Riyazi, *Kulliyat-i Riyazi*, p. 245.

227. Nancy Tapper, 'Abd'ur Rahman and the Pashtun Colonization of Afghanistan Turkistan' in Richard Tapper (ed.), *The Conflict of Tribe and State in Iran and Afghanistan* (London: Croom Helm, 1983), p. 235.

228. Edwards, *Moral Fault Lines*, p. 98.

229. Ibid., p. 111.

230. Robert Johnson, 'The Penjdeh Incident, 1885', *Archives*, XXIV, 100 (April 1999), pp. 28–48.

231. Sir Peter Lumsden to Earl Granville, 29 March 1885, FO 65/1238. NA; Johnson, 'The Penjdeh Incident', p. 43.

232. Gladstone to Earl Granville, 24 April 1885, PRO 30/29/129. NA.

233. Roberts to Sir Henry Rawlinson, 3 May 1885, 97–1/CXXX, Roberts Papers, National Army Museum.

234. H. M. Durand, cited in P. Sykes, *Sir Mortimer Durand* (London: Cassell and Co., 1926), pp. 146 and 154.

235. Kayz Mohammed, *Saraj al-Tawarikh*, p. 466; M. Nabi, *Sawal wa Jawab-i Dawlati* (The Amir's Interviews with the Viceroy of India) (Kabul: Government of Afghanistan Publication, 1885), p. 15.

236. Sultan Mahommed, *Life of Abdur Rahman* (London: John Murray, 1900), I, p. 283. Muhammed Yousaf Riyazi estimated the number as 60,000. M. Y. Riyazi, 'Ayn Waqai' in *Kulliyat-i Riyazi* (The Collected Works of Riyazi) (Meshed, 1907), pp. 2–5 and 8.

237. Cited in P. Sykes, *Sir Mortimer Durand* (London: Cassell and Co., 1926), p. 198.

238. Kakar, *Government and Society in Afghanistan*, p. 176.

239. Government of India to India Office, 7 September 1888, Correspondence with India, L/PS/7/55 IOR.

240. Kakar, *Government and Society in Afghanistan*, p. xxii.

241. Viceroy to Foreign Office, 4 August 1892; Morier to Foreign Office, 26 September 1892; India Office to Foreign Office, 23 August 1892 in Foreign Office Memorandum, 24 January 1893, FO65/1460. NA.

242. Kakar, *Government and Society in Afghanistan*, p. 175.

243. Ibid., p. 177.

244. Abdur Rahman, *Risala-i Muwaizza* (Book of Advice) (Kabul, 1894), pp. 59–60; Mullah Abu Bakr et al., *Taqwim al Din* (The Calendar of the Religion) (Kabul, 1889), pp. 67–74.

4. THE PASHTUN RISING, 1897–8

1. Colonel H. D. Hutchinson, *The Campaign in Tirah, 1897–98* (London, 1898), p. 1.

2. K. M. L. Saxena, *The Military System of India, 1859–1900* (New Delhi, 1974), pp. 268–9.

3. A. K. Slessor, 'Why and How the Afridis Rose', [*Colburn's*] *United Services Magazine*, 20 (1899–1900), pp. 388–400.

4. W. K. Fraser-Tytler, *Afghanistan* (Oxford: Oxford University Press, 1950), p. 196; Robert Warburton, *Eighteen Years in the Khyber, 1879–97* (London: John Murray, 1900). The mullah conspiracy was advocated most strongly by R. I. Bruce, *The Forward Policy and its Results* (London, 1900).

5. Captain H. L. Nevill, *Campaigns on the North West Frontier* (London, 1912), pp. 275–6.

6. The contemporary view of the military threat to India was exemplified by Major General Sir C. M. MacGregor, *The Defence of India: A Strategical Study* (Simla, 1884). The Russian view can be found in V. I. Bovykin, *Ocherki istoriivneshnei politiki Rossii* (Essays in the History of Russia's Foreign Policy) (Moscow, 1960). See also E. L. Steinberg, 'Angliiskikaia versiia o "russkoi ugroze" Indii v XIX-XX v.v'. (The English Version of the 'Russian Threat' to India), *IZ*, 33 (1950), pp. 47–66. The most prominent scholarship on the question of the Russian threat includes D. R. Gilliard, *The Struggle for Asia 1828–1914* (London, 1977); Edward Ingram, *The Beginnings of the Great Game in Asia, 1828–34* (Oxford: Oxford University Press, 1979); M. Yapp, *Strategies of British India* (Oxford: Oxford University Press, 1980); G. J. Alder, *British India's Northern Frontier, 1865–1895* (London, 1963) and A. P. Thornton, 'The Reopening of the Central Asian Question', *Historical Journal* (1956), pp. 123–36.

7. R. A. Johnson, '"Russians at the Gates of India"? Planning the Defence of India, 1885–1900', *Journal of Military History*, 67 (July 2003), pp. 679–744.

8. Christian Tripodi, 'Peacemaking through bribes or cultural empathy? The political officer and Britain's strategy towards the North-West Frontier, 1901–1945', *Journal of Strategic Studies*, 31, 1 (2008), pp. 123–51; Robert A. Huttenback, 'The

"Great Game" in the Pamirs and the Hindu Kush: The British Conquest of Hunza and Nagar', *Modern Asian Studies*, 9, 1 (1975), pp. 1–29.

9. Lord Roberts to Lord Kitchener, 28 January 1907, WO 30/57/28, Kitchener Papers, National Archives. Roberts planned for the creation of volunteer lines of communication troops and 24,000 were raised by 1893. General Roberts, Principles of Army Administration in India, 1 April 1893, L/Mil/7/7056 IOR.
10. D. Edwards, *Heroes of the Age: Moral Fault Lines on the Afghan Frontier* (Berkeley, CA.: University of California Press, 1997), p. 83.
11. The Amir defeated the pretender to the throne, Ayub Khan, in 1881; the Ghilzai revolt (1886) L/PS/7/44 and L/PS/7/47 IOR; the Badakshan revolt (1888) L/PS/7/55 IOR; and the Hazara revolt (1891–3) L/PS/7/55 and Confidential Letters, Durand Papers, D 727/11.
12. General Sir William Lockhart (1841–1900) joined the Bengal Native Infantry in 1858 and served in Bhutan, Abyssinia, Afghanistan, Burma and on the North West Frontier. From 1890 he commanded the Punjab Frontier Force (the 'Piffers') and was promoted to General in 1896. He subsequently became Commander in Chief in India in 1898.
13. Captain H. L. Nevill, *Campaigns on the North West Frontier* (London, 1912), pp. 164–208.
14. Major Deane, Political Agent in Malakand to Foreign Secretary of the Government of India, 9 May 1897, cited in Ahmed, *Millennium and Charisma*, p. 105.
15. Captain A. H. McMahon and Lieutenant A. D. G. Ramsay, *Report on the Tribes of Dir, Swat and Bajaur* (Peshawar, 1916, revised edn), pp. 49ff.
16. General Sir William Lockhart to Foreign Secretary of the Government of India, 19 November 1897, Files of the Government of the Punjab in the Foreign Department, Frontier Branch, no. 78. Peshawar, Pakistan.
17. Yate, 'North West Frontier Warfare', p. 1187. Lieutenant Colonel J. G. Ramsay drew similar conclusions in 'The Tactical Principles and Details Best Suited to Warfare on the Frontiers of India', *Journal of the Royal United Services Institution* (1899), p. 103.
18. Colonel H. C. Wylly, *From the Black Mountain to Waziristan* (London: Macmillan, 1912), p. 314. Of the 2,000 Afridis employed within the Indian Army, some had deserted, prompting the authorities to deploy the remainder away from the theatre of operations. Nevertheless, the majority remained in service and some fought at Malakand despite the entreaties of the Pashtun fighters that they should desert.
19. It was rumoured that 80,000 rifles had been sold by the Amir of Afghanistan to the tribesmen.
20. Wylly, *From the Black Mountain to Waziristan*, p. 384.
21. *Tirah Operations, 1897–98*, report by Captain Flamsted Walters, 1900. L/Mil/17/13/99 IOR.

22. See, for example, James Spain, *The Pathan Borderland* (The Hague, 1963), ch.5; Arthur Swinson, *North West Frontier* (London: Hutchinson, 1967), pp. 283–6; Byron Farwell, *Queen Victoria's Little Wars* (London: Allen Lane, 1973), pp. 318–29.

23. The tribal security system was based on a series of layers of defence. At village level, a *jirga* (council) could nominate up to forty men to act as *arbakai* (constabulary) or its equivalent to tackle recalcitrant locals. *Chelweshtai* and *tsalweshtai* represented larger groupings or small forces with a more extensive remit, including the protection of a larger area of territory or punitive actions against rival clans and factions. The *lashkar* was the largest grouping and could reach numbers of 2,000. It was not tied to any localized defence and, if combined with other groups, could act as the means to raise large numbers of fighters in relatively short periods of time.

24. W. S. Churchill, 'The Ethics of Frontier Policy', *United Services Magazine*, 17 (1898), p. 506, cited in T. R. Moreman, 'The British and Indian Armies and North West Frontier Warfare, 1849–1914', *Journal of Imperial and Commonwealth History*, 20, 1 (1992), p. 40.

25. Cited in Nick Evans, '"Playing the Game off their Own Bats": The Peninsular War, British Light Infantry and the Twentieth Century Legacy', *Mars and Clio: Newsletter of the British Commission for Military History*, 27 (Spring 2010), p. 11.

26. A. K. Slessor, 'Field Fortifications in Tirah', *United Services Magazine*, 19 (1899), pp. 400–09.

27. Hutchinson, *Tirah*, p. 129.

28. Moreman, 'The British and Indian Armies and North West Frontier Warfare', p. 47.

29. T. R. Moreman, 'The Arms Trade and the North West Frontier Pathan Tribes, 1890–1914', *Journal of Imperial and Commonwealth History*, 22, 2 (1994), pp. 193, 198 and 205.

30. A. C. Yate, 'North West Frontier Warfare', *Journal of the Royal United Services Institute of India*, 42, 248 (October 1898), p. 1191.

31. G. F. R. Henderson, *The Science of War: A Collection of Essays and Lectures, 1891–1903* (London: Longmans, Green & Co., 1905), pp. 345–6.

32. E. Peach, 'The Tactical Principles and Details Best Suited to Warfare on the Frontiers of India', *Journal of the Royal United Services Institute of India*, 28, 137 (October 1899), p. 344.

33. Cited in Moreman, p. 55.

34. R. I. Bruce, *The Forward Policy and Its Results* (London: Longmans, Green & Co., 1900), p. 249.

35. Edwards, *Heroes of the Age*, p. 83; S. M. Khan, *The Life of Abdur Rahman Khan* (London, 1906), pp. 175–7.

36. Cited in Charles Miller, *Khyber: British India's North West Frontier* (London: MacDonald and Jane's, 1977), p. 240.

37. Abdur Rahman was confronted by loyal and more belligerent factions in Kabul and had to calibrate his responses carefully, taking care to avoid provocation of the British. Bruce, *The Forward Policy*, pp. 252ff.

38. Confidential Letters, Durand Papers, D 727/8 IOR; P. Sykes, *Sir Mortimer Durand* (London: Cassell and Co., 1926), pp. 199–200.

39. *The Risings of the North West Frontier, 1897–98*, (Allahabad: Pioneer Press), p. 150.

40. Amir Abdur Rahman, 23 September 1897, cited in Hutchinson, *Tirah*, p. 15.

41. Comissioner Peshawar District to Punjab and Simla, 8 and 10 September, and 2 October 1897, telegrams, 78, Frontier Branch, Foreign Department, Government of the Punjab. Directorate of Archives, North West Frontier province, Shahi Bagh, Peshawar.

42. Hutchinson, *Tirah*, pp. 84–5.

43. Khyber Political Diaries, 28 June 1897; 7 August 1897, L/PS/7 IOR.

44. Deputy Commissioner Khyber to Punjab and Simla, 14 and 16 August 1897, telegrams, 76, Frontier Branch, Foreign Department, Government of the Punjab. Directorate of Archives, North West Frontier Province, Shahi Bagh, Peshawar.

45. Adam Khan (Khambar Khel) to his brother Muhammad Zaman Khan, Kabul, 18th Jamadi-ul-Awal 1315 AH (15 October 1897), and Sherdil Khan and Abdul Rahim, son of Malik Sinjab Khan Orakzai to Malik Sinjab Khan, 28th Jamadi-ul-Awal 1315 AH (25 October 1897) in Hutchinson, *Tirah*, pp. 123 and 125.

46. Theodore Pennell, cited in Victoria Schofield, *Every Rock, Every Hill* (London: Buchan and Enright, 1984), p. 139.

47. Callwell, *Tirah*, p. 7; Commissioner Peshawar District to Punjab and Simla, 5 September, 2 and 4 October 1897, telegrams, 78, Frontier Branch, Foreign Department, Government of the Punjab. Directorate of Archives, North West Frontier Province, Shahi Bagh, Peshawar.

48. Assistant Commissioner Thal to Deputy Commissioner Kohat, 8 February 1898, telegrams, 78, Frontier Branch, Foreign Department, Government of the Punjab. Directorate of Archives, North West Frontier Province, Shahi Bagh, Peshawar.

49. Callwell, *Tirah*, p. 31.

50. Callwell, *Tirah*, p. 33.

51. Callwell, *Tirah*, p. 45.

52. Hutchinson, *Tirah*, pp. 52–3. Callwell, *Tirah*, p. 46.

53. Callwell, *Tirah*, p. 50.

54. Ibid., p. 51.

55. Hutchinson, *Tirah*, p. 61.

56. Ibid., p. 62.

57. Ex-army personnel also directed the fire of the tribesmen and provided effective leadership and discipline. Moreman, *The Army in India*, p. 62.

58. Hutchinson, *Tirah*, p. 63.

59. Ibid., p. 77.

60. Hutchinson, *Tirah*, p. 88.

61. Nevill, *Campaigns on the North West Frontier*, p. 317. There was praise for Afridi tactics in H. Woosnam Mills, *The Tirah Campaign* (Lahore, 1898), pp. 119–20 and Field Marshal Lord Birdwood, *Khaki and Gown: An Autobiography* (London, 1942), p. 86.

62. Hutchinson, *Tirah*, p. 121.

63. Enquiry into the circumstances attending the losses sustained by the Northamptonshire Regiment in Tirah, on 9 November 1897, 4 January 1898, L/Mil/7/15882 IOR.

64. Hutchinson, *Tirah*, p. 107.

65. Ibid., p. 132.

66. Ibid., pp. 112–13.

67. General Officer Commanding Tirah Expeditionary Force to Foreign Secretary, 17 November 1897, L/PS/7/99 IOR.

68. Hutchinson, *Tirah*, p. 115.

69. Ibid., p. 127.

70. Ibid., p. 128.

71. Lt Cowie, 1ˢᵗ Dorsets, letter dated 5 December 1897, DMM/1/220, Campaigns and Engagements, 1818–1898, Dorset Regiment Archive, The Keep Military Museum, Dorchester.

72. C. E. Calwell, *Small Wars: their Principles and Practice* (London, 1906 edn), p. 39.

73. Sir Robert Warburton, *Eighteen Years in the Khyber* (London: John Murray, 1900), pp. 298–9.

74. R. I. Bruce, *The Forward Policy and its Results* (London: Longmans, Green & Co., 1900), pp. 140–41.

75. Ahmed, *Millennium and Charisma*, p. 105.

76. Hutchinson, *Tirah*, p. 155.

77. Ibid., pp. 155–6.

78. Miller, *Khyber*, p. 279. It is thought that *c*.100 followers became casualties. General Officer Commanding Tirah Expeditionary Force to Adjutant-General in India, 12 December 1897, L/PS/7/99 IOR.

79. From a letter by an Officer with the Picquet, F Company, KOSBs, cited in Hutchinson, *Tirah*, p. 201.

80. Colonel L. James, *High Pressure: Being Some Record of Activities in the Service of The Times Newspaper* (London, 1929), p. 43, cited in Moreman, *The Army in India*, p. 67.

81. Wylly, *From Black Mountain to Waziristan*, p. 336.

82. Hutchinson, *Tirah*, pp. 166–7. Lieutenant General Sir A. P. Palmer to Chief of Staff, Tirah Expeditionary Force, 31 January 1898, L/Mil/7/15899 IOR.

83. Wylly, *From Black Mountain to Waziristan*, p. 336.

84. Hutchinson, *Tirah*, p. 170.

85. Foreign Department Despatch, 69 of 1898 (Frontier): Settlement with the Afridis and the opening of the Khyber Pass, 5 May 1898, L/PS/7/103 IOR.

86. Wylly, *From Black Mountain to Waziristan*, p. 338.

87. India Office to Governor General of India, Secret Despatch no. 18, 5 August 1898. L/Mil/7/15919 IOR.

88. Colonel Thomas Holdich, *The Indian Borderland* (London: Methuen, 1900), p. 362.

89. Nevill, *Campaigns on the North West Frontier*, p. 322.

90. Hutchinson, *Tirah*, p. 130.

91. Hutchinson, *Tirah*, pp. 166–7.

5. THIRD ANGLO–AFGHAN WAR, 1919, AND WAZIRISTAN, 1936

1. *The Third Afghan War, 1919: Official Account* (Calcutta: Government of India Publication), p. 7.

2. Ibid.

3. Ibid., p. 22.

4. *The Anglo-Russian Convention*, L/PS/10/1125, file 3082/1907/1 IOR.

5. *Afghan Neutrality, 1914*, L/PS/10/461. IOR.

6. *German Agents in Afghanistan*, L/PS/10/593, file 1287, pt.2/1917 IOR.

7. *Copies of Parliamentary Papers*, House of Commons, 1919, XXXVIII, cd324, L/MIL/17/14//61 IOR.

8. Sykes, *Afghanistan*, II, p. 266.

9. Cited in T. A. Heathcote, *The Afghan Wars, 1839–1919* (Staplehurst: Spellmount, 2003 edn), p. 198.

10. Sykes, *Afghanistan*, p. 269.

11. *Report of the Hunter Committee: Disturbances in the Punjab*, CMD 681, 1920; D.George Boyce, 'From Assaye to *The Assaye*: reflections on British Government, Force and Moral Authority in India', *Journal of Military History*, 63, 3 (1999), p. 660.

12. Afghan Post Master to the Amir, 7 May 1919, cited in *The Third Afghan War: Official Account* (Calcutta: Government of India Publication, 1926), p. 29.

13. Ibid., p. 30.

14. Sykes, *Afghanistan*, p. 275; Heathcote, *Afghan Wars*, p. 180.

15. Heathcote, *Afghan Wars*, p. 178.

16. *Third Afghan War: Official Account*, p. 25.

17. Ibid., p. 23.

18. Ibid., p. 23.

19. *Third Afghan War: Official Account*, p. 28; Sykes, *Afghanistan*, p. 274; *Third Afghan War, Diary of Events*, L/MIL/17/14/60 IOR.

20. *Third Afghan War: Official Account*, pp. 33–4; *Third Afghan War, Report on the Action at Bagh*, L/MIL/17/14/63 IOR.

21. *Third Afghan War, Official Account*, p. 40. *Third Afghan War, Report on the Action at Dakka* L/MIL/17/14/64 IOR.
22. *Third Afghan War, Official Account*, p. 43.
23. Ibid., p. 47.
24. *Report on the Action at Spin Boldak.* L/MIL/17/14/65 IOR.
25. *Third Afghan War, Official Account*, p. 104.
26. Ibid.
27. *Third Afghan War, Official Account*, p. 106.
28. Ibid., p. 108.
29. Heathcote, *Afghan Wars*, p. 195.
30. *Relief of Thal.* L/MIL/17/14/65 IOR.
31. Heathcote, *Afghan Wars*, p. 199.
32. Heathcote, *Afghan Wars*, p. 200.
33. Johnson, *Spying for Empire*, p. 241.
34. Sykes, *Afghanistan*, pp. 358–9.
35. *Turkey and the Khalifat*, 26 May 1919, L/PS/11/153, file P3464 IOR.
36. Sykes, *Afghanistan*, p. 286.
37. *The Khost Rebellion*, L/PS/10/1112 IOR.
38. *Afghanistan: Purchase of tanks, armoured cars, etc.* File 4658, pt 2, 1924–1925. L/PS/10/1130 IOR.
39. *Afghanistan: The Amir's Subsidy*, 11 February 1919–22 July 1919. L/PS/11/154, file P3845/1919 IOR.
40. *Afghan Rebellion*, L/PS/10/1285–95 IOR.
41. Sykes, *Afghanistan*, II, p. 313.
42. *Relations with the Government of Nadir Shah.* L/PS/10/1232 IOR.
43. Habibullah was executed when Nadir Shah took Kabul following demands by Ghilzai elders. Sykes, *Afghanistan*, p. 322.
44. *Third Afghan War: Official Account*, p. 135.
45. T. R. Moreman, *The Army in India and the Development of Frontier Warfare, 1849–1947* (London: Macmillan, 1998), pp. 109–11.
46. *Third Afghan War: Official Account*, p. 134.
47. Robert Johnson, *Lessons in Imperial Rule: Instructions for Infantrymen on the Indian Frontier* (London: Frontline, 2008), p. x.
48. Mukulika Banerjee, *The Pathan Unarmed* (Oxford and Karachi: Oxford University Press, 2000).
49. There were thirty-nine raids, thirty-one kidnappings and the murder of ten Hindus, as well as the razing of sixty houses, the theft of cattle and sheep, and the looting of trucks on the road.
50. 'Note on the Faqir of Ipi', File 514/VII, IOR R/12/72; Supplement 3 to Intelligence Summary 6, 17–23 June 1937, Appendix A, IOR L/MIL/5/1065; Alan Warren, *Waziristan, The Faqir of Ipi and the Indian Army: The North West Frontier Revolt* (Oxford: Oxford University Press, 2000), pp. 98–9.

51. Warren, *Waziristan*, p. 86.

52. 7–11 November 1936, L/PS/12/3230 IOR.

53. Maj. J. A. Robinson, 'The Disturbances of 1936–7 in Waziristan', North Waziristan Affairs, Waziristan Disturbances, 1936–38, L/PS/12/3232 IOR. *Operations on the North West Frontier, Intelligence Summaries, 1936–37*, p. 16, L/PS/12/3192 IOR.

54. Report on the Operations in Waziristan, 25 November 1936 to 16 January 1937, 21 June 1937, L/Mil7/16971 IOR; Moreman, *Army in India*, p. 156.

55. *Operations on the North West Frontiers, Intelligence Summaries, 1936–7*, L/PS/12/3192 IOR; File 514/IV, Resident to Governor North West Frontier Province, 18 Feb 1937, pp. 38–41, R/12/69 IOR.

56. Warren, *Waziristan*, pp. 146 and 148.

57. 'Attack on the convoy at Shahur Tangi on 9th April, 1937', *Journal of the United Services Institution India*, 67/288, (April and July 1937), pp. 261–5.

58. *Operations North West Frontier, Intelligence Summaries*, 1936–7, pp. 90–93, L/PS/12/3192 IOR; Warren, *Waziristan*, pp. 178 and 180–81.

59. John Masters, *Bugles and a Tiger* (London: Michael Joseph Ltd, 1956), pp. 225–31.

60. Robert Taber, *War of the Flea* (New York: L. Stuart, 1965; new edn, Washington, DC.: Potomac Books, 2004), p. 11; American doctrine suggests that there must usually be 20–25 counter-insurgents for every 1,000 residents in an operational area. *Counterinsurgency Field Manual* FM3–24 (Chicago, IL.: University of Chicago Press, 2007), p. 23.

61. Moreman, *The Army in India*, pp. 179–80.

62. Arthur Swinson, *North West Frontier* (London: Hutchinson, 1967), p. 377.

63. When a British officer was captured, castrated and flayed—his skin being pegged out nearby—his Indian troops were ordered to beat a wounded Pashtun. Swinson, *North West Frontier*, p. 378.

64. Masters, *Bugles and a Tiger*, p. 205. If withdrawing, troops had to maintain continual observation of the hostile tribesmen throughout, and only then could they attack. Usually they had to be in contact for thirty minutes to take firm action from the air, but an area of 2 miles around could be considered a combat zone. *Instructions governing the employment of armed forces in the maintenance of tribal control of the NWF of India and in Baluchistan, 1940*, Confidential (Government of India, Defence Dept) L/PS/20/B308 IOR.

65. Ibid.

66. In certain circumstances, action could be taken by ground and air forces without the sanction of the Government of India, but all 'Deliberate Operations' had to have official sanction with clearly defined political objectives. In periods of Watch and Ward, including maintaining the security of communications or action against gun runners and raiders, the civil authority could call on the Indian Army for sup-

port, but when a situation arose which could not be controlled by the Civil Armed Forces, the deployment of regular troops became imperative and control would naturally shift to the local military commander. Nevertheless, the Government of India insisted on the full cooperation of the civilians and the military, and 'political control' could be transferred *only* by the Government of India. The army was expected to consult the Political Officer before entering tribal areas, except in maintenance of security in 'road open' days, although the army and air force could be deployed in readiness for action.

67. 'Birds of Death', directed by George Case, a Wall to Wall television production for Channel 4, broadcast in Britain by Channel 4, 21 April 1996. Transcript at: http://www.cambridgeclarion.org/birds_of_death/transcript.html.

68. Weekly Summaries North Waziristan 1938–43, Edward Lydall Papers, IOR MSS Eur D923.

69. Swinson, *North West Frontier*, p. 388.

70. *Handbook of Kandahar Province* (Simla: GSI, 1933). L/MIL/17/14/7. IOR. p. 8.

71. Milan Hauner, 'One Man Against the Empire: The Faqir of Ipi and the British in Central Asia on the Eve of and During the Second World War', *Journal of Contemporary History*, 16, 1 (January 1981), pp. 183–212.

72. *Military Training Pamphlet no. 7 (India) Extensive Warfare (Notes on warfare in mountainous country between modern forces in Eastern theatres)* (Simla, 1941), p. 3, L/MIL/17/5/2248 IOR cited in Moreman, *Army in India*, p. 180.

73. In January 1942, an ambush of the Assistant District Officer, Mr Morgan and his frontier constabulary escort resulted in the death of Morgan and a Havildar. In the subsequent skirmish, two more frontier Sepoys were also killed, but the raiders lost twelve killed and wounded, largely because of the hot pursuit of the frontier forces, including a running battle through crops of sugar cane. *NWFP Governor's Fortnightly Intelligence Reports*, Secret, 24 Jan 1942, L/PJ/5/219 IOR.

74. *NWFP Governor's Fortnightly Intelligence Reports*, Secret, no. 4, 23 Feb 1942, L/PJ/5/219 IOR.

75. *NWFP Governor's Fortnightly Intelligence Reports*, Secret, Report for first half of August 1942, L/PJ/5/219 IOR.

76. *NWFP Governor's Fortnightly Intelligence Reports*, Secret, no. 18, 23 Sep. 1942, L/PJ/5/219 IOR.

77. *NWFP Governor's Fortnightly Intelligence Reports*, Secret, no. 10, 23 May1942, L/PJ/5/219 IOR.

78. *NWFP Governor's Fortnightly Intelligence Report*, Confidential, no. 23, 8 Dec. 1942, L/PJ/5/219 IOR.

79. *NWFP Governor's Fortnightly Intelligence Report*, Confidential, no. 2, 19 Nov. 1942, L/PJ/5/219 IOR.

6. THE SOVIET WAR: THE MUJAHIDEEN, IDEOLOGY AND GUERRILLA WAR, 1978–89

1. Sana Haroon, *Frontier of Faith: Islam in the Indo-Afghan Borderland* (London: Hurst & Co., 2007), p. 192.
2. Alam Payind, 'Soviet-Afghan Relations from Cooperation to Occupation', *International Journal of Middle East Studies*, 21, 1 (February 1989), pp. 107–28.
3. Mohammad Yousaf and Mark Adkin, *Afghanistan: The Bear Trap* (London: Leo Cooper, 1992), p. 142.
4. A. Lyakhovski and S. Davitaya, *Igra Afghanistana* (Moscow, 2009), p. 135.
5. Cited in Edward Giradet, *Afghanistan: The Soviet War* (London: Croom Helm, 1985), pp. 163–4.
6. S. Belanovski and S. Marzeeva, *Dedovshchina v Sovietskoi Armii* (Moscow, 1991) accessible at www.sbelan.ru/content/дедовщина-в-советской-армии. Accessed December 2010.
7. Giradet, *Afghanistan: The Soviet War*, p. 37.
8. A. Maiorov, *Pravda ob afganskoi voine* (Moscow, 1996), p. 110.
9. Artemy Kalinovski, *The Blind Leading the Blind: Soviet Advisors, Counter-insurgency and Nation-Building in Afghanistan*, CWIHP Working Paper 60, January 2010; Memorandum from Chairman of USSR GOSPLAN, N. K. Baybakov, 'Regarding Additional Aid to the DRA', 8 October 1980, International Department (RGANI), fund 5, Op. 77, D.802, p. 44. Harvard University.
10. Yousaf, *Afghanistan: Bear Trap*, p. 127.
11. Ibid., p. 64; David Galula, *Counterinsurgency Warfare: Theory and Practice* (Westport, CO.: Praeger Security International, 1964), pp. 11–28.
12. Yousaf, *Afghanistan: Bear Trap*, pp. 68–9.
13. Ibid., p. 68.
14. Giradet, *Afghanistan: Soviet War*, p. 81.
15. Yousaf, *Afghanistan: Bear Trap*, p. 69.
16. Cited in Carlotta Gall and Thomas de Waal, *Chechnya: A Small Victorious War* (London: Pan Books, 1997), p. 97.
17. Yousaf, *Afghanistan: Bear Trap*, p. 59.
18. Giradet, *Afghanistan: Soviet War*, p. 181.
19. The population of Afghanistan was 15.5 million, of which just over 900,000 lived in Kabul, according to the last census before the war taken in 1979. The population of Kabul swelled rapidly during the war.
20. Lester Grau, *The Soviet-Afghan War: Superpower Mired in the Mountains*, available at http://www.smallwars.quantico.usmc.mil/search/LessonsLearned/afghanistan/miredinmount.asp Accessed December 2010; V. Korolev, *Uroki voiny v Afganistane 1979–1989 godov*, available at http://www.sdrvdv.org/node/159 Accessed December 2010.
21. S. Kozlov (ed.), *SpetsNaz GRU: Afganistan* (Moscow, 2009), p. 25.

22. Giradet, *Afghanistan: Soviet War*, p. 38.
23. Giradet, *Afghanistan: Soviet War*, p. 61.
24. According to Gorelov, the senior Soviet military advisor in Afghanistan, the Afghans had 145,000 men, 650 tanks, 87 infantry fighting vehicles, 780 armoured personnel carriers, 1,919 guns, 150 aircraft and 25 helicopters.
25. Mark Galeotti, *Afghanistan: The Soviet Union's Last War* (London: Frank Cass, 1995), p. 7.
26. Yousaf, *Afghanistan: Bear Trap*, p. 57.
27. Loc. cit.
28. Mark Urban, *War in Afghanistan* (London: Macmillan, 1990), p. 106; Gilles Dorronosoro, *Revolution Unending: Afghanistan, 1979 to the Present* (New York, 2005), p. 188.
29. Yousaf, *Afghanistan: Bear Trap*, p. 58.
30. G. Bobrov, *Soldatskaya Saga* (Moscow, 2007), pp. 237–40.
31. V. Ogryzko, *Pesni afganskogo pokhoda* (Moscow, 2000), p. 49, cited in R. Braithwaite, *Afgantsy* (London: Profile Books, 2011), p. 143.
32. Braithwaite, *Afgantsy*, p. 218.
33. L. Kucherova, *SpetsNaz KGB v Afganistane* (Moscow, 2009), pp. 321 and 319.
34. D. Gai and V. Snegirev, *Vtorzhenie* (Moscow, 1991), p. 137.
35. Kalinovsky, *Blind Leading the Blind*, p. 19.
36. Lester Grau (ed.), *The Soviet-Afghan War*, p. 27.
37. Jon Lee Anderson, *Guerrillas: Journeys in the Insurgent World* (London: Abacus, 2006 edn), pp. 148–9.
38. A. Greshnov, *Afganistan: Zalozhniki vremeni* (Moscow, 2006), p. 133.
39. Yousaf, *Afghanistan: Bear Trap*, p. 35.
40. Ibid., pp. 32 and 75.
41. Anderson, *Guerrillas*, p. 153.
42. Yousaf, *Afghanistan: Bear Trap*, p. 33.
43. Giradet, *Afghanistan, Soviet War*, p. 183; Abdul Salam Zaeef, *My Life with the Taliban* (London: Hurst & Co., 2010), p. 26.
44. Giradet, *Afghanistan, Soviet War*, p. 185.
45. Gai and Snegirev, *Vtorzhenie*, p. 236; Yu Lapshin, *Afganski Dnevnik* (Moscow, 2004), p. 101.
46. Ali Ahmad Jalali and Lester Grau, *Afghan Guerrilla Warfare* (St Paul, MN.: MBI, 2006); first pub. as *The Other Side of the Mountain*, 3 vols. (Lawrence, KS.: University Press of Kansas, 1995), p. 405.
47. Jalali and Grau, *Afghan Guerrilla Warfare*, p. 400.
48. Loc. cit.
49. Yousaf, *Afghanistan: Bear Trap*, p. 124.
50. Jalali and Grau, *Afghan Guerilla Warfare*, p. 404.
51. Yousaf, *Afghanistan: Bear Trap*, p. 36.

52. Giradet, *Afghanistan: Soviet War*, p. 60.

53. Steve Coll, *Ghost Wars* (London: Penguin, 2004), p. 149.

54. A. Lyakhovski, *Tragedia i doblest Afgana*, p. 370.

55. Gai and Snegirev, *Vtorzhenie*, pp. 227–9.

56. Braithwaite, *Afgantsy*, p. 230.

57. Ibid., pp. 228–9.

58. Zaeef, *My Life with the Taliban*, p. 24.

59. Yousaf, *Afghanistan: Bear Trap*, p. 166.

60. D. Cordovez and S. Harrison, *Out of Afghanistan* (Oxford: Oxford University Press, 1995), p. 198.

61. Yousaf, *Afghanistan: Bear Trap*, p. 186.

62. M. Gareev, *Moya Poslednaya Voina*, p. 102, available at http://militera.lib.ru/memo/russian/gareev_ma/index Accessed December 2010.

63. Yousaf, *Afghanistan: Bear Trap*, p. 116.

64. Zaeef, *My Life with the Taliban*, p. 34; Yousaf, *Afghanistan: Bear Trap*, p. 31.

65. Giradet, *Afghanistan: Soviet War*, p. 213.

66. Jalali and Grau, *Afghan Guerilla Warfare*, p. 405.

67. Yousaf, *Afghanistan: Bear Trap*, p. 126.

68. Yousaf, *Afghanistan: Bear Trap*, p. 41.

69. Giradet, *Afghanistan: Soviet War*, p. 64.

70. Yousaf, *Afghanistan: Bear Trap*, p. 154.

71. Ibid., p. 156.

72. Giradet, *Afghanistan: Soviet War*, p. 185.

73. Ibid., p. 186.

74. Yousaf, *Afghanistan: Bear Trap*, p. 43.

75. Ibid., p. 43.

76. Yousaf, *Afghanistan: Bear Trap*, p. 126.

77. His son, Sirajuddin Haqqani, led the 'Haqqani network' resistance to the American-led occupation from 2003.

78. Jalali and Grau, *Afghan Guerrilla Warfare*, p. 319.

79. Gai and Snegirev, *Vtorzhenie*, p. 139.

80. Yousaf, *Afghanistan: Bear Trap*, p. 160.

81. Ibid., p. 162.

82. Lieutenant Omar and Mawlawi Nezamuddin Haqani, 'Zhawar one' in Jalali and Grau, *Afghan Guerrilla Warfare*, p. 319.

83. Omar and Haqani, 'Zhawar one', p. 320.

84. Yousaf, *Afghanistan: Bear Trap*, p. 162.

85. Ibid., p. 167.

86. Lieutenant Omar, Mawlawi Nezamuddin Haqani and Mawlawi Abdul Rahman, 'Zhawar Two' in Jalali and Grau, *Afghan Guerrilla Warfare*, p. 324.

87. Yousaf, *Afghanistan: Bear Trap*, p. 171; Lieutenant Omar, Mawlawi Nezamuddin Haqani and Mawlawi Abdul Rahman, loc. cit.

88. Lieutenant Omar,Mawlawi Nezamuddin Haqani and Mawlawi Abdul Rahman, loc. cit.
89. Yousaf, *Afghanistan: Bear Trap*, p. 169.
90. Lieutenant Omar, Mawlawi Nezamuddin Haqani and Mawlawi Abdul Rahman, 'Zhawar Two' in Jalali and Grau, *Afghan Guerrilla Warfare*, p. 325.
91. Lyakhovski, *Tragedia i doblest Afgana*, p. 439.
92. Giradet, *Afghanistan: Soviet War*, p. 193.
93. Giradet, *Afghanistan: Soviet War*, p. 54.
94. Yousaf, *Afghanistan: Bear Trap*, p. 36.
95. Ibid., p. 39.
96. Ibid., p. 42.
97. Ibid., p. 137.
98. Ibid., p. 56.
99. Ibid., p. 135.
100. Ibid., pp. 130–31.
101. Dorronosoro, *Revolution Unending*, p. 152.
102. Yousaf, *Afghanistan: Bear Trap*, p. 131.
103. Giradet, *Afghanistan: Soviet War*, p. 197; Rob Johnson, *The Iran-Iraq War* (New York and Basingstoke: Palgrave, 2010).
104. Giradet, *Afghanistan: Soviet War*, p. 199.
105. Ibid., p. 195.
106. Yousaf, *Afghanistan: Bear Trap*, p. 33.
107. Giradet, *Afghanistan: Soviet War*, p. 60.
108. Yousaf, *Afghanistan: Bear Trap*, p. 40.
109. Ibid., p. 71.
110. Giradet, *Afghanistan: Soviet War*, p. 196.
111. Ibid., p. 77.
112. Ahmad Shah Masoud's father had been an Afghan Army officer and a native of the Panjshir from a prestigious and influential family. He studied engineering at the university in Kabul, and joined the Muslim Youth organization, which derived its inspiration from the Muslim Brotherhood of Egypt. The Muslim Youth organization consisted of wings that favoured militant Jihadism, led by Gulbuddin Hekmatyar, and moderate Islamism, led by Berkhanuddin Rabbani. They split, formally, into new parties: respectively the Islamic Party of Afghanistan and the Islamic Society of Afghanistan.
113. A. Lyakhovski and V. Nekrasov, *Grazhdanin, Politik, Voin: Pamyati Akhmad Shakha Masuda* (Moscow, 2007), pp. 24ff.
114. A. Lyakhovski, *Tragedia i doblest Afgana*, p. 10; Giradet, *Afghanistan: Soviet War*, pp. 78–80.
115. Giradet, *Afghanistan: Soviet War*, p. 82.
116. Ibid., p. 83.

117. Ibid., p. 183.
118. Ibid., p. 187.
119. Ibid., p. 175.
120. Ibid., p. 188.
121. Robert Johnson, *Spying for Empire: The Great Game in Central and South Asia, 1757–1947* (London: Greenhill, 2006), p. 36.
122. Zaeef, *My Life with the Taliban*, p. 22.
123. Yousaf, *Afghanistan: Bear Trap*, p. 33.
124. Anderson, *Guerrillas*, pp. 152–3.
125. Ibid., p. 155.
126. Giradet, *Afghanistan: Soviet War*, p. 215.
127. Zaeef, *My Life with the Taliban*, p. 25.
128. Giradet, *Afghanistan: Soviet War*, p. 226.
129. Anderson, *Guerrillas*, p. 148.
130. Braithwaite, *Afgantsy*, p. 221.
131. Giradet, *Afghanistan: Soviet War*, p. 226.
132. Roy, cited in Giradet, *Afghanistan: Soviet War*, p. 183.
133. Afghanistan Justice Project, *Casting Shadows: War Crimes and Crimes against Humanity, 1978–2001* (2005), p. 56.
134. V. Krivenko, *Ekipazh Mashiny Boevoi* (St Petersburg, 2004), p. 351.
135. Giradet, *Afghanistan: Soviet War*, p. 182.
136. Yousaf, *Afghanistan: Bear Trap*, pp. 133–4.
137. Cited in Yousaf, *Afghanistan: Bear Trap*, p. 147.
138. Giradet, *Afghanistan: Soviet War*, p. 180.
139. Ibid., p. 182.
140. Yousaf, *Afghanistan: Bear Trap*, p. 49.
141. Gai and Snegirev, *Vtorzhenie*, p. 367.
142. D. Cordovez and S. Harrison, *Out of Afghanistan* (Oxford: Oxford University Press, 1995), p. 65; A. Lyakhovski, *Tragedia i doblest Afgana* (Moscow, 2004).
143. A. Chernyaev et al., *V Politburo TsK KPSS* (Moscow, 2006), p. 108.
144. Angelo Rasanayagam, *Afghanistan*, p. 130; Barnett R. Rubin, *The Fragmentation of Afghanistan*, pp. 159–60.
145. Alexandr Kartsev, *Shelkovy Put* (privately published, 2004), ch.13.
146. A. Greshnov, *Afganistan: Zalozhniki vremeni* (Moscow, 2006), p. 148.
147. Boris V. Gromov, *Ogranichennyi kontingent* (Moscow: Izdatel'skaya gruppa, 'Progress-Kultura', 1994), p. 192: Giradet, *Afghanistan: Soviet War*, p. 85.
148. Olivier Roy, *Islam and Resistance in Afghanistan* (Cambridge: Cambridge University Press, 1990), p. 199; William Maley, *The Afghanistan Wars* (London and New York: Palgrave Macmillan, 2002), p. 90.
149. Giradet, *Afghanistan: Soviet War*, p. 87.
150. James G. Hershberg (ed.), 'New Evidence on Soviet Intervention in Afghanistan', *Cold War International History Bulletin*, 8–9 (1996–9), p. 169.

151. Maley, *Afghanistan's Wars*, p. 136.
152. Cordovez and Harrision, *Out of Afghanistan*, pp. 303–6.
153. Herschberg, 'New Evidence', p. 177.
154. *Department of State Bulletin*, 88, 2135 (June 1988) p. 55.
155. Imitiaz H. Bokhari, 'Internal negotiations Among Many Actors: Afghanistan' in I. William Zartman (ed.), *Elusive Peace: Negotiating an End to Civil Wars* (Washington, DC.: Brookings Institute, 1995), p. 261.
156. Ibid.
157. Maley, *Afghanistan Wars*, p. 142.

7. THE CIVIL WAR, THE TALIBAN AND THE INSURGENCY, 1990–2011

1. Antonio Giustozzi, *Empires of Mud* (London: Hurst & Co., 2009), pp. 54–7.
2. Dorronosoro, *Revolution Unending: Afghanistan, 1979 to the Present*, pp. 227–8.
3. Vladimir Snegirev, *Ryzhy* (Moscow, 2000), p. 156.
4. A. Greshnov, *Afganistan: Zalozhniki vremeni* (Moscow, 2006), pp. 71 and 74; Mark Urban, *War in Afghanistan* (London, 1990), pp. 274ff.
5. Yousaf, *Afghanistan: The Bear Trap*, pp. 227–33.
6. As quoted in A. Seierstad, *The Bookseller of Kabul* (London: Little, Brown, 2003), p. 150.
7. Zaeef, *My Life with the Taliban*, pp. 234–5.
8. Zaeef, *My Life with the Taliban*, pp. 62 and 65.
9. James Fergusson, *Taliban* (London: Bantam Press, 2010), p. 19.
10. Fergusson, *Taliban*, p. 11.
11. Zaeef, *My Life with the Taliban*, p. 72.
12. Fergusson, *Taliban*, p. 42.
13. Matinuddin, *The Taliban Phenomenon*, p. 71.
14. Ibid., pp. 76–7.
15. Matinuddin, *The Taliban Phenomenon*, p. 86.
16. Fergusson, *Taliban*, p. 43.
17. Fergusson, *Taliban*, p. 34.
18. According to Zaeef, Masoud had rejected peace overtures with the Taliban in 1998. Zaeef, *My Life with the Taliban*, pp. 87–8.
19. Fergusson, *Taliban*, p. 85.
20. Kamal Matinuddin, *The Taliban Phenomenon: Afghanistan, 1994–1997* (Oxford: Oxford University Press, 1999), p. 59.
21. Neamatollah Nojumi, *The Rise of the Taliban in Afghanistan* (New York: Palgrave Macmillan, 2002), pp. 154, 180 and 189.
22. Fergusson, *Taliban*, p. 38; Anderson, *Guerrillas*, op. cit.
23. Zaeef, *My Life with the Taliban*, pp. 136–44; Fergusson, *Taliban*, p. 87.
24. Fergusson, *Taliban*, p. 89.

25. Sami Yousafzai and Ron Moreau, 'The Taliban in Their Own Words', *Newsweek*, 5 October 2009.

26. Sami Yousafzai and Ron Moreau, 'The Taliban in Their Own Words', *Newsweek*, 5 October 2009, p. 1.

27. Yousafzai and Moreau, 'The Taliban in Their Own Words', p. 2; Fergusson, *Taliban*, p. 113.

28. See James Dobbins, *After the Taliban* (Washington, DC.: Potomac Books, 2008).

29. Giustozzi, *Empires of Mud*, op. cit.

30. Jane Perlez, 'Rebuffing US, Pakistan balks at crackdown', *New York Times*, 14 December 2009.

31. Yousafzai and Moreau, 'The Taliban in Their Own Words', p. 11.

32. Mohammad Yousaf and Mark Adkin, *The Battle for Afghanistan: The Soviets Versus the Majahideen During the 1980s* (Barnsley: Pen and Sword Books, 2007 edn), pp. 40 and 130.

33. Olivier Roy, *Islam and Resistance in Afghanistan* (Cambridge: Cambridge Middle East Library, 1986), p. 224.

34. Roy, *Islam and Resistance in Afghanistan*, p. 224.

35. Loc. cit.

36. Ibid., p. 225.

37. David B. Edwards, *Before Taliban: Genealogies of the Afghan Jihad* (Berkeley, CA.: University of California Press, 2002).

38. Cited in Chris Johnson and Jolyon Leslie, *Afghanistan: The Mirage of Peace* (London: Zed Books, 2008), p. 67.

39. Ibid., p. 68.

40. Yousafzai and Moreau, 'The Taliban in Their Own Words', p. 3.

41. Ibid., p. 4.

42. Ibid., p. 6.

43. Ibid., p. 7.

44. Ibid., p. 7.

45. Ibid., p. 9.

46. Ibid., p. 10.

47. Bill Roggio, 'Taliban Losses in Afghanistan, Gains in Pakistan', *Long War Journal*, 25 June 2006.

48. Yousafzai and Moreau, 'The Taliban in Their Own Words', p. 9.

49. Yousafzai and Moreau, 'The Taliban in Their Own Words', p. 10.

50. Fergusson, *Taliban*, p. 140.

51. Ibid., p. 136.

52. Loc. cit.

53. Yousafzai and Moreau, 'The Taliban in Their Own Words', p. 11.

54. Fergusson, *Taliban*, p. 144.

55. David Loyn, 'Travelling with the Taleban', *BBC News*, 24 October 2006.

56. Loc. cit.
57. Loc. cit.
58. David B. Edwards, *Before Taliban: Genealogies of the Afghan Jihad* (Berkeley, CA.: University of California Press, 2002).
59. Robert D. Crews and Tarzi Amin, *The Taliban and the Crisis of Afghanistan* (Cambridge, MA.: Harvard University Press, 2008), p. 86.
60. Ibid., p. 77.
61. Ibid., p. 76.
62. Antonio Giustozzi, *Koran, Kalashnikov and Laptop: The Neo-Taliban Insurgency in Afghanistan* (London: Hurst & Co., 2007), p. 101.
63. Crews and Amin, *The Taliban and the Crisis of Afghanistan*, p. 87.
64. Ibid., p. 80.
65. Giustozzi, *Koran, Kalashnikov and Laptop*, p. 101.
66. Loc. cit.
67. Loc. cit.
68. Johnson and Jolyon, *Afghanistan: The Mirage of Peace*, p. 31.
69. Giustozzi, *Koran, Kalashnikov and Laptop*, p. 110.
70. Ibid., p. 112.
71. Loc. cit.
72. Ibid., p. 117.
73. Loc. cit.
74. Johnson and Jolyon, *Afghanistan: The Mirage of Peace*, p. 57; Fergusson, *Taliban*, p. 186.
75. Johnson and Jolyon, *Afghanistan: The Mirage of Peace*, p. 66.
76. Giustozzi, *Koran, Kalashnikov and Laptop*, p. 117.
77. Ibid., p. 119.
78. David B. Edwards, *Before Taliban: Genealogies of the Afghan Jihad* (Berkeley, CA.: University of California Press, 2002).
79. Ibid.
80. Ibid.
81. Ibid.
82. 'Taliban Out-Governing Afghan Government', *ABC News*, 31 August 2009. http://www.abc.net.au/news/stories/2009/08/31/2672485.htm   Accessed December 2010.
83. Johnson and Jolyon, *Afghanistan: The Mirage of Peace*, p. 6.
84. Crews and Amin, *The Taliban and the Crisis of Afghanistan*, p. 88.
85. UNAMA, January 2010.
86. Fergusson, *Taliban*, p. 158.
87. Aryn Baker, 'Taking Aim at the Taliban', *Time Magazine*, 16 August 2007.
88. Loc. cit.
89. In one example, local police in Shin Kalay in Nad-e Ali, Helmand, were domi-

nated by the Noorzai clan who were rivals of the local Kharotei. While two Kharotei mullahs joined the Taliban, village elders remained uncommitted. The elders changed sides to support the government only when they felt their status was being undermined by the aggressive and demanding mullahs. Names purposely omitted. Similar conflicts characterize Achakzai and Nurzai rivalries in Spin Boldak.

90. Tom Coghlan, 'The Taliban in Helmand: An Oral History' in Antonio Giustozzi (ed.), *Decoding the New Taliban* (London: Hurst & Co., 2009), pp. 119–53.

91. Giustozzi, *Koran, Kalashnikov and Laptop*, p. 86.

92. Johnson and Jolyon, *Afghanistan: The Mirage of Peace*, p. 132.

93. Fergusson, *Taliban*, p. 161.

94. Giustozzi, *Koran, Kalashnikov, and Laptop*, p. 86.

95. Loc. cit.

96. Johnson and Jolyon, *Afghanistan: The Mirage of Peace*, p. 50.

97. Ibid., p. 90.

98. Giustozzi, *Koran, Kalashnikov and Laptop*, p. 93.

99. Syed Saleem Shahzad, 'Taliban's New Commander Ready for a Fight', *Asia Times Online*, 20 May 2006.

100. Yousafzai and Moreau, 'The Taliban in Their Own Words', p. 12.

101. Ibid., p. 14.

102. Ibid., pp. 11–12.

103. Ibid., p. 14.

104. Ibid., p. 15.

105. Thomas H. Johnson, 'The Taliban Insurgency and an Analysis of *Shabnamah*', *Small Wars and Insurgencies*, 18, 3 (September 2007), pp. 317–44.

106. Yousafzai and Moreau, 'The Taliban in Their Own Words', p. 13.

107. General Sir David Richards, speech at the Royal Geographical Society, 2 December 2010.

108. For theoretical and practical analyses of reconciliation see David Bloomfield, Teresa Barnes and Luc Huyse (eds), *Reconciliation After Violent Conflict: A Handbook* (Stockholm: IDEA, 2003) and R. Nets-Zehngut, 'Analysing the Reconciliation Process', *International Journal on World Peace*, 24 (2007).

109. Zaeef, *My Life with the Taliban*.

110. David Loyn, *Butcher and Bolt* (London: Hutchinson, 2008), p. 283.

111. The List, as at the end of 2008, consisted of 243 individuals and 113 groups allegedly linked to al Qaeda. Fergusson, *Taliban*, p. 171.

112. Cited in Loyn, *Butcher and Bolt*, p. 295.

113. John Keane, *Reflections on Violence* (London: Verso, 1996), p. 134.

114. Talatbek Masadykov, Antonio Giustozzi and James Michael Page, 'Negotiating with the Taliban: Towards a Solution to the Afghan Conflict' (London School of Economics Crisis States Research Centre: Working Paper 66, Jan. 2010), p. 3.

115. 'Negotiating with the Taliban', p. 5.
116. Ibid., p. 9.

8. LESSONS LEARNED?

1. C. E. Callwell, *Small Wars: Their Principles and Practice* (London, 3rd edn, 1906), pp. 99 and 40–42.
2. *Report on the Administration of the Border of the North West Frontier Province* (Peshawar: Government Press, 1921–38).
3. See, for example, *Waziristan and the Lessons of the last 60 years* (Simla: Government Central Press, 1921).
4. Moreman, *The Army in India and the Development of Frontier Warfare* (London: Macmillan, 1998), pp. 129 and 135.
5. John Charles Edward Bowen, *Plain Tales of the Afghan Border* (London: Springwood Books), p. 13.

SELECT BIBLIOGRAPHY

Archival Sources

India Office Records, London
Home Correspondence
   H543–46.
Military Records
   L/MIL/3 Correspondence with India.
   L/MIL/7 Collections of Papers relating to the NW Frontier and Afghanistan.
   L/MIL/17/14 A and B, Library of Military Records, Central Asia and Afghani-
   stan.
Political and Secret Records
   L/PS/3 Home Correspondence, 1807–1911.
   L/PS/5 Secret Letters from India.
   L/PS/6 Political Letters from India.
   L/PS/8 Demi-Official Correspondence, 1862–1912.
   L/PS/9 Correspondence outside India.
   L/PS/20 Library of Political and Secret Records.
Proceedings of the Government of India
European Manuscripts
   Mss Eur F439/6 Papers of Major General Nott.
   Mss Eur D727 Papers of Sir Henry Mortimer Durand.
   Mss Eur E218 papers of the First Earl of Lytton.

National Archives, Kew, London
   PRO 30/12 Papers of Lord Ellenborough.

Gorbachev Foundation, Moscow
   Papers relating to the decision to withdraw from Afghanistan.

Wilson Center, Washington DC
   Papers relating to the Soviet intervention in Afghanistan.

Library of Congress, Washington DC

Blood, P. (ed.), *Afghanistan: A Country Study* (2001).

General Alexander Lyakhovski, *Tragedia i Doblest Afgana* (The Tragedy and Glory of the Afghan War) (Moscow, 1985 edn).

Historic Published Works (pre-1900)

Abdur Rahman, *The Life of Abdur Rahman* (London, 1900).

Abdur Rahman, *Risala-i Muwaizza* (Book of Advice) (Kabul, 1894).

Mullah Abu Bakr et al., *Taqwim al Din* (The Calendar of the Religion) (Kabul, 1889).

Bellew, H. W., *The Races of Afghanistan, being a brief Account of the Principal Nations Inhabiting that Country* (Calcutta: Thacker and Spink, 1880).

Bruce, R. I., *The Forward Policy and its Results* (London, 1900).

Churchill, W. S., 'The Ethics of Frontier Policy', *United Services Magazine*, 17 (1898).

Durand, Major General H. M., *The First Afghan War* (London, 1879).

Elphinstone, Mountstuart, *An Account of the Kingdom of Cabaul* (Karachi, 1839).

Anon. [G. R. Elsmie], *Epitome of Correspondence Regarding Our Relations with Afghanistan and Herat* (Lahore: Government Press, 1863).

Eyre, Vincent, *The Kabul Insurrection of 1841–2* (ed.), G. B. Malleson (London, 1879).

Ferrier, Joseph P., *History of the Afghans* (London: John Murray, 1858).

Forbes, Archibald, *The Afghan Wars, 1839–42 and 1878–80* (London: Seely & Co., 1892).

Havelock, Captain Henry, *Narrative of the War in Affghanistan*, 2 vols. (London: Henry Colburn, 1840).

Harris, Captain, *Reports and Narratives of Officers who were Engaged at the Battle of Maiwand, 27 July 1880* (India Intelligence Branch, 1881).

Hensman, Howard, *The Afghan War of 1879–80* (London, 1881, reprinted New Delhi: Lancer, 2008).

Holdich, Colonel Thomas, *The Indian Borderland* (London: Methuen, 1900).

Hutchinson, Colonel H. D., *The Campaign in Tirah, 1897–98* (London, 1898).

Kaye, John William, *History of the War in Afghanistan*, 3 vols. (London: Richard Bentley, 1857).

Lal, Mohan, *Amir Dost Mohammed Khan*, 2 vols., (pubd 1846; reprinted Oxford, 1978).

MacGregor, Charles Metcalfe, *Central Asia*, II, *A Contribution Towards the Better Knowledge of the Topography, Ethnology, Resources and History of Afghanistan* (Calcutta: Government of India Publication, 1871).

MacGregor, Major General Sir C. M., *The Defence of India: A Strategical Study* (Simla, 1884).

MacGregor, Charles Metcalfe, *The Second Afghan War: Official Account* (London: 1908 edn).

Mills, H. Woosnam, *The Tirah Campaign* (Lahore, 1898).

Nabi, M., *Sawal wa Jawab-i Dawlati* (The Amir's Interviews with the Viceroy of India) (Kabul: Government of Afghanistan Publication, 1885).

Nash, Charles (ed.), *History of the War in Affghanistan* (London, 1843).

Nott, William, *Memoirs and Correspondence of Major-General Sir William Nott* (ed.), J. H. Stocqueler, 2 vols. (London, 1854).

Ramsay, Lieutenant Colonel J. G., 'The Tactical Principles and Details Best Suited to Warfare on the Frontiers of India', *Journal of the Royal United Services Institution* (1899).

Riyazi, M.Y., 'Ayn Waqai' in *Kulliyat-i Riyazi* (The Collected Works of Riyazi) (Meshed, 1907).

Roberts, Lord F. S., *Forty-One Years in India* (London: Macmillan, 1898).

Sale, Lady Florentina, *A Journal of the disasters in Affghanistan, 1841–42* (London: 1843).

Slessor, A. K., 'Field Fortifications in Tirah', *United Services Magazine*, 19 (1899).

Slessor, A. K., 'Why and How the Afridis Rose', [*Colburn's*] *United Services Magazine*, 20 (1899–1900).

Warburton, Robert, *Eighteen Years in the Khyber, 1879–97* (London: John Murray, 1900).

Wheeler, Stephen, *The Ameer Abdur Rahman* (London: Bliss, Sands and Foster, 1895).

Yate, A. C., 'North West Frontier Warfare', *Journal of the Royal United Services Institution* (May 1900).

Yate, A. C., 'Sixty Years of Frontier Warfare', *Journal of the Royal United Services Institute*, (March 1900).

The Era of Afghan State Formation and British Intervention

Ahmed, A. S., 'The Colonial Encounter on the North West Frontier', *Asian Affairs*, 9 (1978).

Ahmed, Akbar S., *Millennium and Charisma among Pathans* (London: Routledge and Kegan Paul, 1976).

Alder, G. J., *British India's Northern Frontier, 1865–1895* (London: Longman, 1963).

Anderson, David M. and David Killingray (eds), *Policing the Empire: Government, Authority and Control, 1830–1940* (Manchester: Manchester University Press, 1991).

Babakhdzhayev, M. A., *Bor'ba Afganistana za nyezavisimost (1838–42)* (Afghanistan's War for Independence) (Moscow: Oriental Literature Press for the Institute of Oriental Studies of the Soviet Union's Academy of Sciences, 1960).

Banerjea, Mukulika, *The Pathan Unarmed: Opposition and Memory in the North West Frontier* (Santa Fe, NM.: School of American Research Press, 2000).

Barfield, Thomas, *Afghanistan: A Cultural and Political History* (Princeton and Oxford: Princeton University Press, 2010).

Barth, Fredrik, *Political Leadership Among Swat Pathans* (London: London School of Economics Monograph, 1959).

Barthorp, Michael, *The North West Frontier: British India and Afghanistan* (Blandford, 1982).

Beckett, Ian F. W., 'Cavagnari's *Coup de Main*', *Soldiers of the Queen: Journal of the Victorian Military Society*, 82 (September 1995).

Beckett, Ian F. W., *The Victorians at War* (London: Hambledon, 2003).

Belich, James, *The New Zealand Wars and the Victorian Interpretation of Racial Conflict* (Auckland: Auckland University Press, 1987).

Bond, Brian, *Victorian Military Campaigns* (London: Hutchinson, 1967).

Bosworth, E., *The Medieval History of Iran, Afghanistan and Central Asia* (London: Valorium Reprints, 1977).

Bovykin, V.I., *Ocherki istoriivneshnei politiki Rossii* (Essays in the History of Russia's Foreign Policy) (Moscow, 1960).

Boyce, D. George, 'From Assaye to *The Assaye*: reflections on British Government, Force and Moral Authority in India', *Journal of Military History*, 63, 3 (1999).

Calwell, C. E., *Small Wars: their Principles and Practice* (London, 1906 edn).

Callwell, C. E., *Tirah, 1897* (London, 1911, republished with a new Introduction by Rob Johnson, Williamsburg, VA., 2010).

Caroe, Sir Olaf, *The Pathans* (London: Macmillan, 1958).

Comaroff J., and J. Comaroff, *Ethnography and Historical Imagination* (Boulder, CO.: Westview, 1992).

Darling, Linda T., 'Contested Territory: Ottoman Holy War in Comparative Context', *Studia Islamica*, 91 (2000), pp. 133–63.

David, Saul, *Victoria's Wars* (London: Penguin, 2007).

Doherty, Paddy, *The Khyber Pass* (London: Faber, 2007).

Dupree, Louis, 'The Retreat of the British Army from Kabul to Jalalabad in 1842: History and Folklore', *Journal of the Folklore Institute*, 4, 1 (June 1967).

Edwards, David B., *Heroes of the Age: Moral Fault Lines on the Afghan Frontier* (Berkeley, CA.: University of California Press, 1996).

Ewans, Martin, *Afghanistan: A New History* (Richmond: Curzon Press, 2001).

Farwell, Byron, *Queen Victoria's Little Wars* (London: Allen Lane, 1973).

Galbraith, J. S., 'The "Turbulent Frontier" as a factor in British Expansion', *Comparative Studies in Society and History*, 11(1959–60), pp. 150–68.

Gerhard, D., 'The Frontier in Comparative View', Comparative Studies in Society and History, 1 (1959), pp. 205–29.

Ghobar, Ghulam Mohammed, *Afghanistan der Masir-i Tarikh* (Afghanistan on the Highway of History) (Kabul: Book Publishing Institute, 1967).

Gillard, D. R., *The Struggle for Asia 1828–1914* (London: Methuen, 1977).

Gregorian, Vartan, *The Emergence of Modern Afghanistan* (Palo Alto, CA.: Stanford University Press).

Hauner, Milan, 'One Man Against the Empire: The Faqir of Ipi and the British in Central Asia on the Eve of and During the Second World War', *Journal of Contemporary History*, 16, 1 (January 1981).

Heathcote, T. A., *The Afghan Wars* (Oxford: Osprey, 1980).

Hopkins, B. D., *The Making of Modern Afghanistan* (London and New York: Palgrave, 2008).

Hopkirk, Peter, *The Great Game: The Struggle for Empire in Central Asia* (Oxford: Oxford University Press, 1984).

Hutchinson, H. D., *The Campaign in Tirah, 1897–1898* (1898, reprinted New Delhi: Lancer, 2008).

Ingram, Edward, *The Beginnings of the Great Game in Asia, 1828–34* (Oxford: Clarendon Press, 1979).

Johnson, Robert, *Lessons in Imperial Rule: Instructions for Infantrymen on the Indian Frontier* (London: Greenhill, 2008).

Johnson, Robert, 'The Penjdeh Incident, 1885', *Archives*, XXIV, 100 (April 1999), pp. 28–48.

Johnson, Robert, *Spying for Empire* (London: Greenhill, 2006).

Johnson, R. A., '"Russians at the Gates of India?" Planning the defence of India, 1885–1900', *Journal of Military History*, 67 (2003).

Kakar, Hasan Kawun, *Government and Society in Afghanistan: The Reign of Amir Abd'al Rahman Khan* (Austin and London: University of Texas Press, 1979).

Kakar, Hasan, *The Pacification of the Hazaras of Afghanistan* (New York: Afghanistan Council of the Asia Society, 1973).

Khalfin, Nikolai, *Proval Britanskoy agressii v Afganistanye (19 v. nachalo 20 v.)* (The Downfall of British Aggression in Afghanistan) (Moscow: Socio-economic Literature Press, 1959).

Lee, Jonathan, *The 'Ancient Supremacy': Bukhara, Afghanistan and the Battle for Balkh, 1731–1901* (Leiden: Brill, 1996).

Lindholm, Charles, *Generosity and Jealousy* (New York: Columbia University Press, 1982).

Liddell Hart, B. H., *The British Way in Warfare* (London: Faber and Faber, 1932).

MacKenzie, D., 'Expansion in Central Asia: St Petersburg vs the Turkestan Generals (1863–66)', *Canadian Slavonic Studies*, 3 (1969), pp. 286–311.

Macrory, Patrick, *Signal Catastrophe* (London: Longman, 1969).

Martin, F., *Under the Absolute Amir* (London and New York: Harper & Brothers, 1907).

Masters, John, *Bugles and a Tiger* (London: Michael Joseph, 1956).

McMahon Captain A. H., and Lieutenant A. D. G. Ramsay, *Report on the Tribes of Dir, Swat and Bajaur* (Peshawar, 1916, revised edn).

Miller, Charles, *Khyber: The Story of an Imperial Migraine* (London: Macdonald and Jane's, 1977).

Moreman, T. R., *The Army in India and the Development of Frontier Warfare, 1849–1947* (London: Macmillan, 1998).

Moreman, T. R., 'The Arms Trade and the North West Frontier Pathan Tribes, 1890–1914', *Journal of Imperial and Commonwealth History*, 22, 2 (1994).

Moreman, T. R., '"Small Wars" and "Imperial Policing": The British Army and the Theory and Practice of Colonial Warfare in the British Empire, 1919–1939', *Journal of Strategic Studies*, 19, 4 (1996), pp. 105–31.

Morris, P., 'Russia in Central Asia', *Slavonic Review*, 53 (1975).

Nevill, Captain H. L., *Campaigns on the North West Frontier* (London, 1912).

Norris, J. A., *The First Afghan War, 1838–1842* (Cambridge: Cambridge University Press, 1967).

Nukhovich, E., *Vnyeshnaya politika Afganistana* (Afghan Foreign Policy) (Moscow: Institute of International Relations Press, 1962).

O'Balance, Edgar, *The Afghan Wars, 1839 to the Present* (London: Brassey's, 2002).

SELECT BIBLIOGRAPHY

Omissi, David, 'Martial Races: Ethnicity and Security in Colonial India, 1858–1939', *War and Society*, 7 (1991), pp. 1–26.

Pratt, Mary Louise, *Imperial Eyes: Travel Writing and Transculturation* (London: Routledge, 1992).

Rasanayagem, Angelo, *Afghanistan: A Modern History* (London: I. B. Tauris, 2003).

Richards, D. S., *The Savage Frontier: A History of the Anglo Afghan War* (London: Macmillan, 1990).

Rishtiya, Sayyid Mohammed Qasim, *Afghanistan dar qarn-i nuzdah* (Afghanistan in the nineteenth century) (Kabul, 1958).

Robb, P. (ed.), *The Concept of Race in South Asia* (New Dehli, 1995).

Robson, Brian, *Crisis on the Frontier* (London: History Press, 2004).

Robson, Brian, *The Road to Kabul: The Second Afghan War, 1879–81* (London: Arms and Armour Press, 1986).

Roe, Andrew, *Waging War in Waziristan: The British Struggle in the Land of bin Laden* (Lawrence, KS.: University Press of Kansas, 2010).

Saxena, K. M. L., *The Military System of India, 1859–1900* (New Delhi, 1974).

Schofield, Victoria, *Every Rock, Every Hill* (London: Buchan and Enright, 1984).

Shah, S. W. A., *Ethnicity, Islam and Nationalism: Muslim Politics in the North West Frontier Province 1937–47* (Karachi: Oxford University Press, 1999).

Singh, Ganda, *Ahmad Shah Durrani* (Bombay: Asia Publishing House, 1959).

Spain, James, *The Pathan Borderland* (The Hague: Mouton & Co., 1963).

Steinberg, E. L., 'Angliiskikaia versiia o "russkoi ugroze" Indii v XIX-XX v.v'. (*The English Version of the "Russian Threat" to India*), *IZ*, 33 (1950), pp. 47–66.

Stewart, Jules, *The Crimson Snow* (London: History Press, 2008).

Stewart, Jules, *The Khyber Rifles* (London: Sutton, 2006).

Stewart, Jules, *On Afghanistan's Plains* (London: I. B. Tauris, 2011).

Stewart, Jules, *The Savage Border* (London: Sutton, 2007).

Swinson, Arthur, *North West Frontier* (London: Hutchinson, 1967).

Sykes, P., *A History of Afghanistan*, 2 vols. (London, 1940).

Sykes, Sir Percy M., *Sir Mortimer Durand* (London, 1926).

Tanner, Stephen, *Afghanistan: A Military History* (New York: De Capo, 2003).

Tapper, Richard (ed.), *The Conflict of Tribe and State in Iran and Afghanistan* (London: Croom Helm, 1983).

The Third Afghan War, 1919: Official Account (Calcutta: Government of India Publication, 1920).

Thornton, A. P., 'The Reopening of the Central Asian Question', *Historical Journal* (1956), pp. 123–36.

Tripodi, Christian, 'Peacemaking through Bribes or Cultural Empathy? The Political Officer and Britain's Strategy towards the North-West Frontier, 1901–45', *Journal of Strategic Studies*, 31, 1 (February 2008).

Tytler, W. K. Fraser, *Afghanistan* (Oxford: Oxford University Press, 1950).

Warren, Alan, *Waziristan, The Faqir of Ipi and the Indian Army: The North West Frontier Revolt* (Oxford: Oxford University Press, 2000).

Wylly, Colonel H. C., *From the Black Mountain to Waziristan* (London: Macmillan, 1912).

Yapp, Malcolm, 'The Revolutions of 1841–1842 in Afghanistan', *Bulletin of the School of Oriental and African Studies*, 27, 2 (1964).

Yapp, M., *Strategies of British India* (Oxford: Oxford University Press, 1980).

The Era of Revolution and Soviet Intervention

Ahmad, Aisha, and Roger Boase, *Pashtun Tales: From the Pakistan-Afghan Frontier* (London: Saqi, 2003).

Anderson, Jon Lee, *Guerrillas: Journeys in the Insurgent World* (London: Abacus, 2006 edn).

Armstrong, Karen, *Islam: A Short History* (London: Random House, 2001).

Bobrov, G., *Soldatskaya Saga* (Moscow, 2007).

Bogdanov, V., *Afganskaya Voina 1979–1989* (Moscow, 2005).

Borovik, Artem, *The Hidden War: A Russian Journalist's Account of the Soviet War in Afghanistan* (New York: Hippocrene Books, 1990).

Bradsher, Henry S., *Afghan Communism and Soviet Intervention* (Oxford: Oxford University Press, 1999).

Bradsher, Henry S., *Afghanistan and the Soviet Union* (Durham, NC.: Duke University Press, 1985).

Braithwaite, R., *Afgantsy* (London: Profile Books, 2011).

Canfield, Robert L., *Faction and Conversion in a Plural Society: Religious Alignments in the Hindu Kush* (Ann Arbor: University of Michigan Press, 1973).

Cederman, Lars-Erik, Andreas Wimmer, and Brian Min, 'Why Do Ethnic Groups Rebel? New Data and Analysis', *World Politics*, 62, 1 (January 2010).

Coll, Steve, *Ghost Wars* (London: Penguin, 2004).

Collins, Kathleen, *The Logic of Clan Politics in Central Asia* (Cambridge: Cambridge University Press, 2006).

Cordovez, Diego, *Out of Afghanistan: The Inside Story of the Soviet Withdrawal* (New York: Oxford Univesity Press, 1995).

Dupree, Louis, *Afghanistan* (Princeton: Princeton University Press, 1973).

Emadi, Hafizullah, *Culture and Customs of Afghanistan* (Westport, CT.: Greenwood Press, 2005).

Gai, D. and V. Snegirev, *Vtorzhenie* (Moscow, 1991).

Galeotti, Mark, *Afghanistan: The Soviet Union's Last War* (London: Frank Cass, 1995).

Giradet, Edward, *Afghanistan: The Soviet War* (London: Croom Helm, 1985).

Giustozzi, Antonio, *War, Politics and Society in Afghanistan, 1978–1992* (London: Hurst & Co., 2000).

Grau, Lester (ed.), *The Soviet-Afghan War* (Lawrence, KS.: University Press of Kansas, 2002).

Greshnov, A., *Afganistan: Zalozhniki vremeni* (Moscow, 2006).

Gromov, Boris V., *Ogranichennyi kontingent* (Moscow: Izdatel'skaya gruppa, 'Progress-Kultura', 1994).

Hershberg, James G. (ed.), 'New Evidence on Soviet Intervention in Afghanistan', *Cold War International History Bulletin*, 8–9 (1996–7).

SELECT BIBLIOGRAPHY

Jalali, Ali Ahmad and Lester Grau, *Afghan Guerrilla Warfare* (St Paul, MN.: MBI, 2006); first pub. as *The Other Side of the Mountain*, 3 vols. (Lawrence, KS.: University Press of Kansas, 1995).

Kakar, Hasan, *Afghanistan: The Soviet Invasion and the Afghan Response, 1979–1982* (Berkeley, CA.: University of California Press, 1995).

Kalinovsky, A., *A Long Goodbye: The Politics and Diplomacy of the Soviet Withdrawal from Afghanistan, 1980–1992* (Thesis at the London School of Economics, 2009).

Kalinovsky, Artemy, *The Blind Leading the Blind: Soviet Advisors, Counter-insurgency and Nation-Building in Afghanistan*, CWIHP Working Paper 60 (January 2010).

Keller, Shoshana, *To Moscow, Not Mecca: The Soviet Campaign against Islam in Central Asia* (Westport, CT.: Praeger Publishers, 2001).

Kerr, Graham, *Demographic Research in Afghanistan* (New York: Asia Society, Paper 13, 1977).

Kozlov, S. (ed.), *SpetsNaz GRU: Afganistan* (Moscow, 2009).

Krivenko, V., *Ekipazh Mashiny Boevoi* (St Petersburg, 2004).

Kryuchkov, L., *Lichnoe Delo*, I (Moscow, 1996).

Kucherova, L., *SpetsNaz KGB v Afganistane* (Moscow, 2009).

Lewis, Bernard, *The Crisis of Islam* (New York: Random House, 2004).

Lyakhovski, A., and S. Davitaya, *Igra Afghanistana* (Moscow, 2009).

Lyakhovski, A., *Tragedia i doblest Afgana* (Moscow, 2004).

Lyakhovski, A., and V. Nekrasov, *Grazhdanin, Politik, Voin: Pamyati Akhmad Shakha Masuda* (Moscow, 2007).

Magnus, Ralph, and Eden Naby, *Afghanistan: Mullah, Marx and Mujahid* (Westport, CN.: Greenwood Press, 1998).

Maiorov, A., *Pravda ob afganskoi voine* (Moscow, 1996).

Maley, William, *The Afghanistan Wars* (London and New York: Palgrave Macmillan, 2002).

Naby, Eden, 'Ethnicity and Islam in Central Asia', *Central Asian Survey*, xii/2 (1993) pp. 151–68.

Naby, Eden, 'The Ethnic Factor in Soviet-Afghan Relations', *Asian Survey*, 20, 3 (1980).

Payind, Alam, 'Soviet-Afghan Relations from Cooperation to Occupation', *International Journal of Middle East Studies*, 21, 1 (February 1989).

Prados, J., *Safe for Democracy: The Secret Wars of the CIA* (Chicago: Ivan R. Dee, 2006).

Quelquejay, Chantal Lemercier, 'From Tribe to Umma', *Central Asian Survey*, III, 3 (1984) pp. 15–26.

Rasanayagam, Angelo, *Afghanistan* (London: I. B. Tauris, 2003).

Snegirev, Vladimir, *Ryzhy* (Moscow, 2000).

Tanner, Stephen, *Afghanistan: A Military History* (Cambridge, MA.: De Capo Press, 2002).

Urban, Mark, *War in Afghanistan* (London: Macmillan, 1990).

Warikoo, K., *Afghanistan Factor in Central and South Asian Politics* (New Delhi, 1994).

Weinbaum, Marvin G., *Pakistan and Afghanistan: Resistance and Reconstruction* (Boulder, CO.: Westview Press, 1994).

Wimbush, S. Enders, 'The Politics of Identity Change in Soviet Central Asia', *Central Asian Survey*, III/3 (1984) pp. 69–78.

Yousaf, Mohammed and Mark Adkin, *Afghanistan: The Bear Trap* (London: Leo Cooper, 1992) republished as *The Battle for Afghanistan: The Soviets Versus the Mujahedin During the 1980s* (Barnsley: Pen & Sword Military, 2007 edn).

Zahab, Mariam Abou, and Olivier Roy, *Islamic Networks: The Pakistan-Afghan Connection* (London: Hurst & Co., 2004).

Zahid Hussain, *Frontline Pakistan: the Struggle with Militant Islam* (London: I. B. Tauris, 2008).

The Civil War, 1989–2001

Amin, S. H., *Law, Reform, and Revolution in Afghanistan: Implications for Central Asia and the Islamic World* (Glasgow: Royston, 1993).

Anderson, Jon W., *Doing Pakhtu: Social Organization of the Ghilzai Pashtun* (Ann Arbor: University Microfilms International, 1979).

Atwan, Abdel Bari, *The Secret History of Al-Qaida* (Berkeley, CA.: University of California Press, 2006).

Bhatia, Michael Vinay, and Mark Sedra, *Afghanistan, Arms and Conflict: Armed Groups, Disarmament and Security in a Post-war Society* (London: Routledge, 2008).

Brahimi, Alia, *Jihad and Just War in the War on Terror* (Oxford: Oxford University Press, 2010).

Burke, Jason, *Al-Qaeda* (New York: I. B. Tauris, 2003).

Cederman, Lars-Erik, Andreas Wimmer, and Brian Min, 'Why Do Ethnic Groups Rebel? New Data and Analysis', *World Politics*, 62, 1 (January 2010), pp. 87–119.

Crews, Robert and Amin Tarzi, *The Taliban and the Crisis of Afghanistan* (Cambridge, MA.: Harvard University Press, 2008).

Donner, Fred, 'The Sources of Islamic Conceptions of War' in John Kelsay and James Turner Johnson (eds), *Just War and Jihad: Historical and Theoretical perspectives on War and Peace in Western and Islamic Traditions* (New York: Greenwood Press, 1991).

Dorronsoro, Gilles, *Revolution Unending: Afghanistan, 1979 to the Present* (New York: Columbia University Press, 2005).

Edwards, David, *Before Taliban: Genealogies of the Afghan Jihad* (Berkeley, CA.: University of California Press, 2002).

Fearon, James D. and David D. Laitin, 'Ethnicity, Insurgency and Civil War', *American Political Science Review*, 97, 1 (February 2003).

Gilley, Bruce, 'Against the Concept of Ethnic Conflict', *Third World Quarterly*, 25, 6 (2004).

Giustozzi, Antonio, *Empires of Mud* (London: Hurst & Co., 2009).

Gohari, M. J., *The Taliban: Ascent to Power* (Oxford: Oxford University Press, 2001).

Goodson, Larry P., *Afghanistan's Endless War: State Failure, Regional Politics, and the Rise of the Taliban* (Seattle, WA.: University of Washington Press, 2001).

Grosby, Steven, 'The Verdict of History: the inexpungable tie of primordiality—A response to Eller and Coughlan', *Ethnic and Racial Studies*, 17, 1 (1994).

Horowitz, Donald L., *Ethnic Groups in Conflict* (Berkeley, CA.: University of California Press, 1985).

Johnson, Rob, *A Region in Turmoil: South Asian Conflicts since 1947* (London: Reaktion, 2005).

Kalyvas, Stathis, *The Logic of Violence in Civil War* (New York and Cambridge: Cambridge University Press, 2006).

Khalilzad, Zalmay, 'Afghanistan in 1995: Civil War and a Mini-Great Game', *Asian Survey*, 36, 2, *A Survey of Asia in 1995*: Part II (1996), pp. 190–95.

Maley, William, *The Afghanistan Wars* (London and New York: Palgrave Macmillan, 2002).

Matinuddin, Kamal, *The Taliban Phenomenon: Afghanistan 1994–1997* (Oxford: Oxford University Press, 2000).

Modelski, George, 'International Settlement of Internal War', in James Rosenau (ed.), *International Aspects of Civil Strife* (Princeton: Princeton University Press, 1964).

Rashid, Ahmed, *Jihad: The Rise of Militant Islam in Central Asia* (New Haven, CT.: Yale University Press, 2002).

Roy, Olivier, *Islam and Resistance in Afghanistan* (Cambridge: Cambridge Middle East Library, 1986).

Rubin, Barnett R., *The Fragmentation of Afghanistan: State Formation and Collapse in the International System* (New Haven, CT.: Yale University Press, 1995).

Toft, Monica Duffy, *The Geography of Ethnic Violence: Identity, Interests and the Invisibility of Territory* (Princeton, NJ.: Princeton University Press, 2003).

Urban, Mark, *War in Afghanistan* (Basingstoke: Macmillan, 1990).

Zartman, I. William (ed.), *Elusive Peace: Negotiating an End to Civil Wars* (Washington, DC.: Brookings Institute, 1995).

The Taliban, the Neo-Taliban, and Their Allies

Afghanistan Justice Project, *Casting Shadows: War Crimes and Crimes against Humanity, 1978–2001* (2005).

Cook, David, 'The Implications of "Martyrdom Operations" for Contemporary Islam', *Journal of Religious Ethics*, 32, 1 (Spring 2004), pp. 129–151.

Counterinsurgency Field Manual FM3–24 (Chicago, IL.: University of Chicago Press, 2007).

Dobbins, James F., *After the Taliban* (Washington, DC.: Potomac Books, 2008).

Farrell, Theo, 'Culture and Military Power', *Review of International Studies*, 24 (1998), pp. 407–16.

Farrell, Theo and Terry Terriff, *The Sources of Military Change: Culture, Politics, Technology* (Boulder, CO.: Westview, 2002).

Fergusson, James, *Taliban* (London: Bantam Press, 2010).

Giustozzi, Antonio, *Koran, Kalashnikov and Laptop* (London: Hurst & Co., 2007).

Giustozzi, Antonio, *Decoding the New Taliban: Insights from the Afghan Field* (London: Hurst & Co., 2009).

Gohari, M. J., *Taliban: Ascent to Power* (Oxford: Oxford University Press, 2001).

Griffin, Michael, *Reaping the Whirlwind: The Taliban Movement in Afghanistan* (London: Pluto Press, 2001).

SELECT BIBLIOGRAPHY

Haroon, Sana, *Frontier of Faith: Islam in the Indo-Afghan Borderland* (London: Hurst & Co., 2007).

Hyman, Anthony, 'Nationalism in Afghanistan', *International Journal of Middle East Studies*, 34, 2 (May 2002).

Johnson, Chris and Jolyon Leslie, *Afghanistan: The Mirage of Peace* (London: Zed Books, 2008).

Johnson, Rob, *Oil, Islam and Conflict* (London: Reaktion, 2008).

Juergensmeyer, Mark, *Terror in the Mind of God: The Global Rise of Religious Violence* (Berkeley, CA.: University of California Press, 2000).

Licklider, Roy (ed.), *Stopping the Killing: How Civil Wars End* (New York: New York University Press, 1993).

Maley, William, *Fundamentalism Reborn? Afghanistan and the Taliban* (London: Hurst & Co., 1998).

Malik, Iftikar, 'Pakistan in 2001: The Afghanistan Crisis and the Rediscovery of the Frontline State', *Asian Survey*, 42, 1 (2001), pp. 204–12.

Marsden, Peter, *The Taliban: War, Religion and the New Order in Afghanistan* (London: Zed Books,1998).

Masadykov, Talatbek, Antonio Giustozzi and James Michael Page, 'Negotiating with the Taliban: Towards a Solution to the Afghan Conflict' (London School of Economics Crisis States Research Centre: Working Paper 66, Jan 2010).

Matinnudin, Kamal, *The Taliban Phenomenon: Afghanistan, 1994–1997* (Oxford: Oxford University Press, 1999).

Nasr, S. V. R., 'Transnational Islamic Holy Warriors in Kashmir, Afghanistan, Central Asia, Chechnya and Kosovo', *Global Review of Ethno-Politics*, II/3–4 (2003).

Nets-Zehngut, R., 'Analysing the Reconciliation Process', *International Journal on World Peace*, 24 (2007).

Nojumi, Neamatollah, *The Rise of the Taliban in Afghanistan: Mass Mobilisation, Civil War and the Future of the Region* (New York: Palgrave Macmillan, 2002).

Porter, Patrick, *Military Orientalism* (London: Hurst & Co., 2009).

Stanski, Keith, '"So these folks are aggressive": An Orientalist Reading of "Afghan Warlords"', *Security Dialogue*, 40, 73 (2009).

Raiment, Sean, *Into the Killing Zone* (London: Constable, 2008).

Rashid, Ahmed, *Descent into Chaos: The U.S. and the Disaster in Pakistan, Afghanistan, and Central Asia* (London: Penguin, 2009).

Rashid, Ahmed, *The Taliban* (London: Yale University Press, 2001).

Roy, Olivier, *Afghanistan: From Holy War to Civil War* (Princeton: Darwin Press, 1995).

Roy, Olivier, *Globalised Islam* (New York: Columbia University Press, 2004).

Roy, Olivier, *Islam and Resistance in Afghanistan* (Cambridge: Cambridge University Press, 1986).

Rubin, Barnett, *The Search for Peace in Afghanistan: From Buffer State to Failed State* (New Haven, CT.: Yale University Press, 1995).

Rzehak, Lutz, *Die Taliban im Land der Mittagssonne. Geschichten aus der afghanischen Provinz. Erinnerungen und Notizen von Abdurrahman Pahwal der Reihe Erinnerungen an Zentralasien* (Reichert Verlag, 2004).

Sondhaus, Lawrence, *Strategic Culture and Ways of War* (London: Routledge, 2006).

Tse-tung, Mao, *On Guerrilla Warfare* (reprinted University of Illinois Press, 2000).

Walter, Barbara F., *Committing to Peace: The Successful Settlement of Civil Wars* (Princeton: Princeton University Press, 2002).

Wilson, Peter, 'Defining Military Culture', *Journal of Military History*, 71, 1 (2008).

Woodward, Bob, *Obama's War* (New York: Simon & Schuster, 2010).

Zaeef, Abdul Salam, *My Life with the Taliban* (London: Hurst & Co., 2010).

INDEX

363

Cold War: 4; end of, 224; impact on diplomatic strategy, 211

Coleridge, General Sir John: military forces of, 196

Cordovez, Diego: Under-Secretary General for Special Political Affairs, 245

Crimean War (1853–6): Treaty of Paris (1856), 87

Czechoslovakia: Prague Spring (1968), 208–9

Dadullah, Mullah Mansur: 279

Dargai: 161–2

'al-Dawla, Shuja: family of, 76

Dostum, Abdurrashid: 259

Doyle, Michael: 6

Dupree, Louis: use of oral traditions, 28–9, 74

Durand, Maj. Gen. Henry Marion: observation of military strategy of Amir Dost Mohammad, 51

Durand, Sir Henry Mortimer: Foreign Minister of Government of India, 24, 146

Durrani, Ahmad Shah: 40; attempt to adopt Persian practices of, 43; death of (1772), 39, 44; family of, 41, 44, 47; inability to create Pashtun national identity, 15; military forces of, 40

Durranis: 79–80, 137–8, 142, 146, 191; conflict with Ghilzais, 39, 262; cooperation with British forces, 83; factionalism of, 39; Kandahari, 55; Zirak, 88

Dyer, Brigadier General Reginald: imposition of martial law in Amritsar, 179; military forces of, 187

Edwards, David: study of Pashtuns, 33

Egypt: 189

Elphinstone, Mountstuart: first British envoy to Kabul (1808), 22–3; documented ethnic groups, 26; view of Amir Dost Mohammed, 46

Emergency Loya Jirga: led by Hamid Karzai, 259

Eyre, Vincent: 85

Faqir, Mullah: supporters of, 129

Fearon, James: 14

Ferrier, J.P.: 6–7

First Anglo-Afghan War (1838–42): 1, 6–7, 24, 29, 34, 38, 47, 88, 134, 157, 185, 188, 291, 297, 305; attempted negotiations during (1841), 19, 71; Beymaru Heights skirmish (1841), 66–7, 69–70; British abandonment of Bala Hissar (1841), 65; British invasion of Afghanistan (1839), 50; British victory at Bamian (1840), 55; siege of Ghazni (1839), 52–3; Zurmat revolt, 60

First World War (1914–18): 176, 179, 195; Afghan analysis of, 29; impact upon British Empire, 178; participation of Indian Army during, 193; Triple Entente, 32; Western Front, 5

Forbes, Archibald: writings of, 7

Ghaznavid Empire: military of, 13

Ghobar, Mir Ghulam Mohammed: *Afghanistan in the Course of History*, 29

Giradet, Edward: coverage of Soviet-Afghan War, 209, 224, 232

Gladstone, William: British Prime Minister, 145

Gorbachev, Mikhail: General Secretary of CPSU, 239–41

Gough, Brigadier General Charles: military forces of, 117, 123

INDEX